The Battle of the Classics

The Battle of the Classics

*How a Nineteenth-Century Debate Can
Save the Humanities Today*

ERIC ADLER

OXFORD
UNIVERSITY PRESS

OXFORD
UNIVERSITY PRESS

Oxford University Press is a department of the University of Oxford. It furthers
the University's objective of excellence in research, scholarship, and education
by publishing worldwide. Oxford is a registered trade mark of Oxford University
Press in the UK and certain other countries.

Published in the United States of America by Oxford University Press
198 Madison Avenue, New York, NY 10016, United States of America.

Library of Congress Cataloging-in-Publication Data
Names: Adler, Eric, 1973– author. | Oxford University Press.
Title: The battle of the classics : how a nineteenth-century debate can
save the humanities today / by Eric Adler.
Description: First Edition. | New York : Oxford University Press, 2020. |
Includes bibliographical references and index.
Identifiers: LCCN 2020018926 (print) | LCCN 2020018927 (ebook) |
ISBN 9780197518786 (Hardback) | ISBN 9780197518809 (ePub) |
ISBN 9780197518793 (updf) | ISBN 9780197518816 (online)
Subjects: LCSH: Classical education—United States. |
Education, Humanistic—United States. | Culture conflict—United States.
Classification: LCC LC1011 .A319 2020 (print) | LCC LC1011 (ebook) |
DDC 370.1120973—dc23
LC record available at https://lccn.loc.gov/2020018926
LC ebook record available at https://lccn.loc.gov/2020018927

1 3 5 7 9 8 6 4 2

Printed by Sheridan Books, Inc., United States of America

For Callie, Julian, and Lili

Contents

Acknowledgments

In the course of researching and writing this book, I have benefited from the help of many people. Especially since the book is an interdisciplinary project, I was exceedingly fortunate that experts from various disciplines generously agreed to read and comment on portions of the manuscript: Teresa Bejan, Ward Briggs, Roger Geiger, David Hoeveler, Calvert Jones, Jeremy Pienik, Robert Proctor, Claes Ryn, Rachel Singpurwalla, James Turner, and Katherine Wasdin. Their corrections and insightful suggestions have helped rescue me from numerous blunders and made this a much stronger work. It should go without saying that any remaining errors of fact or judgment are my own.

By no means does this exhaust the list of people to whom a debt of gratitude is owed. A variety of others aided the project in various ways. April Armstrong at the Seeley G. Mudd Manuscript Library at Princeton University digitized a portion of a Princeton catalogue for me. Sabina Beauchard at the Massachusetts Historical Society helped grant me the right to reprint from the Charles Francis Adams, Jr., Papers there. Elizabeth Drumm graciously took the time to speak with me about the controversy surrounding Reed College's Hum 110 course. Ethan Hutt and Campbell Scribner made many useful bibliographical suggestions. Roosevelt Montas sent me data on Columbia University's core curriculum. James Barondess, Laura Papish, and Akira Yatsuhashi offered suggestions for Chapter 6. Robert Proctor selflessly sent me a portion of the manuscript on which he was working; over the years I have profited enormously from reading Bob's excellent work and from having the good fortune to speak and correspond with him. The staff of the Harvard University Archives was extraordinarily helpful and gracious; I'd particularly like to thank Virginia Hunt, who offered permission to print portions of the Irving Babbitt Papers housed at the Archives.

Claes Ryn deserves special mention as an unfailing mentor. The foremost interpreter of Irving Babbitt, he agreed to meet with me a few years ago to discuss Babbitt's thought and has been an indefatigable supporter ever since. Claes also allowed me to reprint in Chapter 6 a short, slightly altered portion of an article that appeared in the journal he co-edits: "The Neoliberal University and the Neoliberal Curriculum," *Humanitas* 31.1–2 (2018): 113–25; another article, "Was Irving Babbitt an Educational Counterrevolutionst?," is forthcoming from the same journal and contains earlier versions of some material also found in this book. I am greatly indebted to him for all his efforts.

My colleagues at the University of Maryland have offered much guidance and have made my working life pleasant: Francisco Barrenechea, Jorge Bravo, Lillian Doherty, Rachel Singpurwalla, Gregory Staley, and Katherine Wasdin. The staff of Oxford University Press also deserves praise. Stefan Vranka supported this project from the start, offering much advice and encouragement throughout the editorial process. The book is all the better as a result of his ideas and suggestions. The two anonymous readers for Oxford (one of whom revealed himself as the historian Carl Richard, whose work I have long admired) supplied many useful criticisms and recommendations.

Most of all, I would like to thank my family: Amy Adler, Joel Adler, Julian Calvert Adler, Nancy Adler, Mike Donahue, Calvert Jones, Julian Jones, Lili Katz-Jones, and Patricia Wallace. Callie, Julian, and Lili are my constant confidantes and companions. I cannot thank them enough for all their love and support. Accordingly, I dedicate this book to them.

Introduction

The Sick Man of Higher Education

In education, as elsewhere, it is the fittest that survives.
—Charles W. Eliot, "What Is a Liberal Education?" (1884)

Humanism vs. Best Buy

In the spring of 2012, the liberal arts college where I then taught was gearing up to revise its approach to general education. The institution had boasted a similar set of distribution requirements for decades; its leadership, with at least one eye on the college's marketing potential, aimed to change course, hoping that a fresher, more original take would attract prospective students. Although the college had only just begun its process of revision, the faculty listserv was already humming in anticipation, as various professors offered their visions for the best way to move forward.

One faculty member, a long-standing professor in the economics department, sent his colleagues a lengthy disquisition on an ideal general education curriculum. His approach was neither novel nor daring: in essence, he argued in favor of a simplified version of the system the college already possessed. But one paragraph the economist included created a mini-scandal on campus. In the course of his reflections, he wrote, "I think we should at least discuss the question as to whether all of our students should be required to take a foreign language. For my part, I would prefer that a foreign language requirement be enacted only where it is clearly the case that it is integral to the nature of studies being undertaken by a student." Wading more deeply into controversy, he provided a rationale for his opinion: "The fact that English now seems to be a world language (I know this is probably the result of US imperialistic leanings) greatly reduces the need for a foreign language requirement. Yesterday at Best Buy I saw a device that enables a person to immediately translate their language into a number of different languages, the result of which is then read in the translated language to other people. It is clear to me that it is not too far in the future when we will all carry such devices with us on our travels, making communication instantly possible wherever we happen to be."

As one might imagine, this line of argument encouraged a vigorous response from irked humanists. How could a professor at a liberal arts college deny the importance of language study? One angered English professor on the faculty mocked the idea that carrying "a hand-held translator" would help transform the college's students into "global citizens."

Amidst such impassioned tongue-clucking, a member of the French department chose to provide a fuller response. Replying to the initial provocation on the faculty listserv, he wrote, "Actually, learning another language makes you smarter. This is not a claim, but rather a fact that has been proven through many scientific studies." Attaching an article from *The New York Times* discussing such studies, he averred, "I know of no field, other than the languages and to some extent music, that has been shown to measurably improve overall cognition."

The economist pounced. If it were true, he wrote in a response on the listserv, that studying foreign languages makes an undergraduate smarter, then he would have to agree that the college ought to retain a language requirement for all students. But the studies the French professor cited had not actually measured the cognitive benefits of collegiate language study; instead, the cited studies (and other subsequent ones introduced by his colleague) vouched for the benefits for bilinguals who had learned these languages in infancy. "Now," the economist wrote, "if the greater cognitive ability only takes place in individuals who are bilingual from infancy, then this argument obviously cannot be used to justify requiring that freshmen who are not bilingual from infancy take a foreign language. So, could you direct me to studies that substantiate the claim that taking a language later in life also leads to an increase in cognitive ability?"

It turned out that the French professor could not do so. Although the economist ultimately gave up his attack on the value of language study, I got the sense that he did so out of concern for maintaining collegiality and decorum. He had made his point, but he had also ruffled feathers. So he decided to disengage. In short, no one had convinced him.

This exchange left me deeply disconcerted. Why had one of my fellow humanists chosen to justify the value of his life's work on the basis of a handful of studies conducted by social scientists? Why did he not recognize that by engaging with an economist in this way he was setting himself up for failure? And why did his colleagues (I include myself) not muster more convincing arguments? Were a handful of poorly contextualized examinations of supposed cognitive benefits the only testaments to the value of studying world languages? Could millennia of Western educational history focused on such subjects be so easily dismissed as outdated and wrongheaded? In the conflict prompted by our colleague in the economics department, many of the college's humanities faculty undoubtedly dismissed him as a philistine. But, if language study stands or falls on its "cognitive benefits" alone, what was so philistine about challenging its value? There must, I hoped to myself, be better ways to argue in favor of the languages—and, more broadly, in favor of the humanities.

Down and Out in Colleges and Universities

In the intervening years, many humanists must have harbored similar hopes. If the news media are to be believed, these are not heady times for the humanities in higher education. These days, it seems, nary a week goes by without some dire report in the popular press advertising the humanities' impending collapse. In a 2013 piece in *The New Republic*, for example, Gordon Hutner and Feisal Mohamed intoned, "You've probably heard several times already that the humanities are in 'crisis.' The crisis is real."[1] The authors pointed to the drastic diminution of public funding for state institutions of higher learning. They contended that this has caused in administrative circles a pernicious obsession with the generation of revenue—an obsession that is detrimental to the humanities.[2] Although other observers offer different conclusions about the causes for woe, many have agreed with Hutner and Mohamed that the humanities in the US are in crisis.[3] High-profile reports commissioned

---

[1] Hutner and Mohamed 2013. Cf. Hutner and Mohamed 2016a: esp. 3.

[2] Criticisms of the consumerist, "neo-liberal" character of contemporary American higher education are legion. See, e.g., Verene 2002: xi–xiii; Kirp 2003; Bousquet 2008; Donoghue 2008; Newfield 2008: esp. 9–10, 20, 25; Schrecker 2010: esp. 4, 100–5, 154–224; Di Leo 2013; Jay 2014: 7, 23–24; Roth 2015: 1–2 (but cf. 6, where he praises curricular free election and 72–73, where he lauds Charles Eliot); Prose 2017. Proctor (2014: 26–28) contends that all defenses of liberal education today focus on it as an antidote to industrialized capitalism and the division of labor.

[3] E.g., Newfield 2008: 19; Menand 2010: 16, 59–92; Gaggi 2011; Harpham 2011: 15–16, 18, 22; Jay and Graff 2012; Klinkenborg 2013; MacDonald 2014 ; Bauerlein 2015: 32–33; Jacobs 2015; Geiger 2016; Kleinman 2016: 68; Prose 2017; Sewall 2019. Cf. Nussbaum 2010: 17–18, 124–25; Ferrall 2011; Gutting 2013; Saul 2013; Melin 2016: 2016; McCumber 2016; Nikopoulos 2017.

by Harvard University and the American Academy of Arts and Sciences have undoubtedly helped feed this narrative.[4]

Other writers, though typically recognizing a sense of gloom among humanities faculty nationwide,[5] have challenged the notion that the humanistic disciplines are experiencing a crisis.[6] To some, for example, a sense of catastrophe has long hounded the humanities in America.[7] Others have pointed out that reports advertising the demise of humanistic disciplines on campus typically rely on statistics highlighting decreases in the percentages of humanities majors. Since the passing years have witnessed the growth of many new vocational concentrations in American higher education, they maintain that the focus on such percentages is misleading.[8]

Despite the salience of these claims, it remains difficult to conclude that all is well for the humanities in American higher education. Tracking the percentages of undergraduate humanities concentrators over time may indeed supply an unreliable picture.[9] But such figures undoubtedly influence many college and university administrators, who make decisions about faculty hiring and even program dissolution in part on these (often unreliable) measures. Thus, for instance, institutional leaders typically pointed to the unpopularity of particular majors when justifying the closure of various humanities departments. Recent attempts to shutter humanities programs at the State University of New York at Albany, the University of Pittsburgh, the State University of New York at Stony Brook, Mills College, the University of Wisconsin at Stevens Point, McDaniel College, and Carroll College have only increased a sense of alarm for humanists across the nation.[10] Prominent

[4] See Armitage, Bhabha, et al. 2013 (which focuses on both the arts and the humanities); Brodhead, Rowe, et al. 2013 (which focuses on both the humanities and the social sciences). On these reports, see, e.g., Connor 2013b; Saul 2013.

[5] Many underscore the gloomy mood among contemporary humanists: e.g., Berman 2006–7: 8; Klinkenborg 2013; Saul 2013; Belkin: 2016; Jaschik 2017. Cf. Armitage et al. 2013; Brodhead et al. 2013: 9; Bérubé and Ruth 2015: 10.

[6] See, e.g., Armitage et al. 2013: 7–11; Frantzman 2013; Tworek 2013; Jay 2014: 7–17; Bérubé and Ruth 2015: 1–25; and n. 8.

[7] E.g., Gaggi 2011; Harpham 2011: 15; Jay 2014: 1–2, 8.

[8] This argument has been advanced most effectively by Schmidt 2013a and b. See also anonymous 2013; Connor 2013a, b, and c; Tworek 2013. But Schmidt (2018) has more recently changed his mind about the "crisis" of the humanities—which he now deems to be real.

[9] One should note, however, that these percentages continue to decline. See, e.g., Jaschik 2017 for some of the latest numbers. Cf. Edwards 2016.

[10] On the situation at SUNY Albany, see, e.g., Gaggi 2011; Armitage et al. 2013: 29 n. 17; Hutner and Mohamed 2013. On the elimination of various humanities graduate programs at the University of Pittsburg, see, e.g., Armitage et al. 2013: 29 n. 17; Hutner and Mohamed 2013. On proposed cuts to the humanities at SUNY Stony Brook, see, e.g., Flaherty 2017b. On the proposed elimination of various humanities and social science departments at Mills College, see, e.g., Seltzer 2017. On the plan to eliminate various humanities and social science programs at the University of Wisconsin at

American politicians—of both the Left and the Right—have publicly questioned the value of humanities degrees. This all could lead one to believe that disciplines previously deemed the core of liberal arts instruction (e.g., philosophy and classics) could find themselves on the chopping block.[11] Those more pessimistic about the future of the humanities, moreover, have rightly pointed out that optimists typically work in departments of English or history—the disciplines associated with the humanities that may experience enrollment declines but are sufficiently established in the vast majority of US institutions of higher learning to feel no existential threat. Faculty members who teach, for instance, foreign languages have little reason to mirror this sense of confidence.[12]

Higher Education's Great Amnesia

In this fraught environment, tracts touting the benefits of the contemporary humanities have understandably blossomed.[13] Recent apologetics for the humanities in American colleges and universities have a tendency to look back only a few decades in educational history in order to aid their assertions. Thus, as we shall see in Chapter 1, defenses published in the aftermath of the 2008 financial crisis tend to focus their attention no earlier than the academic culture wars of the 1980s and 1990s. During the culture wars themselves, authors disputing the role of the humanities typically cast their purview only as far as the 1960s.[14] This has inevitable (and detrimental) effects on the arguments for the humanities in America: they often seem rootless, unaware of the humanities' history, and unmindful of the fact that certain contentions about their value have been floated before—oftentimes in the face of compelling counterarguments. This historical myopia, if you

Stevens Point, see, e.g., Dix 2018; Flaherty 2018. On the elimination of five majors and three minors at McDaniel College—all in the humanities and arts—see Jaschik 2019c. On the cutting of five majors and ten minors at Carroll College (including classical studies and ethics and value studies), see Jaschik 2019a.

[11] See, e.g., Rawlings and Aoki 2013; Proctor 2014: 10; Jacobs 2015; Zakaria 2015: 19; anonymous 2016; Geiger 2016: 24; Kleinman 2016: 88. Cohan (2012) urges the dissolution of humanities departments.
[12] See, e.g., Hutner and Mohamed 2016b: 1–3; Jaschik 2019b. Cf. Melin 2016.
[13] For an examination of many such tracts, see Chapter 1, this volume.
[14] On this topic, see Adler 2016: 9–41. Carnochan (1993: 2) notes the ahistorical nature of the culture-wars debate over the curriculum.

will, leaves defenders of the humanities rudderless. They seem constantly to be reinventing the wheel.[15]

The penchant to eschew serious engagement with the broader history of the humanities can weaken contemporary justifications for the humanistic disciplines. This book will demonstrate that a parallel historical case has much to teach us about defenses of the humanities. In the late nineteenth century, American higher education witnessed the so-called Battle of the Classics.[16] At that point in time, much intellectual energy in the nation was expended on attacks on and defenses of the role of the humanities (then commonly conceived as the classical humanities)[17] in US higher learning. Sundry newspapers and journals of the day focused on the topic, which appears to have engaged broad swaths of the American reading public. Traditionalists in the Battle of the Classics hoped to retain the classical languages (in many cases still synonymous with the "humanities") as the pedagogical core of higher education in the US. Their opponents, who were often called "modernists," by contrast, aimed to end curricular prescription and the dominance of Latin and ancient Greek in the American colleges.

Although the disputes associated with the Battle of the Classics are not perfectly analogous to those surrounding the role of the humanities today, they have much to teach prospective defenders of the contemporary humanities. And for good reason: this was a quintessential episode in which disagreements about the place of the humanities in education and American life took center stage. We can thus learn a great deal from the arguments over the classical humanities in this period that will be directly or indirectly applicable to our own situation. What was compelling about the positions promoters of the classical humanities offered during the Battle of the Classics? Which of their arguments failed to resonate—and why? How can the contemporary humanities in higher education benefit from an understanding of these crucial earlier disputes? Though our investigation will focus on the role of the humanities in US colleges and universities, much

---

[15] Proctor 1998 underscores this point in regard to the tracts from the academic culture wars. In its first printing, the book was titled *Education's Great Amnesia*.

[16] Rudolph (1977: 180) reports that college and university histories often give this name to the struggle, which he says took place in the 1880s and 1890s. Kirkland (1965: 191) calls it the "Greek War." As will be addressed later, we shall slightly expand this chronological purview to include the first few decades of the twentieth century. There is historical precedent for this expansion: see anonymous 1917 for the use of the phrase "The Battle of the Classics" for the curricular debates of the 1910s.

[17] On the shift in American higher education from a conception of the humanities based on the classical languages (the *studia humanitatis*) to our current, more capacious, meaning, see Chapter 2, this volume.

that we shall discover will also be applicable and important to other educational contexts. America, after all, is not alone in experiencing a crisis of the humanities.

Among other things, this book will contend—with the history of the Battle of the Classics as part of its evidence—that humanities apologetics that avoid vouching for *specific humanities content* are doomed to failure. Such arguments, as we shall see, inevitably deteriorate into viewing the humanities (and, for that matter, education in general) as little more than a conduit for the inculcation of various skills. And too much focus on skills as the essence of higher learning will lead to defeat.

The book will emphasize that defenders of the humanities need to stress the significance of particular humanities content in their apologetics. The Battle of the Classics ably demonstrates that insistence on the intellectual, aesthetic, and moral value of studying profound works of art, philosophy, religion, and literature remains the strongest rationale for the contemporary humanities. If American institutions of higher learning persist in relying on a skills-based, substanceless approach to pedagogy, the humanities will continue to wither.

Importantly, and notwithstanding the opinions of many traditionalistic culture warriors, this demonstration does not imply that the humanities must stake their claim on the Western canon alone. Works of deep intellectual, aesthetic, and moral significance are linked to a rich variety of human civilizations, past and present. As we shall see in Chapter 5, a thinker who wrote at the tail end of the Battle of the Classics blazed a path forward, illustrating how such diversity of thought and experience can rightly serve at the heart of an appropriate, vigorous, and ethically challenging curriculum. Moreover, he demonstrated that the future health of civilization relies on a proper approach to humanistic education, without which human beings are in danger of courting misery and chaos. As we shall recognize, the world urgently requires a humanistic revival.

Evaluating the Battle of the Classics

When examining the Battle of the Classics, how are we to know which arguments made during the disputes are strong and which are weak? To a great extent, naturally, we shall determine this through an engagement with the arguments themselves, probing and testing their validity. But the responses to various contentions presented in the Battle of the Classics can help us mightily in this regard: as we shall see, some arguments met with thoughtful and compelling counterclaims, whereas others did not.

One could presumably make the case that the squabbles over the role of Latin and ancient Greek in the American college curriculum during the late nineteenth and early twentieth centuries were a sideshow to broader developments in the US. The country, after all, was a changing nation, and it was highly unlikely that it would retain a curricular model adopted prior to its industrialization and greater democratization. As they have elsewhere in the world, such processes of modernization have necessitated important changes in the nature of education.

But ideas also matter. American visions of education were far more than mere reflections of underlying material forces or empty justifications for the economic and political status quo. Would American higher education have charted the exact same path without the instrumental work of John Dewey, to give only one example? Ideas about education and the humanities mattered then, and they matter now.

To be sure, much has changed since the passing of the Battle of the Classics over a century ago. Yet higher education at that time faced a key turning point that is analogous in spirit to the one it currently confronts. The late nineteenth and the early twenty-first centuries are both viewed as eras of globalization, with exhilarating upsurges in interconnectedness, economic exchange, and technological development amid slow but significant alterations in the global distribution of power. And in both eras, the humanities have been questioned as to their "usefulness," even as the forces of globalization furnish good reasons to build the character of young Americans as well as their vocational skills.

During the late nineteenth and early twentieth centuries, traditionalists wanted to maintain the classical languages as the bedrock of higher learning in the United States. In many (though not all) cases, their opponents longed to open up the undergraduate curriculum, to ensure an equal place for the natural and social sciences, as well as the study of some modern European languages and various vocational subjects.

Today, the roles have reversed from the days of the Battle of the Classics: rather than ruling the roost, humanists are now merely pressing to retain their seat at the pedagogical table, in an academic environment increasingly uncongenial to them. Proponents of the STEM fields (science, technology, engineering, and mathematics) and vocational subjects see their disciplines dominating in a way that the classical languages did in early American higher education, and humanists are now the ones scrambling to prove their relevance.

What can this striking reversal tell us about the best ways to defend the humanities in America? What can humanists' failures during the Battle of the Classics teach us? Do their arguments apply today? What do the humanities offer that is unique, and how inclusive can they be in a world that is again experiencing rapid change and globalization?

This book investigates the raison d'être of the humanities. It does so in a way that is attuned to the history—and the politics—of contending ideas about why the humanities matter and what role they should play in higher education. Chapter 1 probes the contemporary intellectual lay of the land, by analyzing numerous apologetics for the humanities that appeared in the aftermath of the 2008 global financial meltdown. It demonstrates that these defenses overwhelmingly vouch for humanistic disciplines through various skills-based rationales. The chapter underscores the weaknesses associated with this approach, highlighting the tenuousness of such well-intentioned arguments. It also notes various misunderstandings and misimpressions found in contemporary apologetics, thus demonstrating the need to present a more historically informed case for the humanities.

Chapter 2 helps supply much-needed historical background. By charting the path of the humanities from Roman antiquity to the present, it gives readers a sense of precisely what the humanities have been and are today. This aids those attempting to define the contemporary humanities, and helps distinguish between the Renaissance conception of the *studia humanitatis* and the broader liberal arts tradition. The chapter also focuses on the shift that took place during the nineteenth century in our understanding of the humanities. At this time, from a conception that formerly embraced the classical languages alone, the humanities came to take on their current, more capacious meaning. This fundamental reimagining makes it exceedingly difficult to defend the humanities today. In touching on the broader contours of the Battle of the Classics, the chapter also reinforces some of the congenital weaknesses of skills-based rationales for the humanities. Only with such knowledge under our belt can we attempt to provide a convincing case for the contemporary humanities.

The book then turns to examine three major episodes in the Battle of the Classics. Chapter 3 analyzes the brouhaha surrounding a Phi Beta Kappa address Charles Francis Adams, Jr., delivered at Harvard University in 1883. Adams's speech, titled "A College Fetich," launched a fierce intellectual controversy, as interlocutors passionately debated Adams's call to end collegiate admission requirements in ancient Greek. The chapter highlights the scattershot nature of Adams's appeal, which relied more on its author's storied family history than its argumentative rigor. But it also underscores the weaknesses of many traditionalist responses to Adams, highlighting their reliance on Christian sectarianism and skills-based rationales. By advancing such arguments, supporters of the classical humanities unwittingly played into the hands of their opponents.

Similar conclusions can be drawn from another prominent incident in the Battle of the Classics, an event that is the focus of Chapter 4. On February 24, 1885, James McCosh, the president of the College of New Jersey (now Princeton University) and Charles W. Eliot, the president of Harvard University, debated the comparative merits of curricular prescription and election in New York City. This debate engaged two giants of the Battle of the Classics: Eliot had already established himself as the most energetic and prominent advocate of the so-called free-elective system, and McCosh had taken up a watered-down version of the traditionalist case. Although Eliot's arguments suffer from serious defects, the chapter contends that in the debate McCosh failed to hit on many of them. His appeal, like lots of responses to Eliot during the Battle of the Classics, ceded too much ground to his opponent, and relied too much on a sectarian worldview and skills-based arguments in favor of the classical languages as providers of "mental discipline."

Chapter 5 examines the heated debates surrounding the work of an often overlooked but crucial figure in the history of the humanities in America. The literary and social critic Irving Babbitt, whose views inaugurated a spirited intellectual ruckus in the early decades of the twentieth century, was the most consequential thinker associated with a movement called New Humanism. Chapter 5 argues that Babbitt crafted the most satisfying case against the opponents of the classical curriculum, a case that highlighted the quintessential importance of the humanistic tradition to the continued flourishing of civilization. Although often viewed today as a reactionary, Babbitt was in many ways a thinker before his time, offering a more inclusive approach to humanism that looked far beyond its Western origins. The chapter also stresses that his opponents, although contributing vituperative criticisms of Babbitt's work, failed to counter successfully the intellectual and ethical undergirding of his approach to higher education. Unfortunately, though, other New Humanists, principally Paul Elmer More and Norman Foerster, diluted Babbitt's message, relying in large part on skills-based rationales that Babbitt had correctly downplayed.

The final chapter uses Babbitt's ideas as a starting point for an intellectually and ethically sound approach to the contemporary humanities. Although Babbitt—and, more generally, traditionalists during the Battle of the Classics—did not present a defense of the humanities completely appropriate for our day and age, his ecumenical and comparatively broad-minded approach can help ground a contemporary rationale that is both novel and satisfying. Chapter 6 argues that contemporary humanists must vouch for the central importance of their subjects in part by expressing the ways in which masterworks of culture (from *all* intellectual traditions, not just Western ones) help contribute to the creation of better human beings. Reliance on a (dubiously grasped) skills-based approach to the contemporary humanities dilutes the importance of the humanistic tradition, unwittingly reinforcing the superior value of the natural and social sciences. Substance-based apologetics also have the benefit of encouraging a revolution in the humanities classroom: they should promote a genuinely humanistic approach to the study of literature, philosophy, religion, and the arts as conduits for students to ponder life's great questions and ultimately to lead more fulfilling lives.

* * *

It goes without saying that the fraught environment for the humanities today compels humanists to muster disparate sorts of arguments to stave off the demise of their disciplines. Different circumstances—and different audiences—will require the use of different tactics.[18] That truism notwithstanding, the present book will demonstrate that the Battle of the Classics suggests a promising foundation for the defense of the contemporary humanities. Today's advocates for the humanities must come to recognize that the *substance* of humanistic education matters profoundly. As we shall argue in the final chapter, this should not entail merely a change in argumentative tactics on the part of American humanists, but also a shift in their

---

[18] See the valuable point made by Small (2013: 3): there is no silver-bullet defense of the humanities that can be offered that will appease all potential critics.

pedagogical strategies and a demand for curricular models more amenable to the spirit of humanism. By the book's end, we shall conclude that any people concerned about personal and civilizational flourishing, regardless of their political commitments, must recognize the crucial role of the humanities in contemporary education.

1

Skills Are the New Canon

An optimum liberal arts curriculum would simply require students to take courses with the college's finest teachers, regardless of discipline or course content.
—Victor E. Ferrall, Jr., *Liberal Arts at the Brink* (2011)

My own preference is to create a canon of methods rather than a canon of specific knowledge or of great books—that is, to define, develop, and require instruction around a set of master skills that together would make one an educated, intellectually empowered, morally aware person.
—Nicholas Lemann, "What Should Graduates Know?" (2016)

The idea that a university education really should have no substantial content, should not be about what John Keats was disposed to call "Soul-making," is one that you might think professors and university presidents would be discreet about. Not so.
—Mark Edmundson, *Why Teach? In Defense of a Real Education* (2013)

Crisis and Response

The news about the current state of the humanities in American higher education appears to be decidedly pessimistic. This situation may be less dire than the incessant media reports announcing the imminent demise of the humanities would suggest. But all is not well for contemporary humanistic disciplines in US colleges and universities. One notes, for example, flagging morale among academic humanists, and a sense of ennui that the lousy job market for prospective professors cannot be responsible for alone. Some American institutions of higher learning have shut down humanities departments altogether.[1] And, as we shall see in this chapter, supporters of the humanities now feel the need to write tracts extolling their virtues in an attempt to stave off their downfall. Hence Helen Small, a professor of English in the UK, chose to compose a monograph entitled *The Value of the Humanities* (2013). No one seems to think a book called *The Value of the Business Major* or *What the Study of Nursing Can Do for You* is urgently required. Formerly the center of higher learning in the US, the humanities now find themselves relegated to the periphery, in an era seemingly uncongenial to broad education as a whole. As Anthony Kronman lamented in the early 2000s, "In the hierarchy of academic authority and prestige, the humanities today stand at the bottom."[2] Sad to say, these words ring even truer now than when Kronman wrote them.

Thus the humanities may not actually be in *crisis* in the US, but they appear to be in trouble. This trouble, as you would imagine, has spawned a massive literature of defense, as humanists and their allies attempt to plump for the value of the humanities in American higher education.[3] Such literature is nothing new: in future chapters, we shall trace it back to the nineteenth century, when earlier generations of academics and intellectuals fretted about the diminished role of the classical humanities (i.e., the *studia humanitatis*) in US colleges.

But in the wake of the 2008 global financial crisis, the apologias for the humanities appear to have taken on an added urgency. As we shall see, such defenses do not always stick to the subject of the humanities; understandably worried about the ever-creeping vocationalism in American higher education, various writers have recently defended the liberal arts as a whole.[4] Even so, since about 2010, scores of authors have dedicated much energy to efforts to ensure a future for the humanities on US college campuses.

In this chapter we shall examine the arguments of many such authors and demonstrate that they present a portrait of the humanities strikingly bereft of substance. Instead of stressing the need for students to contemplate particular works associated with the modern humanities, these defenses typically vouch for the humanities' value on the basis of their purported ability

---

[1] On this topic, see the Introduction.

[2] Kronman 2007: 207.

[3] Some recent contributions to this literature include Nussbaum 2010; Harpham 2011; Di Leo 2013; Edmundson 2013; Small 2013; Jay 2014; Bérubé and Ruth 2015; Hutner and Mohamed 2016.

[4] E.g., Ferrall 2011; Roth 2015; Zakaria 2015. Such authors often—and incorrectly—use the terms *humanities* and *liberal arts* interchangeably, as Proctor (2014: 11, 14) notes in regard to Nussbaum 2010.

to inculcate various skills in students. Such arguments, though not without their merits, possess intrinsic disadvantages and vulnerabilities.

Learning without Content

As late as 1997, the ancient philosopher, political theorist, and public intellectual Martha Nussbaum could announce that "on the whole, higher education in America is in a healthy state."[5] In her monograph *Cultivating Humanity: A Classical Defense of Reform in Liberal Education* (1997), Nussbaum tried to calm the waters of the academic culture wars of the 1980s and 1990s.[6] Appearing toward the tail end of that prolonged conflict, the book attempted to undercut traditionalistic criticisms of the American university, arguing that, despite some minor troubles,[7] all was well in US higher education. In the book's most moving passages, Nussbaum described the bad old days of American colleges, when ethnic and gender prejudices ran rampant.[8] Her traditionalistic opponents, with their reactionary veneration for the Great Books,[9] obscured the serious problems with American higher education in the past.[10] Those bemoaning the politicization and intellectual debasement of the country's universities in the late 1960s, she stressed, misunderstand the valuable changes that had taken place since then. In short, conservative grumbling notwithstanding, higher education in the US was doing just fine.

By 2010, however, Nussbaum had dramatically changed her tune. Her earlier book had attempted to rally behind reforms in American colleges and universities associated with both the humanities and social sciences.[11] In *Not for Profit: Why Democracy Needs the Humanities* (2010), by contrast, Nussbaum slightly shifted her purview. Announcing "a world-wide crisis in

---

[5] Nussbaum 1997: 2. But cf. 297–98, in which Nussbaum views increasing vocationalism as a threat. A few years later, Freedman (2003: 54–55) similarly fears the effects of vocationalism on the liberal arts. Cf. Kronman (2007: 206), who asserts that no one is calling for the dissolution of humanities departments. Would that were so today!

[6] For a history of the academic culture wars, see Adler 2016: 9–41.

[7] E.g., Nussbaum 1997: 2, 7, 173–75, 297.

[8] Ibid. 152–61, 191–93.

[9] Works from the academic culture wars criticized by Nussbaum (e.g., 1997: 132, 297–98) include Bloom 1987; Kimball 1990.

[10] For her criticisms of Great Books curricula, see Nussbaum 1997: 33–35, 170–71. Some recent defenses of the liberal arts similarly disfavor the Great Books approach; see, e.g., Roth 2015: 165; Zakaria 2015: 59–61. Verene (2002: 19–21, 56) argues that the humanities require a canon. But he ultimately supports (60) a personal canon for each undergraduate student.

[11] Nussbaum 1997: 10–11.

education," the latter book lamented, "The humanities and arts are being cut away, both in primary/secondary and college/university education, in virtually every nation in the world."[12] Now distressed about the global state of education, the author of *Not for Profit* rightly highlighted the pernicious effects of discarding a broader, more liberal approach to learning. The result of this abandonment, Nussbaum contended, will be nations that produce "generations of useful machines, rather than complete citizens who can think for themselves, criticize tradition, and understand the significance of another person's sufferings and achievements."[13]

Both of Nussbaum's books defend the value of humanistic disciplines in revealing and instructive ways. One notes, for example, that Nussbaum's vision of the humanities does not hinge on any humanities content. In *Cultivating Humanity* and *Not for Profit*, Nussbaum never highlighted any particular works of fiction, poetry, philosophy, art, music, religion, or history that require study for students to deem themselves educated. The two books, for example, considered philosophy courses essential for all undergraduates.[14] But her focus in both cases was the inculcation of logic through Socratic pedagogy. This Socratic style, which Nussbaum lauded as "one of the hallmarks of modern progressive education,"[15] is the sine qua non of the properly educated person. Nowhere did Nussbaum stress that a high school or college education must introduce students to *particular philosophical works* because of their unparalleled profundity, their grappling with essential issues in meaningful ways, or even their historic importance to culture and the life of the mind. To Nussbaum, it appears, philosophy remains crucial for an educated citizenry because it fosters *a certain mode of inquiry*. The specifics surrounding the content with which students engage do not matter nearly as much.[16] Matthew Arnold's famous invocation of culture as "the best which

---

[12] Nussbaum 2010: 2.

[13] Ibid. Interestingly, Nussbaum (2010: 10, 53, 112) argues that the study of the humanities is good for a nation's economic growth. So, despite the title of the book, it turns out that the humanities are also "for profit." See, on this score, the perceptive criticisms of Proctor (2014). Cf. Jay and Graff 2012; Di Leo (2013: 15) dislikes Nussbaum's focus on growth. For other arguments focusing on the humanities as economically helpful, see, e.g., Small 2013: 4–5; anonymous 2016.

[14] Nussbaum 1997: 42 and 2010: 55, 92. The former specifies one required course, the latter two.

[15] Nussbaum 2010: 56. Small (2013: 129) deems *Not for Profit* "a strikingly unSocratic defence of a Socratic education."

[16] Nussbaum (2010: 57–58) does discuss Rousseau's *Emile*, which could hint that she thinks it is crucial to introduce this work to students. Her high regard for Socratic inquiry, moreover, suggests that she would consider certain works by Plato—particularly the early dialogues—of particular import. But in both cases, Nussbaum's focus is on the methods associated with Socratic pedagogy. She esteems *Emile*, in fact, because it aligns with such pedagogy.

has been thought and said in the world" seems like an idea from a different intellectual universe.[17]

Nussbaum is far from alone in her emphases. One idiosyncrasy associated with many recent apologetics for the humanities surrounds their refusal to argue in favor of any specific humanities content. Jeffrey R. Di Leo's *Corporate Humanities in Higher Education: Moving beyond the Neoliberal Academy* (2013) vouches for an approach the author labels "critical humanities," which its author defined as "studying the humanities through the lens of race, class, gender, sexuality, and so on, amplified by a commitment to social justice and democratic education."[18] For Di Leo, the ideological messages conveyed in the classroom eclipse the focus on the individual works encountered. Thus, when asserting the humanist's need to make students feel intellectually un-comfortable in class, Di Leo proclaimed that recent movies typically work better than time-tested books. He wrote, "Whereas reading and discussion, for example, of Simone de Beauvoir's *The Second Sex* (1949) is often met with disinterest and glazed eyes, introducing it [i.e., critical inquiry] through say a film like director Ridley Scott's *Thelma and Louise* (1991) provides the students with a philosophy lesson that is both entertaining and enlight-ening."[19] To Di Leo, the political message to be learned overshadows the need to introduce students to particular works of literature and art.

The English professor Paul Jay has demonstrated similar preoccupations. In *The Humanities "Crisis" and the Future of Literary Studies* (2014), Jay also downgraded regard for substance. Focusing on the best direction for English departments, Jay candidly asserted that "it could certainly be argued that *the process of canon formation itself* is a more important, historically and intel-lectually compelling paradigm for organizing literary study, especially at the core level, than the great books model is."[20] In his vision, canon formation trumps the canon. Throughout his book, Jay defended the value of critical theory to the collegiate study of literature. Such theory, he argued, lends rigor to the humanities in the first place.[21] But nowhere did Jay specify individual works of high theory with which students ought to be acquainted. Instead, he stressed the value of a postmodern philosophical approach to the study of literature.

[17] Arnold 1869: viii.
[18] Di Leo 2013: 10.
[19] Ibid. 11.
[20] Jay 2014: 91 (emphasis in the original).
[21] Ibid. 24.

This appears to be a popular conclusion among some contemporary defenders of the humanities. Michael Bérubé, an English professor of an outlook similar to Jay's, has recently suggested that the excitement in today's humanities stems from a skeptical postmodern outlook, rather than the works addressed in class. In an essay called "Value and Values," he contended that "the liberal arts we now practice, the disciplines of the humanities that emphasize historical change and the contingency of value, are not only more adequate to the world we actually live in but more *exciting* intellectually: that world is a world in which the meaning and value of Shakespeare or Sophocles or Stephen King are not fixed once and for all but open for continued discussion and contestation . . . as they manifestly are. It is a world in which race and gender, sexuality and disability are not defined once and for all but susceptible to slippage and performativity . . . as they manifestly are."[22] Bérubé's list of Shakespeare, Sophocles, and Stephen King gives away the game: the chief message for students is "the contingency of value" (an idea that, paradoxically, Bérubé does not present as contingent), and it does not seem to matter if the focus of this insight is an age-old classic or an example of contemporary popular fiction.

At times, recent promoters of the humanities and the liberal arts seem so dead set on avoiding a focus on content that they fail to note how this predilection undercuts their broader arguments. In *Liberal Arts at the Brink* (2011), for example, Victor E. Ferrall, Jr., a president emeritus of Beloit College, fretted that "[t]he main story line for higher education during the past half century is the rise in demand for vocational instruction."[23] Ferrall perceptively noted the problems for liberal arts institutions associated with the abandonment of curricular requirements. He wrote, "In an effort to attract students, some liberal arts colleges have reduced and even eliminated course requirements. 'Study only what you like best' is a college recruiter's dream argument. To the extent that colleges eliminate requirements, however, they turn over liberal-education curriculum design to students who are not yet liberally educated, and they create the strong probability that their education will be less broad, less liberal."[24]

Yet when Ferrall turned to the actual content of a liberal arts education, he announced his lack of concern. "The fact is," Ferrall noted, "the curriculum game plan is far less important to educational success than the skill

---

[22] Bérubé 2015: 52 (emphasis in the original).
[23] Ferrall 2011: 44.
[24] Ibid. 109.

and commitment of the individual teachers who implement it."[25] If, as Ferrall contended, quality teaching alone is the crux of the matter,[26] why would increasing vocationalism amount to a problem? According to Ferrall's curricular criterion, one would think that fantastic instruction in, say, engineering or accounting would be superior to inferior introductions to, say, Homer and Plato. How, one wonders, does Ferrall's contentless vision of higher education demonstrate the unique value of the liberal arts? If substance truly does not matter, why will any content not suffice?

Contentless Concerns

To be sure, a few recent works defending the humanities or the liberal arts demonstrate a sense of unease with the popular penchant to avoid discussions of content. Michael S. Roth, the president of Wesleyan University, connected this tendency to a regrettable disinclination on the part of academics to make distinctions of quality. In *Beyond the University: Why Liberal Education Matters* (2015), Roth wrote, "Pushpin, as the founder of utilitarianism Jeremy Bentham put it, is as good as music or poetry. This was why the same distribution requirement might be satisfied by a course in Shakespeare or by a course in amateur filmmaking in Brooklyn. Commonsense civility has led us to a place where we are afraid to make any judgments about the merits of the material studied because to do so might offend somebody."[27] Otherwise critical of the political theorist Allan Bloom's best-selling jeremiad *The Closing of the American Mind* (1987),[28] Roth concluded that "Bloom is right that most universities today don't seem capable of articulating what students should learn. This task should fall to the faculty, but professors are naturally drawn to the subjects they themselves were taught. Nor does hyperspecialized professional training serve them well in thinking about the curriculum as a whole."[29] To Roth, this disinclination to vouch for specific content has allowed critics of broad learning to pounce. Yet even Roth did not argue in favor of a curriculum of his own.

---

[25] Ibid. 148.
[26] Ibid. 148.
[27] Roth 2015: 141.
[28] Ibid. 139–43, 157.
[29] Ibid. 157.

Some other humanists feel similar discomfort with this flight from content. The English professor Mark Bauerlein has contributed a number of articles criticizing the proclivities of recent scholarly champions of the humanities.[30] In a 2013 piece from *The New Criterion*, for example, Bauerlein blamed proponents of postmodern literary criticism for the fecklessness of such apologetics. He stressed that, thanks to the ravages of recondite and politically charged theory, "the works of the ages that fill actual humanities syllabi barely exist in these heartfelt defenses. Instead of highlighting assigned authors, artists, writings, and artworks, they signal what happens after the class ends: the moral, civic, and workplace outcomes."[31]

According to Bauerlein, high theory and what he terms "identitarian"[32] themes are the culprits for this state of affairs. He juxtaposed recent tracts in favor of the humanities with those from the era of the academic culture wars, when the disagreements chiefly surrounded the contents of the undergraduate curriculum.[33] But, as we shall see in Chapter 2, the origins of the problem Bauerlein identifies have an older pedigree than he suggests. Only one side in the academic culture wars of the 1980s and 1990s grounded its arguments for the humanities on specific works of art and literature. Traditionalists such as Bloom and William J. Bennett pined for required coursework based chiefly on the masterworks of Western culture.[34] Their opponents, by contrast, criticized the impetus to prescribe particular courses for all undergraduates, thereby effectively advocating either a series of distribution requirements or some other variant on student free-election.[35] Such anti-traditionalist culture warriors, if you will, may have appealed to obligatory coursework on multicultural topics, but tended not to stress the individual works that such classes would study.[36] Thus we must look further back in the history of American higher education for this humanistic flight from substance. In any

---

[30] E.g., Bauerlein 2013, 2014, and 2015.

[31] Bauerlein 2013: 6. See also Bauerlein 2014 and 2015: 33–34. Others have expressed congruent opinions about the negative effects of postmodern literary theory on the humanities: e.g., Harpham 2011: 30, 105–6; Geiger 2016: 27. Cf. Delbanco 2012: 98; Jay 2014: esp. 3–4, 24, 28.

[32] Bauerlein 2014: 11.

[33] Bauerlein 2015: 35. Cf. Summit 2012: 673.

[34] Bennett 1984; Bloom 1987. Other traditionalistic proponents of a Western core curriculum include Cheney 1988; Kimball 1990; Howe 1991; Ellis 1997.

[35] E.g., Levine et al. 1989; Levine 1996. But see Graff (1990: 53), who criticizes the distribution model of general education. On some incongruities associated with traditionalistic and anti-traditionalistic perspectives in the canon wars, see Adler 2016: 31–35.

[36] E.g., Damon 1989; Gordon and Lubiano 1992: esp. 257.

case, Bauerlein has perceptively touched on a central issue surrounding the recent defense of literature: its authors are contented without content.[37]

Nor do the concerns Bauerlein articulated fester only among traditionalistic humanists. Some who do not share Bauerlein's ideological outlook have voiced similar worries about our current substanceless defenses of the contemporary humanities. According to the English professor Mark Edmundson, scholars' disinclination to evaluate the profundity and quality of various literary works is very strange indeed. In an essay collection published in 2013, Edmundson keenly and archly noted, "Ask a professor what she thinks of the work of Stephen Greenblatt, a leading critic of Shakespeare, and you'll hear it for about an hour. Ask her what her views are on Shakespeare's genius and she's likely to begin questioning the term along with the whole 'discourse of evaluation.'"[38] Here Edmundson's critique dovetails with thoughts Bloom offered decades ago in his bestselling polemic.[39] *The Closing of the American Mind* lambasted what Bloom took to be the pervasive relativism in American intellectual life. What its promoters advertise as broadminded "openness" to different cultures in fact amounts to the close-minded inability to draw conclusions on subjects of crucial import.[40] Hence we find humanists—otherwise eager to advertise the distinct contributions of their disciplines—who appear squeamish about heralding any particular humanities content.

Skills Pay the Bills

So, if vouching for content seems passé, how do contemporary defenses of the humanities envision the value of their disciplines? The answer to this question may be summed up in one word: skills. An obsession with the inculcation of particular skills dominates most recent apologias for the humanities and the liberal arts.[41]

---

[37] Cf. Small (2013), who presents five main arguments to justify (research in) the humanities and focuses very little on content. For her (minor) interest in content, see 151–74. According to Beard (2013: 7), however, the only reason to study Latin is for the content encountered.

[38] Edmundson 2013: 22–23.

[39] This correspondence in views is especially salient, since Edmundson does not share Bloom's ideological commitments in many respects and proved critical of traditionalistic perspectives in the academic culture wars during the time period in question. See Edmundson 1993.

[40] Bloom 1987: esp. 38, 39.

[41] E.g., Nussbaum 2010 (an approach praised by Newfield 2016: 177 n. 4); Jay and Graff 2012; Tworek 2013; Jay 2014; Zakaria 2015: 61–62, 68–69, 71–72, 75, 78–79, 87; anonymous 2016; Lemann 2016; Prose 2017. Cf. Menand 2010: 28, 50; Harpham 2011: 27; Delbanco 2012: 4–5, 85–86; DeNicola

Some are particularly outspoken about the value of this approach. In a coauthored opinion piece from 2012, Paul Jay and Gerald Graff expressed befuddlement with humanists' disinclination to engage in skills-talk when defending their subjects of expertise. "If there is a crisis in the humanities," they wrote, "it stems less from their inherent lack of practical utility, which too often prevents us from taking advantage of the vocational opportunities presented to us."[42] To Jay and Graff, skills are all-important: "In fact," they concluded, "we would argue there is no defense of the humanities that is not ultimately based on the skills it teaches."[43]

It is difficult to intuit why Jay and Graff appeared concerned about humanists' disinclination to focus on skills. Such skills-talk, as we have detected, actually dominates most contemporary defenses of broad learning. Take, for example, the work of Stanley Fish, whose criticisms of some skills-based arguments for the liberal arts Jay and Graff censured.[44] Disbelieving the notion that higher education can improve students' moral capabilities, Fish maintained, "College and university teachers can (legitimately) do two things: (1) introduce students to bodies of knowledge and traditions of inquiry that had not previously been part of their experience; and (2) equip those same students with the analytical skills—of argument, statistical modeling, laboratory procedure—that will enable them to move confidently within those traditions and to engage in independent research after a course is over."[45] Even Fish, with his minimalistic and professionalized vision of higher education,[46] largely (albeit not solely) reduced the value of learning to the inculcation of skills.

Some professors have proven so enthusiastic about the skills regimen that they have argued in favor of using skills as the organizing principle of undergraduate education. According to Nicholas Lemann, a professor and former dean of journalism, undergraduate instruction in the nation's colleges has "something to learn from professional schools about better

---

2012: 25; Edmundson 2013: 46–47, 150; Berrett 2016; Geiger 2016: 27–28; Melin 2016: 106. For other works that focus on skills, see, e.g., Nussbaum 1997; Fish 2008: esp. 12–13, 40–49, 54, 58, 153. Cf. Freedman 2003: 56–58, 64–65.

[42] Jay and Graff 2012. Cf. Jay 2014.

[43] Jay and Graff 2012. Cf. Small (2013: 6, 151–73) and Proctor (2014), who both address arguments in favor of the "uselessness" of the humanities. Such views, as Proctor (2014: 20–22, 27–29) demonstrates, were especially popular in the nineteenth century, both in Britain and the US.

[44] See Jay and Graff 2012.

[45] Fish 2008: 12–13.

[46] See, e.g., Fish 2008: esp. 11, 14, 59, 102–3. Cf. Kronman 2007: esp. 199–203, 240–41.

defining themselves academically."[47] He added, "The great majority of college students in the United States are taking mainly skills courses, which are aimed at getting them jobs in white-collar fields that are not the 'ancient and honorable professions' that college graduates once looked to."[48] Thus Lemann advocated "a canon of methods," which prompted *The Chronicle of Higher Education*'s Dan Berrett to announce that *skills are the new canon*.[49] "Today just about everyone—administrators, students, parents, employers, policy makers, and most professors—has accepted the notion that broad, transferrable skills are the desired product of college," Berrett concluded.[50]

(Un)critical Thinking

What sorts of skills do contemporary defenders of the humanities underscore? By far the most popular answer to that question is *critical thinking*. Numerous apologists for humanistic study ground their arguments on this mystical (and often poorly defined) phrase, which seems to have taken on its current meaning as late as the 1940s.[51] And it's no wonder: According to the educational historian Roger L. Geiger, "an astonishing 99.6 percent of surveyed faculty reported that fostering critical thinking is an essential or very important goal of college."[52] Since educators overwhelmingly associate this skill with effective pedagogy, it stands to reason that humanities professors want to claim critical thinking as their own.

Among the most prominent and energetic advocates of this approach to validating the humanities is Nussbaum. Both books Nussbaum wrote in favor of broad liberal arts education rely heavily on this concept. Thus, for example, in *Not for Profit* Nussbaum bemoaned the fact that a 2006 report from the US Department of Education focuses solely on "national economic gain," almost entirely eschewing regard for the humanities, the arts, and "critical thinking."[53] Her list of worthy goals for a polity's approach to schooling includes the following recommendation: "Vigorously promote critical

---

[47] Lemann 2016.
[48] Ibid.
[49] Berrett 2016.
[50] Ibid.
[51] See Roth 2015: 181–82.
[52] Geiger 2016: 25. Cf. Small 2013: 27.
[53] Nussbaum 2010: 3.

thinking, the skills and courage it requires to raise a dissenting voice."[54] As we have noted, the cardinal importance of critical thinking to her vision of the humanities compelled Nussbaum to require all undergraduate students to take at least one,[55] if not two,[56] courses in philosophy.

Jay proves a similarly enthusiastic advocate for tying humanistic study to critical thinking. In fact, Jay supports the teaching of postmodern literary theory largely on the basis of its supposed effects on students' abilities to think critically. In his aforementioned book he asserted that "courses putting a stress on critical theories and disciplinary methodologies are some of the best ones we have for teaching critical thinking, and for training students to think ethically about social justice, both of which nearly everyone agrees are central to any conception of a humanities education."[57] He concluded that, as a result of the vicissitudes of the modern corporate university, "defending the humanities must be a two-pronged effort, insisting on the important role the humanities play in fostering critical thinking about bottom-line values and the instrumentalization of everyday life, *and* articulating the value of a humanities education in concrete terms that stress the practical skills human-ities students learn."[58] Without such a pragmatic approach to defending their subject matter, humanists will see the crisis of the humanities proceed apace.

The novelist, essayist, and critic Francine Prose deemed critical thinking so essential to humanistic study that she pondered the possibility that ne-farious powerbrokers have knowingly attempted to marginalize and under-mine the humanities in an attempt to turn Americans into docile sheep. In an impassioned opinion piece in *The Guardian* illustratively titled "Humanities Teach Students to Think. Where Would We Be without Them?" Prose asked, "Is it entirely paranoid to wonder if these subjects are under attack *because* they enable students to think in ways that are more complex than the re-ductive simplifications so congenial to our current political and corporate discourse?"[59]

Such widespread enthusiasm for the humanities as conduits for fos-tering critical thinking overlooks key problems with advancing this line of

---

[54] Ibid. 46. Cf. Nussbaum 1997: 9–11. Nussbaum also focuses her skills-based regimen in part on something she calls "the narrative imagination." See, e.g., Nussbaum 1997: 85–112 and 2010: 95–120. Cf. Ferrall 2011: 17.

[55] Nussbaum 1997: 42.

[56] Nussbaum 2010: 55, 92.

[57] Jay 2014: 3–4.

[58] Ibid. 5 (emphasis in the original).

[59] Prose 2017 (emphasis in the original).

argument. First, one notes that these praises of critical thinking seldom identify the skill(s) it signifies. As Ferrall justly asked, "There are few college presidents and admissions officers who do not routinely feature 'critical thinking' in their public utterances. But what exactly is critical thinking? How does it differ from plain old good thinking?"[60] Given the crucial importance of critical thinking to contemporary defenses of the humanities, it is striking that few apologists feel the need to unpack and explain this concept. Why would defenders allow their arguments in favor of the humanities to hinge on a term sufficiently nebulous that Stanley Fish could dismiss it as "a phrase without content"?[61] And Fish is not alone in his criticisms of this concept: some education experts question its validity and pedagogical value.[62]

Nor is this the only downside associated with the scholarly emphasis on critical thinking. In order to convince skeptics that humanistic disciplines must be retained in American higher education, it seems crucial to demonstrate that the humanities provide something that other fields do not. If they do not do so, why do colleges and universities need the humanities? Yet it is far from certain that critical thinking is the sole domain of the academic disciplines making up the contemporary humanities. Thus Ferrall rightly wondered, "Whatever critical thinking may be, why is it more likely to be learned by studying English literature or philosophy than business management? Why would one suppose that English literature or philosophy professors are more likely to inculcate critical thinking in their students than business administration professors? To be blunt, why would one expect English literature or philosophy professors to *be* critical thinkers?"[63] Nussbaum herself admitted that critical thinking can be learned in science courses as well.[64]

Bauerlein agrees. He emphasized that social and natural scientists can argue that they too inculcate this skill.[65] As Small concluded, the humanities do not own critique, and even the discipline of philosophy cannot claim some special province in this regard: "critical and philosophical reflection are indispensible to intellectual work everywhere."[66] If humanities content were truly inconsequential (or, to say the same thing, a matter of individual

---

[60] Ferrall 2011: 107.
[61] Fish 2008: 54. Cf. Peckham 2010: 49.
[62] See, e.g., Wilson 1988; Atkinson 1997; Bailin, Case, et al. 1999; Johnson and Hamby 2015. Cf. Mason (2007: 340), who notes the disparate philosophical conceptions of critical thinking. Peckham (2010: 49–65) criticizes the concept in the context of English composition courses.
[63] Ferrall 2011: 107–8 (emphasis in the original).
[64] Nussbaum 2010: 7–8.
[65] Bauerlein 2013: 7. Cf. Bauerlein 2015: 34–36.
[66] Small 2013: 27; see, more broadly, 26–28, 129.

student preference alone), then would it not be preferable for American colleges and universities to cut out the middleman and have all humanists teach undergraduate courses called "Critical Thinking"? Not for nothing did Geiger include the critical-thinking rationale among his rogue's gallery of bad justifications for the humanities.[67] He concluded that "staking the claims for the humanities on the quicksand of critical thinking comforts the faithful, but will never convince the skeptics."[68]

We can point to another important downside associated with justifying the humanities on the basis of critical thinking. As it turns out, this short-coming plagues all such skills-based arguments. Seemingly unbeknownst to its advocates, basing rationales for the humanities on the instilling of skills ultimately subordinates the humanistic disciplines to the social sciences. In *Not for Profit*, for example, Nussbaum invoked scholarly studies conducted by psychologists to buoy her claims about the inculcation of skills in human-ities students.[69] Other proponents of this line of argument do the same;[70] the sociologists Richard Arum and Josipa Roksa, whose book *Academically Adrift* (2011) made headlines when it first appeared in print, appear to be a popular choice for humanists who want to appeal to the authority of so-cial scientists in an attempt to validate conclusions about the humanities as conduits for promoting desirable skills sets.[71]

Through these means, skill-promoters such as Nussbaum and Jay implic-itly demonstrate that the social sciences—and not the humanities—have the tools to assess value. Thus humanists must turn to social scientists to validate their impressions. Humanists, apparently lacking any useful means to judge the worthiness of their subject matter, must play the social scientists' game. By doing so, they show the superior value of the social sciences—and signal that humanists lack any intrinsic ability to evaluate quality. How valuable can the humanistic disciplines be if they cannot even credibly vouch for their im-portance on their own terms?

This contradiction points to a related problem. Understandably, as it turns out, most humanists make poor social scientists. Take Jay, for instance,

---

[67] Geiger 2016: 25. For other views on the value of critical thinking to defenses of the human-ities, see, e.g., Jay and Graff 2012; Jay 2014: esp. 3–5, 12–13, 24, 28, 55; Roth 2015: 181–88; Prose 2017. Proctor (2014: 27) points out that proto-critical thinking arguments have been important for defenders of the liberal arts since the nineteenth century.

[68] Geiger 2016: 25.

[69] Nussbaum 2010: 40–44.

[70] E.g., Small 2013: 91–92; Jay 2014: 16–17, 163; Kleinman 2016: 95.

[71] E.g., Summit 2012: 673; Jay 2014: 16–17, 163; Kleinman 2016: 95. Cf. Brodhead et al. 2013: 36 n. 6.

who, as we have noted, is among the most strenuous advocates of the skills-based argument for the contemporary humanities. In an attempt to vouch for the value of the humanities in *The Humanities "Crisis" and the Future of Literary Studies*, Jay twice mentioned the studies Arum and Roksa reported on in *Academically Adrift*[72] and thus unwittingly demonstrates the perils for humanists of relying on appeals to social science. The Collegiate Learning Assessment (CLA) on which Arum and Roksa based many of their findings actually groups humanities majors along with those in the social sciences. Thus any benefits of a comparatively high CLA score Jay can attribute to the humanities are in fact *equally attributable to the social sciences*. Further, Arum and Roksa demonstrated that CLA scores among majors in the natural sciences and mathematics are *higher* than those in the humanities and social sciences.[73] If we are to adhere strictly to the skills-based rationale, then, we can conclude only that mathematics and the natural sciences amount to more valuable subjects in which to major. Most crucially, *Academically Adrift*'s overarching thesis is that on the whole undergraduate students in the US *learn very little during their years in college*. The book's subtitle hammers home this argument: *Limited Learning on College Campuses*. Why would humanists want to base their case for the humanities on the notion that concentrations in humanistic fields appear slightly less abysmal than others in inculcating valuable intellectual proficiencies?[74]

The dangers of hitching one's wagon to such justifications should appear obvious. What happens when a group of social scientists conducts a study that shows, say, engineering majors vastly outperforming humanities majors in some skill they associate with collegiate learning? If the humanities must live by the social sciences, they will die by them, too. In short, outsourcing claims about your value to other disciplines is a risky business. And when social scientists cast doubt on the humanities as incubators of valuable aptitudes, you can presume that humanists will do a poor job debunking such conclusions. After all, humanists already agreed to play by the social scientists' rules. Through this means, they have set themselves up for failure.

Nor are social scientists the only group to which skill-promoting humanists appeal when attempting to make their case. Their defenses of both

---

[72] Jay 2014: 16–17, 163.

[73] See, e.g., Arum and Roksa 2011: 105.

[74] It is peculiar, therefore, that Summit (2012: 673) considers *Academically Adrift* "[o]ne of the most resonant recent defenses of the humanities." One should note, moreover, that critics of *Academically Adrift* doubt that the authors have mustered sufficient evidence for their overarching conclusions. See, for example, Astin 2011.

the humanities and the liberal arts often invoke the opinions of an assortment of successful businessmen and businesswomen. Thus, for example,
Jay quoted a major company's chief executive officer (CEO) to provide anecdotal evidence that business leaders want humanities students, thanks to
their "critical thinking skills."[75] The television pundit and public intellectual Fareed Zakaria routinely mentioned the views of Jeff Bezos, Steve Jobs,
and other business titans in his book-length apologia for the liberal arts.[76]
And Ferrall appealed to sympathetic entrepreneurs in his plea to save liberal
education.[77]

The desire to win favor from voices within the business community makes
sense in our age of rampant pre-professionalism. But one should not overlook the dangers involved in staking the case for the humanities on the authority of others. What would happen to such arguments if a large collection
of CEOs denigrated the humanities as worthless? How many prominent
entrepreneurs must be invoked to make a solid argument for the humanities' value? And how feeble are humanists' own justifications for their subject
matter that they are forced to look outside the academy for a rationale? The
education scholar Sheldon Rothblatt offered another good point in regard to
such appeals. Though professors often vouch for the liberal arts by suggesting
business leaders want the skills that liberal arts graduates have, they typically mention figures who are too high up the corporate ladder to do much
hiring themselves.[78] Jeff Bezos may value broad learning, but Jeff Bezos is
not likely to interview your son or daughter for a job. In all, resolutely pragmatic arguments in favor of such un-pragmatic subjects put humanists at the
mercy of outsiders.

The Humanities, Bulwark of Democracy

Thankfully, arguments in favor of critical thinking do not exhaust the intellectual arsenal of contemporary defenders of the humanities. But other
rationales stressed in the literature likewise rely heavily on instrumental
justifications. According to Small, the contention that democracy needs

[75] Jay 2014: 12.
[76] Zakaria 2015: 74, 82, 90.
[77] Ferrall 2011: 160–61. For other examples of defenders of the humanities and liberal arts invoking
supportive businessmen and businesswomen to make their case, see, e.g., Jay and Graff 2012; anonymous 2016; Kleinman 2016: 94–95. Cf. Belkin 2016.
[78] Rothblatt 2016: 34–35.

the humanities amounts to "the most fervently adopted argument for the humanities now."[79] Nussbaum's *Not for Profit* advanced one of the most well-known and impassioned recent versions of this argument.[80] The increasing vocationalism of education within numerous democratic nations, Nussbaum contended, amounts to "a world-wide crisis."[81] "Thirsty for national profit," she continued, "nations, and their systems of education, are heedlessly discarding skills that are needed to keep democracies alive."[82]

Many humanists agree with Nussbaum's emphasis on the humanities as promoters of thoughtful and broadminded democratic citizens. Di Leo, for example, praised Nussbaum for centering her defense of the humanities in part on democratic citizenship.[83] Andrew Delbanco, whose book *College: What It Was, Is, and Should Be* (2012) has been much discussed and recommended, linked democratic citizenship to American higher education as a whole. The idea that democracy requires an educated citizenry, he claimed, "is more true than ever."[84] Thus Delbanco ended his monograph by noting that the US must protect institutions of higher learning because "[d]emocracy depends on it."[85] Even Geoffrey Galt Harpham, who proved cautious about overhyping this line of attack,[86] announced in his book *The Humanities and the Dream of America* that "we may say that the textual emphasis of the humanities implies, as it were, the possibility of truthful knowledge (and the symmetrical, equally bracing, possibility of error), the act of reflection, and the cultivation of democratic citizenship, and fosters as well a sense of freedom and power, opening into an undiscovered future."[87] Some, it seems, are steadfast advocates for the humanities as the bulwark of democracy.[88]

Criticisms of these contentions suggest themselves. In *Not for Profit*, Nussbaum wrote, "I shall argue that cultivated capacities for critical thinking

[79] Small 2013: 9.
[80] Nussbaum 2010: esp. 121–43. Nussbaum 1997 offers congruent contentions. It should be noted that Nussbaum (2010: 10) associates the argument for the humanities that is based on democratic citizenship with the argument for critical thinking.
[81] Nussbaum 2010: 2.
[82] Ibid.
[83] Di Leo 2013: 4.
[84] Delbanco 2012: 29.
[85] Ibid. 177.
[86] Harpham 2011: 27.
[87] Ibid. 28. Cf. 152.
[88] For other recent works in defense of the humanities and/or liberal arts that focus on democratic citizenship, see, e.g., Nussbaum 1997; Freedman 2003: 64–65; Small 2013: 5–6, 9–10, 125–50, 175; Hutner and Mohamed 2016a: 3; Prose 2017.

and reflection are crucial in keeping democracies alive and awake."[89] As we have seen, it is problematic to argue that the humanities are the sole instillers of "critical thinking." Most assuredly, the same may be said for the more nebulous skill of "reflection." Thus it remains unclear why the humanities are essential in this regard. Perhaps in part for this reason, thinkers as varied as Small, Fish, Geiger, and Lemann express reservations about this type of argument.[90]

The focus on the humanistic disciplines as promoters of informed and beneficent democratic citizens seems peculiar in the context of contentless defenses of the humanities. If higher education should be an effective safeguard of democracy, why should colleges and universities across the nation not require all students to study the worldwide history of democracy, and not to encounter particular texts that most effectively highlight its strengths and weaknesses? Surely a healthy democracy cannot rely on "critical thinking and reflection" alone.

Looking Back to Look Forward

It is hard to avoid the conclusion that unmentioned suppositions about humanistic disciplines still pervade our culture (however faintly) and affect the character of recent defenses of the humanities. Although contributors to this literature seldom—if ever—mention as much, it seems that briefs in favor of the humanities in part rely on remnants of the idea that broad learning is gentle(wo)manly learning.[91] Thus those arguing for the humanities as skill-promoters can still capitalize on the sense that opposition to the humanities is philistine. Hence, perhaps, various contemporary arguments for the humanities are less convincing than they might be. But if the humanities possess value only insofar as they offer abilities that can also be conferred by other disciplines outside their orbit, what is philistine about questioning their importance for educated Americans? Despite the obvious good intentions of their authors, one wonders whether these are the best defenses we can muster on behalf of the humanities.

This concern appears to be especially pertinent because of the historical and definitional missteps that trip up various contemporary rationales in

[89] Nussbaum 2010: 10.
[90] Small 2013: 5–6, 9–10, 125–50, 175; Fish 2008: 67–72; Lemann 2016; Geiger 2016: 25.
[91] On this argument in the history of humanities, see, e.g., Proctor 2014: 14–16.

favor of contemporary humanistic disciplines. Numerous apologists either fail to define the modern humanities in their works or provide questionable definitions.[92] Many presume that the *humanities* and the *liberal arts* are synonymous.[93] Others fail to connect the contemporary humanities to the Renaissance conception of the *studia humanitatis* and thus vastly postdate their arrival in American education.[94] Still others rely on polemical accounts of the early American colleges and thus present untrustworthy impressions of their history.[95]

We do not want to make similar mistakes. Thus, before we turn to an examination of key educational disputes that took place during the late nineteenth and early twentieth centuries, it is imperative to examine the history of the humanities themselves. This approach will supply us with the historical context necessary to analyze the Battle of the Classics. And it will help ensure greater precision of our arguments in favor of the contemporary humanities.

[92] For examples of the latter, see, e.g., Nussbaum 1997: 11 and Kronman 2007: 66; Harpham 2011: 17; Jay 2014: 3. Cf. the definition of Verene 2002: x. Proctor (2014: 14) discusses the way in which most people define the humanities today.

[93] E.g., Nussbaum 2010; Jay and Graff 2012; anonymous 2016; Hutner and Mohamed 2016b. Proctor (2014: 12) concludes that the variegated traditions of the liberal arts and the humanities make it difficult for us to define them precisely.

[94] E.g., Marcus 2006: esp. 15; Harpham 2011: 14; Small 2013: 14; Jay 2014: 25, 62.

[95] E.g., Roth 2015: 27, 72, 159; Nussbaum 2010: 57, 141; Zakaria 2015: 75–76. On the misleading nature of much earlier scholarship on the antebellum American colleges, see Winterer 2002: 3, 185 n. 3, 77. Other examples of misunderstandings in recent tracts defending the humanities and liberal arts regarding the history of American higher education include Freedman 2003: 3; Menand 2010: 99; Nussbaum 2010: 57; Harpham 2011: 123–24; Zakaria 2015: 43, 75–76; McCumber 2016.

2

From the *Studia Humanitatis* to
the Modern Humanities

No one today knows what the humanities are. The National
Endowment for the Humanities doesn't define them; it merely lists
the disciplines Congress has empowered it to fund.
                    —Robert E. Proctor, *Defining the Humanities* (1998)

Misimpressions and Complications

"The idea of the humanities," Steven Marcus wrote in a 2006 essay, "first
appeared in the United States early in the twentieth century and has altered
greatly in meaning ever since, thanks to the intellectual, social, cultural, and
educational developments that have taken place in the last hundred years."[1]
Marcus is not alone in tracing the origins of the humanities in America to
the start of the last century.[2] Other scholars, focusing on the humanistic tradition writ large, have pushed these origins slightly further back in time.
According to Jon H. Roberts and James Turner, for example, educators first
employed the plural form of the word *humanity* in the 1870s to describe "liberal culture"—that is, what we might today call the *modern humanities*.[3]

Such views hint at something important: the institutionalization of the
modern humanities as a largely agreed upon group of academic disciplines
developed rather late in the history of American higher education. But this
fact can serve to confuse us, because it separates the modern humanities from
their ancient and Renaissance pasts. As it happens, the phrase *the humanities*

---

[1] Marcus 2006: 15.
[2] For other examples, see, e.g., Harpham 2011: 14; Jay 2014: 25, 62; Small 2013: 14. Cf. Jewett
2012: 98. Such authors disconnect the humanistic tradition from the *studia humanitatis* and associate
the origins of the modern humanities with their institutionalization in US higher education. On this
institutionalization, see, e.g., Summit 2012: 665 and later in this chapter.
[3] Roberts and Turner 2000: 75. See also Winterer 2002: 117–18, who largely follows Roberts and
Turner's account. Cf. Veysey 1979: 54–57; Kuklick 1990: 203.

entered the English language in the eighteenth century.[4] It was originally an English translation of the French term *les humanités*. This, in turn, was the French way of describing the Latin phrase *studia humanitatis* ("the studies of humanity"), which, as we shall see, first appeared in literary works composed during the first century BC, in the final decades of the Roman Republic.[5] We must thus look much earlier than the late nineteenth or early twentieth centuries to unearth the origins of the humanities.

These origins amount to far from the lone confusion surrounding the humanities' history. Some scholars have presumed that the ancient Greeks founded the humanistic tradition.[6] As was the case with those who conflate the *modern* humanities with the humanistic tradition as a whole, one can understand why scholars might come to this conclusion. The ancient Greeks, after all, deeply influenced the humanities and pioneered essentially all the disciplines that were part of their purview in antiquity. But the term *humanitas*, from which we derive the English phrase *the humanities*, is Latin, and, as we shall see, the use of the term *studia humanitatis* to describe a particular approach to education first appears in the extant literature in the work of Cicero.[7] We can be sure that preexisting Greek educational ideals had greatly influenced Cicero when he described his view of the humanities. Cicero, in fact, had employed his Greek friend Tyrannio the Elder as a tutor for his son and nephew, and it seems probable (though ultimately uncertain) that Tyrannio's conception of education rubbed off on him.[8] Though indebted to Greek forbears, however, Cicero, as we shall discuss in later sections, fit this largely Hellenic model to the contours of the aristocratic culture of the late Roman Republic. So, it is the Romans to whom we must first turn in order to grasp the early history of the humanities.

---

[4] See Proctor (1998: 7), who relies on the *Oxford English Dictionary* for this dating. According to Kristeller (1961: 121), the term *the humanities* was coined during the Renaissance.

[5] Thus Proctor (1998: ix, xxiv, 13 and forthcoming) asserts that the humanities used to be synonymous with classical education.

[6] E.g., Jarrett 1973: 1; Jewett 2012: 328. Others contend that the Greeks founded the liberal arts tradition (a tradition that, as we shall see, was one and the same as the *studia humanitatis* in antiquity): e.g., Butts 1971: 20; Rudolph 1977: 29–30. Marrou (1956: 96) believes that no major changes occurred in classical education after the generation following Alexander the Great; according to Marrou (138–39), mature classical education was Hellenistic education, and there never was an autonomous Roman education. Cf. Lucas 1994: 25.

[7] On the distinctions between the Roman *artes liberales/studia humanitatis* and the Greek *enkyklios paideia*, see the section "The Greeks, Forefathers of the Humanities."

[8] For a discussion of Tyrannio the Elder of Amisus and his relationship with Cicero, see, e.g., Bonner 1977: 28–30. On Tyrannio's approach to grammar and philology, see, e.g., Turner 2014: 14.

These sorts of subtleties demonstrate the cardinal importance for our purposes of reviewing the history of the humanistic tradition. We must ensure that misimpressions do not compromise our understanding of the humanities; if they do, we shall have a much harder time offering an intellectually sound case for them in contemporary American education.[9] It stands to reason that *before we can adequately defend the humanities, we need to know what they have been, and what they are today.*

This chapter provides a brief history of the humanities from their origins as the *studia humanitatis* in Roman antiquity to the modern humanities we think of today. By charting this path, it offers a sense of the humanistic tradition in its entirety and explains what is at stake in its prospective downfall. This approach will introduce us to much of the direct historical background for the chapters to come. Only with such knowledge in mind can we attempt to provide as convincing a rationale as possible for the modern humanistic disciplines.

The Roman Origins of Humanitas

In 62 BC, the Roman statesman, orator, and writer Marcus Tullius Cicero (106–43 BC) delivered an atypical and, as it turned out, epochal defense speech on behalf of a man named Archias. Archias, a Greek poet from Antioch, had a close association with his patron, the prominent Roman general and politician Lucius Licinius Lucullus. Lucullus's enemies presumably attempted to irk him by prosecuting the aged Archias for unlawfully claiming Roman citizenship. A trial ensued and Cicero, Rome's master of the bar, represented the poet. Cicero had studied with Archias as a youth,[10] and his defense speech, the *Pro Archia* ("On Behalf of Archias"), which survives from antiquity, demonstrates that Cicero felt great appreciation and fondness for his former tutor.

---

[9] Some misimpressions are understandable—and in some respects unavoidable—because the history of the humanities and, more broadly, of the liberal arts is so complex and less well-documented than we would like. But we must do our best to unearth this history as clearly and precisely as possible.

[10] Cicero *Pro Archia* 1. As a native of Antioch, Archias may have shared the educational ideas offered by Dionysius Thrax and elaborated by his student, Tyrannio the Elder. This is another hint that Tyrannio may have influenced Cicero's conception of the *studia humanitatis*. On Dionysius and Tyrannio, see, e.g., Turner 2014: 14.

Although we cannot be certain, it appears that Archias ultimately won acquittal.[11] But it is not the trial's outcome that rendered it such an important event. Cicero's oration for the defense employed what the author himself called "a certain novel and unusual manner of argument" (*novo quodam et inusitato genere dicendi*).[12] In addition to laying out briefly the legal case for Archias' citizenship, Cicero in the oration maintained that Archias deserves to be a Roman citizen regardless, because Rome needs such learned poets in order to thrive. The speech thus contends that literature plays a crucial role in the health of the Roman state. Unbeknownst to Cicero, the *Pro Archia* became a text of prime importance in the history of Western education.

In order to make his broader case about the great value of literary culture to Rome's vibrancy, Cicero asked of the judges that, given Archias' status as a distinguished poet and scholar, he be permitted to "speak a bit more freely about the studies of civilization and literature" (*de studiis humanitatis ac litterarum paulo loqui liberius*).[13] Although Cicero did not coin *humanitas*,[14] a Latin word with a range of definitions such as "culture," "civilization," "benevolence," and "humanity," he appears to have broadened its meaning.[15] The link between *humanitas* and *studia* ("*the studies* of humanity"), furthermore, could be Cicero's invention: the orator had employed the selfsame phrase in a defense speech from the previous year,[16] and we have no record of its earlier use.

According to Cicero, the *studia humanitatis* are one and the same as the *artes liberales* ("liberal arts," i.e., subjects appropriate for the education of the freeborn),[17] a term that likewise appears first in Cicero's writings in the extant literature.[18] In the *Pro Archia* itself, in fact, Cicero calls the *studia humanitatis* the *optimae artes* (*ab optimarum artium studiis*, "from the studies of the

---

[11] In a letter to his friend Atticus from 61 BC, Cicero mentions Archias without suggesting that he now resided outside of Italy (1.16.15). One can infer from this that Archias remained in Rome and thus the prosecution had failed.

[12] Cicero *Pro Archia* 2. The text of the *Pro Archia* used in this chapter is that of Clark 1911. All translations in this chapter are my own, unless otherwise specified.

[13] Cicero *Pro Archia* 2.

[14] According to Büchner (1967: 1242), we have record of this word being used as far back as the start of the first century BC. But it likely goes further back than this. For a helpful account of the circle of the Roman general and politician Scipio Aemilianus (185–129 BC) and the origins of *humanitas*, see Schadewaldt 1973: 52–58. See also Gwynn 1926: 40–41; Proctor 1998: 213 n. 14.

[15] See Proctor forthcoming.

[16] Cicero *Pro Murena* 29.61.

[17] See Kimball 1995: 78; Proctor 1998: 16–21, 212–14 n. 14 and forthcoming.

[18] Cicero *De inventione* 1.35. According to Kimball (1995: 13), Cicero may have coined the term *artes liberales*.

best arts"),[19] another phrase he occasionally employed to denote the *artes liberales*.[20]

What did Cicero mean by the terms *studia humanitatis* and *artes liberales*? These phrases signified for Cicero a new educational ideal—one rooted in the earlier history of Greek pedagogy and scholarship, but reformulated and recontextualized to fit the nature of Roman aristocratic culture. For Cicero, the *studia humanitatis* and *artes liberales* describe a lifelong educational program encompassing a variety of studies appropriate for a freeborn person.[21] Such a program, Cicero argued, can serve to instill the crucial quality of *humanitas* in human beings.

This argument leads us to ask this question: what did *humanitas* mean to Cicero? Toward the conclusion of the *Pro Archia*, Cicero provided a definition: he urged the trial's judges to protect Archias "in order that he may seem to have been freed by your kindness (*humanitas*), rather than to have been violated by your cruelty (*acerbitas*)" (*ut humanitate vestra levatus potius quam acerbitate violatus esse videatur*).[22] Analyzing this passage, Robert Proctor helpfully explains,

> The opposite of *acerbitas*, *humanitas* in this context clearly means benevolence, kindness, even mercy, expressed in the English word "humanity" when it means "the quality of being humane." As it is used in Cicero's defense of Archias, *humanitas* is thus both a moral *and* an intellectual virtue. Or perhaps it would be better to say that for Cicero *humanitas* is an intellectual virtue that leads to a moral virtue: *litterae*, literature, can make a person kind, benevolent, and adverse to violence.[23]

Ciceronian *humanitas* can be seen as "high culture," exposure to which renders one refined and benevolent.[24] The *studia humanitatis*—more often referred to in Roman antiquity as the *artes liberales*, *bonae artes* ("good arts"), *optimae artes* ("best arts"), or the *ingenuae artes* ("freeborn arts")—then,

---

[19] Cicero *Pro Archia* 1.

[20] Other terms Cicero used to express this idea include *bonae artes, ingenuae artes*, and *artes*. Cicero used the phrase *artes liberales* only once in his extant writings, at *De inventione* 1.35.

[21] On Cicero and the *studia humanitatis*, see, e.g., Gwynn 1926: 57, 59–122; Rand 1932; Marrou 1956: 339–40, 346, 350, 388; Bowen 1972: 177–82; Schadewaldt 1973: 58–61; Morgan 1998: 156; Proctor 1998: 14–21, 59–76, 177, 213 n. 14.

[22] Cicero *Pro Archia* 31.

[23] Proctor forthcoming (emphasis in the original).

[24] For this usage, see Cicero's *Epistulae ad Quintum fratrem* 1.1.

amounted to a broad educational regimen that would inculcate particular intellectual and moral virtues in its devotees.

In a few of his other writings, Cicero specified those subjects whose study can provide this spirit of *humanitas*. Lucius Licinius Crassus, a Roman politician who served as a character in Cicero's dialogue *De oratore* ("Concerning the Orator"), published in 55 BC, states that poetry, geometry, music, and dialectic (i.e., philosophical debate) are examples of arts that can turn people's minds to humanity (*humanitas*) and virtue (*virtus*).[25] Further in the dialogue, Cicero had another statesman, Quintus Lutatius Catulus, underscore the importance of geometry, music, and poetry in this regard, and added literature, the natural sciences (*illa, quae de naturis rerum*), ethics, and political science (*quae de rebus publicis*) to the list.[26] In a letter written in 46 BC to the Roman orator and jurist Servius Sulpicius Rufus, Cicero included philosophy as another subject he deemed "liberal."[27] According to Proctor, these lists of studies demonstrate that, for Cicero, the *studia humanitatis/artes liberales* were one and the same as "ancient education as a whole."[28]

Cicero's conception of the *studia humanitatis* greatly influenced further Roman reflections on a proper elite education. Yet from other ancient discussions of the *artes liberales* we can gather that no complete consensus existed about their constituent elements. Not long after Cicero's death, Marcus Vitruvius Pollio wrote *De architectura* ("Concerning Architecture"), a treatise that includes the author's recommendations for the broad, liberal education he thought suitable for an aspiring architect. Vitruvius listed a wide range of requisite arts: draftsmanship, mathematics, philosophy, music, medicine, law, astronomy, history,[29] and literature.[30] The properly educated architect, he wrote, need not master these studies, but he must not be deficient in any of them.[31]

Our fullest surviving account of this conception of education befitting a freeborn person comes from the Roman rhetorician Marcus Fabius Quintilianus. In the 90s AD, Quintilian (as he is commonly known in English) published the *Institutio oratoria* ("The Education of an Orator"), a

---

[25] Cicero *De oratore* 3.58. The text of the *De oratore* consulted is that of Wilkins 1902.
[26] Cicero *De oratore* 3.127.
[27] Cicero *Epistulae ad familiares* 4.13–14.
[28] Proctor 1998: 16.
[29] Vitruvius *De architectura* 1.1.3.
[30] Ibid. 1.1.4.
[31] Ibid. 1.1.13–14.

work in twelve books devoted to rhetorical theory and practice.[32] Quintilian included a discussion of the requisite subjects for an orator's education. Explicitly basing his conception of the well-trained orator on Cicero's earlier writings,[33] Quintilian highlighted the value of studying grammar,[34] word usage,[35] writing,[36] reading,[37] literature, astronomy, logic,[38] music,[39] geometry,[40] and even a bit of acting[41] and gymnastics.[42]

In a letter detailing the distinction between liberal and manual studies, the Roman Stoic philosopher, political advisor, and playwright Seneca (ca. 4 BC–65 AD) provided a revisionist account of sorts of the *artes liberales*.[43] According to Seneca, only philosophy truly earned the designation "liberal," because only it teaches wisdom and virtue.[44] Even so, Seneca believed that other subjects were prerequisites to philosophy, and he numbered grammar and poetry,[45] music,[46] mathematics,[47] and cosmology[48] among them. Although these authors disagreed on some of the specifics, we may still safely conclude that the *studia humanitatis/artes liberales* ideal in Roman antiquity encompassed a comprehensive approach to education focused on various studies the Greeks pioneered.

The Greeks, Forefathers of the Humanities

The Hellenic patrimony of these subjects clues us into one reason why some observers have credited the Greeks with founding the humanistic tradition.[49]

---

[32] Gwynn (1926: 184–85) dates the work to ca. 93–95 AD. According to Bowen (1972: 200), it was published ca. 96.

[33] Quintilian *Institutio oratoria* 1.10.4.

[34] Ibid. 1.4–5, 9.

[35] Ibid. 1.6.

[36] Ibid. 1.7.

[37] Ibid. 1.8.

[38] Ibid. 1.10.1.

[39] Ibid. 1.10.9–33.

[40] Ibid. 1.10.34–49.

[41] Ibid. 1.11.1–14.

[42] Ibid. 1.11.15–19.

[43] Seneca *Epistulae morales* ("Moral Letters") 88.

[44] Ibid. 88.2–3, 29–30.

[45] Ibid. 88.3.

[46] Ibid. 88.9–10.

[47] Ibid. 88.10–13.

[48] Ibid. 88.14–17.

[49] For examples of scholarship highlighting the Hellenic character of Roman education, see, e.g., Jaeger 1943: 4–5; Marrou 1956: 96, 137–39, 296–97, 325, 335, 386; Butts 1971: 20; Jarrett 1973: 328; Rudolph 1977: 29–30; Lucas 1994: 25. Cf. Bloomer 2011: 2–3, 9.

But there are others. According to many scholars, by the early Hellenistic period (323–31 BC), the Greeks had systematized what we might call Hellenic
"secondary education" into something they deemed the *enkyklios paideia*.
Enkyklios paideia, a term often defined as "general education," describes a
wide-ranging, non-vocational course of studies with obvious parallels to the
Roman conception of the *artes liberales*.[50] Quintilian, in fact, made this connection in his work, when he likened the studies necessary for students who
aspired to train with a professor of rhetoric to the *enkyklios paideia*.[51] In the
fourth century BC, moreover, the Greek philosopher Aristotle distinguished
between liberal and vocational subjects—labeling only the former appropriate for the education of the freeborn.[52] This distinction clearly influenced
Romans such as Cicero and Seneca to proffer similar perspectives on a suitable curriculum for members of the elite.

Another reason for attributing the humanistic tradition to the ancient
Greeks stems from an oft-cited passage in the work of Aulus Gellius. In the
Noctes Atticae ("Attic Nights"), Gellius, a Roman author who lived during
the second century AD, equated the Latin term *humanitas* with the Greek
concept of *paideia* ("culture," "education").[53] Numerous people, he insisted,
incorrectly liken *humanitas* to *philanthropia* ("kindliness").[54] But, Gellius
contended, the word is more correctly seen as akin to *paideia*, a Greek term
Gellius regarded as the equivalent of the Latin *bonae artes*.[55] Some scholars,
taking Gellius at face value, have deemed this passage proof of the Hellenic
foundation of the humanistic tradition.[56]

Much work has challenged Gellius' conclusion, however. According to the
classicist Wolfgang Schadewaldt, for example, the chameleonlike quality of
the word *humanitas* for the Romans demonstrates that Gellius engaged in
a species of simplification.[57] The Romans, moreover, would have used other
words as a translation for the Greek term *paideia*;[58] *humanitas* was not an accurate equivalent.

---

[50] On the *enkyklios paideia* and its definition, see, e.g., Gywnn 1926: 84, 86–88; Marrou 1956: 243–
45, 378; Bowen 1972: 152–65; Kimball 1995: 15, 20–22; Morgan 1998: 33–39, 50–89; Proctor
1998: 212–14 n. 14 and forthcoming; Stein-Hölkeskamp 2003: 71; Christes 2004: esp. 984.

[51] Quintilian *Institutio oratoria* 1.10.1.

[52] Aristotle *Politics* 8.3.

[53] Aulus Gellius *Noctes Atticae* 13.17.

[54] Ibid. 13.17.1.

[55] Ibid.

[56] E.g., Jaeger 1943: 21; Kelley 1991: 2–3.

[57] Schadewaldt 1973: 43–45. Others have remarked on Gellius' simplification. See, e.g., Büchner
1967: 1242–43; Proctor 1998: 212 n. 14; Storch 2005: 560–61. On the ambiguity of the term *humanitas*
for the Romans, see Kristeller 1961: 132.

[58] Schadewaldt 1973: 47.

Similar problems speak against other rationales for tracing *humanitas* back to the Greeks. Although many have presumed that the *enkyklios paideia* was regularized during the early Hellenistic period, we have no attestation of this term's use until the middle of the first century BC.[59] In fact, *Roman* authors are the first to mention the term in the extant literature. Moreover, the *enkyklios paideia*, as we noted previously, described a Hellenic "general education" roughly compatible with our notion of "secondary school." For Cicero, though, the *studia humanitatis* amounted to a lifelong course of studies—a course of studies Cicero nowhere in his writings on education attributed to the Greeks.[60] Despite some important similarities and overlaps, then, there are differences between the Greek conception of the *enkyklios paideia* and the Ciceronian *studia humanitatis/artes liberales*.

If anything, as the classical scholar W. Martin Bloomer has stressed, the Romans overplayed the Hellenic influences on their approach to education and underemphasized their indigenous contributions.[61] As was typical of them, the Romans modified what they borrowed: they pioneered, for example, foreign language study, since the Romans deemed Greek literature indispensable for a properly educated person.[62] Naturally, the Romans assimilated Hellenic education to fit the vicissitudes of their own society—a society that was in many respects more traditionalistic and backward-looking than that of the Greeks. Not for nothing, then, did Cicero maintain, as far as his educational ideals were concerned, that the culture came from Greece, but the virtues came from Rome.[63]

The Nature of the Roman Humanities

Our examination of the *studia humanitatis/artes liberales* in antiquity allows us to come to some key conclusions. This Roman educational tradition, idealized in the writings of Cicero, Quintilian, and others, possessed certain characteristics that would continue to influence the humanities for millennia. For

[59] Christes 2004: 982. Cf. Kimball 1995: 22.

[60] It is also important to recognize that the Renaissance humanists looked back to the Romans (especially Cicero)—not the Greeks—when offering their conceptions of the *studia humanitatis*. On this topic, see, e.g., Rand 1932: 210.

[61] Bloomer 2011: 2–3, 9. See also Proctor forthcoming. Bloomer stresses (2011: 11–12, 201 n. 5) that the Romans' views on education and its Hellenic influences are romanticized.

[62] See Gwynn 1926: 90; Marrou 1956: 342. Morgan (1998: 98–99) informs us that the Romans considered Greek authors more important than Roman ones for the purposes of education.

[63] Cicero, *De oratore* 3.137. On this passage, see Gwynn 1926: 122.

example, the Romans—following the Greeks—conceived of the humanities as a resolutely non-vocational, non-utilitarian course of studies.[64] As far as the ancients were concerned, the non-freeborn person could learn a trade, but such pragmatic fare was too uncultured for the elite. Freeborn people, they thought, should experience an education attuned to higher ideals.

This viewpoint hints at another crucial characteristic of the ancient *studia humanitatis*. It was an educational program focused above all on fostering the student's individual development.[65] The Romans, like the Greeks before them, considered education to be primarily a *moral enterprise*.[66] For this reason, in his exposition of liberal arts education, Seneca stressed that it was better for a man to be good than to be learned.[67] The chief goal of the Roman *studia humanitatis* was the transmitting of wisdom to pupils. To Seneca, for instance, liberal studies prepare one's soul for the inculcation of virtue through philosophy.[68]

Another significant attribute of the *studia humanitatis* in antiquity pertains to their substance: on their literary side, the humanities provided a curriculum that hinged on *particular content*. We can conclude this from both the idealized portraits of the *studia humanitatis* Cicero and later ancient authors offered and the material record.[69] After a thorough examination of papyri from Hellenistic and Roman Egypt, the classicist Teresa Morgan concluded that Greco-Roman literary studies at least as far back as the early Hellenistic period revolved around particular works written by canonical authors. Those aiming at a Greek literary education would invariably read Homer's epics; those aspiring to demonstrate acquaintance with Latin literature would without fail read Vergil's *Aeneid*.[70] For students who continued further along in their studies,[71] the writings of other ancient authors were often encountered; Euripides, Menander, Demosthenes,[72] and Horace[73] appear to have been especially popular pedagogical choices. The papyri show

---

[64] Marrou 1956: 386; Proctor forthcoming.

[65] See, e.g., Marrou 1956: 141–42, 301.

[66] See, e.g., Marrou 1956: 301; Morgan 1998: 95–96. Proctor (1998: 171) notes that, according to the humanistic tradition as a whole, education is predominantly moral.

[67] Seneca, *Epistulae morales* 88.38–39.

[68] Ibid. 88.20.

[69] Morgan (1998: 51) stresses that ancient literary accounts of Greco-Roman education are idealized and thus may not conform to actual practice.

[70] Morgan 1998: 16, 51, 68–88, 93. Cf. Marrou 1956: 29, 33, 225–27, 337.

[71] Morgan (1998: 70) stresses that students regularly abandoned their educations at various times because of a lack of funds.

[72] Morgan 1998: 228.

[73] Ibid. 337.

that the order and specifics of this sort of literary education could be flexible; even so, it contained certain standard elements: above all, Homer's *Iliad* and, starting in the early Roman Empire, Vergil's great epic.[74]

Whatever one's views of the Romans' originality in educational matters, it is clear that they (unlike their Greek forebears) introduced a key component of the humanities that would remain essential to the tradition for millennia: the necessity of foreign language study. Starting in the mid-Republican period, properly educated members of the Roman elite would be bilingual—well-versed in both Greek and Latin learning. The Romans proved so enamored of Greek culture, in fact, that they appear to have overemphasized the Hellenic contribution to their educational traditions. In any case, their approach to pedagogy demanded that Romans devoted to the *studia humanitatis/artes liberales* study Greek grammar and literature just as much as their own.

But in at least one critical respect the Roman take on the humanities differed from later iterations of the tradition. As we have detected, the Roman vision of the humanities was all-encompassing: ancient educational theorists typically considered a wide variety of subjects—including mathematics and the natural sciences—part of humanistic studies. Thus, for example, Vitruvius concluded that all studies are related.[75] Similarly, Seneca deemed every subject "liberal" if it does not focus on money-making.[76] In practice, to be sure, the Roman approach to pedagogy often favored literary studies—perhaps even to the exclusion of other topics.[77] Yet the ancient *studia humanitatis* in theory comprised all those arts not deemed unbecomingly technical and utilitarian. Thus, as we have seen, for the Romans, the humanities and the liberal arts were one and the same.

The Seven Liberal Arts and the Scholastic Transition

We have noted that ancient descriptions of the *studia humanitatis/artes liberales* occasionally differ in their emphases. Quintilian, for example, thought that the aspiring orator should spend some time in training in gymnastics;[78] Seneca, however, debarred this subject from liberal studies.[79] It was

[74] Ibid. 68–88.
[75] Vitruvius, *De architectura* 1.1.12. Cf. Gwynn 1926: 89 regarding Cicero's views on this topic.
[76] Seneca, *Epistulae morales* 88.1–2.
[77] See, e.g., Marrou 1956: 304, 378–79.
[78] Quintilian, *Institutio oratoria* 1.11.15–19.
[79] Seneca, *Epistulae morales* 88.18.

thus left to the late ancient period for the subject matter associated with this tradition to be fully codified. In the fifth century AD, Martianus Capella composed a treatise called *De nuptiis Philologiae et Mercurii* ("On the Marriage of Philology and Mercury"). This work provides the first systematization of the *seven liberal arts* in the extent literature.[80] By the ninth century, these arts had been split up into two groups—the *trivium* ("three roads"): grammar, rhetoric, and dialectic; and the *quadrivium* ("four roads"): arithmetic, geometry, music, and astronomy.[81]

In practice, as mentioned previously, Greco-Roman pedagogy typically focused more on the literary aspects of liberal education (which would ultimately be grouped in the *trivium*) than on other topics.[82] This pedagogical emphasis shifted, however, during the Middle Ages. In the early medieval period, learning in what had formerly been the western portion of the Roman Empire experienced profound changes. Most texts from classical antiquity had been lost; knowledge of the ancient Greek language in medieval Christendom became scarce, especially outside of the Italian peninsula and the Mediterranean coast of France.[83] Not until the eleventh century did medieval European society recover from the chaos surrounding the fall of Rome and its aftermath. Ultimately, European universities, institutions typically owing their origins to the twelfth and thirteenth centuries,[84] would embrace the seven liberal arts that Martianus Capella had enumerated.

The eleventh century also witnessed the foundation of the scholastic movement, which greatly influenced Western education for centuries.[85] Thanks to the rediscovery and translation of various works of Aristotle in the twelfth and thirteenth centuries,[86] this movement gathered increasing strength in European university life, encouraging educators to focus on syllogistic

---

[80] Kimball 1995: 22–23, 30–31. Cf. Bowen 1972: 209, who sees Capella's treatise as largely a copy of Varro's *Nine Books of Disciplines*, but with medicine and architecture removed. According to Marrou (1956: 244–45), the seven liberal arts were definitively formulated in the middle of the first century BC. See also Turner 2014: 17–18.

[81] On the dating, see Schneider 2006: 298. On the terms, see Kimball 1995: 47–51. According to Kimball (47), Boethius coined the term *quadrivium* and anticipated changes in the liberal arts tradition to come in the medieval period by preferring this portion of ancient education to the literary *trivium*. See the following text.

[82] Plato, one of the two chief architects of mature Greek education (Marrou 1956: 96), was anomalous in this regard, since mathematics was essential to his pedagogical vision (see, e.g., Stein-Hölkeskamp 2003: 73; Christes 2004: 984). But the ancient tradition ultimately proved to be more Isocratean than Platonic (see Marrou 1956: esp. 95–118).

[83] See Lucas 1994: 35.

[84] Morison 1935: 6–7; Butts 1971: 28; Lucas 1994: 62; Axtell 2016: 1–3, 7.

[85] Kimball 1995: 56–57. On scholasticism, see, e.g., Kristeller 1961: 6–7, 24–47, 92–119; Lucas 1994: 37–39; Kimball 1995: 56–77; Proctor 1998: 38–39; Axtell 2016: 21, 42, 101.

[86] See, e.g., Kristeller 1961: 96–97; Kimball 1995: 58, 64.

reasoning, metaphysics, and theology. Thomas Aquinas (1224–74), the most influential thinker associated with scholasticism, considered logic the essential feature of the liberal arts.[87] The *quadrivium* was now central to the tradition. By the early Renaissance, many scholastics in European universities had become especially enamored of pure logic and linguistic analysis.[88] The vogue for such skills led scholars to prize the internal logic of various propositions, without much concern for their wider context.[89] In such an intellectual environment, scholars' high regard for the specialized techniques associated with dialectical reasoning eclipsed the importance of introducing students to particular works of literature.

Training in medieval universities was also far more utilitarian in its emphases than were the ancient Roman liberal arts. Classical education had shunned vocationalism as beneath the dignity of a freeborn person. European higher education in the Middle Ages, by contrast, was resolutely occupational.[90] At such institutions, one could study civil and canon law, theology, and medicine, with the aim of turning these studies into a career. Indeed, as the historian Christopher J. Lucas concluded, "The medieval university was first and foremost a professional school for a select few discrete professions."[91]

Rebirth of the Humanities

It was in opposition to the vicissitudes of the scholastic medieval university that the humanities were reborn and reshaped at the start of the Renaissance. This intellectual and pedagogical rebellion commenced in Italy around the beginning of the thirteenth century.[92] At this time, various learned men, who would ultimately be called *umanisti* ("humanists"),[93] became enraptured

---

[87] Kimball 1995: 65–67; Axtell 2016: 20–21 (this shift in favor of the *quadrivium* started around 1200, with the appearance of Aristotle's work in Latin translation).

[88] Proctor 1998: 39; Grendler 2002: 257; Axtell 2016: 20–21.

[89] Proctor 1998: 39.

[90] Cowley and Williams 1991: 45; Lucas 1994: 67; Axtell 2016: 11, 235.

[91] Lucas 1994: 67.

[92] See Witt 2000 and 2015, who argued for an earlier date for the commencement of Renaissance humanism than had previously been supposed.

[93] The English word *humanist* comes from the Italian *umanista*, which was originally school jargon for students of the liberal arts. See, e.g., Kelley 1991: 3. According to Kristeller (1961: 121), the term *umanista* first appears in documents from the late fifteenth century and was commonly used in the sixteenth century (9). Kristeller also specifies (1961: 8–9) that F. J. Niethammer coined the German term Humanismus ("humanism") in 1808.

with classical antiquity, seeing in it an antidote to the scholasticism regnant in European higher education and intellectual life.

The most important early exponent of so-called Renaissance humanism was Francesco Petrarca, who is better known in English as Petrarch (1304–74).[94] To his followers, in fact, Petrarch had revived the *studia humanitatis*,[95] although he had never employed this specific phrase in his work. In various writings, Petrarch demonstrated the supreme value he placed on masterworks from Roman antiquity. Unable to read ancient Greek (knowledge of which was scarce in the West upon the downfall of the Roman Empire), Petrarch deemed particular classical Latin authors key to his moral improvement.[96] By learning about the great deeds of ancient Roman heroes in these works, Petrarch thought, he could persevere through the grief and fear that constantly vexed him. The Black Death plaguing Italy in the mid-fourteenth century claimed many of his loved ones, and Petrarch reported that attempts to emulate ancient Roman examples of bravery and virtue had enabled him to strengthen his revolve in the face of such unimaginable loss.[97]

Although Petrarch provided what the historian Donald Kelley called "the prototype of Renaissance humanism"[98] and perhaps its quintessential expression, it was left to later humanists to lay out an educational program based on this love for classical authors. In 1369, the humanist Coluccio Salutati (1331–1406), having discovered the phrase *studia humanitatis* in Cicero's *Pro Archia*, made the original use of the term during the Renaissance.[99] But it was not until the 1420s that Salutati's student Leonardo Bruni (1370–1444) provided the first systematic definition of the *studia humanitatis* as an educational program from the standpoint of the Italian humanists.[100] Bruni's work *De studiis et literiis* ("Concerning Studies and Literature"), a letter to Battista di Montefeltro, presents a full-scale description of the sort of pedagogy that humanists advocated.

[94] On Petrarch's role in shaping the humanities, see, e.g., Kelley 1991: 7–11; Lucas 1994: 73–74; Kimball 1995: 76–77; Proctor 1998: 25–58.

[95] Proctor 1998: 25–26; Kelley 1991: 7.

[96] On the cardinal importance of moral philosophy to Petrarch and his humanist followers, see, e.g., Grendler 2002: 395.

[97] See, e.g., Proctor 1998: 25–58.

[98] Kelley 1991: 7.

[99] Proctor 1998: 14. On Salutati's influence, see, e.g., Jarrett 1973: 21–22; Proctor 1998: 4, 14.

[100] Proctor 1998: 4–6. On Bruni's pedagogical views and their influence, see, e.g., Jarrett 1973: 21–22; Proctor 1998: xxvi, 4–6, 8–11, 14, 16–24; Grendler 2002: 153, 259. A few earlier pedagogical works from the Renaissance anticipate some of the views Bruni would articulate: e.g., Pietro Paulo Vergerio's *On Liberal Studies* (1401) and *The Character of Studies Befitting a Free-Born Youth* (ca. 1402–3). Bruni provided a more comprehensive discussion than did Vergerio, however.

In this treatise, Bruni suggested that the properly educated person should read only classical authors.[101] The Renaissance humanists dismissed medieval Latin as vulgar and unstylish and thus supported focusing one's studies on ancient Greek and Roman authors alone. Since the arrival of the Byzantine scholar and teacher Manuel Chrysoloras (1350–1415) in Florence in 1397,[102] knowledge of ancient Greek had become increasingly prevalent among the Italian humanists. This trend meant that such scholars could now laud the virtues of ancient Greek literature in the original language. Thus Bruni's treatise vouched for the unparalleled moral and stylistic value of both ancient Greek and Latin works of poetry and prose. According to Bruni, in fact, reading the works of classical philosophers, historians, orators, and poets allowed students to focus on the topics he deemed quintessential for an educated person: moral philosophy and divinity.[103] Although he thought that pupils could learn a bit of geometry, mathematics, and astronomy,[104] Bruni anchored his conception of a good education in the *trivium*: ancient literature provided the sacred and secular wisdom necessary for the perfection of the human being.[105] As Bruni wrote toward the conclusion of his letter, "It is religion and moral philosophy that ought to be our particular studies, I think, and the rest studied in relation to them as their handmaids, in proportion as they aid or illustrate their meaning."[106] For Renaissance humanists such as Bruni, the *studia humanitatis* stood for what we would now designate a *classical education*. The focus was firmly on ancient Greek and Roman writers (encountered in their original languages), at the expense of other topics and eras.

One notes some important overlaps between the ancient and Renaissance conceptions of the *studia humanitatis*. In both eras, theorists saw education primarily as a moral enterprise.[107] They also shunned vocationalism.[108] Further, in regard to literary studies, both approaches revolved around

---

[101] Bruni, *De studiis et literiis* 6–8.
[102] Kelley 1991: 24; Lucas 1994: 74; Grendler 2002: 206–7. Kristeller (1961: 97) contends that ancient Greek learning began to spread in the West after the middle of the fourteenth century.
[103] Bruni, *De studiis et literiis* 15–20.
[104] Ibid. 13.
[105] Cf. Battista Guarino's treatise *A Program of Teaching and Learning* (1459).
[106] Bruni, *De studiis et literiis* 30. The translation is by Kallendorf (2002: 123). For similar regard for moral philosophy among the educational views of the Renaissance humanists, see, e.g., Kallendorf 2002: 257–59.
[107] Proctor 1998: xxvii–xxviii, 3–4, 9–12.
[108] On the movement of Renaissance/Reformation universities back to cultural education and away from vocationalism, see Cowley and Williams 1991: 50–51; Kelley 1991: 6.

exposure to *particular humanities content*. Just as we know that ancient literary education hinged on a canon of masterworks (Homer's *Iliad* and Vergil's *Aeneid* first among them), various educational treatises written by exponents of Renaissance humanism vouch for the unsurpassed value of individual classical authors.[109] Thus, for example, Bruni in his afore-mentioned letter recommended the work of Lactantius,[110] Cicero, Vergil, Livy, Sallust,[111] Tacitus,[112] and Homer,[113] among others. For both the Romans and the Renaissance humanists, the humanities were grounded in substance—works of great wisdom that could perfect students' character and style.

Despite these crucial similarities, we can also detect significant differences between the Ciceronian and Renaissance visions of the *studia humanitatis*. For the Romans, as we discovered, all non-vocational arts played a role in a proper elite education. Thus, as noted previously, Seneca gave the mon-iker *liberal* to all studies not concerned with profitmaking.[114] According to Cicero and other ancient writers on education, then, there was no distinction between the humanities and the liberal arts.

The Renaissance humanists, however, contended that grammar, rhetoric, poetry, history, and moral philosophy comprised the *studia humanitatis*. Although they believed that their pedagogical ideals sprang from Cicero, the Italian humanists had actually made a core change to the tradition by narrowing its purview. Thus, for example, Bruni almost entirely shunned the natural sciences, believing that knowledge of them would not shape a student's character.[115] Similarly, in his treatise from 1450 called *De liberorum educatione* ("Concerning the Education of Boys"), the humanist Aeneas Silvius Piccolomini (1405–64) asserted that one should learn a smattering of astronomy and mathematics, but not too much.[116] The humanities and the liberal arts now signified distinct—albeit overlapping—realms: the former denoted ancient Greek and Latin literature; the latter encompassed these

---

[109] Proctor (1998: xxii–xxvi, 5–6, 16) concludes that the Renaissance approach to the *studia humanitatis* supported a curriculum with particular content.
[110] Bruni, *De studiis et litteriis* 7.
[111] Ibid. 8.
[112] Ibid. 18.
[113] Ibid. 21.
[114] Seneca, *Epistulae morales* 88.1–2.
[115] Bruni, *De studiis et literiis* 13. Cf. Proctor 1998: 11.
[116] Piccolomini, *De liberorum educatione* 93–94.

studies, but also included the non-literary *quadrivium*.[117] The dichotomy between the humanities on the one hand and mathematics and the sciences on the other stems from the Renaissance, not from antiquity.[118]

As far as the historian F. Edward Cranz was concerned, the disentangling of the humanities and the liberal arts in the early Renaissance speaks to a profound change in human consciousness on the part of European peoples.[119] Cicero had in his writings on the *studia humanitatis* encouraged the study of *all* non-vocational arts because he, like the ancients more generally, believed that the goal of education was the contemplation of the universe's perfection.[120] Although individuals could improve their character through education, they could not themselves attain perfection, since they were only one small part of a perfect whole.[121] Cicero's pedagogical outlook demonstrates what Cranz labeled an outward-directed "expansive self."[122]

By the time of the Renaissance, in contrast, inhabitants of western Europe possessed an individualistic, inward-looking conception of the self.[123] Thus, for example, Petrarch turned to ancient Roman examples of heroism in order to achieve what the Italian humanists saw as education's primary goal—the strengthening of character. The ends of a humanistic education had shifted: from contemplation of the universe's perfection, the Renaissance humanists now aimed to perfect themselves. Although Cranz's distinctions may appear overly schematic and are certainly open to criticism, they perhaps explain the fundamental change that took place during the Renaissance in the conception of the humanities. The natural sciences may help one recognize the wonders of the universe, but, for the Italian humanists, they were of distinctly ancillary importance, because they did not improve one's soul. As of the Renaissance, mathematics and the sciences had split off from the humanities.

---

[117] On the Renaissance narrowing of the humanities, see, e.g., Kristeller 1961: 9–10; Kelley 1991: 125; Proctor 1998: 10, 16–24. Kristeller (1961: 110–11) notes that the Renaissance humanists did not deny the importance of the sciences, though they did not stress them.

[118] See Proctor 1998: 23.

[119] For a discussion of this point, see Proctor 1998: esp. 77–83, 109–10. Proctor quotes some of Cranz's (unpublished) work, the contours of which he follows in his book.

[120] See Gwynn 1926: 89; Gwynn asserts (148) that Vitruvius believed the same.

[121] Proctor 1998: 79.

[122] Quoted in Proctor 1998: 78.

[123] See ibid. xxvi–xxviii, 16–24, 44, 49, 58, 71, 76–83. F. Edward Cranz dates this change in outlook to ca. 1100 AD; see ibid. 83.

Coming to America

Although Renaissance humanism, as a movement opposed to scholasticism, commenced and originally proliferated outside the universities, in the fifteenth and sixteenth centuries humanist doctrines made headway in European higher education.[124] By the start of the seventeenth century, the English universities of Oxford and Cambridge had absorbed many of the pedagogical tenets associated with Renaissance humanism.[125] Thus the movement could influence the colonial colleges of America, which were all based on Oxbridge models.[126] In 1636, for example, Harvard College, the first institution of higher learning in the colonies, was founded, with a curriculum that borrowed heavily from the course of studies at the University of Cambridge.[127]

At Harvard and the other eight American colonial colleges (which originally boasted curricula sufficiently similar as to seem almost uniform), the paramount influence of Renaissance humanism meant that the classical languages dominated the course of studies.[128] The colonial American institutions, in proper humanistic fashion, viewed the moral improvement of their students through the inculcation of ancient wisdom as their primary goal.[129] For this reason, most of the colonial college curriculum was classical in its subject matter, and knowledge of Latin and ancient Greek were the lone prerequisites for aspiring students.[130] Even many years after

[124] Kelley 1991: 24; Kimball 1995: 79; Proctor 1998: xxiv, 6.
[125] Hoeveler 2002: 4; Winterer 2002: 11–12; Geiger 2015: xv; Axtell 2016: 77–82.
[126] See Turner and Bernard 2000: 224; Axtell 2016: 43. On the American colonial colleges, see, e.g., Hoeveler 2002; Axtell 2016: 106–46.
[127] On the foundation of Harvard and the influence of Cambridge on its original curriculum, see, e.g., Broome 1903: 15; Morison 1935: esp. 92–107, 161–70; Kraus 1961: 64–65. 75; Rudolph 1962: 3–5, 23–24; Butts 1971: 44–47; Cowley and Williams 1991: 73; Lucas 1994: 104; Cremin 1997: 43, 46; Hoeveler 2002: 8–9, 23–25, 29–30; Geiger 2015: 1; Axtell 2016: 107–14. Originally named New College, the institution became Harvard in 1639; see Broome 1903: 11–12; Morison 1935: 219–21; Cremin 1997: 44; Hoeveler 2002: 29. On the complexities associated with the Oxbridge influence on the American college model, see Hoeveler 2002: esp. 3–21; Mattingly 2017: 36–38. On Harvard's colonial curriculum, see Morison 1935: 246–47, 433–36 and 1936: 139–284; Hoeveler 2002: 32–39, 43–46; Geiger 2015: 3–4, 18–21.
[128] The nine colonial colleges were the following: Harvard (founded in 1636), the College of William and Mary (1693), Yale College (1701), the College of Philadelphia (later the University of Pennsylvania; 1740), the College of New Jersey (later Princeton University; 1746), King's College (later Columbia University; 1754), the College of Rhode Island (later Brown University; 1764), Queen's College (later Rutgers University; 1766), and Dartmouth College (1769). On the curriculum of the American colonial colleges, see, e.g., Meriwether 1907; Rudolph 1962: 23–43 and 1977: 25–53; Cowley and Williams 1991: 85–88; Hoeveler 2002: 29–39, 43–46, 75–76, 85, 122–26, 143–44, 176–77; Geiger 2015: 540–41; Axtell 2016: 116–18, 136–41.
[129] See Kimball 1995: 111; Axtell 2016: 145.
[130] Up until 1745, only Latin and Greek were required for admission to US colleges (Rudolph 1962: 25; see also Geiger 2015: 125); in this year, Yale added arithmetic to the requirements (Broome

the colonial period, roughly half the American college curriculum was classical.[131] American educators, like the Italian humanists before them, viewed ancient Greek and Roman authors—and hence the classical languages—as the essential means to promote proper character formation.

Yet Renaissance humanism was not the lone influence on the early American colleges. As was the case with the universities of Oxford and Cambridge, these institutions had never entirely distanced themselves from scholasticism. Thus, for example, the original course of studies at Harvard demonstrated scholastic influence through required coursework in logic, metaphysics, and mathematics.[132] Disputations, which had played a substantial role in scholastic instruction, served an important pedagogical function in the colonial colleges.[133]

The Protestant Reformation also had a major impact on colonial American higher education. Various Protestant sects founded most of the earliest colleges and competition among religious groups was largely responsible for the spread of these institutions throughout the country.[134] Although the colleges were far more than training grounds for prospective ministers,[135] the highly religious character of early America had deep influences on them. In part for this reason, the first curricula at Harvard College included Hebrew, Syriac, and Aramaic as a portion of the required training in ancient languages.[136] Such studies, along with ancient Greek, would allow students to read the Bible without the mediation of translations.

1903: 30; Rudolph 1977: 52). On the dominance of the classical languages in early American higher education, see, e.g., Meriwether 1907: 147; Kraus 1961; Rudolph 1977: 37; Cowley and Williams 1991: 86–87; Kimball 1995: 107.

[131] Winterer (2002: 2) stresses that this was true up until the late nineteenth century.

[132] Meriwether 1907: 51–59; Morison 1935: 435–36; Kraus 1961: 65; Cremin 1997: 4; Geiger 2015: 29. Over the colonial period, moreover, mathematics and the natural sciences played a larger role in the curriculum, thanks to the influence of the Enlightenment. See, e.g., Butts 1971: 58–73; Rudolph 1977: 33, 53; Geiger 2015: 48–50; Axtell 2016: 137–38; and the following text.

[133] Meriwether 1907: 225–83; Geiger 2015: 2, 29; Axtell 2016: 136–37. On medieval disputations, see Axtell 2016: 21–28.

[134] See Cowley and Williams 1991: 7; Adler 2016: 47.

[135] See, e.g., Rudolph 1962: 7; Butts 1971: 66–67; Cowley and Williams 1991: 88–89; Brubacher and Rudy 1997: 379; Hoeveler 2002: 23; Winterer 2002: 13; Geiger 2015: 7, 79, 540–41; Axtell 2016: 112, 115. *Pace* Earnest 1953: 11.

[136] Kraus 1961: 65, 71; Adler 2016: 47; Geiger 2015: 3; Axtell 2016: 117. The curricular focus on Latin, ancient Greek, and Hebrew also demonstrates that Harvard based its original course of studies on that of the late-Renaissance northern European *collegium trilingue* (sic); see Morison 1936: 165–66; Turner 2014: 41–42. On the decline of Hebrew as a subject at the colonial colleges, see Axtell 2016: 136.

By the end of the colonial period, obligatory senior capstone courses in moral philosophy provided another means through which Protestantism influenced the American colleges prior to the Civil War. College presidents typically taught these classes, which were widespread in American higher education by the late eighteenth century.[137] Steeped in Scottish Common Sense Realism, the moral philosophy capstone courses attempted to provide an intellectual and spiritual summation for undergraduates, reconciling an institution's sacred and secular studies. Such classes, it was hoped, would demonstrate to undergraduates the best way to live their lives.[138]

These and close to every other course in the early American curriculum were required of all students. Prior to the spread of curricular free election in the late nineteenth century, the American colleges provided a course of studies that was almost entirely prescribed. The fixed curricula of early American higher education speak to the tenuous financial circumstances of the colleges. A prescribed course of studies required comparatively few instructors and thus worked well for these institutions, which were always small and typically cash-strapped.

In its early days, very few Americans attended the nation's colleges. Even as late as 1828 students in US colleges were few and far between: the historian David Potts related that in the fall of this year the nation's 50 institutions of higher learning enrolled a grand total of around 3,600 undergraduates.[139] As institutions originally bent on training students for the so-called learned professions (ministry, law, and medicine), the colleges seemed necessary for very few Americans.[140]

---

[137] Turner 1992: 75; Geiger 2000d: 17; Roberts and Turner 2000: 76; Hoeveler 2002: 36; Mattingly 2017: 137. Rudolph (1977: 39) informs us that by the mid-eighteenth century these capstone courses led to the ascendance of moral philosophy in the American undergraduate curriculum. Such courses, Rudolph notes (42) lasted in the curriculum until around 1850. Cf. Turner 1992: 75–77, Kimball 1995: 168, and Jewett 2012: 98. Axtell (2016: 140) notes that these capstone courses "grew out of older courses in divinity."

[138] On these courses, see above all Smith 1956; Howe 1970; Meyer 1972. See also, e.g., Earnest 1953: 28–29; Kraus 1961: 74; Rudolph 1962: 140–41 and 1977: 39–42, 90–94, 139, 150; Ben-David 1972: 52; Kimball 1995: 168; Hoeveler 2002: 36–39; Geiger 2015: 51–52; Axtell 2016: 139–41; Mattingly 2017: 182.

[139] Potts 2010: 9. It was not until the late nineteenth century that American institutions of higher learning began to have larger student bodies. On this topic, see Rudolph 1962: 442 and 1977: 152; Butts 1971: 160; Cowley and Williams 1991: 90; Pearcy 2005: 78–79; Axtell 2016: 277. Even as late as 1900, however, only 4 percent of the college-aged in the US were attending an institution of higher learning (Veysey 1979: 52). And fewer than 1.5 million students enrolled in US colleges during the 1939–40 academic year (see Lucas 1994: xiv). It was with Congress's passage of the Servicemen's Readjustment Act (also known as the G. I. Bill) that the country witnessed a huge increase in its college-going population. See, e.g., Rudolph 1977: 282–83; Cowley and Williams 1991: 188; Lucas 1994: xv; Axtell 2016: 319–25; Mattingly 2017: 280–83.

[140] Geiger 2015: 81, 145–46. This does not mean that only the rich attended these institutions, however. Most colonial American college students were middle-class, and more were poor than were

Such small colleges would naturally boast small faculties. Yet this is not the only striking difference between instruction in pre–Civil War and postbellum American higher education. Prior to the professionalization of collegiate life in the US—a process that commenced in the mid-nineteenth century— almost all instructors at the colleges possessed no formal advanced training. It was presumed that their moral strengths, in addition to their social status and religious beliefs, recommended them for their jobs. Most would eventually leave academia for careers in the ministry.[141] Many college presidents in the early US were also clergymen: only in 1899, for instance, did Yale elect its first non-minister as its leader.[142] Such presidents and faculty members must have seemed ideal for institutions modeled on English boarding schools and focused above all on the inculcation of received wisdom from the ancients.

Naturally, educational institutions like these cared deeply about the moral lives of their students. The colleges took great pains to act in loco parentis.[143] Prior to 1869, for example, Harvard made no distinctions between a student's intellectual attainments and his personal conduct; only in this year did the college remove disciplinary considerations from its calculation of grades.[144]

Unlike today, college leaders in early America played a major role in the classroom. College presidents originally served as their institutions' chief instructor, and they were typically aided by a small collection of tutors, who were most often recent college graduates themselves.[145] As of 1750,

---

rich. See Cowley and Williams 1991: 90. Cf. Rudolph 1977: 28; Geiger 2015: 6–7, 78–81; Mattingly 2017: 15. Lucas (1994: 109) notes that only well into the eighteenth century did US colleges become dominated by wealthy students. Wriston (1939: 306–7) suggests that the American colleges have always had at least some poor students; cf. Axtell 2016: 141–44. On the backgrounds of students who attended the colleges in antebellum America, see above all Burke 1982. On the wealth and social class of American college students in the nineteenth century, see Geiger 2000d: 3–4 and 2015: 126–28.

[141] See, e.g., Geiger 2015: 26; Axtell 2016: 134.

[142] Rudolph 1962: 419; Hall 2000: 213. The leadership of other American colleges became more secular before this time, however. See, e.g., Geiger 2000d: 20 on southern public colleges in the nineteenth century. Axtell (2016: 177) informs us that "over 90 percent of pre-[Civil] war presidents were ordained ministers." According to Hall (2000: 213), "The displacement of clergymen from controlling positions in higher education and charity was a hallmark of American institutional life after 1870." Cf. Hall 2000: 217–18; Axtell 2016: 289–90. Harvard had a layman president as far back as 1708, when John Leverett (1662–1724) began his term; but Leverett became an ordained minister upon becoming president. See Eliot 1923: 4, 44; Geiger 2015: 20–21. According to Eliot (1923: 4, 46), Josiah Quincy (1772–1864) was the first "genuine layman" (4) appointed president of Harvard, in 1829.

[143] On this topic, see Geiger 2000d: 10–14 and 2015: 129–32; Axtell 2016: 132–34, 174, 183–89, 222–23.

[144] James 1930 1: 244; Rudolph 1962: 348 and 1977: 147; Ben-David 1972: 74. On the institution of letter grades at Harvard in 1883, see Rudolph 1977: 147.

[145] See Mattingly 2017: 15. Cf. Geiger 2000d: 17, 277 n. 2.

for example, the four American colleges as a whole were home to only ten professors; the remainder of the collegiate instructional staff was made up of presidents and tutors.[146] These tutors were originally responsible for the entire curriculum. Not until 1766 did Harvard decide to assign tutors to particular subjects, rather than to an entire year's graduating class.[147] At Yale, a more traditional institution than Harvard for much of its history, this reform did not take place until 1830.[148] As hinted at previously, moreover, even professors in the early US had experienced little advanced training in their subjects of expertise.[149] Serious graduate study in America, in fact, did not commence until the last few decades of the nineteenth century.

Historiographical Hostility to the Classical Humanities

The classical humanities played such an outsized role in the early colleges that historians of education occasionally refer to these institutions as the "classical colleges" or the "literary colleges."[150] But Latin and ancient Greek were not the only parts of the early colleges' course of studies. Although many standard elements of contemporary American higher learning did not play much, if any, role in the curriculum (e.g., English, modern foreign languages, and the social sciences),[151] students at these institutions did not simply stick

---

[146] Rudolph 1977: 50–51; Axtell 2016: 134, 176. Cf. Axtell 2016: 122.

[147] Kraus 1961: 69; Geiger 2015: 62, 192; Axtell 2016: 135. Rudolph (1962: 163 and 1977: 44) says that this alteration commenced in 1767.

[148] Rudolph 1962: 163.

[149] On this subject, see, e.g., Axtell 2016: 179–80. Nor did they have formal pedagogical training. See Axtell 2016: 133.

[150] E.g., Rudolph 1962: 32, 104; Roberts and Turner 2000: 75; Winterer 2002: 2, 77; Jewett 2012: 30, 54.

[151] Yale added English grammar and oratory to its curriculum in 1767 (Rudolph 1977: 38). But not until 1857 did a college in the US make the first appointment in English language and comparative philology as stand-alone subjects; in this year, Lafayette College hired Francis A. March as the country's first professor of English literature (Rudolph 1977: 140; Turner 1992: 82; Roberts and Turner 2000: 77). In 1859 Harvard and the University of Michigan introduced English literature as subjects (Turner 1992: 82). Such courses did not appear in the Yale curriculum until 1870 (Turner 1992: 82). French (the first modern foreign language available in the US college course of studies) became a semiofficial course at Harvard in 1720 (Kraus 1961: 71). Provided their parents assented to it, Harvard allowed students to elect French as of 1769 (Butts 1971: 62). The language began to creep into the US college curriculum in the late eighteenth century, Rudolph (1962: 37 and 1977: 51) informs us. But French and other modern European languages typically played a minor role in the course of studies until after the Civil War. The social sciences (which would flower into distinct academic disciplines in the nineteenth century) also had to wait until the postbellum period to become a major element of the US curriculum. But they originally entered the course of studies in the early eighteenth century, via the moral philosophy capstone classes (see Roberts and Turner 2000: 154 n. 2).

to the classical languages. For instance, as mentioned previously, the influence of scholasticism ensured that logic, metaphysics, and mathematics were included in the early college curriculum.

As the Enlightenment wore on, moreover, the American colleges made attempts to change with the times.[152] These were not static institutions. The early colleges experimented with various additions to their fixed curricula. By the end of the seventeenth century, for example, elements of Enlightenment-era science began to appear in Harvard coursework.[153] In 1711, the College of William and Mary, the nation's second-oldest institution of higher learning, established the first chair of mathematics and natural philosophy in America.[154] Tradition-minded Yale added algebra to its curriculum in 1718.[155] Even some inklings of what would be called the social sciences reared their heads in the capstone moral philosophy classes.[156] The course of studies in early America, then, did not perfectly mirror the desires of Renaissance humanists. Although Bruni could shun arithmetic as a subject incapable of perfecting the self and thus unworthy of much pedagogical attention,[157] such an outlook became increasingly difficult to defend in the incipient age of science.[158]

This trend does not mean that the early American colleges were pedagogical trailblazers. As is arguably the case throughout most of US history, these institutions often proved change-resistant. Thus, as we shall see, many American educators during the Battle of the Classics fiercely opposed the push to pioneer the new university system and its attendant curriculum. Instead, campus leaders in the nineteenth century often packed new subjects of study into the latter years of the undergraduate course, while still allowing the old disciplines to dominate the curriculum.[159] The increasing

[152] Lucas (1994: 131) notes that the early US colleges were responsive to demands for curricular reforms, as they experimented with additions and parallel courses of study, especially during the nineteenth century. See also Rudolph 1977: 33; Geiger 2000c; Potts 2000; Winterer 2002: 45; Jewett 2012: 47; Axtell 2016: 197–99. *Pace* Earnest 1953: 20.

[153] Butts 1971: 61; Rudolph 1977: 53. Cf. Geiger 2015: 541.

[154] Kimball 1995: 133–34; Geiger 2015: 14; Axtell 2016: 137–38.

[155] Rudolph 1977: 33. In 1714, Yale received a gift of mathematics books from Jeremiah Dummer, which allowed the subject to play a larger role in the curriculum.

[156] Roberts and Turner (2000: 154 n. 2) specify that this recognition occurred at the start of the eighteenth century. See also Axtell 2016: 306 n. 71.

[157] Proctor 1998: 8–9.

[158] On the publication of Isaac Newton's *Principia mathematica* and its influence on a blossoming age of science in the seventeenth century, see Jarrett 1973: 28–29. For Newton's eventual influence on the colonial curriculum, see Geiger 2015: 16, 31–32, 49–50, 257. On developments in modern science during the sixteenth and seventeenth centuries, see, e.g., Kristeller 1961: 118, 139; Butts 1971: 39.

[159] Geiger (2015: 266) notes downsides of attempts to include the sciences in this manner.

prestige and perceived utility of the sciences necessitated their further inclusion in American higher education. But institutions found ways to innovate that could prove minimally disruptive to the status quo. Harvard and Yale, for example, both founded scientific colleges in 1847; these institutions, with their more pragmatic courses of study, could both ensure a larger role for the sciences and allow Harvard and Yale to retain their classics-heavy A.B. degrees.[160]

But we must recognize that many earlier histories of American higher education have unfairly characterized the nineteenth-century colleges.[161] Such works often treated intellectual history sparingly, and thus failed to articulate the pedagogical goals of Renaissance humanism. Accordingly, they typically portrayed required study of the classical languages as a reactionary exercise in European-style social snobbery unbecoming of the more egalitarian US. Unsurprisingly, perhaps, these histories also managed to miscast the Battle of the Classics, preferring to see it as a dispute between noble, far-sighted reformers and fusty, aristocratic Bible-thumpers.[162] Only since the late 1960s have revisionist historians attempted to provide more balanced perspectives on the antebellum colleges—and, potentially, more balanced perspectives on the role of Latin and Greek in the early college curriculum.[163]

We can point to some key reasons to explain this earlier historiographical hostility. As the historian Caroline Winterer correctly observed, the triumph of the educational reformers in the late nineteenth and early twentieth centuries affected impressions of their opponents.[164] Thus earlier scholars of American higher education often took on the polemical tone of anti-traditionalist diatribes from the Battle of the Classics, and made it seem as if only one side in the disputes had routinely engaged in shrill and dubious argumentation. As we shall see in the chapters to come, this is not true: in

---

[160] Broome 1903: 60; Rudolph 1977: 103–4; Axtell 2016: 198. On the founding of Harvard's Lawrence Scientific School and Yale's Sheffield Scientific School, see, e.g., Eliot 1923: 57–58; Geiger 2000d: 26, 2000e: 155–57, 162–63, and 2015: 263–64, 544.

[161] As Winterer (2002: 185 n. 3) and Geiger (2015: 267) note. See also Potts 2000: 38. For examples of (pre-revisionist) scholars demonstrating hostility to the classical curriculum of the early US colleges, see, e.g., Schmidt 1936: 48, 50, 53; Rogers 1942: 101; Pierson 1952: 74; Earnest 1953: 19–47; Rudolph 1962: 127, 135, 245, 304–5 and 1977: 101, 120, 126, 135, 180–81, 188, 214–15; Veysey 1965: 28–29, 40–41; Butts 1971: 106.

[162] E.g., Meriwether 1907: 286; Veysey 1965: 28–29, 40–41, 182, 201–2, 205, 213–14 and 1979: 54, 73; Butts 1971: 183, 235, 263, 268–78; Rudolph 1977 180–81.

[163] On the revisionist attempts to counter traditional scholarship on the antebellum colleges, see, e.g., the contributions to Geiger 2000a, especially Geiger 2000d; Pak 2008: 32–34; Mattingly 2017: 381 n. 19.

[164] Winterer 2002: 185 n. 3; cf. 32–36, 77.

many debates, overheated prose emanated from both university reformers and their traditionalistic opponents.

To be sure, traditionalists during the conflicts could haughtily dilate on the supposed superiority of Latin and ancient Greek to all other imaginable studies without much in the way of evidence. But their antagonists could prove equally headstrong and unconvincing. Much hostility to the classical languages, for example, radiated from the influential American periodical the *Popular Science Monthly*, a magazine that regularly promoted scientific education during the Battle of the Classics. Its founder and editor, the chemist and science journalist E. L. Youmans (1821–87), condemned the classical languages with great vitriol.[165] He gave titles to unsigned editorials in the journal such as "The Current Study of Classics a Failure" and "Dead-Language Studies Necessarily a Failure."[166] In a piece from 1881, Youmans contended that "Greek is not so ennobling a study as that of sewerage."[167]

In his magazine Youmans also published numerous articles that demonstrated polemical hostility to the classical humanities. Paul Shipman, for example, contributed a piece to the *Popular Science Monthly* in 1880 that attempted to denigrate study of the classical languages as insufficiently masculine. Discussing the insistence of American educators to require students to learn Latin and ancient Greek, Shipman wrote,

> If not abandoned, I am strongly tempted to predict that man, handicapped by the conditions, will be passed by woman, now almost abreast of him, and that before the end of the next century, unless woman gets handicapped herself, our great poets, historians, scientists, and philosophers—the leaders of thought and masters of style—will wear petticoats or Turkish trousers, and the lords of the creation, sent to the rear, will become hewers of words and drawers of grammar to the weaker vessels—the better-halves

---

[165] On Youmans, see, e.g., Haar 1948; Hofstadter 1959: 14, 22–23, 27, 31–34, 47–49, 92, 142; Leverette 1963: esp. 11–62 and 1965; Heyl and Heyl 1976: 45; Jewett 2012: 43, 45, 47, 61–63, 66–68, 74.

[166] Youmans 1883a and b. Leverette (1963: 59) notes that Youmans' brother W. J. Youmans "wrote . . . many of the items appearing under 'Editor's Table,'" and this means it is possible that W. J. Youmans wrote these anonymous editorial notices. For the sake of simplicity, though, throughout this book we shall presume the authorship of E. L. Youmans.

[167] Youmans 1881: 414. Youmans offered this remark in the context of discussing the deaths of students at the College of New Jersey in 1880, because of inadequate sanitation; on this tragedy, see McCosh 1896: 235. Cf. Youmans 1883b: 268.

in very truth—the real architects of mind and acknowledged captains of civilization.[168]

Shipman further opined in the article that "A dead language is the Dead Sea of thought."[169] Both sides in the Battle of the Classics occasionally offered arguments that seem problematic, if not offensive, today.[170]

The combative tone of some nineteenth-century attacks on the classical humanities cannot entirely account for the imbalanced portraits of the Battle of the Classics provided by many histories of American higher education from the early and mid-twentieth century. Supporters of the classical human-ities during the Battle of the Classics insisted that Latin and ancient Greek were the quintessential components of a proper curriculum, without which no person could rightly deem himself or herself educated. Twentieth- and twenty-first-century historians of education typically lack grounding in the ancient languages, since these subjects faded in American schools after the conclusion of the Battle of the Classics. As we detected earlier in the chapter, ever since Greek antiquity, aristocratic associations have attached themselves to the study of classical writers: even before the Romans, Aristotle deemed knowledge of such authors appropriate for the freeborn.

Especially in the US, a nation with strong egalitarian impulses, vouching for the value of the classical languages can thus raise suspicions. The philos-opher of education Kieran Egan summed up the contemporary conventional wisdom among American educators vis-à-vis Latin and Greek thus:

Today, of course, the educational establishment—almost entirely without any knowledge of what was once the backbone or staple of education and almost invariably ignorant of classical languages—takes it for granted that the classics should be treated as an occasional and exotic option for only a few students. The common view of educationalists today is that this shift away from the classics marks a triumph of common sense, a democrati-zation of education, and a recognition that schooling is properly both a

---

[168] Shipman 1880: 155. For a similarly sexist argument promoted by a supporter of the traditional curriculum, see Atwater 1882: 118–19. Rudolph (1962: 324) suggests that co-education at non-technical colleges in the US led to the idea that liberal arts courses are "feminine."

[169] Shipman 1880: 148.

[170] For more examples, see Chapters 3, 4, and 5, this volume. It should be noted that Latin requirements for admission to US colleges could be used to enforce religious and racial prejudice; see Rudolph 1977: 215.

preparation for the everyday life all classes of students will lead in adulthood and an expansion of their experience in the present.[171]

Perhaps more than any other subjects in American higher learning, classical studies have had to endure the misgivings of the educational establishment—misgivings untempered by an understanding of the pedagogical goals of humanism.

In order to get a more accurate sense of the humanities' fate during the Battle of the Classics, we must attempt to be fairer to all sides.[172] It is crucial to recognize, for example, that the perceived threat to pedagogical traditionalism in this era was real. Critics of the prescribed classical curriculum in many cases aimed to reorient the colleges' educational mission. The historian Andrew Jewett has labeled the American academic reformers of the late nineteenth century who shaped the modern university movement the first generation of "scientific democrats."[173] These figures hoped to center American higher education around the natural and social sciences, believing that the scientific method could supply the requisite tools to maintain a cohesive and robust democratic society. It must be noted that the first serious headway in America against the classical curriculum occurred in the years immediately following the Civil War, when Darwinism was all the rage.[174] Scientific democrats, as we shall see, aimed to dethrone curricular prescription in favor of a Darwinian-Spencerian system of educational "survival of the fittest."[175]

The sciences encourage a different view of education's value than do the classical humanities: first and foremost, they hinge on the creation of new knowledge. Such a goal may appear routine today, but at the time it amounted to a fundamental change in orientation. The Italian humanists and their heirs promoted a curriculum that foregrounded the wisdom of the past as a means to shape students' characters. Thus the scientific and humanistic outlooks—the former forward-looking and bent on new discoveries, the latter traditionalistic and focused on the inculcation of received knowledge—would naturally be at crosshairs. What were the goals of US higher education? What

[171] Egan 2002: 120–21.
[172] In this we shall be aided by the work of more recent historians of higher education, who have provided a more balanced assessment of the antebellum colleges. See, e.g., the contributions to Geiger 2000a; Axtell 2016.
[173] Jewett 2012.
[174] Hofstadter 1959: 14, 19. See also Mattingly 2017: 170–73.
[175] See, e.g., Mattingly 2017: 177.

sort of knowledge was most valuable? What kinds of citizens did American colleges aim to create? Participants in the Battle of the Classics at least implicitly needed to answer these crucial questions.

Birth of the Research University

Traditionalists' perspectives on these topics became increasingly embattled in the second half of the nineteenth century, as American higher education began to professionalize. This process encouraged a knowledge-for-its-own-sake ideal that challenged humanistic suppositions about education's value. Unbeknownst to many educators at the time, this challenge helped set the scene for the erosion of the classical humanities as the heart of the US college curriculum.

During the nineteenth century, American educators increasingly began to view the German research university, rather than the English Oxbridge colleges,[176] as the primary intellectual model for advanced instruction and the conceptualization of the professoriate in the US. Starting in the late eighteenth century, German universities underwent the process of professionalization.[177] Given its prominent place in European intellectual culture, it should not prove surprising that the study of Latin and ancient Greek played an outsized role in this reorientation. Critical of the tedious methods of instruction in the ancient languages prevalent in the universities, German classical scholars spearheaded a new rigorous and specialized approach to philology.[178] This necessitated the "scientific" investigation of classical texts, requiring arduous, specialized training in philological methods. German universities pioneered the seminar classroom format, which would allow students to learn scholarly research techniques in an intense and potentially collaborative environment.[179]

By the 1820s, classical studies in Germany had professionalized. German classics professors, motivated by this new spirit of professionalism, now

---

[176] See Axtell 2016: 224.

[177] On this process see, e.g., Turner 1974, 1980, 1981; O'Boyle 1983; Leventhal 1986: Cowley and Williams 1991: 133–34; Pearcy 2005: 15–22; Howard 2006: 116–19.

[178] See, e.g., Leventhal 1986: 247; Geiger 2000d: 30. On professionalized German classical philology, see Turner 1980 and 1981; Grafton 1981 and 1983; Herzog 1983; Leventhal 1986; Kimball 1995: 176; Marchand 1996; Winterer 2002: 50–51; Pearcy 2005: 15–22.

[179] See, e.g., Veysey 1965: 153; Rudolph 1977: 144–45; Leventhal 1986: 258; Pearcy 2005: 21; Howard 2006: 185 n. 195, 261–64.

labeled their discipline *Altertumswissenschaft* ("the science of antiquity").[180] Influenced by the art historian Johann Joachim Winckelmann (1717–1812), these German classicists also broadened their approach to antiquity, conceiving of its study as rightly focused on the Greco-Roman world in its entirety.[181] Professionalized classical scholars looked upon their investigations through a scientific lens; they aimed to make new discoveries about their subject matter, rather than merely serve as stewards of ancient wisdom. This scientific spirit soon spread to other disciplines, leading to the creation of the German research university.

German classical scholars who promoted the *Altertumswissenschaft* ideal did not originally contend that the discovery of new knowledge about the past alone recommended this approach. Rather, the advocates of scientific philology often argued that professionalized classical study would promote a salubrious effect on the inner lives of students. Scholarly investigations of ancient Greek and Roman literature would still introduce pupils to some of antiquity's greatest heroes, and students could thus use these heroes' examples to improve their character.[182] At least part of the scientific philologists' rationale for the study of Latin and ancient Greek, then, connected with pedagogical ideals Petrarch and his followers had articulated in the Renaissance: the pursuit of perfection through an examination of ancient models.

But this rationale, however plaintively vouched for, soon disintegrated in the new atmosphere of narrow, specialized scholarship. The historian Anthony Grafton informs us that students of the classics in nineteenth-century Germany were so bogged down in the acquisition of sub-disciplinary research techniques that they were losing the character-forming and aesthetic qualities of classical literature.[183] Wilhelm von Humboldt (1767–1835), the founder of the University of Berlin and a key advocate of the professionalized research university, believed that scholarly investigations would help shape students on their journey to adulthood.[184] Yet specialized

[180] First among them to do so was F. A. Wolf (1759–1824). See Adler 2016: 53–54 n. 70. On *Altertumswissenschaft*, see, e.g., O'Boyle 1983: 4; Leventhal 1986; Turner 1974: 510; Grafton 1981 and 1983; Herzog 1983; Selden 1990; Winterer 2002: 50–51, 131–32, 154–55; Pearcy 2005: 15–22, 74–80, 106–11; Howard 2006: 116–19, 137–38, 185; Harloe 2013; Turner 2014: 168–83, 275–76.

[181] On Winckelmann and his influence, see, e.g., Pfeiffer 1976: 173–77; Grafton 1981; Howard 2006: 119, 137–38; Harloe 2013.

[182] See, e.g., Turner 1980: 79–80; Grafton 1981: 103 and 1983: 169, 183–84; O'Boyle 1983: 4; Proctor 1998: 103–5; Axtell 2016: 271–72.

[183] Grafton 1983: 169, 183–84. Cf. Shorey 1919: 38.

[184] On the foundation of the University of Berlin, see, e.g., Calder 1966: 217; Butts 1971: 79; Herzog 1983: 283; Cowley and Williams 1991: 133; Howard 2006: 130–211.

classical training invariably sidelined such moral goals. As Grafton noted, "Humboldtian ideals of research came to contradict equally Humboldtian ideals of *Bildung*."[185] In practice, the *Altertumswissenschaft* outlook helped disconnect classical studies from the pedagogical mission of Renaissance humanism. Professionalized classicists were now taking their cues from the sciences: their focus became a quarrying of facts about antiquity—however minute and insignificant.

During the nineteenth century, increasing numbers of American educators looked to the German research university as their prime pedagogical model, particularly, but not only, for what would become graduate instruction in America. Although German higher education, along with, to a more limited extent, other European models, influenced increasing numbers of American educators in these decades, the US colleges would always borrow selectively, ultimately crafting an approach to higher learning that fit with the American experience.[186] In 1819, Edward Everett (1794–1865), the first American classicist to complete rigorous philological training in Germany, returned to his professorship at Harvard and began pushing for academic reforms.[187] He and other veterans of German Ph.D. programs hoped to replace the old grammar-drilling recitations through which the classical languages were taught in the US with lecture and seminar classes.[188] Ancient Greek and Latin, they thought, could offer more to students than "gerund-grinding."[189] Those who had experienced graduate study in Europe also lauded another key German reform: in such institutions, students were

[185] Grafton 1983: 169. On a preference for the research ideal over *Bildung* in early graduate education at the University of Michigan, see Turner and Bernard 2000: 239. See also Axtell 2016: 271–73.

[186] On German influence on American higher education, see, e.g., Turner and Bernard 2000; Geiger 2015: 315–16, 328–32; Axtell 2016: xvi–xvii, 221–75; Mattingly 2017: 256; cf. James 1930 1: 136–38. On American criticism of the German research university in the nineteenth century, see, e.g., Axtell 2016: 244–53.

[187] On Everett and other early American earners of classics Ph.D.'s in Germany, see, e.g., Calder 1966: 217; Reinhold 1984: 182, 189, 204–13; Richard 2009: 11, 14–15; Geiger 2015: 182–83. On Everett's (brief) career at Harvard, see, e.g., McCaughey 1974: 247–55, 263. In nineteenth-century Germany the Ph.D. was the ordinary first degree; American institutions of higher learning turned this degree into a postgraduate certification of research ability. For more on this topic, see the section "Research, Research, Research." O'Brien (2004: 126) contends that early American students at German research universities, despite their attachment to their ideals, seldom had a deep understanding of these institutions. On this topic, see also Axtell 2016: 227, 241–44.

[188] On this topic, see Turner and Bernard 2000: 222, 232, and 337 n. 3; Axtell 2016: 256; Mattingly 2017: 256. According to Turner and Bernard (2000: 232), Charles K. Adams, a history professor at the University of Michigan, in the 1871–72 academic year taught "by some definitions" the first seminar in American higher education. See also Axtell 2016: 260–61.

[189] The phrase is Andrew D. White's (see Schmidt 1936: 57). White was a key university reformer in the late nineteenth century. On White, see the section "The Tide Turns against Prescription."

free to enroll in coursework that interested them.[190] This policy signaled to admirers of German higher education that the fixed curriculum—intrinsic to ancient and Renaissance conceptions of pedagogy—could be usefully abandoned. As it turned out, critics of the classical humanities in the US latched onto this idea, advocating a curricular free-for-all that would remove Greek and Latin from the core of the undergraduate curriculum.

The Classical Humanities Come under Attack

Even before some educators began to see the German research university as a superior model for advanced training in the US, the prescribed classical curriculum had its share of detractors. This is perhaps to be expected, given the pragmatism associated with American culture.[191] In fact, the first known American revolt against the classical course of studies occurred prior to the nation's birth: in 1711, parents pleaded with the Boston Latin School to include more vocational subjects among its offerings.[192] One could find critics of the classical humanities among the Founding Fathers as well. As early as 1749, for example, Benjamin Franklin on utilitarian grounds supported making Latin and ancient Greek optional in the colleges.[193] Thomas Jefferson, although highly enamored of the classical languages, also attempted to give students more say in the selection of their coursework, first at his alma mater, the College of William and Mary, and then at the institution he founded, the University of Virginia.[194]

[190] See, e.g., Lucas 1994: 172; Kimball 1995: 162.
[191] Reinhold (1984: 118–19) reminds us that criticism of the classical curriculum on the grounds of utility existed for centuries in various contexts, despite the dominance of this curriculum from the late Renaissance to the last half of the nineteenth century.
[192] Reinhold 1984: 118.
[193] Ibid. 120; Geiger 2015: 44. See also Burstein 1996: 31, 33. Benjamin Rush, another Founding Father, also became a dogged opponent of the classics. See Reinhold 1984: 72–75, 129; Burstein 1996: 40–41; Richard 2009: 163–64; Geiger 2015: 102–3, 106–7.
[194] According to Butts (1971: 64), Jefferson tried to establish the first elective curriculum at William and Mary in 1779; see also Hawkins 1972: 82; Geiger 2015: 98–100. By 1800 Jefferson had abandoned such ideas for reform because of financial constraints and had set his sights on establishing a new university (Butts 1971: 92). In 1823 Jefferson for the first time wrote up his conception of the elective principle (93–94). But the University of Virginia (established in 1825; see Rudy 1960: 5; Butts 1971: 101; Potts 2010: 18; Geiger 2015: 179; Mattingly 2017: 44–45) did not ultimately allow students to select their own courses; rather, they chose the college at UVA in which they wished to enroll and then took the fixed curriculum mandated by that college (Butts 1971: 95–96; Mattingly 2017: 46). On the curriculum of early UVA, see, e.g., Phillips 1901: 208; Cowley and Williams 1991: 116–17; Geiger 2015: 180–82. On Jefferson's educational views, see Geiger 2015: 25, 98–100; Mattingly 2017: 39–48. Richard (2009: 7–8) notes that students at UVA had to demonstrate proficiency in Latin in order to graduate and thus classical studies thrived there. Jefferson also championed extraordinarily rigorous

Such criticisms of the prescribed classical course of studies only inten-
sified in the nineteenth century. By the early 1800s, the first clear signs of
trouble for the classical humanities had begun to brew, as Latin and ancient Greek started to seem out of touch with the new directions in which
American society was heading.[195] Even in the nation's solidly agrarian
days the classical curriculum had some notable detractors. But now the
US was industrializing, and anchoring American education in the classical languages appeared to be increasingly unpopular. The election of
Andrew Jackson as the nation's president in 1828 only increased skepticism of the classical curriculum. Jackson, the first US president since
George Washington not to attend college, rode a wave of populism to office, which suggested that a classically trained elite would no longer mo-
nopolize control over the nation.[196]

The small US colleges that dotted the landscape had thus far prepared
students for future careers in the so-called learned professions. These
were subjects for which grounding in the classical languages remained
requisite.[197] But in this new age of populism many undoubtedly wondered whether the colleges could also train students for the exponentially
increasing array of vocations associated with an industrializing society.[198]
In the 1820s, a number of US colleges, attuned to criticisms of the classical curriculum, experimented with parallel tracks, which would allow
undergraduates to avoid Latin and ancient Greek.[199] In 1824, for example,
Hobart College (then called Geneva Academy) established one of the first
US college curricula in the English-speaking world without the classical
languages.[200] It soon became a model for non-classical courses of study in
US higher education.[201]

---

classical entrance requirements for UVA's School of Ancient Languages (see Bruce 1920 2: 81–82).
Reinhold (1984: 25) correctly notes that Jefferson was "the advocate par excellence of the classics" in
his age.

[195] See Rudolph 1977: 57.
[196] On this topic, see Potts 2010: 18–19; Axtell 2016: 197–99.
[197] This hints at practical reasons partly responsible for the rise and demise of the *studia
humanitatis*. On this topic, see Meriwether 1907: 63–64; Rudy 1960: 4; Rudolph 1977: 37–38. Proctor
1998: 118–34; Winterer 2002: 104–5.
[198] It is not surprising, then, that Rudolph (1962: 112) concludes that the impetus toward collegiate
reform in the US commenced in the 1820s.
[199] See, e.g., Broome 1903: 43; Potts 2010: 18–19.
[200] Turk 1933: 339. See also Butts 1971: 135–36.
[201] Turk 1933: 345.

The Yale Reports *and the Origins of "Mental Discipline"*

Another institution's attempt to establish a parallel program led to the composition of one of the most influential curricular documents in the history
of American higher education. In 1827, Jacob Abbott, a professor of mathematics and natural philosophy at Amherst College, spearheaded at his institution the creation of a parallel course without required study of Latin and
Greek, a track that would still lead to the earning of a B.A. degree.[202] Although
it had opened only six years prior, Amherst had proven a quick success, and
its curricular innovations earned much attention in the American media.[203]
Yale, then the largest college in the US,[204] felt the need to respond.[205]

Soon Yale would have an official opportunity to reply to Amherst's
innovations. On September 11, 1827, at a meeting of the Yale Corporation,
Noyes Darling, a Yale alumnus and Connecticut state senator, proposed to his
fellow trustees that Yale's curriculum be altered to remove the study of what
Noyes referred to as "the dead languages."[206] The Corporation appointed a
committee of five men to study Darling's motion—a committee that included
both Darling and Connecticut Governor Gideon Tomlinson.[207] It also asked
Yale's faculty what it thought about the proposal.[208] Yale President Jeremiah
Day (1773–1867) and James L. Kingsley (1778–1852), a professor of Latin,
Greek, and Hebrew, each composed a portion of a two-part report in re-
sponse.[209] Tomlinson appended a write-up of the committee's thoughts to
Day's and Kingsley's contribution.[210] By the end of 1828, the resultant docu-
ment, a fifty-six-page pamphlet first read to the Yale Corporation in August

---

[202] See, e.g., Schmidt 1936: 52; Rudolph 1962: 122–24 and 1977: 83; Butts 1971: 83; Richard
2009: 89; Potts 2010: 19, 24–25; Geiger 2015: 185–86. Union College did the same thing in this year
(Potts 2010: 19). On similar reforms attempted in the 1820s, see Geiger 2000c: 139–40. Proponents
of the classics jealously guarded the B.A.: if students could graduate without the classical languages,
these proponents often saw to it that they would have to do so under lesser auspices.

[203] Potts 2010: 19–20; Geiger 2015: 185.

[204] It had the largest graduating class in the US in 1828; see Potts 2010: 23.

[205] See Potts 2010: 20. Pak (2008: 30–31) asserts that George Ticknor's support for turning Latin
and Greek into elective courses in the colleges influenced Yale to write the report. See also Geiger
2015: 183–89.

[206] Herbst 1996: 27; Richard 2009: 94; Potts 2010: 25–26; Geiger 2015: 188. Geiger (188–89)
surmises that the notion of eliminating the classical languages from the Yale curriculum was not earnestly conceived, but rather offered the institution the opportunity to reply to those who proposed
such a move at other colleges.

[207] Potts 2010: 26.

[208] Ibid. 27. Potts mentions the paltry size of the Yale faculty at this time. On the great expansion of
the American college faculty with the onset of curricular free election, see the following text.

[209] Ibid. 27–28.

[210] Ibid. 28.

of that year, was published as *Reports on the Course of Instruction in Yale College; by a Committee of the Corporation, and the Academical Faculty*.[211] A stirring call to retain the fixed classical curriculum, the work is better known today as the Yale *Reports*.[212]

Although contending that Yale's "present plan of education admits of improvement,"[213] President Day in his portion of the document provided numerous reasons to retain the prescribed curriculum. Dismissing vocational studies,[214] Day proposed that the two great features of a superior undergraduate education "are the *discipline* and the *furniture* of the mind; expanding its powers, and storing it with knowledge."[215] Day's report does not entirely dismiss educational content (what he terms the mind's "furniture"), but he considered "discipline" by far "the more important of the two" factors.[216] For this reason, he concluded,

> Those branches of study should be prescribed, and those modes of instruction adopted, which are best calculated to teach the art of fixing attention, directing the train of thought, analyzing a subject proposed for investigation; following, with accurate discrimination, the course of argument; balancing nicely the evidence presented to the judgement; awakening, elevating, and controlling the imagination; arranging, with skill, the treasures which memory gathers; rousing and guiding the powers of genius.[217]

Yale's classics- and mathematics-heavy curriculum should be retained, Day averred, because it most successfully inculcated in students these desirable

---

[211] Potts (2010) has reprinted the full text of the *Reports*. All subsequent quotations from them come from Potts's reprinting.

[212] On the Yale *Reports*, see, e.g., Schmidt 1936: 53–56; Pierson 1952: 72; Earnest 1953: 24; Rudy 1960: iii, 1–5; Rudolph 1962: 130–35, 243–44 and 1977: 65–75; Veysey 1965: 9; Butts 1971: 112, 118–25; Hawkins 1972: 80–81; Reinhold 1984: 193–94; Cowley and Williams 1991: 108; Lucas 1994: 131–34; Kimball 1995: 150–53; Kenney 1998: 4–5; Geiger 2000b: 265, 2000c: 139–40, 2000d: 4–5, 16, and 2015: 187–93, 542–43; Hall 2000: 196–97; Potts 2000: 39–42 and 2010: passim; Roberts and Turner 2000: 20; Turner and Bernard 2000: 224; Winterer 2002: 48–49; Pearcy 2005: 65–71; Pak 2008; Richard 2009: 94–97; Jewett 2012: 30; Adler 2016: 56–57; Axtell 2016: 198–99; Mattingly 2017: 70–74. Pak (2008) convincingly argues that the *Reports* offered a middle ground on curricular matters: they urged the continued prescription of coursework in the classical language but also favored the addition of new subjects to the curriculum. Cf. Geiger 2000d: 4.

[213] In Potts 2010: 5.

[214] Ibid. 14–16.

[215] Ibid. 6 (emphasis in the original).

[216] Ibid. 6.

[217] Ibid. 7.

intellectual traits.[218] For this reason, he deemed it the proper foundation of learning, after experiencing which Yale graduates could most easily turn to vocational training.[219]

As befit the outlook of an instructor of ancient languages, Kingsley spent most of his part of the pamphlet vouching for the superior value of classical studies. Like Day, Kingsley focused on the contribution that the fixed curriculum at Yale makes to students' "mental discipline." About another obligatory portion of Yale's undergraduate studies, he wrote, "The study of mathematics, by the consent of the ablest men who have been conversant with the business of instruction, is especially adapted to sharpen the intellect, to strengthen the faculty of reason, and to induce a general habit of the mind favorable to the discovery of truth and the detection of error."[220] Kingsley further contended that "[i]t is on the same grounds [i.e., that of mental discipline], that the use and necessity of classical literature in a liberal education may be defended."[221] Governor Tomlinson concurred, remarking in his portion of the *Reports* that it "cannot be reasonably denied" that the classical languages offer superior "intellectual discipline" for young persons.[222]

The Yale *Reports* did not present the first defense of Latin and ancient Greek on the basis of "mental discipline."[223] As it turns out, President Zephaniah Swift Moore (1770–1823) of Amherst College had highlighted the value of this concept in his first address there.[224] But the Yale *Reports* commanded great authority.[225] They were so well-received in the American press, in fact, that for decades they helped stifle many attempts at curricular change. In 1829, for example, Amherst's parallel program failed, and the institution

---

[218] It should be noted that Yale's curriculum at this time was not entirely prescribed. See Day's discussion of partial choice offered to students in the junior year: in Potts 2010: 19. See also Mattingly 2017: 73.

[219] Thus Day concluded the following about a graduate of Yale College: "His education is begun, but not completed" (in Potts 2010: 16).

[220] In Potts 2010: 32.

[221] Ibid. 34.

[222] Ibid. 52. Tomlinson offers the only example in the *Reports* of an argument for the classical humanities on the basis of the wisdom contained in literary works from ancient Greece and Rome. See ibid. 53. Still, Tomlinson's focus is firmly on mental discipline.

[223] On the topic of mental discipline and faculty psychology, see, e.g., Pierson 1952: 72; Earnest 1953: 24; Rudy 1960: 1–2, 38; Veysey 1965: 9, 21–25, 54–56, 90–91, 180, 254–55; Butts 1971: 118–19, 128, 164, 165–66, 205, 212–16, 288; Hawkins 1972: 85–91; Jarrett 1973: 42–43; Rudolph 1977: 120, 209–10; Stanic 1986; Cowley and Williams 1991: 107–8; Lucas 1994: 167–69; Kimball 1995: 151–52; Proctor 1998: 99–103, 118, 146–48, 172; Roberts and Turner 2000: 21, 80; Winterer 2002: 49; Potts 2010: 6, 33, 34–36; Geiger 2015: 188–92; Mattingly 2017: 86; and in the following text. Cf. Marrou 1956: 111.

[224] Potts 2010: 20.

[225] On this topic, see Geiger 2015: 190; Mattingly 2017: 73–74.

returned to offering the prescribed course alone.[226] Francis Wayland's ambitious reforms at Brown University, which included the creation of a bachelor of philosophy degree (B.Phil.), similarly collapsed in 1855.[227] Soon after the *Reports* appeared in print, at least, it seemed as if the traditionalists had bested their curricular opponents.[228]

In their attempts to defend the pedagogical status quo, however, such traditionalists ended up radically altering the justification for the classical humanities. As we have seen, Renaissance humanists such as Bruni advocated the study of specific classical authors because their writings offered students wisdom and eloquence. They thus laid out a literary curriculum that allowed pupils to engage in moral and stylistic emulation of the masters. By taking in the examples of great men from the past in canonical works of poetry and prose, students could strengthen their souls and improve their characters. Although the Roman founders of the humanities advanced a less inward-focused approach to education, they too advocated a curriculum of substance: the young were to learn from Greece and Rome's most eloquent writers. To educational theorists from antiquity and the Renaissance, then, the classical humanities had value in large part because of the ability of *specific works of literature* to impart wisdom to the young.

The Yale *Reports'* attention to "mental discipline" represented a seismic shift in arguments for the classical humanities. Proponents of mental discipline theory attempted to connect the liberal arts tradition to so-called faculty psychology.[229] Influenced by Scottish Common Sense philosophy, they viewed the mind through the metaphor of a muscle: just as one needs to exercise one's body in order to grow strong, one must also exercise one's mind to increase the faculties of intellect, the will, and the sensibilities. The authors of the Yale *Reports* trumpeted the prescribed curriculum because they believed that the subjects it included—principally mathematics and the classical languages—offered the most effective form of mental gymnastics.

---

[226] Rudolph 1962: 124; Butts 1971: 136; Potts 2000: 41; Richard 2009: 96; Geiger 2015: 186.

[227] Rudolph 1962: 237–39 and 1977: 109–12; Hawkins 1972: 83–84; Geiger 2000d: 5 and 2000e: 158; Potts 2000: 43–44; Pearcy 2005: 72–73; Richard 2009: 96; Geiger 2015: 227–29, 544; Mattingly 2017: 85. For other examples of such failures around this time, see Adler 2016: 50–51. For an interesting account of Wayland's background and educational views, see Mattingly 2017: 77–95.

[228] On the uncharacteristically successful reforms of Eliphalet Nott at Union College, however, see Broome 1903: 76; Hawkins 1972: 83; Geiger 2000d: 5 and 2015: 186–87; Potts 2000: 42–43; Adler 2016: 51; Mattingly 2017: 78. On Nott's scaling back of student discipline at Union, see Geiger 2015: 216–17.

[229] For a useful explanation of faculty psychology and its origins in the Scots Common Sense School, see Pak 2008: 50. See also Hoeveler 1981: 101–2; Potts 2000: 39–40; Axtell 2016: 262 n. 78.

This drastic change in apologetics for the classical humanities seems to have derived at least in part from the pedagogical realities of the antebellum American colleges. By the nineteenth century—if not earlier—American educators could not earnestly contend that the colleges' approach to classical instruction would allow their students to treat ancient authors as moral and stylistic models.[230] At such institutions, Latin and ancient Greek were the subject of painstaking grammatical analysis. Since tutors, who were often young graduates without much in the way of advanced training, led most of the classes devoted to the ancient languages, they encouraged the rote memorization of textbooks in place of more substantive learning.[231] The recitation method, which turned the classical languages into fodder for relentless oral quizzing, encouraged an obsession with grammatical and syntactical minutiae at the expense of literary appreciation.

Recourse to the *Collectanea Graeca Majora* (1789), the standard Greek textbook of the early nineteenth century, only exacerbated this approach to classical literature. This two-volume collection of short extracts, complete with untranslated Latin endnotes, presented students with decontextualized snippets of ancient writings, which would serve as linguistic exercises shorn of any regard for literary appreciation.[232] Although over the course of the nineteenth century the increasing influence of German philological approaches to classical literature encouraged some American educators to provide a more holistic introduction to classical authors for their pupils,[233] the highly professionalized character of the *Altertumswissenschaft* ideal further distanced ancient studies from the goals of Renaissance humanism. Since their pedagogical practices did not allow them to argue that classical literature offered the benefits vouched for by humanists such as Petrarch and Bruni,[234] antebellum American educators, influenced by Scottish Common Sense philosophy, turned the ancient languages into a form of intellectual calisthenics.[235]

---

[230] Geiger (2015: 53) implies that classical instruction in the late colonial period was superior to the antebellum years, since many ancient authors studied spoke to the concerns of the political present.

[231] See Winterer 2002: 29–37; Geiger 2015: 205–6; Axtell 2016: 194–95. Cf. James 1930 1: 209; Wertenbaker 1946: 234–35.

[232] See, e.g., Winterer 2002: 32–35; Richard 2009: 10; Geiger 2015: 192; Axtell 2016: 201–2.

[233] See, e.g., Richard 2009: xi, 15–17; Axtell 2016: 202.

[234] Bolgar (1973: esp. 10–12), however, argues that to a lesser extent classical instruction during the Renaissance often failed to live up to the ideals vouched for by humanists such as Petrarch and Bruni. The moral content of such training was often highly Christian in orientation and instruction in Greek could prove rudimentary. But by almost all accounts antebellum instruction in the classical languages was especially dreary.

[235] Cf. Mattingly 2017: 169.

Unbeknownst to its devotees, it appears, the argument in favor of the classical humanities on the basis of mental discipline is plagued by intrinsic disadvantages. This approach undercuts the humanistic tradition, because mental discipline theory denies the value of specific educational content. It thus dismisses the chief rationale for the study of classical literature offered since antiquity. As George Stanic explained, "from the point of view of faculty psychology, all that is required is sustained, extended, and rigorous study, with the content of study being relatively unimportant."[236] Without a regard for substance, educators could now argue that *any* activity was a fit subject of curricular attention, provided it proved sufficiently mentally taxing. According to strict proponents of mental discipline theory, the study of Latin and ancient Greek was no more valuable to the young than, say, playing chess.[237] After all, these activities—and countless more, besides—can vigorously exercise the mind. As it turns out, contemporary critics of required classical study typically believed in faculty psychology as well, and thus vouched for the value of curricular election on the same grounds.[238]

Classicists who supported mental discipline theory also undercut the humanities in another crucial way. The theory allowed exponents of the budding social sciences—typically among the strongest critics of the fixed curriculum—to become the rightful judges of educational value. Social scientists, unlike humanists, could test empirically which subjects most effectively promoted mental discipline. The psychologist E. L. Thorndike (1874–1949), for example, reported on a study of high school students he conducted in 1922 and 1923, in which he demonstrated that those who had studied Latin scarcely gained more "general intelligence" than those who had taken stenography classes.[239] Advocates of the new disciplines could now point to their own subjects as inculcators of mental discipline.[240] The

---

[236] Stanic 1986: 40. See also Butts 1971: 164, 212–13; Proctor 1998: xiii, 99–103.

[237] The example given is Proctor's (1998: 101). See also Turner and Bernard 2000: 224.

[238] Pak 2008: 51–52; Geiger 2015: 191. See also Potts 2000: 39–40.

[239] Thorndike 1924: esp. 4, 93. On Thorndike's experiments, see Butts 1971: 263–64; Hawkins 1972: 87. Cf. Youmans 1883b: 266–67. Veysey (1965: 54) notes that Thorndike had been conducting experiments to disprove the theory of mental discipline as early as 1901. For examples of other social scientific experiments supposedly debunking the classical languages' contribution to mental discipline, see Stanic 1986: 41. Stanic suggests that mental discipline theory is a metaphor and as such it cannot ever be fully disproven. Cf. Geiger 2015: 190.

[240] As Pak (2008: 51–52) stresses. And they often did so during the Battle of the Classics. See, e.g., Youmans 1880b: 267; Butts 1971: 165, 214; Stanic 1986: 40–43; Jewett 2012: 71. On this topic, see also Geiger 2000e: 165, 322 n. 48.

traditionalists had unwittingly made social scientists the arbiters of the humanities' value.[241]

This outcome is of crucial importance for us to recognize because, as Potts has noted, mental discipline theory is the nineteenth- and early-twentieth-century version of today's arguments for the humanities on the basis of "critical thinking."[242] In fact, Potts, stressing the continued influence of the Yale *Reports* on contemporary justifications for the liberal arts, concluded that "critical thinking" is mental discipline's "conceptual successor."[243] Our current apologetics for the modern humanities, which routinely genuflect to "critical thinking," are heirs of the *Reports* from 1828. They too suffer from the same flaws.

In highlighting intellectual skills at the expense of educational content, proponents of mental discipline theory were far more in tune with the scholastics against whom the Renaissance humanists had revolted. After all, medieval scholasticism placed paramount value on the techniques associated with syllogistic reasoning. It was in opposition to this spirit that the Italian humanists put forward a curriculum based on the masterworks of ancient Greece and Rome. Despite these serious defects, the Yale *Reports* helped make mental discipline theory all the rage. As we shall see in future chapters, such arguments dominated traditionalistic defenses of the fixed curriculum in the Battle of the Classics. This domination did not bode well for the classical humanities.

The Tide Turns against Prescription

For some time, Yale's 1828 statement on a proper liberal arts curriculum helped to slow educational reform. Despite the new spirit of populism sweeping through US society, the classical languages still possessed

---

[241] Perhaps it is not surprising that Potts (2010: 34) sees Day's notion of mental discipline as stemming from the work of the French astronomer and mathematician Pierre-Simon Laplace. Thus Day took inspiration from a non-humanist. It may also be key to recognize that the Yale *Reports* attempted to defend Yale's liberal arts curriculum as a whole, and not just the classical humanities. That could signal to us why a vague, skills-based justification won out: it would prove difficult to defend the classics, mathematics, and philosophy on the basis of the exact same argument, unless one focuses on skills. In addition to questioning whether the classical languages offered superior mental discipline to students, in the 1880s the so-called New Psychologists began to question the very notion of faculty psychology, which presumes an intellectual sameness among human beings. Human minds, they thought, differed substantially. On this topic, see Butts 1971: 212–16, 263; Jewett 2012: 88.

[242] Potts 2010: 49. See also Proctor 1998: 146–47.

[243] Potts 2010: 49.

tremendous social cachet in polite society. The imprimatur of Yale College— the largest and one of the most eminent institutions of higher learning in the land—influenced many colleges to retain the prescribed course of studies, despite increasingly insistent attacks on it by those itching for changes. But it was not to last. By the time the Civil War began, many of America's colleges were poised for a radical alteration of course.

A major step in this transition occurred in July 1862, when the US Congress passed the First Morrill Land Grant Act.[244] The Land Grant Act donated public lands to US states and territories to found colleges that would provide training in the mechanical arts and agriculture.[245] Although such institutions would also include the study of Latin and ancient Greek among their curricular options,[246] the classical languages would now have to compete for student attention with numerous vocational subjects—many of them entirely new to American higher learning. At first there was little student interest in such pragmatic fare; many Americans likely presumed that one did not need to attend college in order to learn about, say, agriculture.[247] Yet this attitude would soon change.

The Morrill Act represented the founding of a new sort of institution of higher learning in the country, which would rival the old liberal arts colleges. Starting in the late nineteenth century, moreover, the US colleges would have even more challengers. These decades witness the rise of the American research university—an institution heavily modeled on German approaches to higher education.[248]

The "scientific democrats" who inaugurated the American university movement aimed to reorient higher education around the natural and social sciences.[249] Thus they sought to reduce the roles of the classical humanities and Christian theology in the American colleges.[250] The original shapers

[244] On the Morrill Act, see, e.g., Rudolph 1962: 249–62 and 1977: 116–17; Veysey 1965: 15–16; Jencks and Riesman 1968: 157–58, 162, 224–25, 263; Cowley and Williams 1991: 120–21; Lucas 1994: 147–48; Johnson 1997; Proctor 1998: 204; Geiger 2000c: 134–35, 149, 2000d: 26–27, 2000e, and 2015: 281–87, 545; Jewett 2012: 30–31; Axtell 2016: 278–79; Mattingly 2017: 100–13, 169.

[245] Some funds from the First Morrill Act were directed to preexisting colleges. See, e.g., Geiger 2015: 285; Adler 2016: 58; Mattingly 2017: 103–4.

[246] See Geiger 2000e: 154; Mattingly 2017: 102, 108.

[247] On the unpopularity of vocational subjects at the start of the Land Grant institutions, see Veysey 1965: 15–16; Jencks and Riesman 1968: 263; Johnson 1997: 223–26; Mattingly 2017: 104.

[248] Such German influences on American institutions often took different forms, as there was more than one German educational model and American reformers always borrowed selectively. On this topic, see esp. Turner and Bernard 2000.

[249] See Jewett 2012.

[250] Butts (1971: 288–89, 379, 403) stresses that progressive educators—one group of Jewett's scientific democrats—deemed the scientific method of paramount importance to undergraduates. They thus aimed to sideline the humanities in the curriculum.

of the American research universities—many of them social or natural scientists—hoped to transition the "literary colleges" into different sorts of institutions. By the mid-nineteenth century, the historian R. Freeman Butts reported, mathematics and the natural sciences had come to dominate the University of Berlin.[251] It was reasonable to conclude that the same would happen in the US, provided that the American colleges followed the intellectual and curricular ideals of German research universities.

In making their case for a new kind of higher learning, the scientific democrats helped marginalize the classical humanities by connecting the study of Latin and ancient Greek to the Protestantism regnant in the old colleges.[252] They did so, even though Western higher learning for millennia had frequently proved hostile to the ideals and writings of Greek and Roman pagans.[253] As we shall see in future chapters, in the Battle of the Classics the *studia humanitatis* and Christian theology often made for strange bedfellows. But, as American culture was growing more secular in the second half of the nineteenth century, the university reformers clearly recognized the pragmatic value of tying the classical humanities to religious orthodoxy.

Among the most prominent early scientific democrats was Andrew D. White (1832–1918), a professor of modern history and English literature. A disciple of Henry P. Tappan (1805–81), the energetic reformer who attempted to turn the University of Michigan into a Prussian-style university,[254] White served as the first president of Cornell. Chartered in 1865,[255] Cornell is among the earliest of America's modern universities.[256] As an instructor of subjects given little room in the prescribed classical curriculum,[257] White unsurprisingly supported a new course of

[251] Butts 1971: 79.
[252] See Youmans 1880a and various examples in Chapters 3 and 4, this volume. It is true, as Veysey (1965: 25) notes, that in the nineteenth century American supporters of educational traditionalism were often supporters of theological orthodoxy.
[253] On Christian hostility to the pagan classics, see, e.g., Marrou 1956: 426–27; Reinhold 1984: 116–17; Cowley and Williams 1991: 48; Morgan 1998: 45; Winterer 2002: 14–15; Richard 2009: 152–67. Cf. Kristeller 1961: 6, 70–91.
[254] See Bishop 1962: 40, 79; Turner and Bernard 2000; Geiger 2015: 252–54, 288, 316–18. Turner and Bernard note (225, 227) that White learned much from his decade at Tappan's University of Michigan, an institution they call the first American model for a modern university.
[255] Bishop 1962: 64. The institution opened in 1868 (Veysey 1965: 81; Rudolph 1977: 115; Jewett 2012: 32, 54; Geiger 2015: 287), with White as its president (Butts 1971: 185).
[256] *Pace* Rudolph 1977: 116, who perceives that it was America's first modern university. According to Geiger (2015: 287–88), Cornell was "the first American university to be dedicated to the new principles of advanced and practical knowledge."
[257] Fittingly, given White's scholarly background, Cornell established the nation's first chair of American history, in 1881. See Bishop 1962: 104. George Washington Greene (1811–83) had earlier offered courses on the topic at Cornell from 1872 to 1874.

studies that did not compel undergraduates to enroll in Latin and ancient Greek, if they thought that these subjects did not suit them.[258] Originally pioneering a "parallel-group" curriculum, by 1896 Cornell possessed an almost completely unrestricted system of elective courses.[259] The university allowed its undergraduates to study such subjects as agriculture, civil engineering, law, and commerce without being relegated to a scientific college. Cornell was a quick success: nonsectarian from the start[260] and co-educational as of 1872,[261] the university soon attracted a large student body.[262]

Although White, as Cornell's first leader, was among the more influential university reformers, his fame paled in comparison with that of Charles W. Eliot (1834–1926), a chemist and longstanding president of Harvard.[263] Eliot, whom we shall discuss at greater length in Chapters 4 and 5, was far from the first proponent of elective coursework.[264] But, as a staunch critic of the fixed classical curriculum, he became the most tireless and high-profile advocate of free election in America. The recent growth of new disciplines in American academia (e.g., English literature, literature in other modern European languages, modern history, and

[258] Bishop 1962: 75.
[259] See, e.g., Bishop 1962: 75, 155–56, 240–41, 274; Veysey 1965: 118; Butts 1971: 188; Hawkins 1972: 84; Lucas 1994: 170; Geiger 2015: 317.
[260] White envisioned Cornell as nonsectarian; see Bishop 1962: 65, 84; Veysey 1965: 84–85.
[261] Bishop 1962: 143–52; Rudolph 1977: 124; Mattingly 2017: 110. As of 1900, 71 percent of all US colleges and universities were co-educational (Rudolph 1962: 322; Mattingly 2017: 155). Rudolph (1962: 311) and Geiger (2000d: 27 and 2000f: 183) mention that Georgia Female College in Macon, chartered in 1836, was the first women's college in the US. Oberlin College inaugurated co-education in American higher education in the 1830s. See, e.g., Rudolph 1962: 311; Butts 1971: 140; Cowley and Williams 1991: 113; Lucas 1994: 121–22; Geiger 2000c: 142, 2000d: 27–28, 2000f: 183, and 2015: 201, 206, 210–11; Mattingly 2017: 148. As of 1900, around 40 percent of US college students were women (Veysey 1965: 272). Rudolph (1977: 83) and Mattingly (2017: 148) also note that Oberlin was the first institution in the US to allow blacks to enroll; see also Geiger 2015: 201, 470. Cf. Malamud 2016: 26–27.
[262] Rudolph 1962: 267; Mattingly 2017: 111. Geiger (2000e: 167 and 2015: 289) notes, however, that Cornell's early classes had a very high attrition rate. It took a while for the institution to attract students who would graduate in large numbers.
[263] See Hawkins 1972: 80, 85; Mattingly 2017: 115. Veysey (1965: 81) and Geiger (2015: 321 n. 11) note that White resented Eliot, in part because of Eliot's comparative prominence among the scientific democrats.
[264] As Mattingly (2017: 117), notes, "the actual elective system, that is, choice among courses for seniors and gradually for well-schooled underclassmen, could be found at Harvard and other colleges by the 1830s." On elective coursework at German universities, see, e.g., Axtell 2016: 230–31; on its influence on the free-elective system in American higher education, see, e.g., Axtell 2016: 262–66. Eliot himself (1923: 16–24, 53) describes Harvard's wavering support for the election of undergraduate courses prior to his presidency and notes that the first steps toward the elective principle at Harvard occurred during the tenure of John Thornton Kirkland (who served from 1810 to 1828).

botany), Eliot thought, helped render the prescribed curriculum obsolete. In his influential inaugural address as Harvard's new president in 1869, he announced, "The elective system fosters scholarship because it gives free play to natural preferences and inborn aptitudes, makes possible enthusiasm for chosen work, relieves the professor and the ardent disciple of the presence of a body of students who are compelled to an unwelcome task, and enlarges the instruction by substituting many and various lessons given to small, lively classes."[265]

Eliot's curricular proposals met with some furious criticism.[266] But his great success in fundraising allowed him to increase the number of faculty members at Harvard to such a degree that the institution could grant unparalleled choice to undergraduates in their selection of courses. As of 1897, Harvard had eliminated all required classes from its curriculum, save one course in English composition.[267] Thus Eliot had removed the classical humanities from the center of the Harvard course of studies. In 1886, Harvard also eliminated ancient Greek as an entrance requirement; the institution would now allow advanced mathematics and physics as substitutes.[268] Harvard under Eliot signaled that undergraduates did not need to experience any particular content in order to deem themselves educated. Although few American institutions went as far as Eliot's Harvard in embracing free election, the stamp of approval from the nation's oldest and most prestigious university did much to destroy the prescribed curriculum. By the turn of the century, all manner of vocational subjects (e.g., domestic science, sanitary science, and physical education) were becoming established at US universities.[269] As of 1900 most American institutions of higher learning allowed some degree of student election.[270] The elective system was now almost omnipresent, and even educational traditionalists recognized some of its virtues, simply aiming to confine it to the junior and senior years.[271]

[265] Eliot 1969: 11. On this speech and its import, see, e.g., James 1930 1: 224–35; Geiger 2015: 319.
[266] On opposition to Eliot's curricular ideas, see, e.g., Rudolph 1962: 294–300; Veysey 1965: 199, 249–51; Butts 1971: 210–12, 218–19; Carnochan 1993: 51–67; and, Chapters 4 and 5, this volume.
[267] Rudolph 1962: 294 and 1977: 194. Cf. Morison 1942: 346; Hawkins 1972: 95–96, 272; Geiger 2015: 321; Axtell 2016: 263; Mattingly 2017: 119 (who misunderstands Hawkins 1972: 95).
[268] Rudolph 1977: 181, 186. Similarly, in 1884 Eliot eliminated the compulsory study of Latin and Greek for Harvard freshmen (Geiger 2015: 321).
[269] Veysey 1965: 113.
[270] Morison 1942: 384; Butts 1971: 232; Axtell 2016: 263.
[271] Butts 1971: 232.

Research, Research, Research

White's Cornell and Eliot's Harvard provided important models for educational leaders itching to found genuine universities in America. But they differed from their Teutonic predecessors in one crucial respect: in the early years of their respective presidencies neither White nor Eliot especially encouraged faculty members to engage in original research.[272] It was thus left to Daniel Coit Gilman (1831–1908) to lead America's first institution devoted to advanced academic research and graduate study. Gilman had studied geography at Yale, and he ultimately served as the first president of the Johns Hopkins University, which was founded in 1876.[273] Originally intended to support graduate studies alone, Hopkins pioneered serious graduate training in America.[274] The Hopkins model of graduate study quickly earned imitators, from both new institutions (e.g., Clark University and Bryn Mawr College)[275] and traditional

[272] See Hawkins 1972: 53–54, 64–65; Geiger 2015: 317, 319–20. Similarly, Eliot originally doubted that the model of the German research university could be usefully imported to America. See, e.g., Axtell 2016: 254.

[273] On the foundation of Hopkins, see above all Hawkins 1960. See also, e.g., Rudolph 1962: 269–75; Veysey 1965: 158–59; Cowley and Williams 1991: 137; Proctor 1998: 204; Geiger 2000d: 27, 30–31 and 2015: 323–26; Jewett 2012: 32; Axtell 2016: 268; Mattingly 2017: 178–79. On Gilman's educational views, see, e.g., Geiger 2000e: 160–64; Mattingly 2017: 177–80.

[274] On important differences between the German and American Ph.D. degrees (the former the ordinary first degree, the latter a specialized research degree), see Turner and Bernard 2000: 236, 241. Yale had offered the nation's first three Ph.D.'s in 1861; one was awarded in the field of classics, to James Morris Whiton. But serious graduate education commenced with Hopkins, as discussions of Whiton's pamphlet of a dissertation ably demonstrate. On this topic, see Shorey 1919: 40–41; Rudolph 1962: 269, 335; Veysey 1965: 50; Calder 1966: 217; Lucas 1994: 171; Kimball 1995: 161; Geiger 2000d: 32; Axtell 2016: 219–20, 267. According to Shorey (1919: 41) and Calder (1966: 271) Frank B. Tarbell's *Notes on the Philippics*, completed at Yale in 1879, was the first real classical dissertation written in America. Reinhold (1984: 23) notes that, despite the highly classical pedigree of collegiate education, educators in America did not produce even one work of classical scholarship prior to the field's professionalization. Turner (2014: 276) considers William Watson Goodwin's *Syntax of the Moods and Tenses of the Greek Verb* (1860) the first major original US contribution to classical scholarship. According to Rudolph (1977: 154–55), by 1880 Charles Eliot, previously uninterested, began to promote scholarly publication at Harvard, to keep pace with Hopkins (see also Geiger 2015: 322; Mattingly 2017: 129; Chapter 4, this volume). As of this year, Harvard granted sabbaticals to its professors at half pay (see Veysey 1965: 175; Hawkins 1972: 67–68; Axtell 2016: 228, 308 n. 76). Eliot established its Graduate School of Arts and Sciences (formerly the Graduate Department) in 1890 (see, e.g., Rudolph 1962: 335; Geiger 2000d: 33; Mattingly 2017: 129). By 1892, Veysey (1965: 165) reports, Harvard had caught up to Hopkins in the realm of graduate training (cf. Morison 1942: 336). According to Cowley and Williams (1991: 139) scholarly research still had little status in US higher education as of this year. Cf. Veysey 1965: 175.

[275] On the foundation of Bryn Mawr in 1888, see Rudolph 1962: 319); on the foundation of Clark University in 1889, see Cowley and Williams 1991: 141; Geiger 2000d: 31 and 2015: 338–42; Axtell 2016: 268–69.

liberal arts colleges aiming to keep up with the times (e.g., Harvard and Yale).[276]

As befits the legacy of a "scientific democrat" such as Gilman, Johns Hopkins's embrace of the research ideal further moved US higher education away from the classical humanities.[277] Formerly institutions bent on instilling ancient wisdom in undergraduates, American colleges and universities now turned to an intellectual and pedagogical model more conducive to the natural and social sciences: the creation of new knowledge. As the faculty split up into distinct academic departments and a hierarchy of the professoriate was established (assistant professor, associate professor, and full professor),[278] the American colleges were rapidly changing course. By the early years of the twentieth century, prospective professors needed to earn Ph.D. degrees to land jobs in academia.[279] New faculty members were required to be dedicated scholarly specialists.[280] This requirement was just as true for classicists, as the *Altertumswissenschaft* ideal came to dominate the field in America.[281] Obligatory study of the classical languages soon disappeared from higher education in the US. Professionalized classical scholars now saw it as their chief aim to discover new information about the Greco-Roman past, rather than to act as custodians of ancient learning. As research-oriented faculty members began to recast the mission of American

---

[276] On Eliot's embrace of the research ideal in 1879 as a result of competition with Hopkins, see, e.g., McCaughey 1974: 287–91, 297–98; Geiger 2015: 322–23; on Yale's slow road toward the university model, see Geiger 2015: 332–34.

[277] This is the case, despite the fact that the classical scholar Basil L. Gildersleeve was Gilman's first faculty hire. On the hiring of Gildersleeve, see Adler 2016: 79–80 along with the sources mentioned in n. 13; Axtell 2016: 239. Gildersleeve was critical of German scholarly narrowness and worried about its possible effects on American classical studies. See Agard 1953: 148–49; Winterer 2002: 154; Axtell 2016: 240, 248, 264–65.

[278] See, e.g., Axtell 2016: 199, 274, 306. According to Rudolph (1962: 399) and Veysey (1965: 58–59, 320), academic departments were established in large numbers in American colleges during the 1880s and 1890s. These decades also witnessed the creation of academic hierarchies according to rank (Rudolph 1962: 398). By the 1890s, Veysey (1965: 319) notes, most US institutions of higher learning had cemented their faculty ranks. On the first academic department set up in US higher education—at Harvard in 1825—see Rudolph 1977: 77.

[279] See Veysey 1965: 176; Turner and Bernard 2000: 222–23; Winterer 2002: 153; Axtell 2016: 236–38, 306. By contrast, Rudolph (1962: 395) tells us that in 1884, Harvard had 189 faculty members, only 19 of whom had Ph.D.'s. In 1904, however, the City College of New York required all its professors to have earned a Ph.D. (Rudolph 1962: 396). Cf. Kimball (1995: 165) on the increase of American faculty members with Ph.D.'s from 1883 to 1933.

[280] On the professionalization of the faculty in US higher education during the nineteenth century, see, e.g., Finkelstein 1997; O'Boyle 1983: 8, 12, 17, 20–24; Axtell 2016: 199. According to Veysey (1965: 317), not until the late 1870s did the idea of an academic career in the professional sense commence in the US.

[281] On this topic, see Kimball 1995: 176; Pearcy 2005: 79–80; Adler 2016: 64–66.

higher education according to the dictates of professionalized scholarship, the goals of Renaissance humanism were being swept aside.

Birth of the Modern Humanities

All these changes obviously boded poorly for the vibrancy of the classical humanities in America's colleges and universities. During the nineteenth century, moreover, as a new spirit of populism spread in an industrializing US, the classical humanities failed to face the challenges introduced by nationalism and increasing democratization.[282] The study of English, then largely a newcomer to American academia, had the distinct advantage of treating the US's national literature in a manner accessible to the colleges' expanding student body. By comparison, the classical languages—inextricably tied to European education and therefore its more aristocratic ethos—seemed increasingly remote from American populism. Recognizing this dichotomy, in the mid-nineteenth century numerous opponents of academic vocationalism began radically to alter the conception of the humanities.[283] Thanks in large part to the Italian humanists, the *studia humanitatis* for centuries referred to the study of literary masterworks from ancient Greece and Rome. Aware of the troubled future for Latin and ancient Greek in the US,[284] some classical scholars deliberately broadened the humanities to include, as the historian Caroline Winterer puts it, "a kind of elevating, holistic study of literature, music, and art."[285] Now a number of disciplines—English, literature, philosophy, art history, French, and German, among others—were accorded a power previously granted to classical authors alone. The *modern humanities* were born.

Unfortunately, as might be expected, serious problems of categorization soon began to dog the modern humanities. Which disciplines were part of their purview? What was the intellectual and pedagogical rationale for

---

[282] On nationalist criticisms of Greco-Roman antiquity in early America, see Richard 2009: 105–19. Discussing the antebellum period, Richard notes (112), "Rare was the American who refused to declare American superiority to the classical civilizations."

[283] According to Proctor (1998: 7), this commenced in the 1860s; Winterer (2002: 117) dates it to the 1850s. Cf. Roberts and Turner 2000: 75.

[284] Prior to the late 1960s, however, enrollments in Latin at American secondary schools remained healthy. See, e.g., Phinney 1989; LaFleur 2000; Richard 2009: 209; Adler 2016: 71.

[285] Winterer 2002: 117. Music appreciation was actually a later arrival in the American college curriculum, since it relied in large part on the invention of the phonograph. On this topic, see Roberts and Turner 2000: 79.

their study? These questions have never received fully satisfying answers, and this lack of response speaks volumes about the makeshift nature of this nineteenth-century reconceptualization.[286] For example, American educators did not originally consider history part of the modern humanities: prior to 1900, scholars typically relegated the discipline to the social sciences.[287] Even today, historical studies uncomfortably straddle these two intellectual worlds, and this posture suggests problems with the underlying framework for the modern humanities.

Clearly, the modern humanities required some sort of intellectual justification if they were to have a chance to retain anything akin to the gravitas accorded to the old *studia humanitatis*. The most important thinker associated with this justification is Charles Eliot Norton (1827–1908), a polymath faculty member at Harvard, who served as the nation's first professor of art history.[288] Norton, a cousin of Harvard President Charles W. Eliot, became the chief architect of an intellectual rationalization for the modern humanities that ultimately earned the moniker "Western civilization."[289] The historian James Turner, Norton's biographer, helps explain Norton's approach to the topic: to Norton, "a common history had led the peoples of Europe (and their cultural descendants overseas) to share many beliefs and practices. These made them a single civilization, the people of which, despite many differences dividing them, recognized themselves as distinct from the peoples of, say, Chinese or Egyptian civilization."[290] It would be the proper goal of the modern humanities, believed Norton, to trace this common ancestry throughout time, from its supposed origins in Greek antiquity to the present.

---

[286] Cf. Veysey 1979: 51 (the modern humanities may never have had "any intrinsic intellectual coherence"). Thus Jarrett (1973: xvi–xvii, 47), in a book-length history of the humanities, admits that he cannot offer a perfect definition for the modern humanities. Cf. Proctor (1998: 98, 109–10), who contends that the classical humanities died in the nineteenth century and nothing ever took their place.

[287] Turner 1992: 96 n. 24. Cf. Roberts and Turner 2000: 79. Educators originally left history out of the modern humanities' orbit, even though the Italian humanists had regularly included the study of Greek and Roman historians as part of the *studia humanitatis*. US higher education did not feature separate courses on history until Harvard hired Jared Sparks to teach the subject in 1838 (Roberts and Turner 2000: 78–79). By the 1850s, such courses were typical at US colleges and universities (Roberts and Turner 200: 78–79).

[288] On Norton and his advocacy of "liberal culture," see above all Turner 1999. See also Vanderbilt 1959; Veysey 1965: 194–95, 204–5, 223–24 and 1979: 54; Butts 1971: 269–70; Turner 1992: 86–90; Roberts and Turner 2000: 78, 81, 95–88, 99, 102–4; Jewett 2012: 198.

[289] Turner 1999: 384–88. Turner relates (384) that Norton did not use this term, preferring to refer to "our civilization."

[290] Turner 1999: 384. On the origins of Greece and Rome being seen as the foundation of "Western civilization" in the late nineteenth century, see also Winterer (2002): 133–34.

Only then could Westerners understand the development of their society and deem themselves educated.

Norton's vision helped supply an organizing principle for the modern humanities, which could also help ground the newly fractured undergraduate curriculum. As we shall see, it helped inspire numerous Western civilization survey courses that were often required of college students in the mid-twentieth century. But, in comparison with the Renaissance conception of the *studia humanitatis*, "Western civilization" as a foundational concept suffered from serious defects.[291] First, as Norton undoubtedly recognized, the term would have been meaningless in the European past. Greco-Roman authors did not consider themselves "Western," and they often demonstrated strong prejudices against groups that lived farther to the West than they did.[292] The Renaissance humanists, moreover, urged direct communion with writers from classical antiquity. They did not see a grand progression of "Western" history; thus, to humanists such as Bruni, students should ignore medieval European authors as unworthy of their attention. One could reasonably question, furthermore, the decision to select the Greeks as the progenitors of the West. Many ancient Greek authors, after all, had acknowledged profound Egyptian and Near Eastern influences on their society.[293] Why were these civilizations denied a serious role in the wellspring of the Western tradition? This question seems especially pertinent, given the obvious importance of the Judeo-Christian tradition to what came to be called the West. If, to borrow Matthew Arnold's famous phrase, Western history had been a constant fluctuation between Hellenism and Hebraism, why had Near Eastern peoples other than the Jews and early Christians been removed from this continuum?[294]

The very novelty of Norton's vision, furthermore, in comparison with the age-old *studia humanitatis*, may have made it appear artificial. And— importantly, as it turned out—Norton's justification for the modern

---

[291] As Turner (1999: 388) notes, "His [Norton's] rendering of the humanities and their cultural meanings rooted itself widely in American collegiate education. True, the roots proved—and inevitably—shallow; and this point can hardly receive too much stress." For more criticism of the vagueness associated with such support for so-called liberal culture such as Norton's, see Veysey 1965: 202; Turner 1992: 80, 89.

[292] On this topic, see Isaac 2004: esp. 411–39.

[293] This subject was endlessly debated during the academic culture wars of the 1980s and 1990s, thanks to the controversy surrounding Martin Bernal's *Black Athena* project. On this topic, see, e.g., Adler 2016: 113–71.

[294] The conception of Hellenism and Hebraism were key to Arnold 1869. On this conception in Arnold's work and its origins in Heinrich Heine's vision of Western history, see Stone 1998: esp. 181.

humanities could prove salient only as long as the American college curriculum focused the vast majority of its attention on European cultures. It made intellectual sense in an environment in which supporters of the modern languages typically aimed to add only German, French, and (possibly) Italian and Spanish to the American undergraduate curriculum. For proponents of a more globalized approach to higher education, the "Western civilization" rationale would always seem wanting.

Disenchantment with Free Election

Although it quickly pervaded much of American academia,[295] the free-elective system continued to earn criticism from many quarters.[296] Not all the critics were pedagogical traditionalists. Even among the scientific democrats, a new progressive wing worried about the curricular hodgepodge's inability to instill scientific values in the nation's undergraduates.[297] And no wonder: the triumph of free election ushered in a lowering of academic standards, as undergraduates typically selected their institutions' easiest courses and directed their attention to the extra-curriculum.[298] According to many educators, more reforms appeared to be required.

One innovation rapidly took hold and became a quintessential feature of American undergraduate education. In 1877, a Johns Hopkins course catalog offered the first mentions in US higher learning of the terms *major* and *minor* to denote non-preparatory student concentrations.[299] David Starr Jordan (1851–1931), the president of Indiana University, established the major-minor system at his institution in 1885.[300] It then spread like wildfire. By 1910, most US colleges and universities had adopted it.[301] To this day,

[295] By the 1890s, Veysey (1965: 264) reports, only tiny US colleges did not have an elective system of some sort and a graduate school. He further informs readers (119) that the pure elective system peaked around 1903.

[296] See, e.g., Geiger 2015: 408–21; Axtell 2016: 264–65.

[297] See Butts 1971: 9–10; Jewett 2012: 14, 24–26, 74, 114–15, 196–97; Geiger 2015: 457.

[298] See Geiger 2015: 365–421; Adler 2016: 66. In 1903, the average Harvard undergraduate was found to study only fourteen hours per week outside the classroom; see Veysey 1965: 272. In the same year, seniors at Yale only needed one hour or less per day to prepare for all their courses; see Veysey 1965: 359.

[299] Payton 1961: 58. James (1930 1: 245) notes that the revised system of honors at Harvard under Charles W. Eliot encouraged student concentrations akin to the major prior to its official existence.

[300] Butts 1971: 199. Geiger (2015: 342–43) perceives that Jordan was influenced by the course of studies at Cornell (his alma mater) when creating this system at Indiana and then ultimately at Stanford. On Cornell's early curriculum, see the section "The Tide Turns against Prescription."

[301] Rudy 1960: 45 n. 10; Rudolph 1977: 119.

majors and minors remain a virtually omnipresent part of American undergraduate studies.

Such a concentration system at least implicitly criticizes curricular free
election. Typically, students fulfilling a given major are required to experience specific content in their coursework. Thus, for example, English majors
often have to take a class devoted to Shakespeare and sociology majors must
enroll in a course focused on formative theorists such as Marx, Durkheim,
and Weber. If such requirements seem indispensable to many concentrations,
why should the remainder of the undergraduate curriculum not similarly
rely on uniform content?[302]

Despite the salience of this question, the most widely adopted approach
to reform the non-concentration portion of the undergraduate curriculum
does not hinge on educational substance. Upon replacing Eliot as Harvard's
president in 1909, the political scientist A. Lawrence Lowell (1856–1943)
modified his predecessor's elective system, setting up the so-called distribution model in its place.[303] This approach to general education required
students to experience an array of academic disciplines, typically by selecting
a few courses from categories such as the social sciences, the humanities,
the fine arts, and the natural sciences. Although providing more focus than
does a complete curricular free-for-all, the distribution system emphasizes
a skills-based rationale for undergraduate study. For this reason, students
must often enroll in, say, a literature course, but they may choose among a
whole gamut of classes to satisfy this requirement. The key component of
such requirements is for undergraduates to learn to think like literature
professors; the works they read remain almost entirely a matter of student
preference. Undergraduates making their way through the distribution
model, that is to say, need not experience any particular content in order to

---

[302] Disagreements about the best sort of "general education" for undergraduates naturally surfaced
only after the demise of the prescribed curriculum and the advent of student concentrations. Prior to
this time, one might say that the entire course of studies in US colleges was "general education." On
different approaches to so-called general education, see the following text.

[303] Morison 1942: 446; Rudy 1960: 62; Veysey 1965: 247–51; Butts 1971: 245, 247, 409; Hawkins
1972: 278; Rudolph 1977: 229; Geiger 2015: 414; Mattingly 2017: 244. See also Jewett 2012: 198.
Harvard under Lowell also adopted the concentration (i.e., major-minor) system in 1910 (Cowley
and Williams 1991: 146; cf. Morison 1942: 446; Hawkins 1972: 278). On the distribution model as
a whole in US higher education, see Phillips 1901: 211; Rudy 1960: 62–63; Butts 1971: 245, 403–4,
409–10; Rudolph 1977: 254–56; Kimball 1995: 177, 192–93, 212. Harris 1880: 171 seems to anticipate the idea of distribution requirements. In 1905, Cornell established area requirements in its undergraduate curriculum, which anticipated Lowell's distribution model at Harvard; see, e.g., Bishop
1962: 393; Hawkins 1972: 100–1. Hawkins (1972: 278) notes that David Starr Jordan at Stanford
and William DeWitt Hyde at Bowdoin advocated concentration and distribution prior to Lowell's
presidency.

consider themselves educated. This system, popularized by Lowell's Harvard, remains the dominant approach to general education in the nation.[304] By highlighting skills at the expense of substance, it was bound to help sideline the modern humanities.

Many humanists therefore hungered for a system that would be more conducive to their interests. In 1919, Columbia University pioneered coursework that helped cement Norton's vision of Western civilization in the college curriculum. It was in this year that the institution's "War Issues" course transformed into "Introduction to Contemporary Civilization," the class that ultimately inaugurated Columbia's so-called core curriculum.[305] This amounted to the first major attempt after the demise of the antebellum fixed curriculum to supply a program of specific courses with uniform content for undergraduate general education.[306] Columbia ultimately expanded its program into a two-year mandatory sequence, which, in Nortonian style, would introduce students to the West's greatest writers. Undergraduates at the institution read these authors—in translation, for those who did not write in English—in small seminar classes. In 1931, Robert Maynard Hutchins (1899–1977), the president of the University of Chicago, and Mortimer J. Adler (1902–2001), a veteran of the Columbia program, established a famous Great Books program at their institution, which similarly aimed to introduce students to the West's canonical authors.[307] Although never as popular as the distribution model, these core curricula helped midwife survey courses on Western civilization, which were obligatory elements of general education at numerous American colleges and universities. These classes fought back against the curricular smorgasbord, implicitly informing students that they needed to experience specific works of prose and poetry (e.g., Homer's *Iliad*, Plato's *Apology*, Vergil's *Aeneid*, Dante's *Divine Comedy*, and Milton's *Paradise Lost*) to be considered properly educated.

The Great Books programs—though they have not completely disappeared from US higher education—are nowhere near as commonplace as they were in their heyday between the wars. To some extent, they were victims of the

[304] See Rudolph 1977: 254–56; Kimball 1995: 212; Arum and Roksa 2011: 73–74.

[305] See Rudolph 1962: 455 and 1977: 237; Ben-David 1972: 61–62; Allardyce 1982: 698, 703–4; Carnochan 1993: 70; Lucas 1994: 213; Jewett 2012: 203; Geiger 2015: 464–67 (who also notes [464] that Columbia English professor John Erskine originally proposed a two-year Great Books sequence of courses for juniors and seniors in 1916).

[306] Ben-David 1972: 61–62.

[307] Allardyce 1982: 709–16; Geiger 2015: 461–67. On Hutchins's educational views, see also Mattingly 2017: 245–53. Hutchins explicitly denied the necessity of studying the classical languages as part of his Great Books approach to general education. See Hutchins 1995: 82–83.

shallowness associated with Norton's vision from the start. Beginning in the late 1960s, the popularity of the postmodern movement in American academia led to the rise of identity politics on campus. According to many scholars associated with postmodernism, Western civilization surveys are intellectually and ideologically dubious, if not pernicious: centered around a Whiggish grand narrative from Greek antiquity to the present, such classes overlooked much of human history. Numerous critics of the Great Books contended that these courses, with their syllabi devoted to writings by "dead white males," served to marginalize women and minorities.[308]

In some cases, American universities, attuned to these criticisms, turned Western civilization classes into world civilization courses. More often they dropped such required coursework altogether, allowing an Eliot-like spirit of free-market anarchy to re-establish itself in the American college curriculum. In response to student complaints, for example, Amherst College in 1971 decided to scrap all its general education requirements.[309] Most institutions have continued to cling to some version of the distribution model, however. Thus, from the late twentieth century to today, distribution rules the roost, and with it the contentless approach to general education that has further demoted the modern humanistic disciplines. It is in this context that many observers over the past few decades have fretted about the "crisis" plaguing the humanities. Revealingly, the modern humanities now face the same pressures from the democratization of American higher education that formerly hounded the classics: pundits can maintain that the modern humanities are elitist and of little value to a new vocationally oriented student body.

The Manifold Problems for the Modern Humanities Today

Our examination of the history of the humanities from Roman antiquity to the present suggests numerous challenges for defenders of today's modern humanistic disciplines on American college campuses. It should be clear that the humanistic tradition is far more variegated and complex than most contemporary works lamenting their demise recognize. Our current understanding of the humanities—as a vague collection of academic disciplines

---

[308] This was especially the case during the American academic culture wars of the 1980s and 1990s. On this topic, see Adler 2016: esp. 9–41. For further problems with the Great Books tradition as an educational model, see, e.g., Geiger 2015: 465–66.
[309] Rudolph 1977: 272.

mostly, but not entirely, focused on language—is very much an invention of the late nineteenth century. For the great majority of their history, the humanities signified something very different. To Cicero and other ancient educational theorists, the humanities amounted to the sum of Greek and Roman learning. To Bruni and other Renaissance humanists, they denoted engagement with masterworks of Greco-Roman civilizations in their original languages as a means to moral betterment. At least by the nineteenth century, however, the decontextualized, grammar-obsessed classical pedagogy in America disallowed educators to repeat the sorts of humanistic rationales for the study of Latin and ancient Greek that had been prevalent in the Renaissance. Bereft of such arguments, American classicists turned to a skills-based defense that focused on "mental discipline." This shift in apologetics appears to have been a disaster. Accordingly, American educators in the second half of the nineteenth century were forced to re-conceptualize the humanities, turning it into the odd congeries of studies that is easiest to define by negation: the humanities are what is left over from higher education when you remove the natural sciences, the social sciences, the fine arts, and vocational studies.

It naturally proves nearly impossible to present a fully convincing rationale for this disparate group of disciplines. After all, what sort of justification for philosophy will also suffice for, say, the study of Korean? Norton's focus on the grand arc of Western high culture provided one—superficial—avenue of defense, but the politics of inclusion have successfully questioned its appropriateness and concomitantly left the humanities rootless. African art, the *Analects* of Confucius, Japanese Noh drama—these subjects and so much more are part of today's humanities. How can the "Western civilization" narrative offer an adequate rationale for such studies? It cannot. And thus, in this environment, apologists for the modern humanities have been forced once again to muster their skills-based arguments. Much like their predecessors in the nineteenth century, they undoubtedly perceive that the current intellectual and pedagogical status quo leaves them with no other options.[310]

But this resignation serves to turn one's back on the fundamental character of the humanistic tradition from the Italian Renaissance: students grappling with works of profundity and style in order to improve their character. Critical thinking, verbal dexterity, and other skills will naturally follow from such grappling, but they are its byproduct, not its heart. Simply put,

---

[310] Cf. Proctor 1998: xxiv–xxv.

humanists either believe that their subjects can help shape students' souls, or they are not humanists.[311] The humanities thus properly hinge on their substance: masterworks that can most effectively spur on self-reflection and moral improvement. Concomitantly, humanists must defend their tradition chiefly by highlighting the value of studying particular works of literature, art, music, religion, and philosophy. Skills-based apologetics ring hollow in part because they cut against the grain of the humanities. The Italian humanists, after all, reimagined the *studia humanitatis* as an antidote to the skills-focused scholasticism of the Middle Ages. Our investigation of the humanistic tradition demonstrates the cardinal value of specific content to their flourishing. In the history of Western education, the humanities have been at their strongest when educational theorists have zeroed in on the supreme value of engaging with canonical masterworks. Thus, in Roman antiquity—when reading Homer and Vergil was the sine qua non of the liberal arts—the literary portion of the *studia humanitatis* dominated. During the Renaissance and its aftermath, the humanities were viewed as the quintessential object of study for the properly educated person. Albeit to a lesser extent, even the interwar Great Books programs—with their insistence on uniform substance—implicitly contended to students that higher education depended to a goodly extent on the humanities.

By contrast, those eras in which an emphasis on skills held the most sway have witnessed the subordination of the humanities. Medieval higher education, thanks to its focus on syllogistic reasoning and formal logic, emphasized the *quadrivium* at the expense of the literary-based *trivium*. And the bulk of educational history after the demise of the *studia humanitatis* in the late nineteenth century has demonstrated that ditching substance for skills has meant a slow death for the modern humanities. If we are going to mount an adequate defense for the role of the humanistic disciplines in American higher education, we must highlight their substance, and what this substance can mean for students' inner lives.

It is also essential to recognize that standard elements of the contemporary curriculum were crafted deliberately in order to minimize the role of the humanities in the American colleges and universities. The university

---

[311] This is the case, despite the difficulties humanists have long encountered in their attempts to highlight the moral aspects of their pedagogy. See, e.g., Marrou 1956: 234; Veysey 1965: 37; Summit 2012: 671–72. Humanists today encounter this problem: many would like to argue in favor of the moral benefits of humanistic education, but our professionalized approach to our subject matter seldom allows for such concerns to play a role in the classroom. On this problem and how to ameliorate it, see Chapter 6, this volume.

reformers who spread the free-elective system across the nation aimed to sideline the *studia humanitatis* in favor of scientific and/or vocational education.[312] Although the distribution model modestly tamed free election, it left its intellectual rationale undisturbed: discipline-based academic skills remain the quintessential elements of undergraduate studies and the educational substance students encounter remains up to their whims. It seems well-nigh impossible for the modern humanistic disciplines to thrive in curricular systems specifically created to diminish them.

This chapter has also helped us see that the late nineteenth century remains the most crucial period in educational history for those concerned about the fate of the humanities in America. After all, it was during these decades that resistance to the *studia humanitatis* came to a head and, as a result, reformers began to conceptualize the modern humanities to take their place. Thus the Battle of the Classics has much to teach us.

How did the humanities fare during these pivotal years? What can we learn from educational controversies that drew much attention during the Battle of the Classics? The next three chapters investigate these very questions.

---

[312] See Butts 1971; Jewett 2012; and previous text.

3

A College Fetich?

But for science we should still be worshipping fetishes; or, with the hecatombs of victims, propitiating diabolical deities.

—Herbert Spencer, *Education: Intellectual, Moral, and Physical* (1861)

"But you see," replied Mr. Adams, "Greek is the rallying point, the chief fortress of our opponents. If that can be carried by assault and destroyed, the ground will then be clear for any desirable arrangements."

—Edwin Pliny Seaver, "Tribute [to Charles Francis Adams, Jr.]" (1914–15)

A *"Guerrilla Raid"* on the Classical Humanities

It was a blast against the classical humanities seemingly heard nationwide. On Thursday, June 28, 1883, Charles Francis Adams, Jr., (1835–1915) took to the podium in Sanders Theatre on the campus of Harvard University and delivered a fiery address before the institution's Phi Beta Kappa society. By this time, as we noted in the previous chapter, the dominant role of ancient Greek and Latin in the American college curriculum had long aroused controversy.[1] But Adams, a Harvard graduate (class of 1856) and a man of impeccable aristocratic pedigree, somehow managed to reignite the issue.[2] Newspapers from Hartford to Honolulu covered the ensuing brouhaha and

---

[1] Many who took part in the controversy surrounding Adams's speech recognized that this was a matter of longstanding disagreement. See, e.g., anonymous 1883r; Cooke 1883: 1; Morse 1883a: 341 and 1883b: 214; Chamberlain 1884: 5; Frost 1885: 327; Herbermann 1885: 140; Porter 1885: 426–27. Cf. James 1884: 291; Shorey 1910: 599–600 n. 64. Krug (1969: 2) notes that as far back as 1873 William C. Collar, the head of the Roxbury Latin School, caused a commotion by proposing the elimination of ancient Greek as a required subject for entering college.

[2] On the importance of Adams's fame and the illustriousness of the event to the ensuing controversy, see, e.g., Porter 1883: 107; Chamberlain 1884: 5.

nary an intellectual magazine in the country appeared to remain silent on the topic.[3]

In his blistering speech, given the suggestive, if slightly archaic, title "A College Fetich," Adams scorned his alma mater for continuing to require ancient Greek as part of its examination for admission.[4] This requirement, Adams thundered, is "a positive educational wrong,"[5] a "superstition"[6] that had harmed the lives of Adams and his fellow Harvardian family members. To connect Harvard to the modern world, he suggested, the institution should allow French or German to take Greek's place. The text of Adams's oration, soon issued in pamphlet form, sold through three printings, as the American public hotly debated the wisdom of its author's attack on the ancient Greek language. Adams's biographer justly called "A College Fetich" "the most important single document in the 'Greek War' flaring in academe."[7] It was a speech of talismanic importance to the Battle of the Classics.

The nation's classicists and their supporters, sensing grave danger for the ancient Greek language in American education, quickly joined the fray, attacking the speech and presenting various rationales for the classical humanities. Their pleas, however, fell on deaf ears. Harvard's faculty and Board of Overseers soon renewed the debate over the institution's admission examinations.[8] In 1886, Harvard announced that it would alter its requirements, thereby allowing prospective students to drop Greek among the examined subjects.[9] The New Englander and Yale Review lamented

[3] For examples of the voluminous coverage of the controversy over Adams's speech in the popular press, see, e.g., Adams 1883 (which includes a transcription of much of Adams's address); anonymous 1883a, b, c, d, e, f, g, h, i, j, k, l, m, n, o, p, q, r, s, t, u, v, w, x, y, z, ab, ac, and ae; Bolles 1883; Cooke 1883 and 1884; Curry 1883; Jeff 1883 (a humor column focused on the speech); Morse 1883a and b; Wicks 1883; Winthrop 1883; Youmans 1883c; anonymous 1884c; Eggert 1884a and b; Fernald 1884; Fisher 1884; James 1884; Herbermann 1885; Porter 1885.

[4] For the A.B. course; Harvard's Lawrence Scientific School, established in 1847, had different entrance requirements, as did the institution's professional schools. Prior to the advent of the College Board in 1901, Harvard, like other American colleges, administered its own admission examinations. On this topic, see, e.g., Broome 1903; Fuess 1950: 3–11; Geiger 2015: 382–84.

[5] Adams 1884: 16.

[6] Ibid. 17.

[7] Kirkland 1965: 191. The speech had a lasting impact, too: a full fifteen years later, John Dewey could still appeal to Adams's oration in the title of his own work. See Dewey 1940: 18–35 ("The Primary-Education Fetich," originally published in 1898).

[8] Broome 1903: 93.

[9] Various American newspaper articles (e.g., anonymous 1885a, n) reported that the Harvard faculty voted on February 17, 1885, to make only one of the two classical languages required for admission to the A.B. course. In effect, this decision meant that applicants had the option of dropping ancient Greek, since Latin was a far more commonly studied language in American secondary schools. In a piece from May of that year, Porter (1885: 443) suggested that the faculty's decision might not be final. In any case, the new admission policy was first announced in the 1886–87 number of the Harvard University Catalogue, which specifies that the changed requirements will go into effect

the rapidity of Adams's victory. "Even Mr. Charles Francis Adams, Jr.," it moaned, "must be astonished that his guerrilla raid upon the sacred shrine of the long-worshipped Fetich has resulted in so speedy a surrender to the rampant iconoclast."[10] For the first time in Harvard's history, students could gain admission to the institution for a bachelor's degree without any prior experience with ancient Greek. Harvard's example soon set the tone for the nation, as college after college abandoned its Greek entrance requirements. By 1910, the language, formerly propped up by its role as a sine qua non of collegiate admission examinations, had all but disappeared from high schools in the US.[11]

This chapter analyzes Adams's speech and the spirited reactions it engendered. It demonstrates that *skills-based* arguments dominated the appeals offered by supporters of collegiate requirements in ancient Greek. Almost entirely failing to invoke the tenets of humanism, such supporters anchored their apologetics in the concept of "mental discipline." Their opponents, sensing the weaknesses of these appeals, ably countered this defense. At a crucial point in time for the classical humanities in American higher learning, then, skills-based rationales proved a dismal failure. This should go some way toward demonstrating the perils involved in vouching for the humanities through such means.

A Brahmin's Brahmin

Charles Francis Adams, Jr., in many respects lived a charmed life. Born on May 27, 1835, he was third of seven children of a prominent American political family.[12] His father, who lived from 1807 to 1886, served as both a US

---

in 1887 (anonymous 1886d: 74–87). See, e.g., Smyth 1930: 36; Morison 1942: 354, 389; Krug 1969: 29. On the specifics of the new admission examination, see anonymous 1886d: 74–87. For a discussion of the Harvard admission examination around the time Adams delivered his address, see, e.g., Broome 1903: 46–65, 87–96; Wechsler 1977: 5–19, 46, 47, 84–86. Anonymous 1882: 66–69, 75 offers a detailed description of the Harvard admission requirements for the A.B. course for the 1882–83 academic year.

[10] Porter 1885: 424. Kirkland (1965: 247 n. 39) guesses that Noah Porter, Yale's president, wrote this unsigned article. It does read like Porter's work on the controversy: cf. Porter 1883, 1884. But we cannot be sure this is the case; it could also have been written by William Lathrop Kingsley (1824–96), then the editor of the *New Englander and Yale Review*, the youngest son of James Luce Kingsley, a Yale professor who contributed to the Yale *Reports* of 1828. On the *Reports*, see Chapter 2, this volume.

[11] Winterer 2002: 103.

[12] For Adams's biography see especially Adams 1916; Kirkland 1965. Much else of value about Adams's life can be gleaned from the collection of his papers available at the Massachusetts Historical

Congressman from Massachusetts (1859–61) and Lincoln's appointment as the nation's envoy to the UK (1861–68). Earlier Adamses had made an even greater impact on American politics. Adams's grandfather, John Quincy Adams (1767–1848), and great-grandfather, John Adams (1735–1826), had both been US presidents. Although never lacking in funds, Adams's father greatly increased his fortunes upon marrying Abigail Brown Brooks (1808–89), the daughter of one of the wealthiest men in New England.[13]

But Adams never got along well with his father, and their strained relationship contributed to complaints Adams uttered in his "A College Fetich" address.[14] Like many elite Americans at the time, Adams had the good fortune to receive a comparatively thorough education. This commenced with attendance at a dame school; then, at age thirteen, he entered the Boston Public Latin School, a feeder to Harvard that Adams's father had attended and revered.[15] At Boston Latin, with its traditionalistic, Latin-and-Greek-heavy curriculum, Adams proved a dismal failure. In 1851, one year prior to graduation, Adams's father withdrew his son from the school, placing him under the tutelage of a private instructor instead. "Here was a failure Charles could not forget," wrote Adams's biographer. "Instead of blaming himself, he blamed the school and blamed his father for sending him there in the first place."[16]

Despite his rocky time in secondary school, Adams would take up his family's seeming birthright by attending Harvard. Having passed a presumably perfunctory examination for admission, Adams started at Harvard College as a sophomore in 1853.[17] A year later, his younger brother Henry—the future author of the American nonfiction classic *The Education of Henry*

Society (most of it on microfilm; for the collection, see http://www.masshist.org/collection-guides/view/fa0263). This chapter includes quotations from some materials found in these papers. Unfortunately, the collection at the Massachusetts Historical Society does not contain correspondence from 1883 or 1884, the years most pertinent to the controversy surrounding Adams's speech. But Adams's diary and his correspondence from other years offer useful information. Some postmortem tributes to him present revealing glimpses of his personality: see, e.g., Eliot 1914–5; Long 1914–15; Seaver 1914–15; Thayer 1914–15.

[13] Kirkland 1965: 2.

[14] On Adams's dislike for his father, see Adams 1916: xx–xxi, 21–23; Kirkland 1965: 5–6.

[15] On Charles Francis Adams, Sr.'s, great esteem for Boston Latin, see, e.g., Adams 1900: 11 and 1916: 21–23; Richard 2009: 2.

[16] Kirkland 1965: 7.

[17] Adams 1916: 23–24. Adams's brother Henry claimed that his entrance examination for Harvard College was extremely easy; see Samuels 1965: 8. On admission to Harvard College at this time, see Broome 1903: 46–47, 48–49 n. 13. Geiger (2015: 225) notes, however, that by the 1850s Harvard had raised its entrance requirements, such that its examination for admission was an onerous three-day affair.

Adams—would join him at the institution; the two boys roomed together off campus for the remainder of Adams's school days.[18] Like his older brother, Henry would eventually write captiously about his Harvard experience. In *The Education*, Henry memorably noted that "no one took Harvard College seriously. All went there because their friends went there, and the College was their ideal of social self-respect."[19] In the opinionated fashion typical of his family, he mused, "The chief wonder of education is that it does not ruin everybody concerned in it, teachers and taught."[20]

Henry's portrait of his years as a student at Harvard College in *The Education* exhibits similarities with his brother's assessment. In comparison with his time at the Boston Latin School, which in his autobiography Charles Adams deemed "the most depressing" period of his life,[21] Charles gave slightly higher marks to Harvard as a decent, if unserious, place. Charles Adams wrote that "my college life I look back on with pleasure, and a moderate satisfaction."[22] Harvard lacked the personal touch, he reported, offering little guidance when it came time for him to choose the elective portion of his courses in his junior and senior years.[23] Although he enjoyed studying ancient Greek, Adams reported in his autobiography that Professor Cornelius Conway Felton (1807–62) and Evangelinos A. Sophocles (1804–83), then a tutor, beat that love out of him.[24] Underscoring his distaste for the grammar-heavy manner in which the classical languages were then taught at Harvard,

---

[18] Samuels 1965: 8, 10, 40.

[19] H. Adams 1973: 54; on Henry's time at Harvard, see 54–69. For a discussion of Henry's exaggerated portrait of his Harvard days, see Samuels 1965: 8–52. On Henry's brief tenure on the Harvard faculty, see, e.g., Morison 1942: 348–49.

[20] H. Adams 1973: 55.

[21] Adams 1916: 23.

[22] Ibid. 12.

[23] Ibid. 35–36. On the Harvard College curriculum in Adams's undergraduate days, see Walker 1855: 20–26, 1856: 39–45, and 1857: 17–24; Adams 1907: 106. Since both ancient Greek and Latin were required of all sophomores, Adams was compelled to take a year of Latin with George M. Lane (Walker 1855: 21–22) and a year of Greek with Cornelius Felton and Evangelinos Sophocles (Walker 1855: 22). For a discussion of Harvard at this time, see, e.g., Hawkins 1972: 5–10. On Lane and Sophocles, see Smyth 1930: 38; Morison 1942: 298; on Felton, see Eliot 1923: 19–20; McCaughey 1974: 260; Wiesen 1981–82; Richard 2009: 12. The sort of curriculum Adams experienced at Harvard was typical of the A.B. course in his day; see, e.g., Geiger 2000c: 139. Adams would later announce deep-rooted criticisms of Eliot's free-elective curriculum. Eliot was a tutor in mathematics during Adams's junior and senior years (Walker 1856: 44 and 1857: 22).

[24] Adams 1916: 26. Adams's implicit criticism of Felton's teaching seems peculiar, since Felton had criticized the overreliance on rote memorization in the Greek classroom and had promoted a more holistic approach to the study of the ancients; see Wiesen 1981–82; Richard 2009: 15. A major contributing factor to the educational dreariness of Harvard during Adams's student days was the Scale of Merit system, which had been pioneered under the presidency of Josiah Quincy (1772–1864; pr. 1829–45). On this system, see, e.g., Morison 1942: 299; Kirkland 1965: 10–11; Samuels 1965: 10–11.

Adams remarked in his autobiography, "I should have followed Greek and Latin *as literatures.*"[25]

Having graduated with an A.B. in June 1856,[26] Adams, unsure of his calling in life, turned to the law. He took advantage of a family connection and joined the office of Dana and Parker.[27] Although he managed to pass the Massachusetts bar examination—thanks, he suggested, to family connections[28]—Adams discovered that he was both uninterested in and ill-suited for the law.[29] The private practice he had established was soon foundering.[30]

By late 1861, Adams had decided to enlist in the Union Army.[31] Like his family more generally, he was a long-standing abolitionist, and, especially as the son of a quondam Massachusetts congressman and current minister to Great Britain,[32] he deemed it prudent to fight for the Union in the Civil War. Sometime shortly after Christmas, Adams became part of the First Regiment of Massachusetts Cavalry Volunteers.[33] An able officer, in July 1864 he was commissioned as a Lieutenant-Colonel of the Fifth Massachusetts Cavalry, a black regiment.[34] By mid-February of the following year he became the unit's Colonel,[35] before resigning from the Army in August, sickly and weighing not more than 130 pounds.[36]

Loath to remain a lawyer,[37] Adams after the war jump-started a new career in the burgeoning railroad industry.[38] Although lacking in-depth knowledge of the subject, Adams penned an article on the railroad for the prestigious *North American Review*, which appeared in the April 1868 issue of the journal.[39] This helped land Adams a job on the newly created Board of

---

[25] Adams 1916: 32 (emphasis in the original). According to James (1930 1: 209), George Lane, Adams's Latin teacher at Harvard, was atypical of American classicists of his time for his interest in teaching the language in a humane manner.

[26] Ibid. 37.

[27] Ibid. 39; Kirkland 1965: 13.

[28] Adams 1916: 42.

[29] Ibid. xxvi–xxvii, 38–39.

[30] Ibid. 108.

[31] Kirkland 1965: 22–23.

[32] Ibid. 21.

[33] Ibid. 23.

[34] Adams 1916: xxxi; Kirkland 1965: 29.

[35] Kirkland 1965: 30.

[36] Adams 1916: 156–57, 167; Kirkland 1965: 30.

[37] Adams 1916: 170.

[38] He did so after he had regained his health on a trip to Europe. See Adams 1916: 168.

[39] Adams 1868. Adams (1916: 171) mistakenly reported that it was published in April 1867. Adams's Harvard and familial connections surely helped him secure the piece's publication: its editor at the time was fellow Boston aristocrat Charles Eliot Norton. In 1890, Lloyd Bryce, a later editor of the *North American Review*, begged Adams to contribute a piece on the railroad again (see the letter from Bryce to Adams, December 8, 1890, in the papers of Charles Francis Adams, box 1, folder 7).

Railroad Commissioners in Massachusetts, on which he served from 1869 to 1879.[40] In part through this experience he obtained a far greater prize: from May 1884 to November 1890, he was the president of Union Pacific Railroad, then among the largest companies in the nation.[41]

By this time Adams was a seasoned contributor to public service on a number of fronts. In 1872, he began work as a member of the school committee in his native Quincy.[42] Adams in this capacity took the lead in inaugurating a mildly successful and oft-discussed series of reforms commonly called "the Quincy experiment."[43] This helped earn him an appointment from Massachusetts Governor John Davis Long (1838–1915) on the state's Board of Education, on which Adams sat from 1880 to 1881.[44] Most important for our purposes, in June 1882 Adams, like numerous members of his family before him, was elected to Harvard's Board of Overseers.[45] He ultimately remained an overseer for four terms of six years apiece, lasting on the board through 1907, with an interval in 1895.[46]

Interested in contributing research on historical topics as early as 1874,[47] Adams was made president of the Massachusetts Historical Society in 1895.[48] In addition to works of local and American history, Adams composed a biography of his father.[49] All the while, Adams, an aggressive businessman and speculator with familial means, amassed a fortune, chiefly through his land holdings.[50] Harvard's choice to deliver its Phi Beta Kappa address as part of the commencement exercises of 1883 was thus an insider's insider: an alumnus of the College, a member of the storied Adams clan, an overseer, an amateur historian, and a respected businessman, Adams must have checked off many boxes for those hunting for a distinguished speaker.

[40] Adams 1916: xxxiv, 173; Kirkland 1965: 41. Adams had urged the creation of such a board and claimed responsibility for convincing the Massachusetts legislature to consent to it; see Adams 1916: 172.

[41] Adams 1916: xxxix, 193; Kirkland 1965: 81, 126.

[42] Kirkland 1965: 144.

[43] Ibid. 146–48. Adams resigned from the Quincy school committee in 1881; see Kirkland 1965: 148.

[44] Kirkland 1965: 148, 150.

[45] Eliot 1914–15: 390; Adams 1907: 103 and 1916: xli, 198; Kirkland 1965: 8, 189; Veysey 1965: 102 n. 130.

[46] Eliot 1914–15: 390; Adams 1916: xli; Kirkland 1965: 190.

[47] Adams 1916: 179–82>.

[48] Adams 1916: xlvi, 208; Kirkland 1965: 216.

[49] Adams 1900.

[50] Adams experienced some financial bumps in the road on the way to his fortune, however. On this topic, see Kirkland 1965: 125–26, 173–79.

Adams's temperament may also have suggested that he would prove an entertaining orator. Many estimations of Adams's personality highlight his opinionated, contrarian, and even combative character. In a tribute to Adams published soon after his death, for example, Charles W. Eliot, with whom Adams worked in his capacity as an overseer, noted that Adams "experienced in high degree the joy of combat, and the joy was not dependent on immediate or even ultimate victory."[51] "He was dogmatic and masterful," suggested Governor Long, "a fighter, for any position he took, who asked no odds and gave no quarter. He was so strong in his conclusions, he pressed them so confidently, that, paradoxical as it may seem, the very intensity of his convictions often sooner or later led him, as an overloaded gun kicks backward, to question them and to go to the other extreme with equal earnestness."[52]

Indeed, Adams positively relished ruffling feathers. In 1891, having given a deliberately provocative title to an address he delivered at the Massachusetts Historical Society, Adams was disappointed that his remarks were respectfully received.[53] The leaders of Harvard's Phi Beta Kappa chapter may well have recognized that their choice of orator was likely to brew controversy. With a speaker disinclined to stoop to the hoary clichés typical of commencement addresses, the stage was set for an exciting afternoon.

A Tirade against Educational Humbug

In this respect, Adams surely did not disappoint. Although a peculiarly inconsistent creation,[54] "A College Fetich" possesses plenty of firepower. Its delivery to an audience partly made up of Harvard faculty members must have caused much hand-wringing.

Having graduated from the College some twenty-seven years ago, Adams said toward the beginning of his remarks, he now aimed to evaluate the quality of his education there.[55] Harvard, he stressed, "was our gymnasium.

---

[51] Eliot 1914–15: 391. Eliot himself was not lacking in this quality, as James (1930 2: 241) notes.

[52] Long 1914–15: 384–85. This last sentence may be a reference to Adams's views on ancient Greek, since Adams had a change of heart on that subject later in life. On this topic, see later in this chapter. For other assessments of Adams's character, see, e.g., Seaver 1914–15: 416–17; Thayer 1914–15: 405–6. Adams (1907: 103–4) portrayed himself as a contrarian.

[53] Kirkland 1965: 212. The title of the speech was "Some Phases of Sexual Morality and Church Discipline in Colonial New England."

[54] Some at the time noted glaring inconsistencies in the speech. See, e.g., Merrill 1883: 420–21; Porter 1883: 106 and 1884: 196; Herbermann 1885: 144. We shall highlight some of these inconsistencies in this chapter.

[55] Adams 1884: 3–4.

It is now the gymnasium of our children. Thirty years after graduation a man has either won or lost the game. Winner or loser, looking back through the medium of that thirty years of hard experience, how do we see the college now?"[56]

Although he did not prove entirely condemning of his undergraduate days, Adams provided a withering portrait of Harvard in the 1850s. Among a litany of criticisms, he stressed that the college was academically unchallenging,[57] failed to provide adequate training for life,[58] did not allow him to focus on a specialty,[59] and wrongly favored Latin and Greek at the expense of the more useful modern languages of English, French, and German.[60] In a crucial passage of the address, Adams, taking issue with the arguments in favor of the classical languages on the grounds of "mental discipline," announced: "In the first place, I very confidently submit, there is no more mental training in learning the Greek grammar by heart than in learning by heart any other equally difficult and, to a boy, unintelligible book."[61] Although a typical proponent of mental discipline theory, Adams, as was standard for critics of the prescribed classical curriculum, vigorously denied the superiority of the classical languages to train the mind. "As a mere work of memorizing," Adams suggested, "Kant's *Critique of Pure Reason* would be at least as good."[62] Indeed, Adams dismissed the notion that Greek provides "the severest intellectual training" as "unadulterated nonsense."[63]

Most of Adams's censures surrounded Harvard's zeal for the classical languages. In part for this reason, one can understand why many who commented on the speech concluded that "A College Fetich" primarily took aim at collegiate Greek.[64] But for all his grousing about Harvard College, Adams had an earlier target in his sights. His chief complaint about his alma mater was its continued refusal to drop ancient Greek as a requirement for admission.[65] Although content with the use of Latin for this purpose, Adams

[56] Ibid. 4.
[57] Ibid.
[58] Ibid. 4–5.
[59] Ibid. 13.
[60] Ibid. 8, 14. Elsewhere in the speech, however, Adams remarked (16) that he has no qualms with the study of Latin.
[61] Ibid. 18–19.
[62] Ibid. 19.
[63] Ibid. 18.
[64] E.g., anonymous 1883d: 116; Cooke 1883: 1; Curry 1883. Cf. Youmans 1884a: 702. A writer referred to merely by his initials (F. F. 1883: 271) believed that many of Adams's critics had missed the point of "A College Fetich."
[65] Adams 1884: 9.

concluded that the study of ancient Greek "is a mere penalty on going to college."[66] Recalling his misery at Boston Latin, he announced, "When I was fitted for college, the study of Greek took up at least one half of the last three years devoted to active preparation."[67] He viewed this work as "the one gigantic nightmare of youth."[68] Despite his toilsome devotion to the language in his schoolboy days, Adams stressed that he could not so much as read the Greek alphabet now;[69] so little did his wasted studies produce. It was thus, he maintained, incumbent on Harvard to alter its examination for admission, allowing either French or German as suitable replacements for the "dead learning" of ancient Greek.[70]

Familial Complaints

To demonstrate the perniciousness of Harvard's continued insistence on a Greek admission requirement, Adams fastened on the anecdotal evidence of his family. Ever since the school years of his great-grandfather John, the first Adams man to attend the College (class of 1755), a Harvard A.B. was something of a rite of passage for the male members of his family. Adams aimed to show that their Greek studies had proved detrimental to both their careers and their lives. He thus took advantage of his storied lineage to scorn the classics.

His excoriation, naturally enough, commenced with his great-grandfather. When John Adams as a middle-aged man became the representative of the American colonies in France, Adams declared, he was forced to learn French, because he had wasted his time in school with ancient Greek instead.[71] Noting that his great-grandfather late in life established the funds necessary for an academy that required Greek and Latin of its pupils,[72] Adams announced that John Adams's continued devotion to Greek instruction was "fetich-worship, pure and simple."[73] And it was "fetich-worship," Adams

---

[66] Ibid. 17.
[67] Ibid.
[68] Ibid.
[69] Ibid. 18.
[70] Ibid. 10.
[71] Ibid. 22.
[72] Adams Academy in Quincy, Massachusetts, which did not open until 1872 and closed in 1908.
[73] Adams 1884: 23. As Richard (2009: 205) notes, Adams's remarks were intended ironically, since John Adams had declared in his will that he would disown any descendant who questioned his bequeathing of land for his classical academy.

concluded, that his great-grandfather would ultimately lament. The speech quoted from a July 9, 1813, letter written by John Adams to Thomas Jefferson, in which the 79-year-old admitted that his Greek training was all for naught, since he knew little Greek at present.[74]

Adams offered similar treatment to the career of his grandfather, John Quincy Adams. Contending that picking up modern languages as a youngster in Europe was more valuable than all the Greek he trudged through as a Harvard student, Adams doubted that his grandfather could ever really read ancient Greek.[75] He would have been well-served, Adams continued, to drop Latin as well, since he considered John Quincy Adams's classically tinged speeches to be an embarrassment.[76]

The speech even ridiculed the Greek learning of Adams's father, Charles Francis Adams, Sr., then still alive to take notice of his son's address. Unlike John and John Quincy, Charles Sr. had managed to keep up his Greek in adulthood. A lover of the classics from an early age, he continued for decades to read numerous classical works as part of his daily regimen, both in their original languages and in translation.[77] But this habit did not shield Charles Sr. from the barbs of his son. Despite all his efforts, Adams maintained, his father could never read Greek with any familiarity. He opined that it would have been better for Charles Sr. to drill himself in German or French than to persevere with ancient Greek.[78]

Nor did Adams spare himself and his three brothers in his assessment. Harvard men all, they dropped the language as soon as they were able in college. They regretted having to learn ancient Greek, Adams reported, even the one who forced his children to study the language—merely because Harvard required it for admission![79] Speaking of himself, Adams concluded that all he gained from his impoverished Hellenic studies was a sense of discipline, and that this could have been procured from "an equal number of hours spent on a treadmill."[80] He and his family, Adams declared, were but more sacrifices to the "college fetich" for ancient Greek.

---

[74] Ibid. 23–24. Adams also quoted from another letter of his great-grandfather to Jefferson, in which John Adams contended that he received little benefit from trying to piece together some of Plato's prose.

[75] Ibid. 24–25.

[76] Ibid. 25–26.

[77] Richard 2009: 28–29.

[78] Ibid. 26–27.

[79] Ibid. 27.

[80] Ibid. 28.

In proffering many of these contentions, Adams was treading on shaky ground. As a few of his critics noted, one could point to much evidence to question the notion that the male members of his family considered themselves ill-served by Harvard's Greek requirement for admission.[81] Although his great-grandson could quote a few letters critical of his classical learning, for example, John Adams's correspondence with Jefferson was littered with Greek and Latin references.[82] Indeed, John Adams had taunted fellow Founding Father Benjamin Rush for the latter's anti-classical diatribes.[83] He had forgotten his Greek in adulthood, but revered the *Iliad* and deemed the classical masterpieces superior to all modern literature.[84] Deeply invested in his son's and grandsons' training in Latin and Greek,[85] John Adams likened himself to Xenophon[86] and maintained a lifelong identification with Cicero.[87] The vision of mixed governance he promoted for the fledgling US stemmed chiefly from Plato, Aristotle, and Polybius.[88]

Nor was John Quincy Adams a likely denigrator of the pedagogical value of ancient Greek literature. After all, unlike the author of "A College Fetich," who complained that an outdated mania for Greek kept children away from modern tongues when they were most apt to learn them, John Quincy Adams had learned French exceedingly well at a young age.[89] For a brief time the inaugural Boylston Professor of Rhetoric and Oratory at Harvard (1806–9), he translated many classical works for the benefit of his students.[90] An idolizer and imitator of Cicero[91] who was constantly reading the classics, John

---

[81] E.g., Porter 1883: 109, 119–20; Chamberlain 1884: 33–39; Herbermann 1885: 145–47. Richard (2009: 205) notes, "No Adams before Henry and Charles Francis Jr.—certainly not their direct ancestors, John, John Quincy, and Charles Francis—had ever questioned the utility of the classics. On the contrary, each of them had argued passionately, against a vocal minority of critics, that the classics were indispensable to what mattered most: the teaching of virtue and republicanism."

[82] On this topic, see Richard 1994: 27–28.

[83] Ibid. 222. Richard (2009: 205), discussing the educational views of Henry and Charles Francis Adams Jr., justly concluded, "John Adams would certainly have been appalled by both his great-grandsons' assaults on the classics."

[84] Richard 1994: 30. See also Burstein 1996: 35.

[85] Richard 1994: 32–34.

[86] Ibid. 57.

[87] Ibid. 60, 63.

[88] Ibid. 133; Burstein 1996: 37. For more examples of John Adams's high regard for the classics, see, e.g., Richard 1994: 10, 21, 25, 30, 66–67 and 2009: 22–23. On the classical learning of the Adams men as a whole, see esp. Richard 2009: 22–29.

[89] Hecht 1972: 18–26, 32–33. On John Quincy Adams's preparatory education for Harvard, see 30–32, 39–41. On his language training in general, see Levin 2015: 1–2.

[90] Portolano 2013: 427.

[91] Ibid. 442.

Quincy Adams owed his views on rhetoric chiefly to Aristotle, Cicero, and Quintilian.[92]

Adams's father was similarly unlikely to assent to his son's vision of Greek as "a college fetich." As we previously noted, Charles Sr.'s esteem for the traditionalistic Boston Latin School encouraged him to send his sons there, even though the latter professed that its curriculum and teaching methods rendered the place unpalatable.[93] Thanks to his father's appointments abroad, Charles Sr.'s first language was actually French;[94] his high regard for the classics had not constrained his ability to master modern European tongues. At the joint memorial service for John Adams and Thomas Jefferson, furthermore, Charles Francis Adams, Sr., recited the Herodotean story of Solon's trip to Croesus in Lydia; according to the historian Carl Richard, the deceased "would have relished" its inclusion in the ceremony.[95] In all, these did not seem men likely to bewail their classical learning.

But if Adams's anecdotal evidence appeared less than fully convincing, it undoubtedly possessed pragmatic value to the orator. As some contributors to the controversy surrounding Adams's speech suggested, the author of "A College Fetich" ought to have known better than anyone else about the intellectual history of his own family.[96] Adams's distortions of his ancestors' classicism appear to have been the product of his insecurities: after all, he had failed miserably to live up to their example at the Boston Latin School. But who would dare tell an Adams—especially one with an historical interest in his family—about the value of the classics to the Adamses? Although a few critics of "A College Fetich" made attempts, in all they appeared wary of contesting the evidence its author offered about himself and the male members of his clan. On its own, this hesitation did not make Adams's case ironclad, but it offered undeniable benefits to him.

The Virtues of Inconsistency

One could say the same about sundry inconsistences that litter the speech. Indeed, Adams's address was notably scattershot. Here was an

---

[92] Ibid. 428. For more discussion of John Quincy's great esteem for the classics, see Richard 2009: 22–28.

[93] Adams 1900: 10–11.

[94] Ibid. 4–5.

[95] Richard 1994: 69. See also Richard 2009: 29.

[96] E.g., F. F. 1883: 272; Youmans 1883a: 118.

author who seemingly wanted things both ways. He declared that he was
no opponent of the classical languages; Greek, he contended, was only
a "superstition" if required of all students, not if "lovingly learned."[97]
Adams even announced that the ancient languages provided the best
grounding for collegiate study. "I object to no man's causing his children
to approach that goal by the old, time-honored entrance," he opined. "On
the contrary I will admit that, for those who travel it well, it is the best entrance."[98] Wary of being lumped in with pedagogical utilitarians, he also
declared that he was no scientific pragmatist. "In the first place I desire
to say that I am no believer in that narrow scientific and technological
training which now and again we hear extolled. A practical, and too often
mere vulgar, money-making utility seems to be its natural outcome," he
said.[99]

Yet Adams also supplied numerous remarks in the oration that called into
question these judgments. One of his chief criticisms of the required study
of Greek, as opposed to that of Latin, was that the former supposedly has
no modern uses.[100] His grounds for questioning Greek, then, were predominantly utilitarian. Despite conceding that the classical languages provide the
best foundation for the college course and literature of exceeding value,[101]
moreover, he repeatedly attacked ancient authors. "Goethe I hold to be the
equal of Sophocles, and I prefer the philosophy of Montaigne to what seem to
me the platitudes of Cicero," he remarked.[102] Toward the end of the address,
furthermore, Adams concluded,

> I most shrewdly suspect that there is in what are called the educated classes,
> both in this country and in Europe, a very considerable amount of affec-
> tation and credulity in regard to the Greek and Latin masterpieces. That is
> jealousy prized as part of the body of the classics, which if published to-day,
> in German or French or English, would not excite passing notice. There

[97] Adams 1884: 17.
[98] Ibid. 10. Incongruously, though, in a memorial address at the start of Adams's biography, Henry
Cabot Lodge mentions (Adams 1916: xxii–xxiii) that Adams disliked the fact that his father compelled him to attend Boston Latin School, where he was forced to study ancient Greek and Latin. His
father, Adams writes in the autobiography (1916: 21–22), had a "fetish" for the school.
[99] Adams 1884: 10.
[100] Ibid. 16–17. But see also 25–26 (John Quincy Adams should have given up his Latin studies)
and 37 (it is a superstition to require Latin of the educated).
[101] Ibid. 11.
[102] Ibid. 10–11.

are immortal poets, whose immortality, my mature judgment tells me, is wholly due to the fact that they lived two thousand years ago.[103]

Although reckoning that the classics owed their reputation to social snobbery,[104] Adams touted the value of learning French in part because it is the language "of all refined society."[105] Not for nothing did C. G. Herbermann, a critic of Adams, sizing up the published version of "A College Fetich," deem it "[o]ne of the most marvellous [sic] instances of mental polarity which it has been our fortune to meet."[106]

But Herbermann's own conclusions about the address ably demonstrate the benefits of its incongruousness. "Surely," he wrote, "to rank Mr. Adams as an opponent of the classics, or for that matter of Greek, is a delicate and dangerous step."[107] The uneven character of Adams's oration allowed its author to have things both ways. He could offer knocks against the classics that would provoke alarm among traditionalistic educators while at the same time he supplied enough genuflections to the ancients to allow Adams's supporters to claim that he was far from an anti-Hellenic know-nothing.

Thus more extreme denigrators of classical learning could point to "A College Fetich" as proof that even ostensibly moderate, non-utilitarian educational thinkers were fed up with the monopoly Latin and Greek appeared to enjoy in American preparatory studies. Among Adams's champions in the ensuing debate were numerous contributors to the *Popular Science Monthly*, whose founding editor, E. L. Youmans, pilloried the classics with gusto.[108] He and other first-generation scientific democrats[109] used Adams's speech to underscore the superior virtues of an American higher education based on the scientific method.

Although in his address Adams had denied that he wanted to reshape secondary and tertiary education in the US along scientific lines,[110] Youmans and his ilk were correct to note some important intellectual overlap between "A College Fetich" and the curricular views of the scientific democrats. His protestations to the contrary notwithstanding, Adams was in large measure

---

[103] Ibid. 35–36. Cf. 37: "are those transcendent beauties really there" in Greek and Latin literature? "I greatly doubt."
[104] Ibid. 37.
[105] Ibid. 38.
[106] Herbermann 1885: 144.
[107] Ibid. 143–44.
[108] E.g., Youmans 1883a, b, d, e and 1884a, b, c, d.
[109] The term is Jewett's (2012). On the scientific democrats, see also Chapter 2, this volume.
[110] Adams 1884: 10.

utilitarian in his criticisms of the classical humanities. He thought that it was the college's goal to help its students encourage and nourish a specialty, such as Adams's ultimate taste for the business of railroads.[111] The broad learning associated with the humanistic tradition, then, appeared to mean little to him.[112] Adams also nodded to the paramount value of scientific education in the contemporary world. He based his esteem for training in French and German in part on the value these languages possess for modern scientific researchers. "With the exception of law," he announced, "I think I might safely challenge any one of you to name a single modern calling, either learned or scientific, in which a worker who is unable to read and write and speak at least German and French, does not stand at a great and always recurring disadvantage."[113]

An important passage found in Adams's autobiography, furthermore, underscores the compatibility of his thought with that of scientific democrats such as Youmans. Adams reported that one major life-altering event for his intellectual development occurred in November 1865, when he read an essay John Stuart Mill wrote about the sociologist Auguste Comte. Adams related that "that essay of Mill's revolutionized my whole mental attitude. I emerged from the theological stage, in which I had been nurtured, and passed into the scientific." "From reading that compact little volume of Mills," he continued, "I date a changed intellectual and moral being."[114] Adams had become "scientific" in his outlook on the world. Yet it would be some years until Adams would first read the works of Charles Darwin.[115] It seems that he originally learned about evolution through the writings of the British philosopher and scientist Herbert Spencer (1820–1903) and one of his enthusiasts, the American philosopher John Fiske (1842–1901).[116]

This enthusiasm calls to mind some intriguing similarities between Adams's and Spencer's educational thought.[117] Spencer too was a pedagogical

---

[111] Ibid. 13. Cf. Adams 1916: 20.

[112] But, in yet another inconsistency, Adams remarked (1884: 10) that "a broadened culture" "is the true end and aim of the University," a statement applauded by Chamberlain (1884: 12). Still, Adams's overall argument in the speech supports specialization and practicality at the expense of intellectual breadth. Some of his advocates stressed the idea that education was properly career preparation: e.g., Cooke 1883: 1–2; W. M. G. 1883.

[113] Adams 1884: 14.

[114] Adams 1916: 179.

[115] Kirkland 1965: 140 informs us that Adams did not read *The Origin of Species* until the 1880s.

[116] Ibid.

[117] It is important to note that Spencer was a formative thinker on educational topics for the scientific democrats. His influence on major figures such as Charles W. Eliot (with whom Adams seems to have been in intellectual sympathy when he composed "A College Fetich") and John Dewey will be discussed in later chapters.

utilitarian with a flair for the dramatic. In his monograph *Education: Intellectual, Moral, and Physical* (1861), he demonstrated an Adams-like penchant to cause offense. "If we inquire what is the real motive for giving boys a classical education," he wrote in the book,

> we find it to be simply conformity to public opinion. Men dress their children's minds as they do their bodies, in the prevailing fashion. As the Orinoco Indian puts on his paint before leaving his hut, not with a view to any direct benefit, but because he would be ashamed without it; so, a boy's drilling in Latin and Greek is insisted on, not because of their intrinsic value, but that he may not be disgraced by being found ignorant of them— that he may have "the education of a gentleman"—the badge of marking a certain social position, and bringing a consequent respect.[118]

Spencer, like so many of the era's anti-classicists, believed in the theory of mental discipline,[119] but dismissed the notion that Latin and ancient Greek possessed a superior ability to inculcate it in students. He too in his writing on education talked of "fetishes,"[120] just as Adams would some two decades later.

Yet Adams in important respects parted company with Spencer, Youmans, and kindred champions of the sciences. Many boosters of science during the Battle of the Classics saw little value in language learning as a whole. According to Spencer, for example, training in modern European tongues was suspect: "If you ask why Italian and German are learnt," he suggested, "you will find that, under all the sham reasons given, the real reason is, that a knowledge of those tongues is thought ladylike."[121] Even in the realm of aesthetics, which he deemed a comparatively nugatory component of education, Spencer trumpeted the superior value of the sciences over the fine arts and humanities. "And now let us not overlook the further great fact," he argued, "that not only does science underlie sculpture, painting, music, poetry, but that science is itself poetic."[122] Although obviously more extreme in their views than Adams, proponents of science education such as the circle surrounding the *Popular Science Monthly* soon latched onto "A College

---

[118] Spencer 1865: 23. James (1930 1: 349) notes that the essays included in the book were first published in British journals between 1854 and 1859.
[119] Spencer 1865: 37.
[120] Ibid. 95.
[121] Ibid. 24.
[122] Ibid. 81–82.

Fetich" as the work of a famous aristocrat whose views were compatible with their pedagogical ideas.[123]

The Traditionalists Strike Back

Supporters of the classical humanities could be forgiven for deeming Adams's address—and the wide publicity it received—a grave threat to the educational status quo. Unsurprisingly, many quickly chimed in with attacks on "A College Fetich." Frederick Rudolph, an eminent historian of American higher education, portrayed these criticisms—and, more generally, the debate over Adams's speech as a whole—as highly polemical in character.[124]

And, to be sure, some of the critiques of Adams's speech were bellicose in tone and argument. Writing in the *Overland Monthly*, for example, George B. Merrill excoriated Adams for "A College Fetich," even granting the oration an alternate title, "A Plea for Rather Dull Men."[125] Andrew F. West (1853–1943), a Latin professor at Princeton who would later serve as the institution's inaugural dean of the graduate school, defended the classics in part by denigrating the study of modern European languages. "What does English, French or German grammar amount to?" he asked rhetorically. "Simply *débris* of the classical languages, mixed with barbaric elements."[126] Noah Porter (1811–92), the president of Yale College from 1871 to 1886, chimed in with at least two lengthy replies.[127] Their pugnacious tone gives one a sense of the severity of the threat "A College Fetich" offered to Porter's vision of classical liberal education.[128] Porter remarked, for instance, that the

---

[123] For examples of pieces supporting "A College Fetich" in the *Popular Science Monthly*, see Cooke 1883 and 1884; Youmans 1883a, b, c, d and 1884a, b, c, d; Fernald 1884.

[124] E.g., Rudolph 1977: 183–86.

[125] Merrill 1883: 417.

[126] West 1884: 153. C. A. Eggert, a supporter of Adams's address, harped on this statement (1884a: 374–76), focusing on its haughtiness. This helps demonstrate that incendiary retorts to Adams were unlikely to sway the uninitiated: they merely helped traditionalists look like extremists. On West, see, e.g., Hawkins 1972: 97–98; Hoeveler 1981: 290; and Chapter 4, this volume.

[127] Porter 1883, 1884, and 1885. Kirkland (1965: 247 n. 39) suggests that the latter piece, which was unsigned, was likely written by Porter. This may be the case. On this topic, see the previous text. For an interesting perspective on Porter's traditionalistic views on the governance of Yale, see Hall 2000. On Porter's contribution to debates over the nature of American higher education, see, e.g., Geiger 2015: 333–34; Mattingly 2017: 89–90, 173–76. According to Mattingly (174), Porter's book *The American College and the American Public* (1878) supplied "one of the most articulate defenses of the classics at the heart of collegiate discipline."

[128] Rudolph 1977: 186 justly noted that Porter 1883 was a particularly polemical response to Adams.

modernist curriculum Adams promoted "reminds us somewhat of the advertisement of a cheap boarding-school."[129]

Some responses to "A College Fetich," were far more respectful, however. In 1884, Daniel H. Chamberlain (1835–1907), a Yale and Harvard graduate who, prior to his governorship of South Carolina (1874–76),[130] had served during the Civil War under Adams in the Fifth Massachusetts Cavalry,[131] traveled to various venues to deliver a full-scale rebuttal of Adams's positions.[132] Chamberlain gave this speech, first performed at the Yale Kent Club in New Haven,[133] the title "Not 'A College Fetish.'" Since its performance evinced great interest in audiences,[134] the oration ultimately saw light of day as a pamphlet to rival Adams's publication.[135] A regular correspondent on friendly terms with Adams,[136] Chamberlain offered a defense of the classical humanities while remaining consistently deferential to his opponent. In the published version of "Not 'A College Fetish,'" for example, Chamberlain suggested that Adams's appeal encouraged attention in part because of its author's "character, his position as one of the representatives of an illustrious family, the vigor and courage of his address, the confidence of his tone, the personal and family illustrations which enliven his arguments," among other qualities.[137]

Whether mannered or not, educational traditionalists provided an assortment of criticisms of Adams's positions. Perhaps the most glaring deficiency in such retorts is their almost complete disconnect from the spirit of humanism. As we noted in the previous chapter, devotees of the ancients such

[129] Porter 1883: 110.

[130] On Chamberlain's biography, see, e.g., Chamberlain 1907: 174–78; Green 1908. On his governorship, see, above all, Allen 1969.

[131] Green 1908: 7–8. On Adams's command of this unit, see Adams 1916: xxx–xxxi.

[132] Anonymous 1883a; Chamberlain 1884: iii. Chamberlain 1876 demonstrates that its author supported classical studies prior to the controversy surrounding "A College Fetich." He also opposed Charles Eliot's free-elective system; see Chamberlain 1886.

[133] On March 11, 1884; see Chamberlain 1884: iii.

[134] The Boston Globe reported (anonymous 1884d) that Chamberlain's iteration of the address as the Phi Beta Kappa speech at the University of Vermont on June 24 of that year, given the topic, was delivered at a venue that "was crowded to overflowing."

[135] Chamberlain 1884.

[136] The Adams papers at the Massachusetts Historical Society list Chamberlain as a routine letter writer to Adams. In a letter preserved among these papers from October 21, 1891, for example, Chamberlain respectfully refers to their disagreement on the topic of "A College Fetich." He wrote, in part, "I have read the re-statement of your views with interest and respect with which I read all that comes from your pen. I am heartily glad at least for this:—that whether you and I agree or not, you at least are preserving your interest in this and kindred themes to a degree that makes you a striking exception to the great mass of Americans who have opportunity and ought to have the wish to bear a hand in settling to some extent these great questions about education and culture" (box 1, folder 18).

[137] Chamberlain 1884: 5.

as Petrarch and Bruni vouched for the value of classical literature in large measure because of its unparalleled ability to shape one's character. These texts, when read in their original languages, provided appropriate literary and moral models for students, who could intuit from them the way to live a good life. The debate surrounding "A College Fetich," however, demonstrates that by the late nineteenth century such contentions had all but disappeared from apologetics for a traditional approach to the liberal arts. The grammar-heavy, decontextualized nature of classical training in American secondary and tertiary education presumably disallowed proponents of Greek and Latin to mount such a "Petrarchan" defense.

Not that retorts to Adams always failed to vouch for the literary greatness of the ancients. In his riposte to Adams, for example, Chamberlain stressed the superior quality of classical literature. He concluded that Homer, for example, produced "undoubtedly the most valuable poetical monument the world contains."[138] About the earliest of the three great Athenian tragedians, he suggested, "Not to know Aeschylus is not to know what was first in time, and is perhaps highest in conception and style in the whole range of tragic poetry and dramatic art."[139]

Such points have the benefit of stressing the potentially unique value of classical authors. But they suffer from a debilitating vagueness. As we noted, in "A College Fetich" Adams announced that he preferred the works of Montaigne to those of Cicero. How could a quick declaration of the opposite preference prove persuasive? George P. Fisher, vouching for the greatness of ancient Greek literature in the pages of the *Princeton Review*, for example, wrote, "On the whole . . . when we take into view both matter and form, the finest productions in literature are the dramas of Sophocles. Homer and Sophocles! Where shall we look for another two upon a level with them?"[140] As was typical of Adams's critics, he supplied no examples to back up his view, no passages of special beauty or profundity to sway the skeptical. This omission could be, a doubter may well have thought, another instance of the "fetish" for the classics in action.

Most important, nowhere did Fisher and his fellow traditionalists stress the unique benefits of reading such authors in their original tongues. One finds in the critiques of "A College Fetich" no talk of models, and little in

[138] Ibid. 22.
[139] Ibid. 23. Cf. 23–25 for Chamberlain's appreciations of Thucydides, Demosthenes, Plato, and Aristotle.
[140] Fisher 1884: 119. For similar thoughts, see 119–20.

the way of using classical authors as guides to the Good Life. A college edu-cation, wrote the traditionalist E. R. Sill in the pages of *The Atlantic*, should allow a man to "get complete possession of himself—in all his powers: mind, body, and that total of qualities known as 'character'—as is essential to the highest success in any specialty or profession whatever."[141] But even in presenting such an (atypical) appeal, Sill failed to specify the role of the clas-sical humanities in shaping one's character. The entire college curriculum, he intuited, aimed to influence students, and nowhere did he hint that the humanities of necessity played a crucial role in this process.[142] Thereby did such traditionalists undermine age-old humanist rationales for the study of ancient Greek and Latin literature.[143]

Weak Sauce for the Classical Humanities

In the absence of such arguments, Adams's critics typically provided defenses that come across as less than compelling. Some authors, assuredly hoping to win over the scientifically inclined to their cause, stressed that ancient Greek remains of crucial value to modern education because it forms the basis for much scientific terminology. According to E. R. Humphreys, for example, "The majority of all scientific terms are formed directly from the Greek," a fact that renders "Greek a *necessity to the scientific student*."[144] Expanding this argument further, Rev. William G. Frost, a professor of Greek at Oberlin College, stressed, "The Greek has given us directly, or through Latin paraphrases, almost the entire vocabulary of philosophy, of science, and of literary criticism."[145]

---

[141] Sill 1885: 208.

[142] Sill also focused on the shaping of mind and body, which suggests high regard for "mental discipline."

[143] For further examples of traditionalists in the conflict coming closest to providing humanistic rationales for the classical humanities, see, e.g., Sill 1883: 172 and 1885: 208–9; Porter 1884: 211–12 and 1885: 429–30, 434; Frost 1885: 332–33. The modernist Sumner (1884: 136) explicitly rejected the idea that the classics provide any guidance for conduct. Adams (1907: 145) later asserted that he believed in character-building in college. Many opponents of Adams's speech also suggested that its criticisms were outdated: e.g., Morse 1883a: 341–42 and b: 214; Porter 1883: 106, 111. Adams recog-nized (1884: 5), however, that his condemnations of education in his student days were only partially accurate today.

[144] Humphreys 1883 (emphasis in the original).

[145] Frost 1885: 335. For similar arguments from traditionalists in the debate, see, e.g., Curry 1883; Chamberlain 1884: 44–45. Cf. Adams 1884: 14, 16, who denies that Greek helps with scientific terms.

Although well-intentioned, such arguments were unlikely to convince a skeptical public that all aspirants to a bachelor's degree in the US needed to study years of ancient Greek in order to earn admission to college. Did the presence of some Greek-derived terminology really require American students to devote much of their secondary education to translating authors such as Homer and Xenophon? This benefit may reasonably seem to many a slim payoff for hours upon hours of toil.

Some of Adams's opponents took the opposite tack: they argued that German and French, which Adams had seen as requisite for scholars in the contemporary world,[146] had no more utility than did the classics. "It is not by any means provided by the 'modernists,' as they call themselves," sniffed the schoolmaster and intellectual J. H. Morse (1841–1923), for instance, "that French and German as *spoken* languages, are of practical value to more than a tenth of the graduates of our colleges."[147]

Such arguments played into the hands of scientific democrats such as Youmans, who, like his mentor Spencer,[148] dismissed language study tout court. In an unsigned editorial in the *Popular Science Monthly*, Youmans averred, "The study of words, the chief scholarly occupation, is mentally debilitating, because it leaves unexercised, or exercises but very imperfectly, the most important faculties of the mind—those which can only be aroused to vigorous action by direct application to the facts of the phenomenal world."[149] Although aiming his barbs specifically at what he termed "dead-language studies,"[150] Youmans called into question the benefits of studying *any* languages.

By no means did the aforementioned arguments exhaust the contentions of Adams's critics. A few defenders of Greek highlighted the language's religious bona fides. In a specifically Protestant example of this justification, Daniel Curry wrote in the *Western Christian Advocate* that whereas the unlearned can read the Bible in the vernacular, "the Romanist appeals to the

---

[146] Adams 1884: 14.

[147] Morse 1883a: 341 (emphasis in the original). For similar arguments from traditionalists in the conflict, see, e.g., anonymous 1883ad; Chamberlain 1884: 31–32. Chamberlain (1884: 13–14) also suggested that mathematics was not a useful subject for most men's careers, and yet no one questioned the value of the discipline it afforded. Decades after the conflict was over, Shorey (1910: 609–10) still maintained that modern languages were not useful for most students.

[148] Spencer 1865: 24, 74. Youmans 1883d supports Spencer's educational views against Sill 1883. The modernist Fernald (1884: 30) asserts that he believed in educational "survival of the fittest."

[149] Youmans 1883b: 266–67. Youmans here adheres to a view of education rooted in faculty psychology, which stresses the importance of mental discipline.

[150] Ibid. 266.

Vulgate as the infallible Word of God; but back of all these is the originals, in the Greek language, to which the last appeal must come, and beyond which there can be no dispute."[151] Slightly more ecumenically, the clergyman Andrew Preston Peabody (1811–93), a former editor of the *North American Review* and a professor emeritus of Christian morals at Harvard,[152] also noted the supreme value of direct access to the New Testament. "We call ourselves a Christian people," he wrote, "and ill as we deserve the name, it never was so truly ours as now, if we may trust the statistics of the churches and benevolent institutions of all the leading Christian denominations."[153]

This passage hints at an important downside associated with this argument. As historians of higher education have noted, the US during the Battle of the Classics was both industrializing and secularizing, as technological changes helped uproot the nation's traditional patterns of life.[154] The pace of scientific discoveries, combined with the recent mania for Darwinism,[155] suggested to many educated Americans—such as Adams—that they stood at the dawn of a new era, in which religion would rightly play a much smaller role. Thus the scientific democrats aimed to limit theological influence on the American colleges, just as they had hoped to sideline the classical humanities. Although justifications foregrounding the specifically Christian benefits to be derived from learning ancient Greek were likely to retain an appeal among some Americans, the numbers of these citizens were dwindling. Such entreaties on behalf of Greek could also make the classical humanities appear particularly behind the times—ill-equipped to help students navigate a world that Adams and his fellow so-called modernists suggested was decreasingly linked to the values of the past.

Highlighting the significance of reading the New Testament in its original language led to other potential pitfalls for traditionalists. If ancient Greek

---

[151] Curry 1883.

[152] Kirkland (1965: 193) suggests that Peabody was, with Adams, a member of the Harvard Board of Overseers at the time Adams delivered "A College Fetich." But the *Harvard University Catalogue* for the 1882–83 academic year does not list Peabody in this office; see anonymous 1882: 29–30. James (1930 1: 187), Morison (1942: 328), and Hawkins (1972: 45–46) note that Peabody had served as Harvard's acting president between the resignation of Thomas Hill on September 30, 1868, and Charles W. Eliot's assumption of the office. Peabody had been a possible replacement for Hill, but he lost out to Eliot.

[153] Peabody 1884: 75. For similar arguments from traditionalists in the debate, see, e.g., Frost 1885: 335; Herbermann 1885: 161–62; Porter 1885: 424–25, 433.

[154] E.g., Rudolph 1962: 241–42, 248, 346; Ben-David 1972: 51–55; Lucas 1994: 142: Axtell 2016: 276–77.

[155] On the early enthusiasm for Darwin (and social Darwinism) among Americans, see, e.g., Hofstadter 1959. Youmans 1884c: 558 provides a Darwinian view of education.

was largely valuable because it offered Christians direct access to the Bible, what could justify the typical humanist pedagogical focus on so many pagan authors from antiquity? Why should good Protestants spend their time translating the works of Homer, Sophocles, and Plato? Some modernists in the conflict over "A College Fetich," in order to play up the tension between the study of ancient Greek and Christianity, underscored the *anti*-Christian bona fides of Greek literature. Albert S. Bolles (1846–1939), the first professor of business at the University of Pennsylvania, for example, took to the pages of *The Atlantic Monthly* to disparage Porter, Yale's president, for his supposedly unchristian esteem for pagan literature. "We confess our surprise that a clergyman like President Porter, whose Christian living and thinking have been a consistent and fine example," he wrote, "should dwell so fondly on the ancient classics as a means of moral and aesthetic culture."[156] If traditionalists were going to stress the benefits of reading the New Testament, their opponents could easily invoke age-old Christian arguments against the study of pagan authors.[157]

A Pedagogical Problem?

Many traditionalistic critics of "A College Fetich" also attempted to shift the blame from the classics themselves to the unfortunate methods of classical instruction that held sway at many American schools, colleges, and universities.[158] In this respect, some proponents of ancient Greek were willing to concede that Adams's address was not entirely wrongheaded. According to Porter, for example, the classics were not necessarily taught well in the US, and this disadvantage unfortunately made "A College Fetich" sound more plausible than ought to have been the case.[159] Fellow traditionalist Morse agreed, suggesting in the pages of *The Critic* that anti-classical complaints such as Adams's were not voiced in Germany, where instruction was more

---

[156] Bolles 1883: 690.

[157] Some modernists even contended that esteem for the classics was anti-Anglo-Saxon and/or unpatriotic. See, e.g., Gummere 1883: 227; Newton 1885: 148–49. Adams (1884: 41) reported the sentiments of a Yale graduate, who said that when he left college, he knew more about ancient Greece and Rome than about the US.

[158] On these methods and the problems they presented for a humanistic approach to education, see Chapter 2, this volume.

[159] Porter 1883: 121. For Adams's criticisms of classical instruction during his youth, see Adams 1884: 9, 19–20 and 1916: 26–27, 31.

thorough.[160] Chamberlain provided a typical example of this contention, criticizing the hyper-focus on Greek grammar and syntax in the American classroom at the expense of "a better knowledge of the language as a vehicle of thought and a more adequate appreciation and enjoyment of the literature which it embodies."[161] The popular recitation method—according to which ancient Greek and Latin became fodder for intense and relentless oral quizzing on grammar—was a typical target of traditionalistic scorn.[162]

On this score, many of Adams's supporters strongly agreed.[163] In a contribution to the debate over the American college curriculum, the geologist Clarence King (1842–1901), for example, surmised that "gradually, instructors have turned from the *art of language* to the *science of grammar*."[164] Invoking the likely author of the first extant Greek grammar from antiquity, King lamented that American classics teachers, rather than inspire students with the works of Sophocles and Plato, typically forced them to esteem the "children of Dionysius Thrax."[165] Classical pedagogy in America, at both the secondary and tertiary levels, many believed, urgently required improvement.[166]

The traditionalistic attempt to redirect Adams's complaints toward pedagogical issues, however, played into the hands of classical opponents. In an editorial tellingly titled "Dead-Language Studies Necessarily a Failure," for instance, Youmans contended that grievances over poor classical instruction had dogged the subject "for hundreds of years." He continued, "There has been a thousand times more practice in teaching [Latin and ancient Greek]

[160] Morse 1883a: 341.
[161] Chamberlain 1884: 33.
[162] For other examples of traditionalists in the conflict who were blaming the methods of Greek instruction, see, e.g., Humphreys 1883; Porter 1883: 125–27, 1884: 202, and 1885: 435; West 1884: 159. See also the quotations of S. C. Bartlett, the president of Dartmouth, and John E. Todd in anonymous 1883z. Others asserted that classical teaching had recently improved a great deal: e.g., Peabody 1884: 77–78; Chamberlain 1884: 32–33; Fisher 1884: 122–26; Frost 1885: 330; Sill 1885: 215. See also Cooke 1883: 2; James 1884: 305. On the improvement of classical pedagogy in American colleges during the nineteenth century (thanks to the influence of German philological practices on American classical instruction), see, e.g., Axtell 2016: 201–4. For criticisms of the professionalized approach to philology and its impact on instruction, see Chapter 2 and Chapter 5, this volume.
[163] Rudolph (1977: 185–86) noted the agreement of traditionalists and modernists on this point.
[164] King 1888: 373 (emphasis in the original).
[165] Ibid. On Thrax, see, e.g., Turner 2014: 14.
[166] For other criticisms of Greek instruction in America among Adams's supporters, see, e.g., Youmans 1884e: 126. Cf. King 1888: 373–78. Many combatants in the dispute, like King, believed that schools should teach more Greek literature and less Greek grammar: e.g., Todd quoted in anonymous 1883z; Chamberlain 1884: 32–33; Fisher 1884: 122–26. See also King 1888: 373–75, 378–79, 384; Adams 1907: 5–6 and 1916: 33, 35. Newton (1885: 155–57) believed that some use of spoken ancient Greek in the classroom could help with instruction. Sill (1885: 215) maintained that instruction in all languages was poor in American schools.

than in teaching any other languages; the work of learning them is of the same kind as that of learning other languages, and they are said, moreover, to be the most perfect forms of speech, and in that respect would seem to have advantages over other languages."[167] So, there was no excuse, Youmans concluded, for the persistence of such miserable pedagogy. Terrible teaching could not be the root cause of the uprising against the classics, he asserted. "We have," he wrote, "to regard the educational failure of the dead languages as a result of the progress of the human mind, and therefore as a normal and inevitable thing."[168] If the traditionalists hoped to shift the blame to lousy methods of instruction, their opponents would not let them off the hook so easily.

Many of Adams's opponents in the dispute over "A College Fetich" also unwittingly strengthened the contentions of Youmans by focusing so much attention on the exceeding difficulty of ancient Greek. In part by underplaying the goals of humanism articulated in the Renaissance, numerous traditionalists in the debate stressed the benefits of the language that spring from its supposedly unique rigors. For example, Merrill argued that Greek was of special educational value because it proved so challenging to master.[169] By eschewing humanistic rationales and stressing such arduousness, traditionalists were likely to reinforce the impression of classical studies as soul-crushing gerund-grinding.[170] Thus did they strengthen Youmans' vision of "dead-language study" as congenitally ill-suited to the needs of modern life.

Problems plagued other contentions traditionalists presented regarding the pedagogical value of ancient Greek. According to some of Adams's detractors, the classical languages were useful in part because of the benefits they offered in the realm of English composition. Teachers of Latin and Greek, argued Morse, impart "intellectual precision and accuracy" in the young; as a result, those who have studied the ancient languages write "excellent English."[171] "It is a fact which can not be disproved," argued an editorial in a periodical called *The Chautauquan*, "that from a study of the classics

---

[167] Youmans 1883b: 265.
[168] Ibid. 267. See also Youmans 1883a: 122: "We suspect, however, that a good deal more is made of this bad-method pretext than it will bear, and that the study of dead languages as a leading element of higher education in this age must remain a failure, whatever the perfection of the methods employed in their acquisition. Indeed, it becomes a serious question whether, broadly considered, perfected methods would not lead to worse failure than the existing practice."
[169] Merrill 1883: 426.
[170] For complaints of this sort, see, e.g., anonymous 1884c; Fisher 1884: 124; Adams 1916: 33.
[171] Morse 1883b: 214.

comes . . . a mastery of good English, such as can be acquired from nothing else."[172]

But, some opponents reasonably wondered, was this really true? Why could students not learn "a mastery of good English" by studying *English*? Or by reading great works of English literature? According to King, for example, the best modern writers were those who had escaped the drudgery of classical studies.[173] Prior to the controversy over "A College Fetich," Youmans, in a knock against the typical classical pedagogy of his era, had contended that "mere grammarians are generally bad writers."[174] Further, in a contribution to the debate Adams had inaugurated, the modern language instructor C. A. Eggert remarked that English grammar largely derives from German.[175] Thus, he thought, it made more sense for those learning to write English properly and stylishly to study the German language. Traditionalistic pleas notwithstanding, it seemed far from certain that studying the classical languages provided the only key to mastering English.[176]

Discipline, Discipline, Discipline

The chief argument in the arsenal of Adams's critics hinged on "mental discipline." Children of the Yale *Reports* of 1828, traditionalists in the Battle of the Classics crafted apologias for ancient Greek dominated by this consideration. Time and time again, educational traditionalists returned to this theme

[172] Anonymous 1883d. For other arguments about the benefits of the classical languages in this regard, see, e.g., Porter 1883: 119, 121 and 1884: 202–3; Chamberlain 1884: 27; Peabody 1884: 72, 74–75. Even the modernist Sumner (1884: 134) believed this. Cf. Merrill 1883: 421.

[173] King 1888: 376.

[174] Youmans 1900: 10. As a member of the Board of Overseers at Harvard, Adams aimed to prove that translating Latin and ancient Greek did *not* encourage in pupils stylish and grammatically sound writing in English. On the report on this topic that Adams took the lead in preparing, see Adams 1893. Eliot appears to have agreed with this report, which caused consternation among the private schools Adams's committee had tested in regard to the written English of its pupils on admission examinations for Harvard. See Eliot's letter to Adams, November 8, 1892; Adams papers, box 2, folder 8. This letter helps show that Eliot agreed with Adams about reducing the role of the classical humanities in American secondary and tertiary schooling.

[175] Eggert 1884a: 375.

[176] Another common argument traditionalists offered in the dispute over "A College Fetich" focused on the Greeks and Romans as the founders of the West. For examples, see, e.g., Curry 1883; Morse 1883b: 215; Bowker 1884: 101; Chamberlain 1884: 16–18; Dyer 1884: 17; Fisher 1884: 118–19; Bascom 1885: 278–79; Herbermann 1885: 161. Cf. Eggert 1884: 379; West 1884: 156–57; Frost 1885: 345–46; Sill 1885: 212–13; Wright 1886: 21. This argument helps demonstrate that the idea of "Western civilization," a concept Charles E. Norton had helped fashion, was attractive to traditionalistic American educators decades before the founding of the so-called Great Books tradition in the 1910s. On the Great Books tradition, see, e.g., Adler 2016: 67–71.

in their response to "A College Fetich," highlighting the superior mental discipline purportedly imparted by the study of Greek. A letter writer to *The Nation*, responding to the magazine's discussion of the Adams oration, for example, maintained that "I do not claim for the business man any practical benefit from the study of classics, but I do claim that such methods of instruction as are in use in the Greek department at Harvard will give him as much, if not more, mental discipline than can be obtained from any other branch."[177] According to William Frost, "It is the mental discipline which constitutes its [ancient Greek's] chief claim to superiority."[178] Writing about the benefits of both Greek and Latin, West maintained, "I ground the claim of the classical languages to a preeminent place on their immense superiority over all other languages, either living or dead, as a means of mental discipline."[179] Such contentions dominated the detractors' responses to Adams's speech. If the ancient Greek language possessed any pedagogical value, traditionalists asserted, it was chiefly because of its unparalleled effects on the mental faculties of students.

With at least an implicit tip of the cap to the Yale *Reports*, numerous interlocutors in the battle over "A College Fetich" further maintained that the principal aim of the college was the instilling of mental discipline in young men. On this topic, Chamberlain provided a typical example of the assumption. "Mental power," he said, "the power and faculty to organize and direct the forces of human society—the wants, desires, interests of men—is, in the only sense here under consideration, the object of education."[180] "It is true," wrote an anonymous editorialist for the *Maine Farmer* commenting on the dispute, "that very little that is studied in school enters into the adult life of the man, but the school gives the training of the mind."[181]

---

[177] "A Recent Graduate" 1883.

[178] Frost 1885: 336.

[179] West 1884: 159. Cf. 153. For other arguments to this effect from traditionalists in the conflict, see, e.g., anonymous 1883d, ab: 288; Carter in anonymous 1883x; Bartlett in anonymous 1883z; Merrill 1883: 426–27; Morse 1883a: 342 and 1883b: 214; Porter 1883: 110, 114–15, 1884: 202, and 1885: 432–33; Chamberlain 1884: 19–21, 26, 48; Fisher 1884: 121–22; Philo 1886: 20. Cf. Shorey 1910: 591–92, 598, 607–8. At the time of the controversy, *The Atlanta Constitution* (anonymous 1883h) announced (with some exaggeration), "The one argument of those who insist upon a study of the classical languages is that the process disciplines the mind."

[180] Chamberlain 1884: 13.

[181] Anonymous 1883t. For other examples of this assumption, from both traditionalists and modernists, see, e.g., anonymous 1883ab, ad, ae; Bolles 1883: 687–88; H. G. P. 1883; Merrill 1883: 424–25; Porter 1883: 113; Fisher 1884: 115; Herbermann 1885: 142; Sill 1885: 212; Wright 1886: 6. See also Adams 1907: 119–20, 129 and 1916: 33. Curry (1883) reasonably maintained that mental discipline was the typical defense of collegiate Greek.

Given the stress the debate over "A College Fetich" granted to the topic, one can almost excuse Bolles for presuming that mental discipline had always been the aim of the American college; in a contribution to *The Atlantic*, he claimed that "[a]t the time of founding the earlier American colleges, mental discipline was the chief end of the four years' course of study."[182] So dominated with faculty psychology was the discourse surrounding Adams's address that educationists in the late nineteenth century appear to have forgotten about the commanding intellectual influence of Renaissance humanism on colonial American higher education.[183] As Herbermann concluded about the goals of the college, "[a]ll, or nearly all, are agreed that its object is to prepare the student for life in a general way, to so unfold his faculties and powers as to make him not a specialist but a symmetrically developed man."[184]

Attack of the "Modernists"

This seemingly omnipresent focus on faculty psychology suggests something of crucial import to the debate over "A College Fetich." Just as much as his detractors, Adams's supporters grounded their arguments in the theory of mental discipline.[185] Unlike the group of so-called New Psychologists such as E. L. Thorndike decades later, the modernists in the controversy were equally convinced of the soundness of faculty psychology.[186] Thus, for example, Bolles maintained that the first aim of a college education is "to discipline

---

[182] Bolles 1883: 686.

[183] Perhaps in part for this reason, supporters of Adams's speech were able to associate the prescribed classical curriculum of the antebellum American colleges with the educational desiderata of the Middle Ages: e.g., Bolles 1883: 688; Eggert 1884b: 674. Cf. Youmans 1900: 3.

[184] Herbermann 1885: 142. He continues by providing a typical example of the mind-body metaphor on which the theory of mental discipline was based: "As the young gymnast, to secure the sound and symmetrical development of his body, does not swing the blacksmith's hammer, nor use the carpenter's saw, but has recourse to parallel lines, and cross-bars, and trapezes, which he will never use in after life, so the student, to bring out the powers of the mind, may, nay must, if needful, pursue studies which have no further practical aim." In focusing on symmetry, however, Herbermann overstated his case. Some modernists—Adams included—supported the development of specializations among students, at the expense of well-roundedness: e.g., Adams 1884: 6–7 (but cf. 10) and 1916: 20. See also Cooke 1884: 776; Eliot 1914–15: 390. Traditionalists in the conflict opposed specialization: see, e.g., Chamberlain 1884: 47–48; Bascom 1885: 273–75; Frost 1885: 339.

[185] Adams also agreed with mental discipline theory, as his later speech from 1906 makes clear. See Adams 1907: 119–20, 129.

[186] According to Jewett (2012: 88), the New Psychologists in the 1880s began to argue that human minds differ substantially from one another. This theory would challenge the notion that particular sorts of mental gymnastics were best for all young minds. But this conclusion did not seem to catch on in American educational circles until after the Adams controversy.

the mind."[187] Similarly, toward the conclusion of a letter to the editor of *The Nation*, a mild modernist summed up his argument by writing, "In what has been said above, I have considered the college course simply as a means of mental discipline, leaving the question of acquirement entirely aside."[188] Even Youmans, in one of his numerous pieces on the conflict, praised views of education that highlighted mental discipline.[189] On this score, the traditionalists and the modernists appeared to be on the same metaphorical page.

It should come as no surprise, then, that such modernists crafted contributions to the debate (some polemical in spirit, some less so)[190] that hinged on the notion that ancient Greek did *not* promote unparalleled mental discipline in its students. The reverse had been the chief argumentative arrow in the traditionalists' quiver, and thus it seems only natural that Adams's defenders attacked it with the greatest vigor and attention. As we previously noted, Adams himself had deemed the link between ancient Greek and the attainment of superior mental discipline "unadulterated nonsense."[191] His supporters would soon join him in stressing this point.

In some instances, modernists used pugnacious terms to criticize the ability of Greek to instill mental discipline. According to Youmans, for instance, "Greek and Latin are on trial before the world under indictment for the fatal deficiency of their educational discipline! They are arraigned as in this respect fundamentally defective because they leave in total neglect some of the most essential powers of the mind."[192] James King Newton, a professor of German and French at Oberlin College, contended that English provided just as much—if not more—mental discipline in its students, and that those whose fetish for the classics compels them to think otherwise are "unpatriotic."[193] "Whoever casts dishonor upon the English language demoralizes the English-speaking people," he charged.[194]

Regardless of the tone of their writings, many modernists provided reasonable criticisms of the traditionalistic contention that ancient Greek

---

[187]   Bolles 1883: 687.
[188]   H. G. P. 1883: 184.
[189]   Youmans 1884b: 702. Youmans believed firmly in faculty psychology as far back as 1867; see Youmans 1900. On this essay, see Leverette 1963: 35–43.
[190]   For examples of writings in support of Adams's speech, see, e.g., anonymous 1883a, c, e, h, k, n, u; Bolles 1883; Cooke 1883 and 1884; Youmans 1883a, b, c, e and 1884a, b, c, e; Eggert 1884a; Fernald 1884; James 1884; Sumner 1884; Newton 1885.
[191]   Adams 1884: 18–19.
[192]   Youmans 1884b: 703.
[193]   Newton 1885: 148–50 (quotation on 149).
[194]   Ibid. 149.

offered unparalleled mental discipline. Even prior to the brouhaha over "A College Fetich," Youmans had justly deemed social scientists the appropriate judges of faculty psychology. Vouching for the superiority of the scientific method in this regard, he wrote, "nothing is more certain than that in the future, mind is to be studied in connection with the organism by which it is conditioned: when we begin to deal with the problem of mental discipline, metaphysics will no longer avail; it is the organism with which we finally have to deal."[195] For all the bellicosity of his prose, Youmans had correctly recognized that psychologists would be the rightful arbiters of mental discipline.

The traditionalists, many of Adams's supporters recognized, had provided scarcely little evidence to make their case. What proof did they have that ancient Greek instilled more mental discipline in students than did any other intellectually taxing activity? In response to traditionalistic assertions about the paramount discipline ancient Greek afforded, various modernists vouched for the disciplinary value of numerous non-classical subjects. Some of Adams's champions went to great lengths in this regard. According to Frederik A. Fernald (1859–1931), a regular contributor to the *Popular Science Monthly*, scientists and professors of modern languages equally claim a role for their subjects in properly disciplining students' minds.[196] Thus he argued that just as it is foolish to believe that one sort of physical exertion alone properly exercises the body, the same is true "with the brain."[197] Similarly, Bolles suggested that great "discipline of mind and body would be acquired" by students, provided that "the studies proposed were taught with as much thoroughness as the studies now prescribed."[198] Some modern European languages, the social and natural sciences—all now rightfully laid claim to a part of this disciplinary process.

A few proponents of the sciences went even further, claiming that the sciences alone provide the requisite discipline. In an editorial in the *Popular Science Monthly*, for example, Youmans asked rhetorically, "Can the great revolution of ideas in regard to nature fail to bring about a corresponding revolution in the mental cultivation of mankind? The simple question is, whether the minds of our youths are to be developed in future by means of the lower or by means of the highest and most perfect forms of knowledge."[199]

[195] Youmans 1900: 13.
[196] Fernald 1884: 25.
[197] Ibid. 26.
[198] Bolles 1883: 693.
[199] Youmans 1883d: 118. This editorial was published a month or so before Adams delivered "A College Fetich."

In another editorial he similarly championed the sciences at the expense of the classical humanities:

> Modern studies have become the rivals of ancient studies, and the discipline of science the rival of classical discipline. The discipline of science is superior to lingual and literary discipline because it involves all the mental processes, because it takes effect upon the realities of experience, because it is a discipline in the pursuit of truth, because it is a preparation for practical life-work, because it uses the most perfected knowledge as its means of culture, and because it brings the mind into intimate and intelligent relation with the system of natural things, which it is the first interest as it is also the highest pleasure of man to understand.[200]

Such criticism of ancient Greek's role in disciplining the mind was rife in the work of Adams's boosters.[201]

As we have already seen, the scientists did not supply the only doubts about the link between ancient Greek and mental discipline. In a defense of the study of some modern European languages, Newton perhaps provided the most detailed and specific rebuke to traditionalists attempting to assert the superiority of Greek in this realm. "It can easily be shown that many of the arguments used in favor of Greek as against German, both as to discipline and culture, are as true of the German as of the Greek," he averred.[202] In a convincing reply to the traditionalists, Newton cleverly juxtaposed grammatical, lexical, and syntactical components of ancient Greek and German, demonstrating the similarities between the two languages.[203] For example, he asked, "Who has proved that it is a better discipline for the memory to learn [ancient Greek] consonantal changes, rather than the changes which the radical vowel undergoes in the principal parts of German verbs of the old conjugation?"[204] In the conflict over Adams's speech, classicists seemed incapable of supplying a specific refutation of such a position. Their conclusions about mental discipline centered on hunches, not evidence.

---

[200] Youmans 1884b: 704.
[201] For other examples, see, e.g., Bolles 1883: 687–88, 690, 693; W. M. G. 1883; Youmans 1883b: 266–67, e: 270 and 1884b: 702–4, c: 558–59; Eggert 1884a: 377–79; Fernald 1884; James 1884: 304; Sumner 1884: 136–38; Newton 1885: 142–48, 157. Spencer (1865: 85–89) had earlier claimed that the sciences inculcate mental discipline more effectively than does language study. Anonymous 1884c found this argument the soundest among those of the modernists.
[202] Newton 1885: 142.
[203] Ibid. 142–48.
[204] Ibid.143. For a similar argument, see Eggert 1884a: 377–79.

By focusing their arguments so heavily on mental discipline, the curricular traditionalists had undercut the classical humanities. Highlighting skills at the expense of substance, they had turned psychologists into the rightful judges of the classics. After all, according to Edmund J. James, "[t]he most advanced thinkers on pedagogics are coming to agree that the subject taught has much less to do with its value as a disciplinary and liberalizing study than the method of teaching it."[205] Thanks to the focus on mental discipline from both sides in the conflict, a college education had been largely reduced to a set of skills. Petrarch's notion that particular works of literature were conduits for self-improvement and moral resolve had given way to ancient Greek and Latin as a species of mental gymnastics. Strangely enough, in the nineteenth century curricular traditionalists, enraptured with skills as the byproduct of education, chose to provide an essentially scholastic case for the classical humanities.

An Unlevel Playing Field

The debate surrounding Adams's oration quickly demonstrated the pitfalls associated with the traditionalists' skills-based, scholastic-style vouching for the classical liberal arts. Among the very few bits of evidence Adams's critics invoked to demonstrate the purportedly superior preparation for college provided by ancient Greek and Latin was the so-called Berlin Report.[206] Many educational traditionalists in the conflict discussed this document in their contributions to the controversy, on occasion even chastising Adams for failing to mention it in his original remarks.[207] According to these traditionalists, the Berlin Report offered unimpeachable empirical proof that modern subjects were less successful at preparing students for college than were the ancient languages.

This report, created a few years prior to the controversy surrounding "A College Fetich," pertained to the fitness for university study of graduates of two different types of German secondary schools: *Gymnasien* ("gymnasia," which boasted a traditional curriculum, featuring much ancient Greek,

---

[205] James 1884: 304.
[206] Hofmann 1883 is an English translation of the report, which was originally an address delivered on October 15, 1880.
[207] See, e.g., Humphreys 1883; Porter 1883: 123–24; anonymous 1884b; Chamberlain 1884: 38–43; Peabody 1884: 78–79; Cary 1885: 168; Herbermann 1885: 159–60. Cf. Morse 1883b: 214. R. 1883 provides another example of a flawed attempt to supply empirical support for ancient Greek.

Latin, and mathematics) and *Realschulen* ("real schools," which offered some training in modern languages and the natural sciences, with concomitantly less Latin and no Greek).[208] Whereas previously only those who had completed their secondary training at a gymnasium could attend Prussian universities, as of 1871 the Prussian government for the first time allowed graduates of the real schools to matriculate in some university departments. This change was controversial among German faculty members. Consequently, in late 1879 a professor at the University of Berlin successfully urged his institution to gather faculty members' opinions about the two groups of students. Berlin's dean of the faculty incorporated the statements of many professors in a report of March 1880. The great majority of instructors concluded that the gymnasia graduates had received superior preparation to those who had attended the real schools.

According to many of Adams's detractors, this conclusively demonstrated that the curricular recommendations in "A College Fetich" were misguided. President Porter, deeming the Berlin Report "a practical trial,"[209] noted, for example, that almost all the professors at Berlin attested to the supremacy of the gymnasia curriculum.[210] Referring in part to the Berlin Report in a reply to Adams in the *Journal of Education*, E. R. Humphreys suggested, "Several educational reports have appeared in Great Britain and Germany during the last fifteen years attest the fact that the most successful students in the scientific and professional courses have been those who have had at least a good elementary training in Greek and Latin."[211] Even Adams, in an appendix to the published version of his speech, noted that, thanks to the Berlin Report, "the weight of evidence from observation and experience is for the time being in favor of the classical course."[212]

But a few social scientists among the modernists soon obliterated such contentions. The most cogent rebuttal came from Edmund J. James (1855–1925), an economist and the future president of the University of Illinois, who supplied a lengthy article on the topic in the *Popular Science Monthly*.[213] In it James noted numerous reasons why the Berlin Report did *not* settle the

---

[208] For the fullest account of the Berlin Report's genesis, see James 1884.

[209] Porter 1883: 123.

[210] Ibid. 123–24.

[211] Humphreys 1883.

[212] Adams 1884: 44. But on the Berlin Report as a whole Adams proves less supportive: he concurred with many of the criticisms James (1884) presented. On these criticisms, see the following text.

[213] James 1884. For other modernist criticisms on this topic, see, e.g., Eggert 1884: 378–79 (an especially strong rebuttal); Fernald 1884.

case as the traditionalists had argued. Indeed, he stressed that it was posi-tively useless for adjudicating the dispute over "A College Fetich."

Porter was wrong, James wrote, to contend that the report offers "a prac-tical trial" of the traditional and modern curricula. Instead, he noted, it re-ally speaks to "the question of the relative superiority of the graduates of the German gymnasia and the real schools, as they exist to-day in Germany."[214] The report was not a proper experiment: it did not control for various other factors that could have affected the comparative performance of gymnasium and real-school graduates. The gymnasia, as the traditional route to univer-sity study in Prussia, naturally boasted the most impressive students; prior to 1871, all real-school students went directly to the job market after gradua-tion.[215] Moreover, since "the traditions of Germany are classical," James wrote, the gymnasia are at the top of the "educational hierarchy."[216] Consequently, they are much better funded and are home to superior teachers.[217] The real schools are not even twenty-five years old, he noted; it would be prudent to wait more time for them to prove their merits.[218] James further doubted that the Berlin faculty provided unbiased assessments of the students, since they had all graduated from gymnasia themselves;[219] the faculty did not even ex-amine the records of students when drawing their conclusions.[220]

Most important, James demonstrated that the Berlin Report was not a proper experiment, and thus it could not be used to demonstrate the supe-riority of a classical course to a modernist one.[221] While waiting for the pro-duction of an "actual experiment," he wrote, "it will be wise for the classicists to avoid quoting reports that have nothing to do with the question, and ap-pealing to authority which, upon investigation, turns out to be squarely on the other side of the dispute."[222] Even Porter had to admit that James's re-buttal possessed merits.[223]

---

[214] James 1884: 294.
[215] Ibid. 295.
[216] Ibid. 296.
[217] Ibid. 294, 298.
[218] Ibid. 295. James also specified (1884: 294) that the real schools do not have a curriculum that fits with the desires of most educational modernists in the US.
[219] Ibid. 299–300.
[220] Ibid. 300–1.
[221] See ibid. 305.
[222] Ibid. 306. On this point *The Independent* (anonymous 1884b) was correct to recognize that James was capable of overstating his case: if the report is not germane to the topic, it cannot also aid the modernist position. Yet *The Independent* was too condemning of James's piece as a whole; it provides many sound rejoinders to the traditionalists.
[223] Porter 1884: 217–18. Cf. Chamberlain 1884: 42.

Ancient Greek and the Social Broadening
of American Academia

A perusal of much scholarship on the history of American higher education would suggest that the curricular battles of the late nineteenth century
chiefly pertained to the social broadening of the college-going population in
the US.[224] One can easily understand why historians would treat the Battle
of the Classics this way: very few secondary schools in the country offered
courses in ancient Greek at this time.[225] There was scarcely little public
support for instruction in the language.[226] In part for this reason, very few
American students who did not employ private classical tutors had an opportunity to study ancient Greek. In the 1889–90 school year, for example,
only 3 percent of high school students and only 7 percent of private secondary school students were enrolled in courses on the language.[227] Since
few young Americans at this time graduated from high school,[228] colleges
such as Harvard, which lacked a preparatory department and insisted on an
ancient Greek admission requirement for a bachelor's degree, were open to a
tiny sliver of the US population. Moreover, at least one prominent combatant
in the Battle of the Classics found the social expansion of the American undergraduate population desirable. Harvard's President Eliot (who agreed
with the main thrust of Adams's address) had hoped to broaden the undergraduate body at his institution, aiming to attract more public-school
graduates.[229]

---

[224] E.g., James 1930 1: 366–67; Butts 1971: 371; Ben-David 1972: 67; Rudolph 1977: 286; Cowley
and Williams 1991: 121, 218; Pearcy 2005: 22–23 (cf. 78–79). Cf. Wright 1940: 112–13, 115 on the
importance of a classical education to the ruling class of colonial Virginia; Geiger 2015: 107–8.

[225] On this topic, see, e.g., Krug 1969: 4–6, 34; Reese 1995: 50, 92; Karabel 2005: 22–23. See also
Saveth 1989: 367–71.

[226] On this topic, see Burton 1880: 185, a high school principal who maintained that his community would revolt if Greek was added to the curriculum. Geiger (2000b: 267) notes, "The unwilling-
ness of high schools to teach Greek . . . contributed significantly to the demise of the classical course."

[227] Krug 1969: 34; Hawkins 1972: 351 n. 18.

[228] See Reese 1995: xvii; Geiger 2000b: 265–66. On the dramatic increase in secondary schooling
in the US during the 1880s, see, e.g., Geiger 2000b: 265.

[229] See James 1930 1: 366–67 and 2: 150–52; Hawkins 1972: 230–31; Karabel 2005: 44. But see also
Mattingly 2017: 229, who perceives that Eliot contemplated attracting graduates of Boston public
high schools in the 1890s only as a result of desperation. In any case, Eliot did not much succeed
in this regard: Hawkins (1972: 172–73) notes that public school enrollment at Harvard was never
very high during his presidency. Cf. Kirkland 1965: 194–95. According to Mattingly (2017: 122–23),
Eliot hoped to expand the pool of students capable of matriculating to Harvard, but recognized that
such students would overwhelmingly come from affluent backgrounds. Still, Mattingly suggests
(125) that Eliot favored "a class-neutral admissions process." Many discussing the debate believed
that Eliot agreed with Adams's position: e.g., anonymous 1883l, v, ae; Porter 1883: 105 and 1884: 195;
Chamberlain 1884: iv; Fisher 1884: 111; Youmans 1884e: 125; anonymous 1885a, b. Anonymous
1883z quotes Eliot agreeing; Eliot suggests that he proposed such a change to Harvard's admission

It is odd, then, that the debate surrounding "A College Fetich" scarcely ever focused on the social broadening of American candidates for a B.A. degree. In his oration Adams never mentioned that his plea to alter Harvard's admission policies could attract a more diverse crowd of applicants to the institution. Nor did contributions to the ensuing fracas expend much energy on the topic.[230] Even Eliot, when the *Boston Globe* canvassed his opinion on "A College Fetich," did not discuss the social changes that Adams's proposed reforms could introduce.[231]

Those aware of Adams's background and outlook should not be surprised that his speech did not champion the social and ethnic diversification of the elite colleges. In his autobiography, for example, Adams was unapologetic about his snobbery. "I don't associate with the laborers on my place," he wrote, "nor would the association be agreeable to either of us. Their customs, language, habits and conventionalities differ from mine; as do their children. I believe in school life; and I believe in the equality of men before the law; but social equality, whether for man or child is altogether another thing."[232] Such a person was unlikely to propose educational reforms in the hopes of attracting a more diverse population of students to his alma mater.[233] In fact, one could argue that Adams's recommendations in "A College Fetich," if followed, would *decrease* social mobility in the country. His great-grandfather, the middle-class John Adams, had used the classical languages as a means to insinuate himself among the elite.[234] Now John Adams's great-grandson, a consummate blue blood, aimed to remove the classical languages as a means for middle-class Americans to rise in status. "By the Gilded Age," argued Carl Richard, "the very time when the classics seemed to be losing

---

examination a full decade prior. Eliot (1914–15: 387) later praised Adams for the speech. Cf. Kirkland 1965: 192; Hawkins 1972: 173; Wechsler 1977: 84; Karabel 2005: 44.

[230] Cf. anonymous 1883t; Cooke 1884: 774–75; Newton 1885: 160–61.

[231] Anonymous 1883z.

[232] Adams 1916: 15–16. For another example of Adams's opposition to social equality, see Adams 1907: 105. According to Kirkland (1965: 183), Adams occasionally doubted the wisdom of democracy.

[233] In some of his writings Adams also demonstrated racial prejudices. See, e.g., Adams 1861: 451–52, 454, 459, 1906, and 1916: 166. Cf. Adams 1907: 51–97. On Adams's ethnocentrism, see Kirkland 1965: 29–30, 156, 159–60, 181. Kirkland (1965: 140) detects traces of social Darwinism in Adams's ideas. For other examples of pedagogical modernists opposing required ancient Greek with arguments that demonstrate racial prejudice, see, e.g., anonymous 1883e; Youmans 1883c: 704. The modernists were not the only members of the debate to harbor racial prejudices. Chamberlain, although an abolitionist and proponent of civil rights for much of his life, ultimately changed his mind and announced his anti-black prejudices. See Chamberlain 1904, an open letter to Lord Bryce. Adams was also friends with Bryce (see Adams 1916: 215), as was Eliot (James 1930 1: 331, 2: 50–52, 247).

[234] Richard 1994: 30 and 2009: xiii; Geiger 2015: 80.

their intellectual utility, the American elite had lost their age-old monopoly on them, so that they no longer served as a reliable badge of social status."[235] Thus aristocrats such as Adams, the historic apologists for the classics against their utilitarian critics, no longer proved such tireless defenders.

The Greek Retreat

In any case, the educational traditionalists clearly lost the debate over "A College Fetich." As of the 1887–88 academic year, Harvard no longer required ancient Greek for admission to its bachelor's course.[236] And President Eliot would ultimately take further steps to marginalize the classical humanities at his institution. As it turned out, despite the new requirements, few candidates for admission omitted ancient Greek from their entrance examinations.[237] Thus in 1894 Eliot established yet another admission system, which allowed for a broader range of subjects in which to be tested.[238] Many other institutions, following the lead of the nation's oldest and most prestigious university, soon dropped their Greek entrance requirements as well. Williams College, for example, no longer deemed Greek an obligatory feature of its examinations for admission in 1894.[239] Columbia followed suit three years later.[240] In 1904, even tradition-minded Yale bowed to the zeitgeist, abandoning required Greek for its admission examinations.[241] The days of obligatory ancient Greek in American preparatory schools were over.[242]

It is far from clear that sounder arguments on the part of educational traditionalists would have retained Harvard's Greek admission requirement much longer. But we must not presume that this consequential change for American higher education was destined to take place when it did. Although

---

[235] Richard 2009: 207. See also x–xi.

[236] On this topic, see the previous text.

[237] Wechsler (1977: 84) stresses that as late as 1894, only 7 percent of candidates for admission to Harvard's A.B. course did not take Greek.

[238] See Hawkins 1972: 174–75; Wechsler 1977: 84. This new system again required only one ancient language for admission. Harvard revised its admission requirements yet again in 1898; see Broome 1903: 96–99.

[239] Rudolph 1977: 182.

[240] Veysey 1965: 118; Rudolph 1977: 213. Columbia dropped Latin as an entrance requirement in 1900; see Veysey 1965: 118; Rudolph 1977: 213.

[241] Veysey 1965: 235. Winterer (2002: 102) observes that by 1905 the majority of US colleges no longer required Greek for admission.

[242] By 1910, even Shorey (1910: 616), a traditionalistic classicist, viewed ancient Greek as a luxury and focused on saving prescribed Latin.

in retrospect the dethroning of the classical humanities in the American college curriculum may seem inevitable, this was not seen to be the case during the controversy. Much of the American academic establishment—particularly at the most venerable institutions—was opposed to Adams and his fellow modernists. When, shortly after Adams delivered his address, Harvard contemplated altering its admission examinations, the presidents and overseers at numerous New England institutions sent letters to Eliot, pleading that he not make this change.[243] The reaction of Dartmouth President Samuel C. Bartlett (1817–98) to the brouhaha helps indicate that the dislodging of the classics was uncertain. Asked for his take on Adams's oration, Bartlett responded, "I believe that the opposition to the ancient languages, which is no greater now than many years ago, if so great, is destined gradually to give way before certain obvious facts."[244] But these facts—however obvious to the president of Dartmouth—ultimately failed to convince.

Indeed, regardless of the reforms to its admission requirements that Eliot's Harvard made in the debate's aftermath, we have seen that traditionalists in the fracas over "A College Fetich" were trounced. Their skills-heavy, humanism-less arguments proved underwhelming. They seemed incapable of criticizing the utilitarian worldview of Adams and his supporters and providing a competing rationale for higher education. The traditionalists also manifestly failed to demonstrate that the classical humanities serve a unique function in the curriculum and that their removal would thus come at great cost. Even at a very early stage in the development of the social sciences, proponents of the classical humanities made a grave error in appealing to the Berlin Report, a supposed scientific experiment, to win the debate. This miscalculation shifted the argument to the social scientists' turf, which further weakened the humanist case for the classical languages. In the end, the traditionalists' insistence on defending the classical humanities on the grounds of mental discipline allowed the modernists to triumph.[245]

[243] See Kirkland 1965: 193; Rudolph 1977: 181.

[244] Quoted in anonymous 1883z. On Bartlett, a controversial and myopic leader devoted to the old-school disciplinary regime at Dartmouth, see, e.g., Geiger 2015: 376; Mattingly 2017: 91–94.

[245] It was a triumph that Adams himself would come to lament. On June 12, 1906, Adams delivered another Phi Beta Kappa speech, this time at Columbia University, in which he bemoaned the free-elective curriculum and wished that he had been forced to continue his study of ancient Greek. For the text of this address, see Adams 1907: 101–47. For discussion of this speech, see, e.g., anonymous 1906a, b, c; Carnochan 1993: 56–59. On the timing of the speech (which coincided with Adams's departure from the Harvard Board of Overseers), see Adams 1907: 101 n. 1 and 1916: 201. Adams claimed (1907: v–vi) that the 1906 address was consistent with his remarks in "A College Fetich." This claim is exceedingly difficult to square with the text of the two orations. Unsurprisingly, then,

What were other disputes in the Battle of the Classics like? Did traditionalists provide more convincing rationales? In Chapter 4, we shall turn to another consequential educational debate of the late nineteenth century and see that religious arguments—especially when based on a similar skills-based defense of the classical humanities—fared no better.

many believed that Adams had altered his opinion about higher education: e.g., Seaver 1914–15: 419; Smyth 1930: 34; Rogers: 1942: 215–16; Pierson 1952: 264–65. Cf. anonymous 1906a, b, c; Hawkins 1972: 280. Adams barely mentioned "A College Fetich" in his autobiography (Adams 1916: 197). This omission hints that he may have been remorseful about the speech later in life. Kirkland (1965: 190, 199) notes that Adams and Eliot had similar educational views through the 1890s, but that Adams broke with Eliot later, in part thanks to their disagreement over Harvard's tuition (see Adams 1904; Eliot's letter to Adams, quoted in James 1930 2: 150–52). On Adams 1906 as a repudiation of Eliot, see Carnochan 1993: 56–58.

4

Darwin Meets the Curriculum

Eliot, well versed in Adam Smith's description of the division of labor, and vividly aware of the importance Darwinism attached to individual variation, sought to elaborate these ideas in educational theory.
　　　　　　　—Hugh Hawkins, *Between Harvard and America* (1972)

It is certain that a college which does not require Greek will not prepare many to go forth as ministers or missionaries. This would be a great evil not only to the churches, but to the community generally.
　　　　　　　—James McCosh, *Twenty Years of Princeton* College (1888)

The War of Two Titans

On Tuesday, February 24, 1885, members of the Nineteenth Century Club, a tony intellectual organization in New York City, witnessed a momentous struggle in the Battle of the Classics. The home of Courtlandt Palmer (1843–88), the club's wealthy founder and president,[1] played host to a debate that engaged two titans of American higher education in the late nineteenth century. Charles W. Eliot, the energetic leader of Harvard University and the country's most prominent advocate of the elective system, delivered an address titled "In a University the Student Must Choose His Studies and Govern Himself."[2] The Rev. James McCosh (1811–94), the president of an institution then named the College of New Jersey but more commonly called Princeton,[3] provided a spirited

[1] On Palmer and his views, see, e.g., Palmer 1886; Thompson 1888. For the Nineteenth Century Club's rules, membership, and a list of its events, see anonymous 1891. Palmer founded the club in 1883 (see anonymous 1891: 13).

[2] For this original title, see anonymous 1891: 31. McCosh (1885b: 3) suggests that Eliot gave it this title himself. When publishing this speech in a later collection, Eliot called it "Liberty in Education." See Eliot 1898: 123–48.

[3] The College of New Jersey would change its name to Princeton University in 1896, two years after McCosh's death. See, e.g., Hoeveler 1981: 342–33; Kemeny 1998: 60. In 1885, McCosh had proposed

rebuttal.[4] Although in his memoirs McCosh referred to his role that evening as that of a defender of "Greek as an obligatory study in our colleges,"[5] the discussion encompassed far more intellectual territory. Eliot and McCosh provided disparate impressions of the optimum undergraduate curriculum and opposing conceptions of the proper manner in which institutions of higher learning in the US ought to conceive of their students.

That night, the presidents of Harvard and Princeton offered their respective visions of American higher education and its goals in shaping the nation's young. Naturally, such intellectual jousting involving the leaders of two elite institutions received much coverage in the nation's press. Soon after the debate concluded, manifold newspapers and popular periodicals joined the fray, weighing in with further arguments and adjudicating the contest.[6] The event provided sundry opinion leaders the opportunity to take stock of the changing face of higher learning in America, at a time when striking alterations in the nation's colleges were occurring. It gave McCosh, the proponent of required study of Greek and Latin for candidates aiming to earn an A.B. degree, the chance to make the case for the classical humanities in the country's colleges and universities.

This chapter analyzes this consequential dispute, probing the strengths and weaknesses of the arguments Eliot and McCosh articulated. It contends that Eliot's laissez-faire approach to higher learning possessed shortcomings, but that McCosh failed to unearth and expound on many of them. Wedded to a skills-based-education rationale based on the principles of faculty psychology, McCosh delivered a rebuke to Eliot that relied too much on mockery and innuendo. Notably, his rebuttal, although capable of scoring

this name change as part of his campaign to make Princeton a university (see, e.g., Hoeveler 1981: 326; Kemeny 1998: 59; cf. Kemeny 1998: 83), a step the college's board of trustees rejected in 1887 (see, e.g., Wertenbaker 1946: 340; Hoeveler 1981: 327; Kemeny 1998: 84).

[4] *The New Departure in College Education,* as McCosh called it, was published as a pamphlet in the same year (see McCosh 1885b). The Nineteenth Century Club did not bestow it with a title; see anonymous 1891: 31.

[5] McCosh 1896: 199. See also McCosh 1888: 17–18, which provides the same view. According to anonymous 1885e, the Eliot-McCosh debate of 1885 did not prominently discuss ancient Greek, but the dispute itself hinged on the role of the language in the college curriculum.

[6] See, e.g., anonymous 1885b, c, d, e, g, h, i, j, l, m, p; Nemo 1885; anonymous 1886; Patton 1885. Hawkins (1964: 198 n. 26) notes that the Eliot-McCosh debate of 1885 received more attention than did their follow-up debate a year later. Carnochan (1993: 10–11) maintains that the 1885 debate generated huge interest in the country. See also Marsden 1994: 199. For scholarly discussion of the 1885 Eliot-McCosh debate, see, e.g., Morison 1942: 353; Wertenbaker 1946: 305–7; Hawkins 1964: 198 and 1972: 59, 97, 124; Hoeveler 1981: 235–37; Carnochan 1993: 9–21; Marsden 1994: 199; Kemeny 1998: 34–38; Geiger 2015: 336.

some important points, did not provide a humanistic justification for the ancient languages and, concomitantly, embraced no classical content as obligatory for properly educated Americans. The chapter also stresses that McCosh's defense of required Greek centered on theological concerns: to Princeton's president, the end of prescribed Greek in the college course was disastrous because its disappearance from higher education would mean the undoing of America's Christian character. Especially given the nonsectarian directions in which elite institutions of higher learning were heading in the coming decades, this brand of defense soon rang hollow. The 1885 Eliot-McCosh debate thus amounted to a lost opportunity for supporters of the classical humanities. McCosh's contentless apologetics for the ancient languages have much to teach proponents of the contemporary humanities in America. We must avoid similar strategies today.

Toward an Evangelical Enlightenment

Although by the time they debated in 1885 McCosh and Eliot had held similar leadership roles in American higher education for well over a decade,[7] the two men came from different backgrounds and possessed very different characters. McCosh, a Presbyterian minister and academic philosopher, was born on April 1, 1811, in Patna, a village in the western portion of the Scottish Lowlands.[8] He was the lone surviving son of Andrew and Jean Carson McCosh, wealthy, middle-class farmers.[9] Although his father passed away when McCosh was only nine, Andrew appears to have had a formative influence on his son. In fact, McCosh followed his father's wish by giving up a life in farming and seeking out a ministerial calling instead.[10] This vocational

---

[7] McCosh began his presidency in 1868, Eliot in 1869.

[8] On McCosh's birthplace, see McCosh 1896: 20; Hoveler 1981: 33 and 2007: 91; Morris 2014: 364. On McCosh's life, see McCosh 1896; Wertenbaker 1946: 290–343; Hoeveler 1981; Marsden 1994: 196–97; Kemeny 1998: 17–86; Bow 2013: 663–68; Morris 2014: 364–68; Geiger 2015: 335–37. See also McCosh 1888; Segrest 2010: 18, 101–32. Numerous scholars mention McCosh's hotheadedness and arrogance (e.g., Hoeveler 1981: xi, 267–69; Carnochan 1993: 16; Morris 2014: 364; Geiger 2015: 336), but also stress his kindheartedness (e.g., Hoeveler 1981: 269; Morris 2014: 364). Hoeveler 1981: 351–69 provides a bibliography of McCosh's published works. William Milligan Sloane is typically credited as the editor of McCosh 1896, but it is clear from the text that he wrote some of the contents himself. Sloane (1850–1928) was a professor at Princeton and McCosh's choice to succeed him in the presidency. But Princeton's board of trustees chose Francis Landey Patton (1843–1932) instead.

[9] James was the fifth-born among their seven children; see Hoeveler 1981: 35.

[10] See Hoeveler 1981: 37.

trajectory also fit with the area of Ayrshire in which McCosh was raised—
then a fiercely Protestant region of Scotland.[11]

An interest in ministry helped define McCosh's educational path. He first
attended a parish school, where he studied predominantly Latin, Christian
theology, and the Bible.[12] Even as a youth McCosh was convinced of the pernicious influence of Moderatism in Scotland: he deemed drunkenness and
fornication serious problems in his homeland that naturally resulted from
theological liberalism. Such baleful trends encouraged the boy to identify
with evangelical Presbyterianism.

In 1824, at the tender age of thirteen, McCosh got his first taste of university life. Beginning with some time in a preparatory department, McCosh
spent five years at the University of Glasgow, where he studied the subjects
traditional to Scottish higher education in the early nineteenth century: Latin and ancient Greek, logic, metaphysics, moral philosophy, physics,
and mathematics.[13] The faculty at Glasgow—an institutional hotbed of
Moderatism—spent little time policing the moral lives of its students.[14] Such
neglect dispirited McCosh, who, as we shall see, later articulated an approach
to American higher learning greatly invested in college faculty members
acting in loco parentis.

From Glasgow McCosh departed to the University of Edinburgh, where
he would ultimately earn an M.A. in divinity.[15] Here he encountered the
two most integral influences on his thought and spiritual development: Sir
William Hamilton (1788–1856), Edinburgh's chair of universal and civil
history,[16] and Thomas Chalmers (1780–1847), the institution's chair of divinity.[17] These two men, in fact, together embodied the guiding passions
of McCosh's life. From Hamilton, a religious Moderate and philosopher
of profound importance to the Scottish Common Sense school, McCosh
imbibed the spirit of the Scottish Enlightenment.[18] The humanism,

[11] Ibid. 33.
[12] Ibid. 37–38. Hoeveler (38) notes that the parish school also likely introduced McCosh to more
pragmatic subjects: "bookkeeping, surveying, and navigation."
[13] Ibid. 44.
[14] Ibid. 45–46, 250, 254–55.
[15] Hoeveler 1981: 71 and 2007: 91; Morris 2014: 365. Hoeveler (1981: 19) notes that Edinburgh
possessed an elective system as far back as 1708.
[16] Hamilton was first a professor of these subjects at Edinburgh. In 1836 he would become a professor of logic and metaphysics there; see Hoeveler 1981: 56–57.
[17] On McCosh's study with these two men and their influence on him, see, e.g., McCosh 1896: 37–
44, 52; Hoeveler 1981: ix–xi, 47–53, 54–62 and 2007: 91; Marsden 1994: 197; Morris 2014: 365.
McCosh's biographical history of Scottish philosophy (McCosh 1874) concludes with Hamilton.
[18] Hoeveler 1981: 20–21 discusses the theistic liberalism that pervaded the Scottish Enlightenment.

rationalism, and empiricism of this movement, which led to substantive advances in numerous areas such as philosophy, botany, and economics, appealed deeply to McCosh.[19] At the same time, McCosh remained devoted to an energetic brand of Protestantism. Chalmers, a prominent neo-Puritan leader and opponent of Moderatism, served as McCosh's chief theological inspiration. Throughout his career, McCosh attempted to blend these two intellectual traditions, defending an evangelical take on the Scottish Enlightenment.[20]

Upon his graduation in 1834, McCosh took up his ministerial calling, first as a pastor at Arbroath, a fishing town to the northeast of Edinburgh.[21] McCosh became a popular minister there, although he lacked the charisma and vocal firepower of more esteemed preachers.[22] In early 1839, he moved to Brechin, a town around fourteen miles north of Arbroath.[23] There the twenty-eight-year-old would serve in his second ministerial position, at the town's Cathedral Church.

It was in Brechin that McCosh took part in a religious dispute of great consequence for the history of Scottish Protestantism and significant for McCosh's future career. On May 18, 1843, after numerous intractable theological disputes with Moderates, Scottish Evangelicals officially split from the Church of Scotland.[24] This event, called the Disruption, marked the commencement of the evangelical Free Church of Scotland. McCosh, an evangelical suddenly without a flock, promptly established the new West Free Church of Brechin.[25] One year after transferring to the town's East Free Church,[26] McCosh married Isabella Guthrie in 1845.[27]

McCosh's path altered dramatically upon the publication of his first book, *The Method of Divine Government* (1850). This lengthy tome, an attempt to reconcile the Scottish Enlightenment and the evangelical movement, received a broad and enthusiastic reception.[28] The reception was

[19] On the Scottish Enlightenment of the eighteenth and early nineteenth centuries, see, e.g., Hoeveler 1981: 3–32.

[20] On this topic, see Hoeveler 1981: 47–48 and 2007: 91.

[21] McCosh 1896: 50; Hoeveler 1981: 72. On McCosh's licensing with the Presbytery of Ayr, see Hoeveler 1981: 71.

[22] See Hoeveler 1981: 75–77, 94–95.

[23] McCosh 1896: 68; Hoeveler 1981: 78.

[24] See, e.g., Hoeveler 1981: 87 and 2007: 91–92; Brown 1991: 286; Marsden 1994: 197; Morris 2014: 365–66.

[25] Hoeveler 1981: 89.

[26] McCosh 1896: 75; Hoeveler 1981: 91–93.

[27] On September 29 of that year; see Hoeveler 1981: 93.

[28] McCosh 1896: 105–6; Hoeveler 1981: 100 and 2007: 92; Morris 2014: 366.

so enthusiastic, in fact, that it earned McCosh a post as a philosophy professor at Queen's College, Belfast, then Ireland's newest institution of higher learning.[29] Although not forsaking his ministerial inclinations (he continued to preach sporadically during his sixteen years in Belfast), McCosh now taught logic and metaphysics and authored his most consequential philosophical works.[30] An amateur naturalist,[31] he also cowrote *Typical Forms and Special Ends in Creation* (1856) with the biologist George Dickie, the first published sign of his lifelong interest in the natural sciences.[32]

A telegram McCosh received in early May 1868 changed his life once again. From this message McCosh learned that the College of New Jersey's Board of Trustees had elected him its new president.[33] Many qualities recommended McCosh for the job: as a stalwart evangelical, he fit well with the spiritual atmosphere of Princeton, an institution founded in 1746 by New Light Presbyterians under the influence of the Great Awakening.[34] McCosh also wedded his evangelicalism to the Scottish Enlightenment, and this choice suggested that he could partially modernize Princeton's curriculum while holding true to the institution's religious aims. By the time Princeton elected McCosh, Scottish Common Sense philosophy had maintained a long and lasting influence on American higher education.[35] Thus, in late 1868, one hundred years after another influential Scottish philosopher, John Witherspoon (1723–94), had taken up the helm in Princeton, the College of New Jersey welcomed McCosh as its new president.[36]

---

[29] McCosh delivered his final sermon at Brechin on December 29, 1851 (see Hoeveler 1981: 107) and took up the professorship in January 1852 (ibid. 112 and 2007: 92). Queen's College was established in 1846. Hoeveler (1981: 112) notes that the college, which hoped to blend classical and practical studies, made ancient Greek an optional subject.

[30] See Hoeveler 1981: 114.

[31] McCosh 1890: x.

[32] Morris 2014: 367; cf. Hoeveler 2007: 92, who claims that it was first published in 1855.

[33] Princeton's board unanimously elected McCosh president on April 29, 1868: see McCosh 1868: v; Wertenbaker 1946: 291; see also Hoeveler 2007: 95; Morris 2014: 367. McCosh received the telegram notifying him of his election in early May; see McCosh 1888: 5 and 1896: 184; Hoeveler 1981: 178, 229.

[34] See, e.g., Wertenbaker 1946: 22; Hoeveler 1981: 216; Richard 2009: 153; Bow 2013: 652. McCosh's trip to the US in 1866, during which he visited various colleges and attended a gathering of Presbyterians in St. Louis, likely put McCosh in the minds of Princeton's board. On this trip, see McCosh 1896: 163–65; Hoeveler 1981: 225.

[35] On this topic, see above all Segrest 2010. See also Hoeveler 1981: 4

[36] McCosh and his family arrived at Princeton on October 20, 1868, where he was welcomed as the new president. See McCosh 1868: v and 1896: 187. On Witherspoon, see, e.g., Wertenbaker 1946: 48–79, 91; Hoeveler 1981: 216–17; Segrest 2010: esp. 64–100; Bow 2013: esp. 652–56.

Significant Reforms under a Moderate Guise

Although his 1885 debate with Eliot helped cement the perception that he was an educational reactionary,[37] McCosh instituted numerous and significant reforms at Princeton. Importantly, he introduced a modest version of the elective system at Princeton: for the first time in the college's history, juniors and seniors were granted partial choice in their coursework.[38] Through this innovation, McCosh ultimately enabled students at Princeton to encounter some of the new disciplines in nineteenth-century American higher education, while still experiencing such time-honored subjects as ancient Greek, Latin, and mathematics.

McCosh also expanded and professionalized Princeton's teaching staff. When he was first appointed, the College of New Jersey boasted a faculty of sixteen.[39] By the time McCosh retired two decades later, this staff had blossomed to forty members.[40] Just as important as this numerical growth was the sort of professor McCosh hired. Viewing the faculty inbreeding at Princeton a threat to the institution's teaching and research quality,[41] McCosh searched for scholars outside the ranks of Presbyterian evangelicals. Although he hoped to lure believing Protestants to Princeton, McCosh welcomed scholars from other denominations whose training, research

[37] The popular press analyzing the 1885 debate occasionally referred to McCosh as an educational conservative, something he denied in the debate itself (McCosh 1885b: 4). See, e.g., anonymous 1885d, h. Kemeny (1998: 36, 38) notes that McCosh has often been wrongly portrayed as an educational "paleoconservative." McCosh's memoirs (McCosh 1896: 189) suggest that he was a reformer akin to Frederick Barnard, Eliot, and Daniel C. Gilman. Hoeveler (1981: x–xi) correctly notes that McCosh was a reformer from the very start of his presidency. According to Carnochan (1993: 22–23) McCosh disagreed more profoundly with Eliot in the debate than he intimated but did not want to come across as conservative. In his inaugural address (McCosh 1868), McCosh criticized an overreliance on Latin, Greek, and mathematics in the college curriculum (37); announced that he did not aim to revolutionize Princeton (38); and claimed that English had the chief linguistic claim to curricular attention (59–60). From the start of his presidency, then, his views appear to have been a hodge-podge of traditionalism and modernism. Patton (1885): 342–43 portrayed McCosh's curriculum at Princeton as middle-of-the-road. According to Marsden (1994: 199), Noah Porter, Yale's president and another invited participant in the debate, was supposed to play the role of the conservative that evening (cf. Geiger 2015: 335).

[38] McCosh 1888: 16 and 1896: 198–99; Wertenbaker 1946: 293, 304; Hawkins 1964: 198; Hoeveler 1981: 233; Bow 2013: 667. Wertenbaker (1946: 235) notes that prior to McCosh's presidency Princeton had some electives, but they were confined to the extra-curriculum. Anonymous 1870: 22–27 offers an overview of McCosh's curriculum at Princeton in its earliest iteration. On Princeton's curriculum under McCosh, see also anonymous 1878: 22–25, 30 and 1886a: 48–50; McCosh 1884: esp. 7 (the course of study as of late 1884); McCosh 1888: 15–20 and 1896: 203–4, 209; Hawkins 1972: 98; Kemeny 1998: 67–68, 259 n. 29; Geiger 2015: 336.

[39] Bow 2013: 666–67.

[40] Ibid. For more on the growth in Princeton's faculty under McCosh, see McCosh 1888: 22–23; Wertenbaker 1946: 300, 342; Hoeveler 1981: 335.

[41] See Hoeveler 1981: 238; Geiger 2015: 335.

accomplishments, and teaching prowess recommended them for their positions.[42] This way, McCosh hoped, the College of New Jersey could supply a quality evangelical alternative to the sort of education American students could attain at the theologically liberal Harvard.[43]

A few years after his arrival, Princeton's ambitious leader also inaugurated the institution's School of Science.[44] Students at Princeton could now earn a B.S. degree and avoid the prescribed classical languages associated with the A.B. course.[45] Although the requirement of Latin for admission to the School appears to have kept enrollment low in its early years,[46] the College of New Jersey now had the means to provide the semblance of scientific instruction on its premises. Combined with a dramatic boost in enrollment at Princeton[47] and the first inklings of graduate education there,[48] these developments might give observers the sense that McCosh aimed to transform the College of New Jersey into a full-fledged university. And indeed, seemingly heartened by the perceived success of his 1885 debate with Eliot, in June of that year McCosh proposed to the Board of Trustees that the college officially change its name to Princeton University.[49] He considered the board's rejection of this suggestion two years later a major blow, which rendered his presidency only a partial but not complete success.[50]

Nor were such moves the lone signs of McCosh's reformist bona fides. He was also among the earliest Christian supporters of evolution in America.

[42] See, e.g., Hoeveler 1981: 239–44; Kemeny 1998: 61–65.

[43] McCosh also cultivated promising Princeton graduates amenable to his outlook as future faculty members. To this end, he sent some to Europe for advanced training, hoping that they would return to Princeton as incipient scholars. On this topic, see, e.g., Kemeny 1998: 63–64; Geiger 2015: 335.

[44] The College of New Jersey's School of Science opened in 1873; see Kemeny 1998: 68. This school could help Princeton compete with elite institutions that boasted scientific colleges of earlier vintage: e.g., Harvard and Yale.

[45] See, e.g., Wertenbaker 1946: 308.

[46] See McCosh 1888: 26, who stresses that all must study Latin to gain admission to the School of Science, save prospective students of engineering, who needed French instead; see also Wertenbaker 1946: 386. Hawkins (1972: 212) notes that Harvard's Lawrence Scientific School maintained a Latin requirement until 1888.

[47] See McCosh 1888: 34 and 1896: 213. McCosh (1888: 34) reports a dip in student enrollment from 1882 to 1886, which contributed to problems for McCosh's continued leadership at Princeton. By the 1886–87 academic year, however, the numbers began to recover.

[48] E.g., Princeton offered its first earned M.A. in 1877 (Kemeny 1998: 70) and its first Ph.D. two years later (ibid. 64; Geiger 2015: 336). Wertenbaker (1946: 301–2) notes that McCosh granted fellowships to seniors for advanced study as early as 1869 and deems this the start of graduate studies at Princeton.

[49] Hoeveler 1981: 326; Kemeny 1998: 59; cf. Kemeny 1998: 83.

[50] On June 20, 1887. See Wertenbaker 1946: 340; Hoeveler 1981: 327; Kemeny 1998: 84. For McCosh's disappointment with the board's decision, see, e.g., Wertenbaker 1946: 341. In 1896, two years after McCosh's death, the board moved to change the institution's name to Princeton University. See Hoeveler 1981: 342–43; Kemeny 1998: 60.

In various speeches and writings, McCosh stressed the compatibility of Darwin's theory with revealed religion. Deeming anti-science rhetoric a threat to Christianity's future, he attacked the belief systems of agnostic and atheistic proponents of evolution such as Herbert Spencer and promoted the notion that Darwinism demonstrated the truth of Christianity.[51] This stance caused much consternation on campus, especially among old-school evangelicals associated with the Princeton Theological Seminary,[52] a nominally unaffiliated institution deeply tied up in the governance of the college.

McCosh, then, was far from a hardline traditionalist among college leaders during the second half of the nineteenth century. The Nineteenth Century Club, in fact, appears originally to have cast him as the moderate in the debate with Eliot: the organization also invited Noah Porter, Yale's more reliably conservative leader, to take part in the discussion. Porter, as we noted in the previous chapter, had already mustered many arguments in favor of required Latin and Greek for the A.B. course.[53] But Porter could not attend, and left McCosh the lone critic of Eliot's "new departure" at Harvard.[54]

In his debate with Eliot that evening McCosh ably demonstrated his preferred manner of tamping down criticism from religious and educational conservatives. Throughout his presidency, he attempted to underscore his inherent moderateness, stressing that he should be considered neither a pedagogical revolutionary nor a fusty reactionary.[55] McCosh's partial opposition to the elective principle in the discussion in New York City likely helped reinforce his standing among traditionalists. Indeed, many Princetonians seemed enthused about their president's performance.[56] McCosh's repeated

[51] On McCosh's views on evolution, see, e.g., McCosh 1890; Wertenbaker 1946: 311–12; Hoeveler 1981: 180–211 and 2007: 78, 90–101; Marsden 1994: 197; Segrest 2010: 115; Bow 2013: 665; Morris 2014: esp. 369–81; Geiger 2015: 335. McCosh 1885a presents a full-scale critique of Spencer's worldview (cf. Hoeveler 1981: 196–202).

[52] On criticism of McCosh's support for evolution, see, e.g., Hoeveler 1981: 273–79; Bow 2013: 665.

[53] But Yale too inaugurated a modest amount of election in the A.B. curriculum under Porter's leadership: in 1876 it first offered some curricular choices. See Pierson 1952: 69. Geiger (2015: 335) notes that McCosh favored more robust election in the college course than did Porter (see also Hoeveler 1981: 235), though Princeton's system under McCosh was nowhere near as liberal as Eliot's at Harvard.

[54] As noted by anonymous 1885p; McCosh 1885b: 3 n. 1; Hoeveler 1981: 235; Marsden 1994: 199. Discussing the reputation of both these men, Marsden (1994: 197) wrote, "Unlike Noah Porter, McCosh could not be written off as a local reactionary." Anonymous (1891: 33) informs us that Porter spoke on the topic of evolution under the auspices of the Nineteenth Century Club on May 25, 1886.

[55] Although we know that he was a hardline abolitionist and supporter of the Union in the American Civil War (see Hoeveler 1981: 224–25), it is difficult to intuit many of McCosh's political views, since he, unlike Eliot, was seldom openly political. On this topic, see, e.g., Hoeveler 1981: 52–53, 257–60; Segrest 2010: 101.

[56] See, e.g., anonymous 1885f; Cuyler 1885; Patton 1885; anonymous 1886c. Cf. anonymous 1887; Kemeny 1998: 59.

mentions during the debate of his commitment to maintain a theologically sound College of New Jersey must have further helped this cause. Even so, McCosh remained a controversial figure at Princeton. As with so much else he did as the institution's leader, in his encounter with Eliot McCosh had to proceed carefully.

The Rise of a Pedagogical Spencerian

Charles W. Eliot was a consummate Harvardian. Scion of influential Boston stock, Eliot had a family with longstanding connections to the nation's oldest institution of higher learning. His paternal grandfather, Samuel Eliot (1749–1820), amassed a huge fortune, ultimately endowing the Eliot Greek Professorship at Harvard and ensuring the wealth of his progeny.[57] Eliot's father, Samuel Atkins Eliot (1798–1862), a Harvard graduate (class of 1817),[58] onetime mayor of Boston and, for a brief spell, a Congressman from Massachusetts,[59] served as the college's treasurer from 1842 to 1853 and a member of its governing board.[60] Born on March 20, 1834, Charles Eliot grew up in his family's mansion on Beacon Street in Boston. The third of five children to survive infancy and the lone son, Eliot possessed undeniable advantages in life.

But not everything came so easily for Eliot. A large birthmark on the right side of his face made him the object of ridicule as a youth, seemingly contributing to his aloof and standoffish nature.[61] Still, Eliot demonstrated great intellectual promise, first at a dame school, then at a church private school, and later at the hallowed Boston Latin School, where he was a few classes above Charles Francis Adams, Jr.[62] Like Adams, Eliot disesteemed Boston Latin's traditionalistic curriculum,[63] even though, unlike Adams, he excelled

---

[57] James 1930 1: 7–8. Theodore Lyman, Eliot's maternal grandfather, had grown wealthy in trade: see James 1930 1: 9. On the life of Charles W. Eliot, see, above all, James 1930 1–2; Hawkins 1972. See also Eliot 1923: 15–16, 27–28, 31–33, 54–57; Mattingly 2017: 115–39.

[58] James 1930 1: 10–11.

[59] Ibid. 27.

[60] Ibid. 29. Charles Eliot's uncle-in-law was George Ticknor, a former Harvard professor who had attempted to modernize the school's curriculum. On Ticknor, see, e.g., Morison 1942: 225–26, 232–38, 276, 343.

[61] See James 1930 1: 12–15. On Eliot's personality, see Morison 1942: 358.

[62] See James 1930 1: 16–17. For Eliot's discussion of his time at the Boston Latin School, see Eliot 1924: 4–5. On Adams, see Chapter 3, this volume.

[63] James 1930 1: 17.

there, especially in Latin. After graduating in 1849,[64] Eliot earned admission to Harvard, where he began studies in September of that year.[65]

In later writings Eliot portrayed Harvard in his undergraduate days as an uninspiring place.[66] Although, thanks to his uncle George Ticknor, the college had instituted a degree of election as far back as 1825,[67] the curriculum Eliot encountered as an undergraduate was overwhelmingly prescribed. Under the recent leadership of the erstwhile reformer Edward Everett (pr. 1846–49) and Jared Sparks (pr. 1849–53), Harvard found itself in a conservative curricular era, when the institution compelled students to stick closely to a traditional classical course. In a recollection of his student years at Harvard written late in his life, Eliot lamented, "I was able to make a choice of mathematics instead of Greek in my junior year, and to carry out that preference for mathematics through my senior year; but that was the only real option I had while I was an undergraduate."[68]

Although he worked sufficiently hard to graduate second in his class,[69] Eliot had no particular esteem for collegiate Greek or Latin. His main intellectual passion sprang from his relationship with the Harvard chemist Josiah P. Cooke (1827–94), with whom he worked as a volunteer in Cooke's laboratory and on various geological jaunts in the northeast and Canada.[70] This self-directed educational enthusiasm, combined with the comparatively lowly place accorded to chemistry and mineralogy at mid-nineteenth-century Harvard, must have helped spur on Eliot's later esteem for the elective principle.[71] In any case, by the time he graduated in July 1853, Eliot recognized that he wanted to pursue a career in science, but was not certain how best to proceed.[72]

As of fall of the next year, Eliot had earned a spot as a tutor in mathematics at his alma mater.[73] In the spring of 1858 he was promoted to an assistant professorship in mathematics and chemistry, a role he would have for the following three years.[74] Although a comparatively inspired teacher in the

[64] Ibid. 18.
[65] Ibid. 36; Hawkins 1972: 3.
[66] See, e.g., Eliot 1923: 15–16.
[67] Rudolph 1962: 119; Hawkins 1972: 82. As of 1826, students could substitute modern languages for half the work required in Latin and ancient Greek.
[68] Eliot 1923: 15–16. On Eliot's undergraduate years, see James 1930 1: 36–66.
[69] James 1930 1: 50; Hawkins 1972: 9.
[70] Eliot 1923: 54–57; James 1930 1: 42 n. 2, 45–46, 53–54.
[71] It should be mentioned, however, that Eliot did not especially stress the importance of election to American higher education until he was president of Harvard.
[72] See James 1930 1: 56.
[73] Ibid. 67; Hawkins 1972: 14.
[74] James 1930 1: 69; Hawkins 1972: 14.

classroom, Eliot remained unpopular with undergraduates, thanks in large measure to the diligence with which he carried out the unwelcome task of checking up on his students and policing their activities.[75] It was in his early days as a Harvard faculty member, however, that Eliot discovered his great talent at a more agreeable undertaking: administrative work. In 1859, in fact, the Harvard Corporation granted him an extra $300 per annum, demonstrating its appreciation for the twenty-four-year-old acting as de facto assistant to the president, James Walker (pr. 1853–60).[76]

After he became a chemistry professor at Harvard's Lawrence Scientific School in 1861,[77] Eliot's career hit a significant snag: two years later, he was passed up for the much-coveted Rumford Professorship of Chemistry, when Harvard decided to appoint Wolcott Gibbs (1822–1908), a far more accomplished researcher, instead.[78] Irked about this turn of events, Eliot resigned from Harvard.[79] Although by this time his financial fortunes had changed considerably (his father unexpectedly sank into poverty in 1857[80] and passed away in 1862),[81] Eliot, thanks to his sound investment of a bequest from his mother's father, set sail in September 1863 for what would be a two-year trip to Europe with his family.[82]

During his stay in France, Switzerland, Germany, the Netherlands, and England, Eliot carefully observed European educational systems, in the hunt for ideas for useful reforms in America. He also worked briefly at the University of Marburg in Hesse, in the laboratory of the eminent chemist Hermann Kolbe, although, thanks in part to Eliot's rudimentary German, the training was insufficient to serve as the basis for a career producing scientific scholarship.[83] Even so, Eliot remained wedded to life as

---

[75] James 1930 1: 67–68. Morison (1942: 358) notes that students tended to dislike Eliot when he was president, although (398) they eventually grew to respect him. See also James 1930 2: 89.

[76] Hawkins 1972: 16.

[77] James 1930 1: 88. Eliot also served as the School's acting dean for the 1862–63 academic year (see James 1930 1: 94; Hawkins 1972: 22).

[78] See James 1930 1: 98–110; Morison 1942: 325; Hawkins 1972: 25–27; McCaughey 1974: 267–68. On Gibbs and his credentials for the professorship, see McCaughey 1974: 267–68. It is a peculiarity worth mentioning that Eliot—the foremost advocate of student choice in regard to coursework—was seemingly incapable of choosing for himself a course of studies that would have led him to earn the Rumford Professorship. Eliot had taken a job as a tutor at Harvard, when it would have been far more valuable for him to gain training in chemistry in Europe.

[79] He was also irritated because then-president Thomas Hill had made a feeble attempt to retain Eliot under lesser auspices, even venturing to raise money from his family for his salary. See James 1930 1: 108–10; Hawkins 1972: 26–27.

[80] James 1930 1: 73–74; Hawkins 1972: 19.

[81] James 1930 1: 89; Hawkins 1972: 22.

[82] Hawkins 1972: 28–29. On Eliot's trip to Europe, see James 1930 1: 115–58.

[83] James 1930 1: 135–36.

an academic: offered a well-remunerated position as a mill superintendent in Lowell, Massachusetts,[84] he passed it up and ultimately agreed to a professorship in chemistry at the newly founded Massachusetts Institute of Technology (MIT).[85]

Eliot would not stay away from Harvard for long. While still a faculty member at MIT, he decided to write down some of his thoughts about higher learning in the US, partially encouraged by his experiences in Europe. By this time, Eliot had been greatly affected by the two chief educational influences of his life: Ralph Waldo Emerson[86] and, especially, Herbert Spencer.[87] In 1861 Spencer, as we mentioned in the previous chapter, had published *Education: Intellectual, Moral, and Physical,* a polemical collection of essays vouching for the innate superiority of the sciences and the comparative uselessness of literature for pedagogical purposes. Eliot, who composed an appreciative forward for a later edition of this monograph,[88] was not as extreme in his argumentation as Spencer, but he still considered all the theses Spencer articulated in the book sound. Unsurprisingly, then, Eliot's vision of higher education, like Spencer's, had a strong social Darwinian flavor. William Boyd, summing up Eliot's pedagogical views a few years after his death, maintained that "Eliot indeed was Spencer's greatest disciple, almost, one might say, Spencer's only disciple."[89] Spencer's pedagogical philosophy helped inform the two-part broadside Eliot contributed to *The Atlantic Monthly,* collectively called "The New Education: Its Organization."[90]

These pieces, which appeared in the February and March numbers of *The Atlantic* in 1869, focused chiefly on the nature and promise of polytechnical instruction in the US. But in them Eliot also presented reflections on the

[84] This offer was made to Eliot in May 1865; see James 1930 1: 143–47; Hawkins 1972: 33.

[85] Eliot was contacted with an offer for this position weeks after declining the mill job. MIT was to open in the fall of 1865. On the offer, see James 1930 1: 151–52; Morison 1942: 325; Hawkins 1972: 33–35; McCaughey 1974: 276–77.

[86] On Emerson's influence on Eliot, see, e.g., James 1930 1: 349; Hawkins 1972: 143–44; Carnochan 1993: 13.

[87] For scholarly discussions of Spencer's influence on Eliot's educational ideas, see, e.g., James 1930 1: 349–51 and 2: 233; Boyd 1934; Hawkins 1972: 52, 87, 93, 152, 289; Carnochan 1993: 13–16. Hawkins (1972: 143) also notes that Spencer influenced Eliot's political philosophy. On Eliot's political views, see, e.g., Eliot 1897: 159–69, 209; Few 1909: esp. 185 and 190; James 1930 2: 226, 228, 272; Morison 1942: 343; Hawkins 1972: 139–67, 201.

[88] See Eliot 1911.

[89] Boyd 1934: 34. For examples of Spencer's influence on Eliot's educational views, see, e.g., Eliot 1869a: 204, 1911: esp. viii–ix, xvi, and 1917: 355. Cf. Eliot 1916: esp. 290–92.

[90] Eliot 1869a, b. Hawkins (1972: 41–42) informs us that Eliot wrote these articles in the fall of 1868.

current state of the nation's colleges.[91] The articles helped demonstrate that Eliot was a stalwart pedagogical modernist. They included a few jabs at the classical humanities, and thus demonstrated his Spencerian inclination to deem language study a worthless exercise in signaling one's cultural capital. In a lengthy sentence that could have come from Spencer's pen, for example, Eliot wrote,

> If it were the custom of all young men, whose parents were able to let them spend one third of the average human span in preparation for the rest, to study Chinese ten years or more; if scraps of Chinese had the same potent effect on the popular imagination as have classical quotations in Parliament, and selections from Plutarch in Congress; if, in short, acquaintance with Chinese were the accepted evidence of having studied till twenty-one or twenty-five years of age before beginning to earn a living,—it might well be a matter of serious consideration for a careful parent, whether his son had not better devote the unusual number of years to the study of that tongue.[92]

Vouching for the ability of polytechnic schools to instill the same sort of mental discipline in their students as do traditional colleges,[93] Eliot stated his preference for English literature over the classical[94] and signaled the unimportance of ancient Greek for science students.[95]

By the time these thoughts appeared in print, Eliot had become a serious candidate for the Harvard presidency. After the resignation of Thomas Hill (pr. 1862–68) at the end of September 1868,[96] Harvard had to hunt for a new leader.[97] Once Charles Francis Adams, Sr., had declined the

---

[91] For scholarly discussion of these articles, see, e.g., James 1930 1: 166–71; Morison 1942: 325–26; Hawkins 1964: 191 and 1972: 41–44; Mattingly 2017: 120.

[92] Eliot 1869a: 204.

[93] Ibid. 215.

[94] Eliot 1869b: 359. According to this article, though, Eliot deemed Latin second in importance to English.

[95] Eliot 1869b: 362. In his writings, Eliot offered many criticisms of the study of the classics. See, e.g., Eliot 1869a: 204, 1869b: 358–59, 361, 1898: 98, 101, 105, 404–5, and 1917: esp. 357; James 1930 1: 135–37. James (1930 1: 94–95) notes that Eliot, as acting dean of the Lawrence Scientific School, did not want Latin and Greek in the curriculum. He also concludes (1930 2: 79) that Eliot lacked an aesthetic sense for literature. According to Mattingly (2017: 128), Eliot had performed poorly on the Greek portion of his Harvard admission examination. Boyd (1934: 34) perceives that Eliot, like Spencer, had no use for the classics. Hawkins (1972: 10), however, mentions that Eliot enjoyed Latin as an elective when he was a Harvard senior. Cf. James 1930 1: 52.

[96] See James 1930 1: 184; Morison 1942: 325; Hawkins 1972: 45.

[97] Andrew Preston Peabody served as interim president until Eliot's official election. He was also a candidate for the presidency, favored by more traditionalistic Harvardians (see James 1930 1: 187; Morison 1942: 328; Hawkins 1964: 196 and 1972: 45–46). On Peabody, see Chapter 3, this volume.

post,[98] the Harvard Corporation flirted with offering the presidency to Eliot.[99] It proved more difficult to win the favor of Harvard's more traditionalistic Board of Overseers, but on May 19, 1869, Eliot was officially marked as Hill's replacement.[100] The thirty-five-year-old Eliot was poised to transform Harvard into a university.[101]

The Revolution in Cambridge

The transformative nature of Eliot's leadership became apparent from the start. At his inauguration on October 19, 1869, Eliot delivered one of the most consequential addresses in the history of American higher education. In this speech, he laid out most of the key priorities of the newly envisioned university system, which ultimately presaged the demise of the antebellum classical colleges.[102] Eliot now presented himself as an enthusiastic supporter of curricular free election.[103] No longer, Eliot proposed, should Harvard students be confined to the study of a handful of subjects. "We would have them all," he announced, "and at their best."[104] In fact, Eliot deemed the content students encountered in their coursework unworthy of much concern. "The actual problem to be solved," he opined, "is not what to teach, but how to teach."[105]

[98] By late February 1869, if not earlier, Harvard offered Adams the presidency, which he immediately declined. See James 1930 1: 191–92; Hawkins 1972: 46.

[99] According to James (1930 1: 192–93), the Harvard Corporation approached Eliot about the presidency on March 10. It then elected Eliot on March 12 (Morison 1942: 327). Although news of this election was made public on March 18 (James 1930 1: 195), the election would not be official until it was approved by the Board of Overseers. This approval did not occur until May.

[100] On this date, the Board of Overseers officially approved (by a 16-to-8 vote) the Corporation's choice of Eliot as Harvard's next president (see James 1930 1: 198; Morison 1942: 328; Hawkins 1972: 48). According to Hawkins (1972: 48), Eliot started his new job immediately.

[101] On March 13, 1869, a day after the Harvard Corporation chose Eliot as the institution's president, Eliot's first wife, Ellen (Derby) Peabody Eliot passed away. See James 1930 1: 194–95; Hawkins 1972: 47.

[102] Eliot 1969. On this speech, see, e.g., James 1930 1: 194–95, 225; Morison 1942: 329–31; Rudolph 1962: 244 and 1977: 132; Butts 1971: 176; Hawkins 1972: 48; Lucas 1994: 165–66; Jewett 2012: 32. According to Roberts and Turner (2000: 160 n. 34), Eliot's inauguration signaled the end of the prescribed classical curriculum.

[103] According to Hawkins (1972: 92), Eliot's curricular ideas prior to his inaugural address appear similar to those McCosh later championed.

[104] Eliot 1969: 1.

[105] Ibid. 2. For Eliot's similar focus on educational methods at the expense of educational content, see, e.g., Eliot 1898: 80, 227.

Eliot soon made good his plans to revolutionize Harvard's undergraduate curriculum.[106] In 1872 Eliot's Harvard abandoned all subject requirements for seniors.[107] Seven years later, the institution abolished all prescribed courses for juniors.[108] Sophomore required coursework was next to go, in 1884.[109] During the year in which Eliot and McCosh would wrangle over the virtues and vices of the elective system, Harvard even managed to reduce subject requirements for freshmen.[110] Undaunted by McCosh's criticisms in the 1885 debate, Eliot spread election still further: by 1894, his institution required only one specific class of A.B. candidates—English rhetoric.[111]

Harvard's enterprising president hoped that this new curricular free-for-all would compel the disciplines to fight for students, supposedly for the betterment of the students and the disciplines themselves. Eliot advertised the perceived benefits of this scheme with evolutionary vocabulary. Thus, in an article originally published in 1884, he claimed, "In education, as elsewhere, it is the fittest that survives. The Classics, like other studies, must stand upon their own merits; for it is not the proper business of universities to force subjects of study, or particular kinds of mental discipline upon unwilling generations."[112] If Eliot's curricular smorgasbord called to mind a brand of pedagogical Darwinism, his insistence on eschewing Harvard's erstwhile regard for monitoring student discipline had a similar ring. Indeed, Eliot had a Spencerian approach to college discipline: if students took advantage of skipping classes, for example, he thought that they would ultimately learn their lesson or suffer the consequences.[113]

Naturally, the move from a prescriptive to an elective curriculum would necessitate a greatly expanded faculty.[114] Eliot, after all, wanted Harvard to

---

[106] On the nature of the Harvard A.B. curriculum in the 1868–69 academic year—the year before Eliot's inauguration—see James 1930 2: 102–11, 335–42; Morison 1942: 344–45, 397–98; Hawkins 1972: 95. Hawkins notes that all freshman studies were prescribed; half the sophomore studies were required; and slightly less than half the coursework for juniors and seniors was mandated as well.

[107] Rudolph 1962: 294; Butts 1971: 176; Hawkins 1972: 96. For a broader discussion of curricular changes during Eliot's presidency, see Morison 1942: 345–55. West 1885 criticizes many of these changes.

[108] Rudolph 1962: 294; Butts 1971: 176.

[109] Rudolph 1962: 294; Butts 1971: 176. Cf. Smyth 1930: 35; Rogers 1942: 101.

[110] Rudolph 1962: 294; Butts 1971: 176.

[111] Rudolph 1962: 294; Butts 1971: 176. Cf. Jewett 2012: 197. Harvard at this time also required one modern language class, although students could choose between French and German (see Morison 1942: 346). According to Hawkins (1972: 96), the free-elective curriculum at Harvard reached its peak in 1899.

[112] Eliot 1898: 120. For similar points, see also Eliot 1898: 127, 145.

[113] Hoeveler 1981: 245. On this subject, see also Hawkins 1972: 110–11; Kemeny 1998: 36; and the following text.

[114] As Eliot asserted in the 1885 debate with McCosh: see Eliot 1898: 125–26.

provide advanced instruction in all subjects he deemed liberal,[115] and this would require hiring scores of new professors and instructors. The president's grand successes in raising capital for Harvard helped drive his innovations, allowing Eliot ultimately to best his many critics at the institution. A dynamic reformer of Harvard's underperforming professional schools,[116] Eliot also inaugurated organized graduate study in the arts and sciences.[117]

In comparison with his steadfast support for the elective principle, however, Eliot was originally uninterested in encouraging faculty research. His earlier faculty hires, for instance, demonstrated less regard for the spirit of the professionalized academy than one might expect.[118] Despite his many talents, Eliot never showed much aptitude for the production of academic scholarship, and this drawback may have led him to underemphasize its import to the American university movement he otherwise championed. Yet competition with the Johns Hopkins University and other American bastions of advanced research soon changed Eliot's attitude. In 1880, for example, Harvard began to grant research sabbaticals to professors at half-pay.[119] To the chagrin of many traditionalists, Eliot had quickly succeeded in transforming the educational experience at Harvard and was eagerly proselytizing for his reforms.

Give Me Liberty or Give Me Death!

Members of the Nineteenth Century Club had good reason to look forward to the debate between Eliot and McCosh in late February 1885. Engaging two major figures associated with the curricular wars on American college campuses and occurring soon after the fracas regarding Adams's "A College Fetich" speech,[120] the skirmish seemed destined to become a memorable

---

[115] By this, Eliot meant that Harvard would not offer classes in preprofessional or technical subjects. Hawkins (1972: 202) demonstrates that this was not accurate: as of 1886, for example, Harvard allowed engineering courses to count as electives for the A.B. course.

[116] See, e.g., Eliot 1923: 31–33; Morison 1942: 336–41.

[117] This innovation was first accomplished in January 1872, when Eliot established the Graduate Department (see Flexner 1930: 73 n. 32; Morison 1942: 334; Hawkins 1972: 55). In 1890, the Graduate Department was renamed the Graduate School of Arts and Sciences (see James 1930 2: 65; Hawkins 1972: 57, 72).

[118] On this topic, see McCaughey 1974: esp. 245.

[119] Veysey 1965: 165.

[120] This speech appears to have remained in people's minds in 1885, as a newspaper's reference to McCosh in the aftermath of the debate makes clear. According to the Washington *Evening Critic*, McCosh "worships the Greek fetich which President Eliot has manfully tried to overthrow." See anonymous 1885h.

event. It should also be mentioned that this intellectual grudge match took place at an especially challenging time for both participants. Lower student enrollments began to haunt McCosh's administration in 1882 and continued through 1885.[121] Eliot faced similar pressures in the lead-up to the debate, which encouraged a burst of anti-reformist sentiment at Harvard.[122] Although they naturally did not intimate as much, a sense of desperation clung to the speakers, who aimed not only to best their opponent, but also to defend the educational apparatus that they had nurtured at their respective institutions—and that now was in danger of unraveling.

Eliot spoke first that evening and appears to have mustered every bit of his considerable oratorical power[123] and talent for producing sprightly, unadorned prose as a means to defend his pedagogical "new departure" at Harvard. Cutting to the chase, he announced toward his speech's start, "To-night I hope to convince you that a university of liberal arts and sciences must give its students three things: I. Freedom in choice of studies. II. Opportunity to win academic distinction in single subjects or special lines of study. III. A discipline which distinctly imposes on each individual the responsibility of forming his own habits and guiding his own conduct."[124] As was in keeping with his enthusiasms, Eliot in the oration devoted the most time to his first contention: that the university curriculum should be defined by the elective principle.[125]

He attempted to prove this contention in manifold ways. In one line of attack, Eliot made clear that he viewed undergraduate students as customers and considered the proper curriculum a kind of intellectual free market.[126] A university, he stressed, "must try to teach every subject, above the grade of its admission requirements, for which there is any demand."[127] Eliot also attempted to assuage fears that incoming freshmen were incapable of choosing appropriate coursework for themselves. Demonstrating his rosy

---

[121] See Hoeveler 1981: 322. Cf. Wertenbaker 1946: 315.

[122] According to Morison (1942: 359), 1885 and 1886 were the two most challenging years for the Eliot administration. Hawkins (1972: 78) notes that anti-Eliot sentiment reached its peak at Harvard during these years.

[123] On Eliot's gifts as a speaker, see James 1930 2: 102–11; Morison 1942: 397–98; Hawkins 1972: 9.

[124] Eliot 1898: 125.

[125] As Eliot (1898: 125) noted in the speech that he would do.

[126] See Levermore (1886: 296), who criticized Eliot for treating colleges like businesses. Eliot (1898: 413) believed that universities should be run in this manner. According to Carnochan (1993: 18), McCosh's criticisms of Eliot in the 1885 debate chiefly surrounded Eliot's treatment of higher education as a business.

[127] Eliot 1898: 127.

estimation of human nature,[128] he asserted, "A young man is much affected by the expectations which his elders entertain of him. If they expect him to behave like a child, his lingering childishness will oftener rule his actions; if they expect him to behave like a man, his incipient manhood will oftener assert itself."[129] This charitable impression of adolescents' conduct would open up for McCosh his most successful line of attack.

One can catch hints of the evolutionary underpinnings of Eliot's curricular views throughout the address. "Every youth of eighteen is an infinitely complex organization," he said, "the duplicate of which neither does nor ever will exist."[130] Such individual variation necessitated an individualized curriculum, which would allow young men to nurture their supposedly unique gifts.[131] Although a firm believer in the concept of mental discipline,[132] Harvard's president did not support the notion—integral to faculty psychology—that adolescents were sufficiently similar to warrant the same sort of education to encourage their capacities to flourish. Instead, he stressed human difference, suggesting that a one-size-fits-all approach to learning would not suffice and reinforcing his Darwinian take on pedagogy.

Elsewhere in his published writings, in fact, Eliot stressed that education should increase natural inequalities. In a lecture delivered in 1896, for example, he contended,

> The vague desire for equality in democracy has worked great mischief in democratic schools. There is no such thing as equality of gifts, or powers, or faculties, among either children or adults. On the contrary, there is the utmost diversity; and education and all the experiences of life increase these diversities, because school, and the earning of a livelihood, and the reaction of the individual upon his surroundings, all tend strongly to magnify innate diversities.[133]

---

[128] According to Eliot (1924: 233), a lifelong Unitarian, Unitarians believe in the essential goodness of human nature.

[129] Eliot 1898: 128–29. See also 132–33 on the supposed superior fitness of an eighteen-year-old to select his own courses.

[130] Ibid. 133.

[131] For similar ideas elsewhere in Eliot's work, see Eliot 1893: 83, 85, 1898: 117. According to Hawkins (1972: 89–90), individual variation was key to Eliot's conception of education. Cf. McCosh 1868: 73, which justifies curricular election on similar bases.

[132] See, e.g., Eliot 1869a: 215, 1869b: 359, 1898: 92–94, 109, 144, 1908: 166, 1917: 359, and 1924: 93. On this topic, see Hawkins 1972: 43, 85–91, 203, 319; Hoeveler 1981: 234. Cf. Eliot 1891.

[133] Eliot 1898: 409. For more of Eliot's (sometimes incongruous) thoughts on the relationship between education and equality, see, e.g., Eliot 1893: 86, 1898: 416, and 1897: 163. According to Hawkins (1972: 168), course election was for Eliot a metaphor for social inequalities.

In the address he offered during his 1885 debate with McCosh, Eliot also perceived that the goal of higher education was service to society. "The individual enjoys most that intellectual labor for which he is most fit," he ventured, "and society is best served when every man's peculiar skill, faculty, or aptitude is developed and utilized to the highest possible degree."[134] Here Eliot showed his support for a conception of education anathema to Renaissance humanism: for him, the goal was not the perfection of the individual but instead bestowing the individual with the tools necessary to aid in ameliorating society's ills.

Eliot tempered his fervor for the elective principle in one important respect: he maintained that Harvard did not allow its A.B. candidates to study any subjects they desire, but merely those that "are liberal or pure, no technical or professional studies being admissible."[135] So, students could not choose *any* discipline that fit their fancy; rather, they were compelled to pick from only "liberal" or "pure" options. But Eliot never defined what he meant by "liberal" and "pure," and Harvard's subsequent embrace of engineering as a fit subject for the A.B. course in 1886 should lead one to question the sincerity of this contention.[136] In a speech he delivered in 1891, Eliot, echoing vocationalists such as Ezra Cornell, uncomplicatedly announced that the American university should teach everything.[137] Why the difference? If Eliot had little faith in confining American education to the age-old seven liberal arts, what made a subject worthy of study? If the ultimate end of education was, as Eliot had it, humanitarian service to one's community, on what basis should preprofessional subjects be inadmissible in the A.B. curriculum? Unfortunately, in his oration, Eliot offered no answers to these questions.

Nevertheless, Eliot provided even more ammunition for his argument in favor of curricular choice. A few of his contentions demonstrated his elitist regard for the nation's "best and brightest." He maintained, for example, that the proper course of studies should chiefly focus on the needs of an institution's preeminent pupils. To Eliot, "a university should aim at meeting the wants of the best students at any rate, and the wants of inferior students only so far as it can meet them without impairing the privileges of the

---

[134] Eliot 1898: 134.
[135] Ibid. 139.
[136] See Hawkins 1972: 202.
[137] Eliot 1898: 227–28.

best."[138] Still, he also believed that the elective principle worked effectively for slackers. After all, as he articulated in another speech defending curricular choice in 1908, "Any human being, whether child or adult, whether hard-worker or brain-worker, will always work harder and accomplish more in a task which interests him."[139] This conclusion potentially caused problems for Eliot's insistence on human variation: in this regard, it seems, he vouched for the inherent similarity of all people, since they all supposedly act in the same manner when accorded a degree of choice.

As if recognizing the potential weaknesses of his position, Eliot in his 1885 oration attempted to provide even more arguments in favor of the elective principle. Trying to gainsay the value of tradition to determining the optimum answers to the day's educational controversies, he remarked that

> free choice implies that there are no studies which are recognized as of supreme merit, so that every young man unquestionably ought to pursue them. Can this be? Is it possible that the accumulated wisdom of the race cannot prescribe with certainty the studies which will best develop the human mind in general between the ages of eighteen and twenty-two? At first it certainly seems strange that we have to answer no; but when we reflect how very brief the acquaintance of the race has been with the great majority of the subjects which are now taught in a university the negative answer seems less surprising.[140]

Emphasizing the novelty of various disciplines that could play a part in the university curriculum, Eliot downplayed the past as a guide for the present. This hints at the fundamental incompatibility of Eliot's views with the spirit of humanism. Given his outlook, it should not surprise us that in a speech celebrating his ninetieth birthday, Eliot repeated to undergraduates the advice of the historian and minister Edward Everett Hale (1822–1909): "Look forward and not backward—Look out and not in."[141] An Italian humanist such as Bruni, of course, would have advocated the reverse.

---

[138] Ibid. 142.
[139] Eliot 1908: 134.
[140] Eliot 1898: 142.
[141] Quoted in James 1930 2: 309.

In comparison with the time he spent vouching for the superiority of the elective principle, Eliot made quick work of the other theses he mentioned at the debate's start. He stated his preference for bestowing academic honors at graduation on students who had completed meritorious work in particular subjects. Eliot lauded such a system on competitive, even evolutionary, grounds: "These honors," he announced, "encourage students to push far on single lines; whence arises a demand for advanced instruction in all departments in which honors can be won, and this demand, taken in connection with the competition which naturally springs up between different departments, stimulates the teachers, who in turn stimulate their pupils."[142] In yet another demonstration of his disavowal of the humanistic tradition, Eliot further embraced specialization. To him, the system of granting honors to undergraduates was crucial to the university's flourishing because it aims "to promote specialization of work and therefore to develop advanced instruction."[143] For the American university to flourish, the ancient regard for well-roundedness must perish. Eliot's approach, clued in to the perceived needs of a changing society, encouraged the kind of specialization that had made industrialization possible.

Eliot in the speech also briefly trumpeted the paramount value of liberty in the realm of student conduct. Deeming the *"in loco parentis* theory" "an ancient fiction which ought no longer to deceive anybody,"[144] he proclaimed,

> It is a distinct advantage of the genuine university method that it does not pretend to maintain any parental or monastic discipline over its students, but frankly tells them that they must govern themselves. The moral purpose of a university's policy should be to train young men to self-control and self-reliance through liberty.[145]

Considering it impractical for institutions of higher learning to police their students, Eliot again argued in favor of the laissez-faire strategy. In contrast with his brief for the elective principle, he provided little elaboration on this score, presumably deeming the points he made against the in loco parentis theory obviously superior.

---

[142] Eliot 1898: 145.
[143] Ibid. 146. Elsewhere in his work, however, Eliot argued against too much specialization. See, e.g., Eliot 1908: 154.
[144] Eliot 1898: 147.
[145] Ibid. 148.

A More Jaundiced Impression of Human Nature

McCosh was now given the opportunity to present his rejoinder. After some self-deprecating throat-clearing[146] and an attempt to dismiss the notion that he was an educational conservative,[147] he got down to brass tacks. McCosh commenced with his strongest argument. Although advanced under the noble-seeming label of liberty, in practice the free-elective system would encourage indolence. If one grants to a student the pleasing ability to select his own coursework, McCosh maintained, "I can tell you what he will possibly or probably choose. Those who are in the secrets of college know how skillful certain students are in choosing their subjects. They can choose branches which will cost them least study, and put themselves under the popular professors who give them the highest grades with the least labor."[148] In an almost Tacitean turn of phrase, McCosh announced, "I am for liberty but not licentiousness, which always ends in servitude."[149]

Unfortunately, McCosh's riposte to Eliot on this score possesses a great deal of truth. The historian Samuel Eliot Morison, discussing Harvard's embrace of free election under Eliot, notes that it had precisely the effects McCosh warned—and that students loved the system because it made their undergraduate days less challenging.[150] The same holds true for institutions other than Harvard, of course. Those with some experience of American higher education (as pupils and/or faculty members) will easily recognize

---

[146] McCosh 1885b: 4. Such humility may have rung hollow, since McCosh was known for his arrogance, egotism, and fiery temper. See, e.g., Hoeveler 1981: xi, 267; Morris 2014: 364; Geiger 2015: 336. These qualities appear to have manifested themselves when McCosh departed in a huff from Harvard's 250th anniversary celebration in November 1886. He believed that Harvard had insulted Princeton and was especially irked by a few lines in a poem Oliver Wendell Holmes read at the festivities. On this brouhaha, which temporarily strained McCosh's and Eliot's friendship, see, e.g., anonymous 1886b, e; McCosh 1886b; Morison 1942: 362–63; Wertenbaker 1946: 333–35; Hawkins 1964: 198 n. 26; Hoeveler 1981: 268; Kemeny 1998: 22. But McCosh was also capable of great compassion: see, e.g., Hoeveler 1981: 269; Morris 2014: 364. According to Hoeveler (1981: 233–34), McCosh and Eliot were sometimes allies and sometimes foes.

[147] McCosh 1885b: 4.

[148] Ibid. 5. For similar arguments, see also McCosh 1884: 4; 1885c: 5. Eliot 1891 and 1908: 159–60 provide weak rejoinders to such points. According to Carnochan (1993: 17) McCosh's argument on this score offers an example of McCosh meeting Eliot on his own intellectual ground. Cf. McCosh 1868: 72 (here McCosh thinks that students will mostly select their courses properly).

[149] McCosh 1885b: 5.

[150] Morison 1942: 384. For a more general discussion of the ways in which free election lowered academic standards in colleges and universities, see, e.g., Rudolph 1962: 306; Geiger 2015: 365–421; Adler 2016: 66; and Chapter 2, this volume.

the salience of McCosh's point: many students, given the power to choose their own courses, will hunt for the easiest options.[151]

But the point with which McCosh ended his otherwise strong, albeit pessimistic, assertion introduces an important issue he did not address. Is the difficulty of particular courses always associated with their object of study, or does the character of individual instructors matter? McCosh hinted that the latter remains a potentially important factor, but he never came to terms with what this might mean for his broader argument. If it is theoretically possible for students to take an easy course in ancient Greek and a taxing course in, say, German poetry, why should only the former play a required role in the undergraduate curriculum?

Despite failing to address this matter, McCosh announced, "*First, there should be branches required of all students who pursue the full course and seek a degree.*"[152] Unsurprisingly, given his bona fides as a philosopher in the Scottish Common Sense tradition, McCosh argued that the required elements of the A.B. course should possess disciplinary value: the obligatory studies, he maintained in the speech, "should all be fitted to enlarge or refine the mind. They should be fundamental, as forming the basis on which other knowledge is built. They should be disciplinary, as training the mind for further pursuits."[153] This line of reasoning calls to mind the same strong objections we noted in the debate surrounding Adams's "A College Fetich." By reducing liberal arts study to the disciplining of the faculties, McCosh unwittingly made psychologists the rightful arbiters of the curriculum. Eliot, after all, vouched for the equal disciplinary value of the new subjects, and McCosh provided little concrete evidence that he was mistaken.

McCosh's attempt to provide some evidence, in fact, underscores the weaknesses inherent in this approach. While arguing in favor of particular obligatory ingredients of an A.B. degree, the leader of Princeton remarked, "President Eliot has a high opinion of German Universities, but the eminent men in their Greatest University, that of Berlin, have testified that a far

---

[151] Online discussion boards for students can help present dramatic illustrations of this contention. Each semester, my university's Reddit page, for example, features a so-called Course Registration Megathread, which is peppered with anonymous queries such as "What is the easiest lab to take?," "Anyone know any bullshit 2 credit classes?," and "Is astr[ology] 315 hard?" For these specific comments, see https://www.reddit.com/r/UMD/comments/9s9ajg/course_registration_megathread_spring_2019/.

[152] McCosh 1885b: 7 (emphasis in the original).

[153] McCosh 1885b: 7. For other examples of McCosh's support for the concept of mental discipline and its import, see, e.g., McCosh 1868: 40–44, 62; 1884: 3–5; 1885b: 7–12, 16–17, 1885c: 5, 8. On this topic, see Hawkins 1972: 86; Hoeveler 1981: 101–2, 231–32. Cf. West 1885: 433 and 1886: 4.

higher training is given in the Classical Gymnasia than in the scientific Real Schule."[154] Apparently, McCosh, like many opponents of Adams's "A College Fetich" oration, failed to recognize that the so-called Berlin Report did not provide a proper experiment attuned to the question at hand and thus did not supply the sort of definitive proof he craved. As we detected in the previous chapter, recourse to the Report ably demonstrated the dangers for traditionalists of waging curricular war on the social scientists' turf.[155]

In place of the curricular hodgepodge Eliot supported, McCosh, in the most memorable portion of his address, appealed to a term of recent vintage at the College of New Jersey. "We in Princeton," he said, "believe in a Trinity of studies: in Language and Literature, in Science, and in Philosophy. Every educated man should know so much of each of these. Without this, man's varied faculties are not trained, his nature is not fully developed and may become malformed."[156] This trinity, with its obviously intended Christian resonances, allowed McCosh to argue in favor of something concrete to fight against Eliot's curricular anarchy.

But in crucial respects it did not embody a radical critique of Eliot's position. After all, McCosh, like Eliot, grounded his conception of a proper education in the concept of mental discipline.[157] His cheerleading for a curricular trinity, while clever, suggested that the benefits to be gained from higher education came from discipline-specific skills—exactly as Eliot had asserted. In explicating his trinity, McCosh presented no examples of educational content that students must encounter to deem themselves educated. All came down to faculty psychology, and McCosh provided no proof that age-old subjects provided more mental discipline than did the newer studies. Nor did Princeton's president question the premises underlying Eliot's curricular views. Was education best viewed as a Spencerian exercise in the "survival of the fittest"? Were students properly seen as customers? Strangely, given his philosophical background, nowhere did McCosh analyze these fundamental issues.

Rather, McCosh seemed content to stick to more quotidian concerns. In his rejoinder he provided a dramatic way to castigate Eliot's free-elective system.

[154] McCosh 1885b: 10.
[155] See Chapter 3, this volume.
[156] McCosh 1885b: 11. McCosh 1884: 3 vouches for these three branches as obligatory for all Princeton students; cf. McCosh 1896: 199. McCosh 1868: 71, however, spoke of the value of a curricular quartet, not a trio.
[157] According to anonymous 1885e, the 1885 Eliot-McCosh debate hinged on the subject of mental discipline. Cf. Hawkins 1972: 88; Kemeny 1998: 35.

From his scan of Harvard's bountiful course catalogue, he presented a prospective post-freshman course of studies,[158] which he then ridiculed as trifling. McCosh's selection of an intentionally nugatory curriculum was as follows:

In the sophomore year: "French Literature of the Seventeenth Century"; "Medieval and Modern European History"; "Elementary Course in Fine Art, with collateral instruction in Water-coloring"; "Counterpoint (in music)."

In the junior year: "French Literature of the Eighteenth Century"; "Early Medieval History"; "Botany"; "History of Music."

In the senior year: "French Literature of the Nineteenth Century"; "Elementary Spanish"; "Greek Art"; "Free Thematic Music."[159]

About this handpicked course of studies, McCosh announced, "There are twenty such dilettanti courses which may be taken at Harvard. I cannot allow that this is an advance in scholarship."[160]

Today's readers of McCosh's speech will likely be perplexed by this conclusion. In comparison with the vocational fare on offer at many contemporary institutions of higher learning, this curriculum appears to demonstrate a serious (if slightly narrow) commitment to liberal learning. One also notes in his choices McCosh's implicitly critical attitude toward elements of the modern humanities: to him, music (including mathematics-soaked counterpoint!) and fine arts seemed unserious.[161] McCosh's evaluation of this list may also fail to convince in light of his broader curricular claims. Elsewhere in the address, McCosh (like Eliot) underscored the cardinal importance of English literature in the undergraduate curriculum.[162] In fact, he—justly—criticized Eliot's system at Harvard because it

---

[158] McCosh left out the freshman year, because in the last iteration of the Harvard course catalogue he found the freshman year still had some prescribed coursework.

[159] This choice of courses is found in McCosh 1885b: 12.

[160] McCosh 1885b: 12.

[161] Cf. McCosh 1885c: 5, 8, which does much the same. Hoeveler (1981: 290–91) notes that, despite the attitude on display in such passages, McCosh inaugurated the study of art at Princeton. McCosh also believed that history was an unnecessarily easy subject. See McCosh 1885b: 11 n. 1.

[162] McCosh 1885b: 12–13. See also McCosh 1868: 56–57, 60. For Eliot's view that English is of cardinal importance for American students, see, e.g., Eliot 1869b: 359–60, 1898: 98–99, and 1917: 358. Boyd (1934: 35) notes that Eliot, unlike Spencer, saw value in studying English literature.

did not require the study of English past the freshman year.[163] But why was the repeated study of English literature valuable, whereas to McCosh devotion to French literature could be belittled as dilettantism?[164] McCosh never provided a clue to help us answer this question, and this omission leads one to conclude that his argument relied more on mockery than on logic.[165] He presumably felt most troubled by the perceived lopsidedness of this potential curriculum; after all, as Princeton's president he called for the expansion of modern European languages in the course of studies.[166] But this conclusion was also open to criticism: some modernists had contended that the traditional focus on the classical languages and mathematics was itself an example of curricular lopsidedness.[167]

McCosh seemed to tread on firmer ground when he turned to issues of student discipline. Here he had the benefit of engaging with Eliot's laissez-faire worldview, which led Eliot to promote a radically hands-off approach to the subject. McCosh made clear that he thought class attendance should be mandatory[168] and noted that German universities could prove more lackadaisical on this score because they required comprehensive postgraduation examinations for entry into various professions, which naturally reinforced collegiate discipline.[169]

In response to Eliot's praise for specialization, McCosh deftly coopted Spencer's ideas for his own purposes. He said, "In Nature, as Herbert Spencer has shown, there is differentiation which scatters, but there is also concentration which holds things together. There should be the same in education."[170]

---

[163] McCosh 1885b: 12–13.

[164] The same may be said in response to West (1886: 10–11), another Princetonian who considered French unchallenging, but not English. Of modern languages, Eliot was especially supportive of the study of French and German: see, e.g., Eliot 1898: 101–4. Cf. Eliot 1898: 116. In his inaugural address, McCosh also supported the study of French and German (McCosh 1868: 59).

[165] Hence Morison (1942: 353) could himself mock McCosh's views on this subject. According to anonymous (1885l), the audience at the debate laughed at McCosh's invocation of French and music as dilettante studies. For a classist defense of McCosh's position in the debate from Princeton students, see anonymous 1885f: 279.

[166] Hoeveler 1981: 238.

[167] E.g., Cooke 1884: 776, who argued that forcing boys to learn the classics amounts to support for specialization.

[168] McCosh 1885b: 13–14. On McCosh's support for the college acting in loco parentis, see, e.g., McCosh 1878, 1888: 35–43, and 1896: 224–25; Wertenbaker 1942: 315–23; Kemeny 1998: 36. See also Marsden 1994: 201; Bow 2013: 667–68.

[169] McCosh 1885b: 14. Some commentary on the Eliot-McCosh debate of 1885 centered on the differences between American and German education: see, e.g., Levermore 1886: 292–93. Cf. West 1885: 436–39. According to Hawkins (1972: 106), noting such differences was part of the criticism of Eliot's educational vision as a whole.

[170] McCosh 1885b: 16.

Students should have specialties, then, but should also become well-rounded, since specialization compels one "to be narrow, partial, malformed, one-sided."[171] For someone eager to cast aside the label of a reactionary, this strategy seemed well-suited to McCosh's purposes.

The same could be said about another masterful attempt on McCosh's part to turn the tables on Eliot. In his speech McCosh announced, "From the close of Freshman year on it is perfectly practicable for a student to pass through Harvard and receive the degree of Bachelor of Arts, without taking any course in Latin, Greek, Mathematics, Chemistry, Physics, Astronomy, Geology, Logic, Psychology, Ethics, Political Economy, German, or even English!"[172] His list is instructive—and damning. How could Eliot, a steadfast booster of scientific education, allow Harvardians to eschew the study of the natural sciences? What was so modern and superior about a curricular system that allowed such avoidance? This list reinforced the impression that the elective system chiefly encouraged undergraduates to circumvent taxing coursework. It further painted McCosh as a moderate at home with the expansion of the natural and social sciences in the A.B. curriculum.

But confusion continued when McCosh again returned to the subject of the optimum course of studies. Agreeing with Eliot that all men possess "special talents," he stated that undergraduates should thus be allowed to select a portion of their coursework.[173] But he never provided a firm rationale for this conclusion. If, as McCosh earlier argued, the elective principle encouraged laziness, why should it *ever* be allowed in the curriculum? How could McCosh be certain that students would use their partial freedom to choose classes associated with their inner strengths? How could he be sure that they would not simply gravitate toward the least demanding subjects instead? This quandary may not be unsurmountable; indeed, one could imagine numerous arguments that could justify partial election in the undergraduate curriculum. But McCosh did not appear to notice the incongruity in his arguments. Further, the president of Princeton's distinctions between obligatory and elective studies lacked concrete justifications. He thought, for example, that many of "the highest languages" should be part of the required course,[174] but never explained what made a language "high" in the first place. Here, McCosh's failure to focus on content caused problems: without

---

[171] Ibid. 16.
[172] Ibid. 12–13.
[173] Ibid. 15.
[174] Ibid. 16.

stressing the value of individual works of literature to the education of youth, his preferences could appear arbitrary.

The Heart of the Matter

Toward the end of his remarks, McCosh offered a hypothetical scenario featuring a young undergraduate that clarifies his chief objection to the free-elective system. A student, he suggested, may arrive at college and choose French in place of ancient Greek, thanks to the reputation of a popular French instructor. Then, as a junior, he could discover that he is called to the ministry. But it is now too late: because of his former fateful choice, he remains likely to give up his calling, rather than go back to school.[175] "The Churches of Christ," McCosh announced, "will do well to look to this new departure, for they may find that they have fewer candidates for the office of ministry."[176]

Here we get to the heart of McCosh's concerns. The evangelical president of Princeton recognized that future ministers must be able to read the New Testament and thus considered it a grave threat to the nation that Eliot's Harvard did not require ancient Greek of its aspirants to the A.B. degree. The New Testament, in fact, amounts to the lone example of educational content McCosh vouched for in his entire speech. Although during his presidency he demonstrated his pragmatism and willingness to compromise, the potential effects on religious life of the abandonment of required ancient Greek were for McCosh too much to stomach. Further demonstrating the Protestant underpinnings of his curricular views, at his address's conclusion McCosh proposed another debate with Eliot: "*This club should have another meeting*," he urged, "*in which President Eliot will defend the new departure in the religion of colleges, and I engage with God's help to meet him.*"[177] More

---

[175] Ibid. 18.

[176] Ibid. 18.

[177] Ibid. 22 (emphasis in the original). For McCosh's speech in this later debate, which took place in 1886, see McCosh 1886a. Eliot's contribution to the debate remained unpublished, despite McCosh's hope (1886a: 3; cf. anonymous 1886e) that they would be published side-by-side. Since Eliot in his address advocated a position on compulsory chapel services that Harvard soon abandoned (see Morison 1942: 366–67), he decided not to publish it. A typescript copy of Eliot's oration can be found among his papers in the Harvard archives, however. On the 1886 Eliot-McCosh debate on the role of religion in the colleges see, e.g., Hawkins 1972: 124–25; Hoeveler 1981: xi, 251–53; Marsden 1994: 199–200; Kemeny 1998: 3–4, 17–22; Mattingly 2017: 243. See also anonymous 1886f; Palmer 1886. For other examples of Eliot discussing the role of religion in American higher education, see, e.g., Eliot 1898: 42–43, 235–36. As far back as 1869, Eliot had criticized the clerical leadership of the nation's colleges, a view that was unlikely to win him McCosh's favor: see Eliot 1869b: 366. For Eliot's

than anything, McCosh's anxieties about the worrisome future of Protestant evangelicalism drove his objections to Eliot's "new departure." This is why, it seems, McCosh later characterized his 1885 debate with Eliot as a defense of ancient Greek in the college curriculum: for him, much hinged on the supply of prospective ministers.[178]

McCosh had ample reasons to be distressed on this front. Even at Princeton, with its obligatory classical study, the percentage of graduates heading toward careers in ministry was dwindling under his leadership.[179] McCosh's theology informed his vision of the classics' value.[180] Thus he repeatedly stressed in his writings that only Christianity can answer life's great questions: despite his genuflections to the classical languages, he was not above criticizing the perceived limitations of pagan Greek literature for this crucial purpose.[181] As the historian P. C. Kemeny put it, for McCosh Eliot's elective system "imperiled the Christian character of American civilization."[182] Hence, he proved an energetic critic of Eliot's educational scheme, even though, as we have detected, he partially agreed with Eliot's pedagogical rationales.

The religious foundation of McCosh's objections to the free-elective system naturally won the president of Princeton his share of pious admirers.[183] But the numbers of such boosters were bound to decline, as elite higher education in the US grew increasingly nonsectarian in the decades that followed.

In addition, McCosh's paramount focus on the obligatory study of the New Testament ultimately undercut his regard for the classical humanities. In keeping with the humanistic tradition, Princeton required its candidates for the A.B. degree to study the works of many pagan authors such as Homer, Herodotus, Demosthenes, Cicero, and Tacitus.[184] Although at the end of his

discussion of the education of ministers, see Eliot 1898: 61–86. For Eliot's views on religion, see, e.g., James 1930 1: 34, 1930 2: 187; Hawkins 1964: esp. 194–95 and 1972: 120–38; Kemeny 1998: 22–26.

[178]   See McCosh 1888: 17–18 and 1896: 199.
[179]   Wertenbaker 1946: 331–32. According to Kemeny (1998: 77), this loss troubled McCosh as early as 1877.
[180]   Cf. Kemeny 1998: 36–37.
[181]   See, e.g., McCosh 1886a: 10, 15–16. For other examples of McCosh demonstrating the religious foundation of his approach to higher education see, e.g., McCosh 1868: 57–58, 1884: 8, 1885b: 18, 22, 1885c: 5, 1888: 51–61, and 1896: 202–3. For scholarly discussion of religion's role in McCosh's pedagogical program, see Hoeveler 1981: 237–38; Carnochan 1993: 21; Marsden 1994: 198; Kemeny 1998: 15, 36–37; Bow 2013: 664; Geiger 2015: 335.
[182]   Kemeny 1998: 37.
[183]   See, e.g., anonymous 1885c and e; Cuyler 1885; Nemo 1885; Patton 1885.
[184]   For specifics from a Princeton course catalogue from McCosh's early tenure as president, see anonymous 1870: 23–25; See also Hoeveler 1981: 232.

1885 speech McCosh belatedly referred to ancient Greek as "the most perfect language, the grandest literature, the most elevated thinking of all antiquity,"[185] as we have discovered, he was capable of disparaging Greek and Latin learning when he aimed to highlight the superiority of the New Testament. If only the Bible—and not pagan literature—could properly address life's foundational concerns, why should Princeton students focus so much of their attention on classical authors? On this question, as with so many thorny issues introduced by his speech, McCosh remained silent.

Who Won? Short-Term Losses, Long-Term Gains

The great attention paid to the 1885 Eliot-McCosh debate and the high stakes involved in the conflict naturally encourage us to wonder who won the battle. In the aftermath of the event itself, it must have seemed difficult for unbiased observers to tell. Some preferred Eliot's arguments;[186] others preferred McCosh's.[187] As Kemeny observed, the mixed response in the press might lead one to conclude that the evening ended in a draw.[188]

With benefit of hindsight, the outcome of the skirmish may seem very different, however. According to W. B. Carnochan, who provided an astute analysis of the debate,[189] McCosh argued in his speech for what would ultimately be called the distribution model of general education. In the McCosh tradition, Carnochan stressed, educators today "would say students need some acquaintance with several 'fields' of knowledge."[190] One can see his point: on the surface, McCosh's trinity of studies sounds like the precursor of contemporary universities' regard for requiring coursework in divisions such as the arts and humanities, the social sciences, and the natural sciences. But this likeness does not hold up to more careful scrutiny. McCosh's Princeton

---

[185] McCosh 1885b: 23.

[186] E.g., anonymous 1885g, h, i, o, and p.

[187] E.g., anonymous c, e, f, k, and m; Chamberlain 1885; Cuyler 1885; Nemo 1885; Patton 1885; anonymous 1886c; Levermore 1886; Kemeny 1998: 247 n. 73 (quotes a letter praising McCosh's performance).

[188] Kemeny 1998: 247 n. 73. Wertenbaker (1946: 307) contends that McCosh won the debate, but his book aimed to celebrate Princeton's achievements as part of the institution's bicentennial (v) and cites only one letter to the press to make his case: that of Daniel Chamberlain (1885), who, as we saw in Chapter 3, was strongly disposed to McCosh's case from the start. Many reports on the debate also came from the pens of Princetonians and/or those writing for religious periodicals. Cf. Kemeny 1998: 59.

[189] Carnochan 1993: 9–21.

[190] Ibid. 18.

required particular courses of its students,[191] not, as Norman Foerster memorably put it, "required electives" from different disciplinary branches, as today's colleges and universities tend to do.[192] The rationales seem similar, but Princeton's curriculum in the late nineteenth century did not provide the model for the dominant approach to general education today.

In any case, McCosh's contribution to the 1885 debate with Eliot helps demonstrate the weaknesses of the distribution model to general education from a humanist perspective: it leaves untouched Eliot's skills-based conception of higher education.[193] This is a major shortcoming, especially since Eliot and other first-generation scientific democrats latched onto the skills-based approach to learning as a means to limit the role of the classical humanities in American higher education. Thus, though A. Lawrence Lowell, as Eliot's successor at Harvard, reformed the institution's free-elective curriculum by adding distributional requirements and the concentration system,[194] Eliot's overarching rationale for higher education has remained dominant in the US. Despite the mild tempering of Eliot's curricular anarchy, Eliot's competitive, laissez-faire vision of university life rules the roost.[195] It is in this environment—Eliot's environment—that the modern humanities see themselves incessantly threatened.

Meanwhile, McCosh's plea to retain prescribed Greek on religious grounds soon proved unsuccessful. As Princeton, partly under McCosh's guidance, transformed into a research university, it began to shed its evangelical religiosity in ways that McCosh himself would have found disconcerting.[196] Ultimately, McCosh's theologically centered and skills-based arguments for the classical humanities lost out in the Battle of the Classics. In his debate with Eliot, McCosh did not entirely go astray: he offered a number of strong retorts, chiefly about the likely motivations of undergraduates. But he failed to provide a radical critique of Eliot's position, which questioned the value of his utilitarian, skills-based, and consumerist vision of education. McCosh

---

[191] See, e.g., McCosh 1884: 7; anonymous 1886a: 48. Although Princeton's grouping of senior electives in accordance with the trinity (see anonymous 1886a: 48–49) can be seen as a closer approximation of a distribution system, this is not really the case, since students at Princeton could choose any electives they liked and did not need to spread their electives among different divisions.

[192] Foerster 1969: 47.

[193] Thus, as Morison (1942: 446) notes, the distribution system pertains to the management of electives, not to the reintroduction of uniform content. For examples of McCosh offering a defense of his preferred curriculum on the basis of the branches of instruction introduced, rather than content, see, e.g., McCosh 1868: 73 and 1888: 20.

[194] On this topic, see Chapter 2, this volume.

[195] Cf. Carnochan 1993: 11.

[196] See Hoeveler 1981: 347–48; Kemeny 1998: esp. 15, 78.

never noted how distant Eliot's pedagogical philosophy was from the tenets of Renaissance humanism and did not explain the value of a humanist approach to higher learning. In all, Princeton's president offered some sound critiques of Eliot's policies in their specifics but left the ideological foundation of Eliot's system unchallenged.

Did anyone involved in the late-nineteenth- and early-twentieth-century disputes over the classical languages provide a different—and more convincing—rationale for the humanities? In the next chapter, we shall encounter a thinker who did just that.

5

Humanism vs. Humanitarianism

The truly free man wants only what he can do and does only what he pleases. That is my fundamental maxim. It need only be applied to childhood for all the rules of education to flow from it.

— Jean-Jacques Rousseau, *Emile* (1762)

From the present tendency to regard humanism as an abbreviated and convenient form for humanitarianism there must arise every manner of confusion.

— Irving Babbitt, *Literature and the American College* (1908)

An Intellectual Battle Royal

"Emerson once wondered whether America would ever grow up to the point where there could be a first-class, Nation-wide dispute about something intellectually important," announced *The Boston Globe* in a cheeky column from June 1930. "Well, Emerson died too soon: this, apparently, is IT."[1] Fifteen writers associated with the so-called New Humanism,[2] an informal movement of literary and social criticism, had recently published *Humanism and America*, a collective manifesto of sorts.[3] Five weeks before the *Globe* attempted to explicate the intellectual battle royal that the book's publication helped spark, Irving Babbitt (1865–1933), the most insightful thinker associated with New Humanism and its intellectual progenitor, debated the American critics Carl Van Doren (1885–1950) and Henry Seidel Canby (1878–1961) on the merits and demerits of his movement in front of a packed

---

[1] Anonymous 1930 (emphasis in the original).
[2] The movement was also branded *American Humanism*. From here on, the capitalization of *Humanism* and *Humanist* will refer to New Humanism and New Humanist, whereas the lower-case terms will describe *humanism* and *humanist* generically.
[3] Foerster 1930a.

audience at Carnegie Hall in New York City.[4] Later that month, a band of detractors, including such luminaries as Edmund Wilson, Lewis Mumford, and Allen Tate, responded with *The Critique of Humanism*, a book-length assault on Babbitt and company.[5] The result, the *Globe* maintained, was "such a din and such a frantic tumult of name calling as nothing else in the recent chronicles of Time and Western Man."[6] For a brief spell, New Humanism seemed to be all the rage.

But this was a din and tumult of long gestation. Babbitt and his confrère Paul Elmer More (1864–1937), the elder statesmen of the movement, had been contributing pieces in favor of New Humanism as far back as the 1890s.[7] As its name suggests, New Humanism maintained a firm connection with higher education and the classical languages. In fact, Babbitt's first published essay, which appeared in the March 1897 issue of *The Atlantic Monthly*, was called "The Rational Study of the Classics."[8] This article, in turn, became an essential part of Babbitt's first monograph, *Literature and the American College: Essays in Defense of the Humanities* (1908),[9] a book in which Babbitt presented a full-scale critique of the American university movement and provided a strikingly different apologia for ancient Greek and Latin from those appearing earlier in the Battle of the Classics.

Throughout the course of a productive academic career, Babbitt composed numerous books and articles,[10] all of which differ in their focus and emphases. But the main thrust of all Babbitt's work was the exposition of his philosophy of life, which would come to bear the moniker New Humanism. Since Babbitt connected his Humanism (a label he preferred to New

---

[4] On this debate, which took place on May 9, 1930, see, e.g., Colum 1930; Levin 1966: 339; Hoeveler 1977: 25; Slayton 1986: 235; Ryn 1995b: xx; Panichas 1999: 204; Jewett 2012: 219.

[5] Grattan 1930a. An April 30, 1930, letter to Babbitt from Josiah Titzall, who worked for Brewer and Warren, the publisher of *The Critique of Humanism*, mentions that the press would publish the book on May 26 of that year (Irving Babbitt Papers, HUG 1185 at the Harvard University Archives, Box 11, "B, 1898–1933"). For more on the Babbitt Papers, see n. 15.

[6] Anonymous 1930. For other pieces discussing the controversy over New Humanism, see, e.g., Jones 1928; Canby 1930; Colum 1930; Rand 1932; Maynard 1935.

[7] Hoeveler (1977: 12) notes, however, that Babbitt's *Literature and the American College*, originally published in 1908, was the first major outline of New Humanism.

[8] Babbitt 1897. See Foerster 1930b: vii; Slayton 1986: 230; Panichas 1999: 198. This article was based on an 1895 lecture of the same name Babbitt delivered at the University of Wisconsin.

[9] Babbitt 1986.

[10] For a complete chronological listing of Babbitt's writings, see Babbitt 1940: 251–59, reprinted in Babbitt 1995: 251–59 (this book is a new edition of Babbitt 1940). Both these books contain an index to Babbitt's collected works (Babbitt 1940: 263–360 and 1995: 263–360).

Humanism)[11] to education, all Babbitt's writings contain at least some reflection on curricular matters. *Literature and the American College*, however, amounts to the fullest expression of Babbitt's pedagogical ideals. For this reason, those interested in New Humanism's defense of the classics must pay particular attention to it. But Babbitt later supplemented this work with further reflections on American higher education: as we shall see, Babbitt's 1920 essay "English and the Discipline of Ideas,"[12] and a piece from 1929 called "President Eliot and American Education"[13] prove especially valuable windows into Babbitt's pedagogical philosophy.

This chapter surveys Babbitt's writings in defense of the classical and modern humanities. Although historians of higher education have typically viewed Babbitt as an educational reactionary,[14] it will demonstrate that he was nothing of the sort. In fact, Babbitt's critique of the American research university and its philosophical underpinnings provides a more satisfying intellectual foundation for the humanities and their upstream, productive role in society than do typical contemporary defenses. The chapter will demonstrate that Babbitt offered a radical critique of professionalized American higher education and the problematic conception of human nature that informs it. It will show that Babbitt, with one foot firmly anchored in the ancient and Renaissance past, fundamentally recast the humanistic tradition to fit the needs of the contemporary world. Importantly, the chapter argues that Babbitt avoided the skills-based rationales for Latin and ancient Greek that had proved so underwhelming during the Battle of the Classics. In their place, Babbitt underscored the unique role that specific humanistic works must play in American higher learning in order for the nation to flourish. Although by no means foolproof or perfectly suited to the vicissitudes of the present, his ideas have much to teach today's beleaguered proponents of the humanistic disciplines.

---

[11] Brennan and Yarbrough 1987: 19.

[12] Babbitt 1920.

[13] Reprinted in Babbitt 1940: 198–224, the piece originally appeared in the January 1929 issue of *The Forum*.

[14] E.g., Harris 1970: 49–79; Butts 1971: esp. 347; Barney 1974: 147–51; Hoeveler 1977: 107; Rudolph 1977: 239; Spanos 1985: 29–50, esp. 38–39; Smilie 2016: esp. 113–14. Cf. Hovey 1986. Smilie (2010: esp. 199) recognizes that Babbitt did not advocate a return to the classical colleges. For discussions of Babbitt's philosophy of education, see, e.g., Mercier 1928: 55–59; McMahon 1931: 42–45; Barney 1974: 105–56; Brennan and Yarbrough 1987: 103–12; Carnochan 1993: 63; Hindus 1994: 45; Davis 2006; Smilie 2010, 2012, 2013, and 2016; Jewett 2012: 198–200, 216–19.

"The Warring Buddha of Harvard"

Although scholarly preoccupation with his educational elitism may lead one to think otherwise, Irving Babbitt in his early days experienced something of a rough-and-tumble existence. He was born in Dayton, Ohio, on August 2, 1865, the fourth of five children of Edwin and Augusta (Darling) Babbitt.[15] Though discussions of Babbitt's life occasionally refer to Edwin Babbitt as a physician, this may be a technically accurate but misleading characterization of his career.[16] Edwin Babbitt was something of a theosophically inclined crackpot. At various points throughout his life, for example, he deemed himself a "magnetist," a "psycho-physician," and a "cromo-therapist," who vouched for the supposed health benefits of colored lights.[17] Although he authored numerous self-help books and served as the dean of a presumably short-lived institution called the College of Fine Forces, Edwin was never capable of roping in a sufficient number of wealthy patients and thus was a poor provider for his family. This seems like important biographical information for those attempting to understand the thought of Edwin's son Irving, since one can read much of Irving Babbitt's work as a repudiation of his father's sentimental spiritualism.

Thanks to his father's precarious ventures, Irving moved around a fair amount as a youngster, ultimately graduating second in his class from Woodward High School, a public institution in Cincinnati, Ohio.[18] Since his family did not possess enough money for him to attend his dream school of Harvard,[19] Babbitt spent a further year at Woodward High, studying

[15] On Babbitt's biography, see, e.g., the contributions to Manchester and Shepard 1941; Barney 1974: 29–58; Hoeveler 1977: 5–10; Nevin 1984: 5–7, 12–32; Slayton 1986; Brennan and Yarbrough 1987: 1–27, 58–78; Ryn 1991: xii–xix, 1995b: xv–xix, and 1997b: 10–12; Panichas 1999: 194–206; Dillon 2006: 59–60. Many details of Babbitt's life come from a brief but valuable biographical sketch his widow, Dora Drew Babbitt (1877–1944), provided for the Manchester and Shepard 1941 collection (ix–xiii). This chapter supplements published biographical material about Babbitt with information from the Irving Babbitt Papers found in the Harvard University Archives (HUG 1185; henceforth referred to as IBP; courtesy of the Harvard University Archives).

[16] In an August 30, 1898, letter to his son (IBP, Box 1, "Family Correspondence, 1865, 1884–1937"), Edwin Babbitt's letterhead refers to him as possessing both an M.D. and an LL.D. It is unclear how accurate these designations are; see Levin 1966: 331.

[17] Brennan and Yarbrough 1987: 8. On Edwin Babbitt, see, e.g., D. Babbitt in Manchester and Shepard 1941: ix; Warren 1956: 145–46; Levin 1966: 331–32; Barney 1974: 30–31; Hoeveler 1977: 5, 153; Nevin 1984: 5; Slayton 1986: 227–28; Brennan and Yarbrough 1987: 3–10, 17; Ryn 1991: xii; Hindus 1994: 18; Panichas 1999: 194.

[18] This graduation occurred in 1884. See D. Babbitt in Manchester and Shepard 1941: x; Slayton 1986: 228. Cf. Ryn 1991: xiii; Panichas 1999: 195. In 1876, Babbitt's mother passed away when he was around eleven. See D. Babbitt in Manchester and Shepard 1941: ix; Ryn 1991: xii–xiii; Panichas 1999: 195.

[19] D. Babbitt in Manchester and Shepard 1941: xi; Slayton 1986: 228.

chemistry and civil engineering.[20] Ultimately, Babbitt's uncles loaned him the requisite funds, and in the fall of 1885 Babbitt traveled to Cambridge, Massachusetts, to study as an undergraduate at the nation's oldest institution of higher learning.[21] By this time President Charles W. Eliot's free-elective curriculum had transformed Harvard, allowing undergraduates great choice in regard to coursework. Babbitt stuck mostly to the ancient and modern languages, graduating in 1889 magna cum laude with high honors in classics.[22]

It was during his undergraduate days that Babbitt would begin to move away from his father's intellectual influence and develop many of the ideas that would become key to New Humanism.[23] Although he excelled at language study in college, Babbitt quickly grew critical of the scholarly ideals of many literature professors there.[24] In a contribution to a collection of reflections on Babbitt's life, William F. Giese (1864–1943), an undergraduate classmate and lifelong friend, explained Babbitt's run-ins with a Harvard professoriate turning rapidly toward the professionalized spirit of philological study emanating from Germany. Giese wrote,

Harvard had at that time a shining galaxy of classical scholars, but they were in general specialists of that straiter sect which the prestige of Germany had set in the high places. Babbitt was to speak of them and their colleagues in the modern field as the Philological Syndicate. While never refusing to pay high tribute to their scholarship, the exacting standards of which he emulated, he took their pedagogy half humorously and half satirically. He especially rallied the professional tone of awe with which they discussed their learned mysteries and the contented narrowness of vision which confinement in didactic grooves is so apt to generate.[25]

"He was," Giese continued, "perpetually girding at" the "pedantry" the Philological Syndicate displayed in the classroom, consenting "to suffer from

[20] This occurred in the 1884–85 academic year (Ryn 1997b: 65–66), after Babbitt spent a summer working on his uncle Albert's ranch in Cheyenne, Wyoming (D. Babbitt in Manchester and Shepard 1941: x; Slayton 1986: 228).
[21] Ryn 1991: xiii and 1995b: xvi.
[22] D. Babbitt in Manchester and Shepard 1941: xi; Levin 1966: 333; Slayton 1986: 229; Ryn 1991: xiii; Panichas 1999: 197. For a list of Babbitt's undergraduate coursework, see Barney 1974: 238.
[23] On Babbitt's intellectual consistency, see, e.g., More in Manchester and Shepard 1941: 325; Warren 1956: 144; Dakin 1960: 323; Hoeveler 1977: 9; Panichas 1999: 40; Smilie 2010: 26.
[24] This disapproval was especially the case in regard to George Lyman Kittredge (1860–1941), a professor of English literature who would become a bête noire for Babbitt.
[25] Giese in Manchester and Shepard 1941: 15. Babbitt referred in print to the Philological Syndicate: e.g., Babbitt 1986: 141, 148.

it as little as was humanly possible."[26] This attitude, which incurred some of the faculty's acute displeasure,[27] would have an undeniable effect on Babbitt's academic career.

Immediately upon graduation, Babbitt, needing to repay the money his family had loaned to him, took the first job a teachers' agency had offered, at the College of Montana in Deer Lodge, a small Presbyterian outfit in a dilapidated mill town, where he taught introductory Latin and ancient Greek for two years.[28] With money saved up from his time in Montana, Babbitt then completed graduate work in Sanskrit and Pali at both the Sorbonne[29] and Harvard.[30] While earning his A.M. at Harvard,[31] he met Paul Elmer More, who would later become a prominent literary critic, editor, academic, lifelong confidante, and one of Babbitt's first converts to New Humanism.[32] Babbitt also had the good fortune to experience a graduate course on Dante with Harvard's Charles Eliot Norton, a polymath professor whose capacious, moralistic approach to the modern humanities provided a pedagogical model far more attractive to the young Babbitt than those on offer through the auspices of the Philological Syndicate.[33] Deciding against the earning of a Ph.D., whose Teutonic narrowness he abhorred, Babbitt in the fall of 1893 procured a year-long appointment as a sabbatical replacement in French, Spanish, and Italian at Williams College.[34]

Although it would be his dream to teach the classics at the university level, Babbitt's unfashionable views on scientific philology and scholarly

[26] Giese in Manchester and Shepard 1941: 15. Babbitt took it as a badge of honor that at one time during his undergraduate career he had the record for the most skipped classes at Harvard (Giese in Manchester and Shepard 1941: 15).

[27] This was particularly true in regard to Kittredge: in his senior year, Babbitt earned a C– in Kittredge's English 2 course (Barney 1974: 238). On Kitteridge as the key figure in Babbitt's portrayal of the Philological Syndicate, see Levin 1991: 28.

[28] D. Babbitt in Manchester and Shepard 1941: xi–xii; Slayton 1986: 229; Hoeveler 1977: 8; Brennan and Yarbrough 1987: 15–16.

[29] At the Sorbonne during the 1891–92 academic year Babbitt studied Sanskrit, Pali, and Indian philosophy with the Indologist and orientalist Sylvain Lévi (1863–1935). See D. Babbitt in Manchester and Shepard 1941: xii; Slayton 1986: 229.

[30] Babbitt completed his graduate work at Harvard in the 1892–93 academic year, with Charles R. Lanman (1850–1941) as his chief mentor. On Babbitt's and/or More's days as graduate students at Harvard, see, e.g., D. Babbitt in Manchester and Shepard 1941: xii; Dakin 1960: 48–49; Duggan 1966: 15; Slayton 1986: 229; Brennan and Yarbrough: 1987: 18; Ryn 1991: xiv; Panichas 1999: 197.

[31] For a list of Babbitt's graduate coursework at Harvard, see Barney 1974: 239.

[32] On More's life and work, see, e.g., Mercier 1928: 126–87; Shafer 1935; Leander 1937 and 1974; Elliott 1938: esp. 46–65; Dakin 1960: Duggan 1966; Hoeveler 1977: esp. 10–12.

[33] On Norton's influence on Babbitt, see, e.g., Giese in Manchester and Shepard 1941: 14–15; Levin 1966: 329; Barney 1974: 39; Nevin 1984: 17–18; Brennan and Yarbrough 1987: 19–20; Turner 1999: 345. Babbitt (1986: 70) thanked Norton in the preface to his first book.

[34] See D. Babbitt in Manchester and Shepard 1941: xii; Slayton 1986: 230.

specialization ensured that he had a rockier career than he had hoped. In the fall of 1894, Babbitt returned to Harvard, where he had longed to join the classics department. Unfortunately, this department, hobbled by lower enrollments due to the implementation of President Eliot's free-elective curriculum,[35] had no openings, and it is distinctly possible that its faculty members, recalling Babbitt as an obstreperous undergraduate, would have wanted nothing to do with him.[36] But the removal of an instructor in the French department for plagiarism compelled its chairman to hunt for a last-minute replacement and thus Babbitt was hired as an instructor in French.[37] He would remain a faculty member of French and, ultimately, comparative literature at Harvard from 1894 until his death in 1933.[38] Yet Babbitt's perspective on education and academia caused trouble for him at Harvard. The institution's classicists and even many of his colleagues in the French department routinely dismissed his ideas. Babbitt's forceful personality and powerful opinions seem to have encouraged strong reactions: not for nothing did G. R. Elliott (1883–1963), another convert to New Humanism, call Babbitt the "Warring Buddha of Harvard."[39] It most certainly did not help Babbitt's prospects that he expressed deep criticisms of the free-elective system and thus took strong exception to the very curricular model that was Charles Eliot's signature as Harvard's president from 1869 until his retirement in 1909.[40]

Almost let go from Harvard at various points in his career, Babbitt after numerous years as an instructor finally earned a promotion to the rank of assistant professor in 1902.[41] He was granted a full professorship in 1912,

[35] Ryn 1991: xiv.

[36] See, e.g., Harris 1970: 9, 71; Hoeveler 1977: 9; Panichas 1999: 198. On Babbitt's flustering of a Greek professor while an undergraduate at Harvard, see Giese in Manchester and Shepard 1941: 1.

[37] Brennan and Yarbrough 1987: 20. On Babbitt's initial appointment at Harvard, see also Mercier 1928: 49; D. Babbitt in Manchester and Shepard 1941: xii; Slayton 1986: 230; Ryn 1995b: xvi–xvii.

[38] As of 1896, Babbitt was supplementing his Harvard salary by teaching extra classes at Radcliffe College (see Slayton 1986: 231; Brennan and Yarbrough 1987: 21). Thus he met his future wife, Dora (May) Drew Babbitt, a Radcliffe graduate whom he wed on June 12, 1900. See Nevin 1984: 13; Slayton 1986: 231; Ryn 1991: xv and 1995b: xviii; Panichas 1999: 199.

[39] Elliott 1938: 56. On the Buddhist influence on Babbitt's thought, see the sections "The Particular and the Universal" and "Is Humanism a Religion?," this chapter. See also Dakin 1960: 93.

[40] For Babbitt's criticisms of Eliot's approach to higher education, see, e.g., Babbitt 1924: 301–2; 1940: 198–224; 1968: 227–28; 1986: 95–99, 122, 204. On this topic, see Veysey 1965: 248; Hawkins 1972: 298; Hoeveler 1977: 9; Smilie 2010: 135–69. In an April 1, 1906, letter to More (IBP, Box 9, "Babbitt-More Correspondence, December 1895–April 1914, pages 1–167"), Babbitt mentions that he considers *Literature and the American College* an attack on Eliot. Babbitt spoke positively about Eliot's upbringing and character (e.g., Babbitt 1940: 198–99), however.

[41] D. Babbitt in Manchester and Shepard 1941: xii; Nevin 1984: 13; Slayton 1986: 231; Brennan and Yarbrough 1987: 22; Ryn 1991: xiv–xv; Panichas 1999: 199. Prior to this promotion, Babbitt began to inquire through More about vacancies in the classics department at Bryn Mawr and through Giese

in large part, it seems, because he had received an outside offer of employ-
ment from the University of Illinois.[42] Ultimately, Babbitt became a popular
and influential teacher at Harvard, where he numbered T. S. Eliot, Walter
Lippmann, Van Wyck Brooks, and the future Harvard president Nathan
Pusey among his students.[43] Despite his unfashionable approach to education and scholarship, Babbitt developed into a prominent academic, earning
distinguished lectureships at universities such as Yale, Stanford, and the
Sorbonne, and winning election to the French Institute in 1926[44] and the
Academy of Arts and Letters in 1930.[45]

The Two Humanisms

From the start of his writing career, Babbitt demonstrated a keener interest
in connecting his pedagogical ideals to the history of the humanities than
did many traditionalists of his era. Thus, for example, Babbitt commenced
his first monograph with a chapter called "What Is Humanism?"[46] Here and
in other writings,[47] Babbitt implicitly supplied two definitions. One might
call the first historical, or lower-case humanism: Babbitt traced the origins
of the humanistic movement in antiquity to the Latin words *humanus* and
humanitas and dilated on the second-century-AD Roman author Aulus
Gellius' definition of the latter term in his *Attic Nights*.[48] Further, Babbitt

---

about vacancies at the University of Wisconsin. See Babbitt's letter of March 5, 1896, to More (IBP,
Box 9, "Babbitt-More Correspondence, December 1895–April 1914, pages 1–167").

[42] D. Babbitt in Manchester and Shepard 1941: xii; Dakin 1960: 113; Levin 1966: 321–22; Nevin
1984: 24; Slayton 1986: 232; Ryn 1991: xv and 1995b: xviii; Panichas 1999: 201.

[43] Although he ultimately made a partial break with Babbitt over religious matters, Eliot deemed
himself originally "a disciple of Mr. Babbitt" (Eliot 1964: 429). As an undergraduate, Lippmann
disagreed with Babbitt, but his later work demonstrates Babbitt's influence. See, e.g., Ryn 1991: x.
Brooks disliked Babbitt's ideas but respected him (Hoeveler 1977: 8–9; Nevin 1984: 25). Pusey, a
devoted pupil of Babbitt (see, e.g., Levin 1966: 326), established the Irving Babbitt Professorship in
Comparative Literature at Harvard in 1960.

[44] D. Babbitt in Manchester and Shepard 1941: xii; Brennan and Yarbrough 1987: 72–73; Panichas
1999: 203.

[45] D. Babbitt in Manchester and Shepard 1941: xii–xiii; Slayton 1986: 235; Ryn 1991: xviii.

[46] Babbitt 1986: 71–87. The soundest examinations of Babbitt include Leander 1974; Ryn 1977 and
1991; Nevin 1984. See also Leander 1937 (with important changes later regarding the concept of the
inner check; see Ryn 1995b: xxiv n. 11).

[47] See, e.g., Babbitt 1930 and 1968: xi–xliv. See also Babbitt 1940: 229–30 (on the goals of
humanism).

[48] Babbitt 1986: 73–76. On Gellius and his definition of *humanitas*, see Chapter 2, this volume.
Babbitt rightly concluded that Gellius' definition was partially inaccurate.

noted that intellectuals did not self-identify as "humanists" until the Renaissance and that the noun *humanism* was of even later origin.[49]

Babbitt's second vision of humanism—what we might call upper-case Humanism or New Humanism—used the first definition as a launching point but amounted to a full-scale synthesis and reimagining, which repacked the movement as a distinct philosophy of life and civilization. This bipartite vision of the humanities left Babbitt open to charges that he misled readers: he confused the historical humanistic movement (which in his scholarship he took pains to elucidate and thus clearly understood) with his own idiosyncratic approach to the Good Life.[50]

Such criticism possesses some merits. Babbitt did not merely unearth humanistic history; rather, he also provided a creative refashioning of the movement, and thus he could even prove capable of criticizing such quintessential humanistic figures as Petrarch for failing to live up to his standards.[51] But Babbitt's reimagined Humanism has much to recommend it, in both its philosophical and pragmatic dimensions. In fact, Babbitt's attempt to encapsulate humanist wisdom from the past enabled him to proffer a fuller philosophical description of the movement as a way of life. Far more specifically than did his Renaissance predecessors, Babbitt explained the goals and values associated with humanistic education. In addition, Babbitt promoted a greatly broadened humanism. This equipped New Humanism to encompass far more than strictly historical humanism allowed—thus rendering the movement more suitable to the needs of an industrializing and democratizing America in the early twentieth century. And Babbitt's expanded vision remains highly valuable for those pondering the potential strengths of a humanistic education today.

The Higher and Lower Will

In the 1880s, as we have noted in previous chapters, defenders of the classical humanities had quibbled with reformers such as Charles Eliot over the comparative effects of various academic subjects on students' mental faculties.

---

[49] Babbitt 1930: 26 and 1986: 77.

[50] For examples of such charges, see Cowley 1930: 64–65; Hazlitt 1930: 96; Wilson 1930: 47–48.

[51] For Babbitt's criticisms of Petrarch, see, e.g., Babbitt 1986: 91, 138, 164. Cf. 187–88. Babbitt also occasionally criticized Renaissance humanism: e.g., Babbitt 1910: 88; 1986: 76–79. Cf. Babbitt 1977: 222. On this topic, see, e.g., Mercier 1928: 51; McMahon 1931: 17.

Through this means they implicitly demonstrated that they agreed with their modernist opponents on first principles. For both sides in the early debates of the Battle of the Classics, the chief goal of education was the disciplining and training of the mind. Babbitt, by contrast, provided a radical critique of scientific democrats such as Eliot, which highlighted the unrealistic vision of human nature that informed their approach to higher education.

As far back as his first book, Babbitt anchored his conception of humanism in its historical inception as the *studia humanitatis* in Cicero's Rome. In sympathy with Renaissance humanists such as Petrarch and Leonardo Bruni, he also stressed that a proper education amounted to the improvement of the self through the use of models from the past. Unlike fellow advocates of "liberal culture" from his era, Babbitt attempted to offer a philosophically precise rationale for this inward-directed education.

In accordance with what he took to be much classical, Christian, and Buddhist thought, Babbitt stressed the duality of human nature.[52] To Babbitt, human beings possess both impulsive desires (what the philosopher Henri Bergson, Babbitt's contemporary, called the *élan vital*)[53] and the ability to restrain or affirm these desires (what Babbitt called the *frein vital*, "inner check," or "higher will").[54] While the term "inner check" (confusingly) suggests pure restraint, in Babbitt's view it serves more as an ethical compass or means of calibrating moral life, with both a restraining and an affirming component.[55] With a nod to Diderot, Babbitt referred to the struggle between one's impulsive desires and one's inner check as "the civil war in the cave,"[56] and he believed that a humanistic education must present students with works of great profundity and insight that engage students' imaginations.[57] Such works, he believed, would enable them to strengthen the inner check on their longings. Through this means, human beings could limit their

---

[52] See, e.g., Babbitt 1936: 82, 104–8, 1968: 77–79, 254, and 1991: 147, 374.

[53] On Bergson's so-called vitalism and its popularity in America, see Jewett 2012: 152–53. For Babbitt's criticisms of Bergson, see, e.g., Babbitt 1912, 1977: 382–83. For criticisms of Babbitt's views on Bergson from a critic of New Humanism, see Grabo 1933: 33–34.

[54] For helpful examinations of what Babbitt and Paul More meant by "inner check," see Leander 1974: esp. 3–4, 6–7, 20; Ryn 1977: esp. 254, 1991: xxxiii–xxxvi, and 1997: 30–32, 150.

[55] Leander (1974: 4) explained the process of Babbitt's and More's concept of the inner check thus: "The working of the moral sense (i.e., the awareness of the ethical ultimate) on the passions, accordingly, has two inseparable aspects: negating and affirming, checking and approving. The moral sense begins its work as an inner check but proceeds by means of deliberation to acceptance of some course of action as good. The course of action which is approved participates in the good; the initial check ('Is this good?') which sets us deliberating, is an intuition of the ethical ultimate, the One, the good, or whatever we prefer to call it."

[56] E.g., Babbitt 1940: 155, 157 and 1991: 150, 187.

[57] On this topic, see, e.g., Davis 2006: esp. 5.

expansive desires when such desires are excessive, as in the early twentieth century, in his view, or affirm them in conditions of excessive self-restraint, as in the medieval West.[58] Thus they might live sounder and happier lives. Of cardinal importance to Babbitt's humanism, then, was the analysis of literary and artistic masterworks that would provide for the young the most compelling visions of the good, the true, and the beautiful.[59]

The Romantic Revolt against Humanism

Unfortunately, thought Babbitt, university reformers such as Eliot had abandoned this conception of education—and thus had abandoned humanism. As far as he was concerned, modern American higher education had traded in its erstwhile commitment to humanism for a shortsighted, all-encompassing devotion to humanitarianism. He identified two types of humanitarianism that, in the absence of a humanist counterweight, were together destroying higher learning in the US:[60] scientific naturalism (which he identified with Francis Bacon)[61] and sentimental naturalism (which he identified with Jean-Jacques Rousseau as the quintessential exponent of romanticism).[62]

Like the romantics more generally, Rousseau denied the duality of human nature: he believed that human beings were intrinsically good and that society and its institutions had corrupted them. Thus sentimental naturalists

[58] See Ryn 1991: xxxvi.

[59] One might presume that Babbitt's inclination to link a proper liberal arts education to the cultivation of one's inner check was itself a kind of skills-boosterism and thus conclude that his approach to higher learning did not eschew the instrumental rationales offered during the Battle of the Classics. But it is simplifying and distorting to suggest that Babbitt's notion of cultivating one's inner check is a skill. The inner check for Babbitt is not simply a reining in of impulse. Rather, Babbitt posited that it was one and the same as a human being's higher will. If this sort of soul-shaping can be deemed a "skill," it is such a complicated and amorphous skill that one could deem any human activity a skill. Further, even if one insists on reducing the cultivation of the higher will to a skill, it is a skill that, according to Babbitt, requires literary, philosophical, religious, and artistic masterworks to achieve. It thus requires the humanities.

[60] Babbitt thought that these two types of humanitarianism may appear to be working at cross purposes but were actually mutually reinforcing and based on the same philosophical principles.

[61] See esp. Babbitt 1986: 89–101.

[62] See esp. Babbitt 1940: 225–47, 1986: esp. 88–108, and 1991. Similarly, Hirsch (1987: xiv–xv, 118–19) perceived that Rousseau was the chief intellectual influence on American education in the twentieth century. Hirsch, however, thought (1–2) that cultural literacy was valuable largely because it made economic prosperity possible. As we shall see, Babbitt's rationale for literary study was different. On the pedagogical conceptions of Babbitt and Hirsch, see Smilie 2013. The comparatively late appearance in the Battle of the Classics of Babbitt's argument about the romantic influence on American higher education does not imply that romanticism had an impact on the colleges after Darwinism did.

such as Rousseau preached the cultivation of one's innate impulses. To such thinkers, there was nothing to be learned from tradition; or, to put things slightly differently, there was only one thing to be learned—that it was bad.

Babbitt viewed Rousseau as the intellectual inspiration for Eliot's free-elective system.[63] In Eliot's scheme, Babbitt concluded, "There is no general norm, no law for man, as the humanist believed, with reference to which the individual should select [courses]; he should make his selection entirely with reference to his own temperament and its (supposedly) unique requirements. The wisdom of all the ages is to be naught as compared with the inclination of a sophomore."[64] To the sentimental naturalist, with his rosy and unrealistic impression of human nature, there was no need for young people to improve their characters, because human beings were by nature good. Thus, thought Babbitt, scientific naturalists, following the path of Francis Bacon, could eschew the goal of character development in favor of the false path of gaining power over the natural world. Humanitarians—whether of the sentimental or utilitarian variety—denied the "civil war in the cave," replacing it with a war between human being and society.[65] But without regard for personal improvement through the cultivation of one's higher will, Babbitt feared, supposed humanitarianism would unleash horrors on the world.[66]

Through his critique of the philosophy behind the scientific democrats' views on education, Babbitt exposed their fundamental hostility to humanism. As we discussed in the previous chapter, at his ninetieth birthday celebration, Eliot himself—whom Babbitt considered a scientific naturalist par excellence—offered some revealing advice to the students in attendance: "Look forward and not backward—Look out and not in."[67] Here, according to Babbitt's terminology, Eliot provided a textbook illustration of the denial of the civil war of the cave. As Eliot often contended, the purpose of education was training for service and power.[68] To the humanist, by contrast,

---

[63] E.g., Babbitt 1986: 96, 120–21. See Rousseau (1979: 84) for an example of what Babbitt meant by the Rousseauistic influence on free election.

[64] Babbitt 1986: 96. This conclusion does not imply, however, that Babbitt aimed simply to reintroduce the prescribed curricula of the early American colleges. See, e.g., Babbitt 1986: 184. But cf. Babbitt 1986: 115–16, 126, 165. Interestingly, Eliot claimed that he favored curricular free election because it encouraged self-control in students; see Eliot 1911: xi.

[65] See, e.g., Babbitt 1991: 130, 187.

[66] On this topic, see, e.g., Mercier 1928: 64–65, which focuses on Babbitt's linking of naturalism to the outbreak of World War I.

[67] Quoted in James 1930 2: 309. Babbitt (1940: 207, 228) noted this advice and linked it to Eliot's belief that happiness was to be found outside the individual. See Smilie 2012: 95.

[68] For examples of Eliot viewing undergraduate education as training for service and/or power, see, e.g., Eliot 1899: 441, 1923: 36, 39, and 1926: 168, 171. According to Boyd (1934: 33), Eliot was a Baconian.

education's goals were wisdom and character. This contrast goes some way toward demonstrating the hostility of the scientific democrats—the architects of the modern university in America—to the humanist project. Implicitly vouching for an altruistic human nature, such humanitarians neglected the inner-focused work of soul-crafting, presuming that the young would naturally use the skills they had acquired in their schooling in beneficent service to society.[69]

The unmasking of the philosophy underpinning the modernists' views on education helps situate the troubles besetting the humanities in American higher learning from the late nineteenth century onward. According to Babbitt, the free-elective curriculum is the product of a romantic conception of education, which is typically aligned with scientific naturalism. Undergraduates, like consumers, can supposedly best determine the coursework necessary for them to become educated. This system thus minimizes—if it does not entirely extinguish—the wisdom of the past as a model for the present. As Babbitt put it in a summation of the views of Eliot and like-minded humanitarians, "This philosophy culminates in a doctrine of progress that would seem to be in serious conflict with the wisdom of the ages; for it is plain that there can be no such wisdom without the assumption in some form of a core of normal human experience that is set above the shifting tides of circumstance."[70] The scientific democrats, with their cult of progress, cut students off from tradition.[71]

As Babbitt keenly recognized, curricular free election, which leaves all up to a student's fancy, embodies the presentist outlook of the scientific naturalist and the sentimental naturalist.[72] It thus undercuts the humanities, which, arguably more than any other facet of American higher education, are centered on the evaluation of meaningful works of art, literature, philosophy, and religion from the past. The same holds true for the distribution requirements system that mildly modified curricular free election in the early twentieth century and that the political scientist A. Lawrence Lowell introduced at Harvard upon his replacement of Eliot as the institution's

---

[69] According to Smilie (2016: 121), for example, John Dewey believed that children naturally aim to serve others.

[70] Babbitt 1940: 199.

[71] As noted previously, this criticism does not mean that Babbitt favored a return to complete curricular prescription. See, e.g., Babbitt 1986: 121.

[72] On the innate hostility of the sentimental naturalist to the experience of the past, see, e.g., Babbitt 1910: 202–3.

president.[73] This system, which typically requires students to sample a smattering of courses from different divisions such as the natural sciences, social sciences, the arts, and the humanities, leaves the substance of undergraduates' education up to their whims. Thus, for example, students must often enroll in a course devoted to literature, but the content of this course remains a matter of a pupil's choice. Shakespeare, comic books, the *Bhagavad Gita*, penny dreadfuls: rather than be guided by a thoughtfully crafted curriculum to experience works that most effectively provide models of conduct and suggest answers to life's great questions, students are left to pick whatever fits their fancy.

Like free election, the distribution requirements system promotes the message that discipline-specific skills are the lone attainments of an educated person. This is not a curriculum that will allow humanism to thrive. Moreover, Babbitt stressed that such a curricular approach is based on an appealing, but ultimately unsound, foundation: that young people can rightly eschew the goal of self-improvement in favor of turning their attention toward improving the world. To Babbitt, the complete replacement of humanism with supposed humanitarianism provides a recipe for civilizational disaster: "The man who does not rein in his will to power and is at the same time very active according to the natural law," he wrote in his book *Rousseau and Romanticism*, "is in a fair way to become an efficient megalomaniac."[74]

Mental Discipline vs. the Discipline of Ideas

It was therefore disastrous, thought Babbitt, that classical scholars, along with exponents of the modern humanities, had themselves chosen to abandon humanism in favor of a professionalization Babbitt linked to scientific naturalism. In *Literature and the American College*, Babbitt referred to philologists in his day as "our modern linguistic Baconians."[75] They did not aim to use the wisdom of the past as a means to provide standards of conduct

---

[73] On Lowell's introduction of the distribution and concentration systems at Harvard, see Chapter 2, this volume. Babbitt originally preferred Lowell to other candidates for the Harvard presidency. But Babbitt was ultimately disappointed by Lowell's performance in the job (see, e.g., Babbitt's February 13, 1912, letter to More [IBP, Box 9, "Babbitt-More Correspondence, December 1895–April 1914, pages 1–167"]).

[74] Babbitt 1991: 366. As this sentence intimates, Babbitt was a critic of Nietzsche's championing of a "will to power"; see, e.g., Babbitt 1924: 259.

[75] Babbitt 1986: 135. Cf. Babbitt 1940: 191.

that would enable the young to live meaningful and happy lives. Rather, they deliberately avoided the age-old emphasis on cultivating well-roundedness, preferring a narrow specialization conducive to the scientific naturalist's cult of progress. About such scholars Babbitt complained, "The present generation of classical philologists, indeed, reminds one of a certain sect of Japanese Buddhists which believes that salvation is to be attained by arriving at a knowledge of the infinitely small. Men have recently shown their fitness for teaching the humanities by writing theses on the ancient horse-bridle and the Roman doorknob."[76]

This assessment clues us into the ways in which the professionalization of American academia in the late nineteenth and early twentieth centuries presents a profound obstacle to the humanities today. Since the old prescribed curriculum had elitist associations and American educational reformers such as Charles Eliot and Cornell's Andrew White added new vocational subjects of study to the curriculum,[77] many observers may see the move from the old classical colleges to the new research universities as a victory for democracy. But such a view fails to recognize that advocates for the American research imperative did not necessarily support vocationalism.[78] Rather, their outlook mandated that their subject matter was now in *their purview alone*. As Babbitt might have put it, Baconian humanities professors, with their Ph.D.'s and university appointments, successfully removed their subjects from the lives of normal educated people. Hence the rampant suspicion fostered among academic humanists for so-called popularizing work; serious scholars supposedly care only about their audience of fellow professionals.

Although, as we have seen in previous chapters, opponents of the prescribed curriculum often contended that its removal would make higher education less elitist, its departure has not swept in a wave of egalitarianism. This is not a surprise: as much research on the emergence of the German and American research universities has demonstrated, one of the chief appeals of this new approach to higher learning was the greater social capital and higher salaries it afforded to the professoriate.[79] The historian Laurence Veysey also

---

[76] Babbitt 1986: 154. Babbitt did see some value in German philological methods, however. See Babbitt 1986: 152–53.

[77] On this topic, see Chapter 2, this volume. Eliot criticized the lack of vocational subjects at Harvard in his inaugural address; see Eliot 1969: 10.

[78] As we detected in the previous chapter, Eliot said that he did not support vocationalism: although he included engineering as a new subject for undergraduates at Harvard, in his writings he claimed that he would admit only liberal studies in the curriculum.

[79] See, e.g., Rudolph 1962: 272; Turner 1974: esp. 508; O'Boyle 1983; and Chapter 2, this volume.

informs us that the professionalization of the humanities should not be confused with its social broadening: in the new professionalized American university there were now litmus tests *both* for one's disciplinary training *and*
for one's "social acceptability."[80] Proponents of academic reform, moreover,
despite their nods to curricular populism, remained mindful of and deferential to existing academic hierarchies. According to the historian Lenore
O'Boyle, academic professionalization set up a kind of "aristocracy of intellect."[81] Thus, for example, scholars were—and are—more likely to take
seriously claims made by professors affiliated with prestigious academic
institutions, and graduate students who train at such institutions stood—and
stand—a better chance of landing academic appointments in the first place.
This state of affairs can be described in many ways, but "egalitarian" certainly
does not seem to be an apt adjective. Following Babbitt, we might suppose
that it would be far more egalitarian, in fact, to give nonprofessionals a clear
sense of why the humanities are worth studying for *anyone* who wants to lead
a serious and satisfying life.

But, as Babbitt continually lamented in his writings, professionalized
classical scholars—along with their colleagues in the modern humanities—
had little interest in such crucial matters. According to Babbitt, as a result
of classicists' choice to discard the urgent work of cultivating humanistic
standards in favor of glorying in linguistic minutiae, classics courses were
populated only by "grinds" who aim to teach the classics themselves.[82] By
disconnecting the classics from humanism, scientific philologists had rendered the ancients meaningless and unappealing to the vast majority of the
nation's undergraduates. The flight from humanism, thought Babbitt, had
allowed twin threats to the wisdom of the ages to dominate the study of literature in US colleges: dilettantes, whose romantic aesthetical doctrine of art for
art's sake eschewed the character-building function of literary masterpieces;
and scientific philologists, whose linguistic trifling ultimately served naturalistic, rather than humanistic, ends. Separating true humanism from both
these pernicious influences, Babbitt continually stressed the urgent need to
study literature in order to determine the proper moral parameters for living.
"The true point at issue," he wrote in a letter to his friend More in 1913, "is
not whether a man has a love of literature but whether he believes that there
are any standards or discipline in life apart from the discipline of scientific

[80] Veysey 1979: 63.
[81] O'Boyle 1983: 9.
[82] Babbitt 1986: 149.

fact. If the basis of a sound humanistic *discipline* is once established, the 'love' will take care of itself."[83]

One will be unsurprised to learn that Babbitt, deeply critical of the Philological Syndicate, had little interest in mental-discipline-based justifications for the classical humanities. Unlike the apologists for the old prescribed curricula of the antebellum colleges, he did *not* anchor his educational philosophy in faculty psychology.[84] In fact, Babbitt would have scorned the reduction of masterworks of classical culture to conduits for mental calisthenics.[85]

Perhaps the clearest example of this can be found in a comparatively obscure essay Babbitt wrote for a periodical called *The English Journal* in 1920, entitled "English and the Discipline of Ideas." At the article's start, Babbitt pondered the possibility that students flock to courses on English literature because they prove easier than classes devoted to physics and the classical languages.[86] Asking whether one could justify English literature courses on "cultural and disciplinary" grounds,[87] Babbitt answered his own question in the affirmative. His response to this query is instructive: "My own conviction," he wrote, "is that if English is to be thus justified it must be primarily by what I am terming the discipline of ideas."[88] More specifically, he contended that the study of English literature should focus on the examination and creation of "sound ethical standards that the old-fashioned American college with all its limitations did do something to promote."[89] "Thus to study English with reference to its intellectual content," Babbitt concluded, "will do more than anything to make it a serious cultural discipline."[90]

Through this means, Babbitt replaced mental discipline—an educational rationale that encouraged laborious gerund-grinding for its own sake—with

[83] September 19, 1913, letter from Babbitt to More (IBP, Box 9, "Babbitt-More Correspondence, December 1895–April 1914, pages 1–167") (emphasis in the original).
[84] *Pace* Hazlitt 1930: 98–99 n. 2; Butts 1971: 262. For an uncharacteristic mention of the difficulty of the classical languages on Babbitt's part, see Babbitt 1986: 169. Cf. 157. Babbitt (e.g., 1986: 164) did make occasional nods to the ability of masterworks to sharpen one's faculties, but this was always of ancillary importance to him in comparison with the messages contained in these works. Much confusion among modern scholars of American higher education seems to surround Babbitt's views on the matter because of his repeated use of the word *discipline*, which some critics seem to have taken as a nod to faculty psychology but was seldom intended as such.
[85] Cf. Harris (1970: 55): "He [Babbitt] conceded that faculty psychology was outdated." *Pace* Hazlitt 1930: 98–99 n. 2; Butts 1971: 272.
[86] Babbitt 1920: 61.
[87] Ibid. 61.
[88] Ibid. 61.
[89] Ibid. 63.
[90] Ibid. 70.

the "discipline of ideas." His dislike for nitpicking philology encouraged Babbitt to jettison the popular notion that the value of Latin and ancient Greek stemmed from their grammatical and syntactical rigor. For him, the humanities were essential to the properly educated person because profound works of art, philosophy, religion, and literature at their best encapsulate the wisdom of the past, which can compel the young to determine a sound philosophy of life.

In many places in his writings, Babbitt demonstrated disdain for the lifeless manner in which pedagogical traditionalists had approached the classics. About the neoclassical Jesuitical training from which Rousseau rebelled, for example, he wrote, "The Greek and especially the Latin classics are taught in such a way as to become literary playthings rather than the basis of a philosophy of life; a humanism is thus encouraged that is external and rhetorical rather than vital."[91] To Babbitt, classical study stripped of the ideas contained in literary masterworks from Greek and Roman antiquity proved trivial, inconsequential. Thanks to the dominance of humanitarianism in the modern American university, Babbitt lamented, "Language interests us, not for the absolute human values it expresses, but only in so far as it is a collection of facts and relates itself to nature. With the invasion of this hard literalness, the humanities themselves have ceased to be humane."[92]

The Particular and the Universal

This was far from the lone example of Babbitt's impetus to provide a starkly different rationale for the humanities from those typical of his time. Another surrounded what he termed the Platonic problem of the One and the Many. Babbitt referred to this issue as far back as his earliest monograph, quoting from Plato's *Phaedrus* (266b) and contending that "nations have perished from their failure to" harmonize the two.[93] For Plato, the One and the Many amounted to a metaphysical problem. In the early dialogues he wondered what is the one thing common to all, say, pious actions, which makes them pious. Babbitt, however, transferred the problem of the One and the Many

---

[91] Babbitt 1991: 118. For other examples of Babbitt's criticisms of neoclassical formalism, see, e.g., Babbitt 1910: 64, 202, 1940: 186–88, 1986: 77, 79, 81, 123–24, 172, and 186–87, 197. On this topic, see, e.g., Mercier 1928: 58–59.
[92] Babbitt 1986: 119.
[93] Ibid. 84.

to the human soul. He equated the lower will—a human being's impulsive, quotidian desires—with the Many, and he deemed the higher will—the inner check—the One.[94]

In *Rousseau and Romanticism*, Babbitt, discussing Plato's most famous student, elaborated further: "Like all the great Greeks," he wrote, "Aristotle recognizes that man is the creature of two laws: he has an ordinary or natural self of impulse and a human self that is known practically as a power of control over impulse and desire. If man is to become human he must not let impulse and desire run wild, but must oppose to everything excessive in his ordinary self, whether in thought or deed or emotion, the law of measure. This insistence on restraint and proportion is rightly taken to be the essence not merely of the Greek spirit but of the classical spirit in general."[95] One's ordinary impulses (that is, one's *élan vital*) serve to distance people from one another; whereas the inner check, which Babbitt linked to both Eastern philosophy and the Christian spirit of grace, speaks to what is common among human beings. To Babbitt, it is characteristic of literary masterworks, from whatever cultural traditions, that they go beyond the realm of the particular, to grant readers a sense of what human life is really like in toto. For example, Babbitt stressed that "Classical literature, at its best, does not so much tend to induce in us a certain state of feelings, much less a certain state of nerves; it appeals rather to our high reason and imagination—to those faculties which afford us an avenue of escape from ourselves, and enable us to become participants in the universal life."[96] Similarly, in a review for *The Nation*, Babbitt suggested that "the creator of the first class gets his general truth without any sacrifice of his peculiar personal note; he is at once unique and universal."[97] It was the fault of the romantic movement, overreacting to a desiccated neoclassical formalism, that it glorified and reveled in impulse and thereby the particular, at the expense of a more profound examination of the human condition.

This focus on universals helps demonstrate the strong syncretistic character of Babbitt's thought. He presented a blueprint for a truly multicultural humanism. In his book *Democracy and Leadership*, for example, he made

[94] For examples of Babbitt's discussions of the One and the Many, see, e.g., Babbitt 1910: 216, 245, 1912: 453–55, 1930: 32, 1940: 220, and 1986: 84–86, 163. On this topic, see, e.g., Mercier 1928: 52 and 1936: 70; McMahon 1931: 64, 80; Hoeveler 1977: 36–38; Ryn 1977: 252–53 and 1997: 29–30.

[95] Babbitt 1991: 16.

[96] Ibid. 163. In this passage we see Babbitt uncharacteristically referring to an element of mental-discipline theory but employing it to different effect.

[97] Babbitt 1918: 139.

clear that he considered Buddhism and Confucianism quintessential elements of his expanded humanistic tradition: "One is tempted to say, indeed," he wrote, "that, if there is such a thing as the wisdom of the ages, a central core of normal human experience, this wisdom is, on the religious level, found in Buddha and Christ and, on the humanistic level, in Confucius and Aristotle. These teachers may be regarded both in themselves and in their influence as the four outstanding figures in the spiritual history of mankind."[98] Similarly, in the introduction to *Rousseau and Romanticism*, Babbitt contended that Eastern wisdom was of critical importance in the fight against naturalism. On this subject, he suggested that "the experience of the Far East completes and confirms in a most interesting way that of the Occident. We can scarcely afford to neglect it if we hope to work out a truly ecumenical wisdom to oppose the sinister one-sidedness of our current naturalism."[99]

Decades before educators in the US fought over the place of the Western canon in American undergraduate education during the academic culture wars, Babbitt, in a spirit of intellectual ecumenism, had greatly expanded that canon beyond its Occidental confines. This signals a desire on Babbitt's part to update the humanistic canon in a way more intellectually satisfying than Norton's focus on "Western civilization."[100] One could indeed contend that Babbitt was arguing for a transformation of humanism akin to Cicero's transformation of Greek *paideia*. Whereas the ancient Greeks had rooted their education in their own culture's literary classics, the Romans focused on studying a foreign culture as much as their own. At its inception, the humanistic tradition was bicultural; in Babbitt's view, it should grow more multicultural still. With his deep regard for the problem of the One and the Many, Babbitt naturally stressed that there was such a thing as a common humanity. All human traditions, he posited, have contributed to the wisdom of the ages, a nucleus of universal human experience that could help us determine salubrious standards for life.

It is crucial to recognize that Babbitt's contention that Buddha and Confucius were two quintessential figures in the humanistic tradition was no mere Orientalizing flourish, a quick nod to the compatibility of some

---

[98]   Babbitt 1924: 163. Cf. Babbitt 1930: 30–31.

[99]   Babbitt 1991: lxxix. For other examples of Babbitt's expansive vision of humanism that encompasses the East, see, e.g., Babbitt 1921, 1924: 34, 163, 1930: 27–28, 30–31, 37, 40–41, 1936: 65–121, 1940: 141–69, 190, 202–5, 1968: xvi, xxxvii, 54, 235–61, 1986: 83, 206, and 1991: 148, 150, 343. On Babbitt's cosmopolitanism, see, e.g., Mercier 1928: vi; Hitchcock 1930: 214–15; McMahon 1931: 18–19; Ryn 1995b: xlix and 1997: 26; Smilie 2010: 155.

[100]   On this topic, see Chapter 2, this volume.

Eastern ideas with Western thought. Rather, Babbitt, as we have discussed, was a serious student of Eastern religion and philosophy. He peppered many of his books with what he took to be Eastern wisdom and, explicating the differences separating Confucianism from Taoism, spied the same tension between humanistic and naturalistic philosophies that he recognized in Western thought.[101]

In his later years, Babbitt worked on a translation of the Buddhist sacred text the *Dhammapada*, which was posthumously published in 1936. Affixed to this translation Babbitt added a famous essay he wrote called "Buddha and the Occident."[102] The essay begins thus:

> The special danger of the present time would seem to be an increasing material contact between national and racial groups that remain spiritually alien. The chief obstacle to a better understanding between East and West in particular is a certain type of Occidental who is wont to assume almost unconsciously that the East has everything to learn from the West and little or nothing to give in return. One may distinguish three main forms of this assumption of superiority on the part of the Occidental: first, the assumption of racial superiority, an almost mystical faith in the preeminent virtues of the white peoples (especially Nordic blonds) as compared with the brown or yellow races; secondly, the assumption of superiority based on the achievements of physical science and the type of "progress" it has promoted, a tendency to regard as general inferiority the inferiority of the Oriental in material efficiency; thirdly, the assumption of religious superiority, less marked now than formerly, the tendency to dismiss non-Christian Asiatics *en masse* as "heathen," or else to recognize the value in their religious beliefs, notably in Buddhism, only in so far as they conform to the pattern set by Christianity.[103]

This passage may seem unremarkable now, or even at least faintly objectionable, with its strong demarcation between Occidental and Oriental civilizations. But such a conclusion fails to recognize how forward-looking Babbitt's syncretism was for the early twentieth century. As we detected in

---

[101] See, e.g., Babbitt 1968: 253–55 and 1991: lxxix, 395–98. On this topic, see Aldridge (1993: 335–36), who notes Babbitt's reductionist view of Taoism; Hindus 1994: 44.

[102] In a September 22, 1927, letter to More, Babbitt claims that he has "at last" completed this essay (IBP, Box 9, "Babbitt-More Correspondence, May 1914–April 1921, pages 168–306"). Cf. Hoeveler 1977: 23; Slayton 1986: 234; Brennan and Yarbrough 1987: 130.

[103] Babbitt 1936: 65.

the previous chapters, many of the architects of the American research university and opponents of prescribed classical study grounded their views in laissez-faire politics and social Darwinism. According to the historians Jon Roberts and James Turner, the newly professionalized academy's critique of the old belief in a unity of knowledge was akin to nineteenth-century esteem for racism and nationalism.[104] The preeminent guiding light for the scientific democrats in the second half of the nineteenth century was Herbert Spencer, whose opinions about supposedly superior racial groups influenced his curricular views.[105] Proponents of student choice in regard to coursework such as Eliot saw the free-elective system as the curricular embodiment of Darwinism, according to which the fittest subjects of study would thrive and the unfit would perish.[106] Babbitt's inclination to delineate broad similarities between ancient cultures of East and West must be seen as an antidote to this sort of bigoted thinking.[107] His paramount regard for an essential unity to human knowledge deliberately opposed the social Darwinian impulse to split up humanity according to a pseudoscientific hierarchy of races.

A comparison between Babbitt's defense of the humanities with a more typical example of humanistic apologetics from his era underscores the far-sighted nature of Babbitt's approach to education and the downsides that would come to be associated with the Nortonian vision of Western civilization as a pedagogical organizing principle. In 1916, the Oxford don Sir R. W. Livingstone (1880–1960) published a book called *A Defence of Classical Education*, a monograph that presents numerous arguments for the study of Greek and Latin that were popular during the Battle of the Classics. For example, Livingstone argued,

> It is not true that we only study Latin because men spoke it in the Middle Ages, and Greek because there was a time when the fullest knowledge of various sciences was contained in Greek books. But it is true that the history of Greece and Rome is the history of the origins of the modern world and that this is one of the reasons why we study them. We live in the West; our ideals are not those of an Indian or a Chinese; our energies

---

[104] Roberts and Turner 2000: 86–87.

[105] For analysis of Spencer's racism and its relation to his pedagogical philosophy, see Egan 2002: esp. 23–24, 28.

[106] On this topic, see Chapter 4, this volume.

[107] Babbitt was highly critical of Spencer, whom he considered (1986: 95) "a scientific humanitarian of the purest water." See, e.g., Babbitt 1912: 452 and 1986: 95, 120, 131–32. Leander (1937: 96) touches on the similarities between Rousseau's and Spencer's approaches to education.

are otherwise directed. We admire activity where they seek calm; we believe in knowledge where they rest on hoary tradition; we respect energy,
they dignity; we have a vocabulary of ideals—progress, democracy, originality, empire—which repel or leave them indifferent. Whence came
this Western attitude so foreign to the East? What fixed this deep gulf to
divide humanity? Who created the spiritual atmosphere we breathe? If
we wish to press the questions, we are thrown back on the history of our
origins, on the makers of Europe.[108]

For a typical classical apologist of the early twentieth century, the study of the
ancient Greeks and Romans served to divide humanity. In that respect, such
educational traditionalists agreed with their pedagogical opponents, whose
embrace of the burgeoning social sciences often included support for eugen-
icist notions about the supposed superiority of white westerners. According
to Babbitt, this attitude stemmed from a naturalistic impulse to overstress the
Many at the expense of the One. Human beings, he noted, are indubitably all
different; but, more importantly, they are also all the same.

The Modern, Critical Spirit

Babbitt's thought differed from that of many earlier humanists in another
crucial respect. He aimed to avoid putting ancient authors on metaphorical pedestals, as purveyors of timeless wisdom whose ideas could not be
improved upon.[109] Babbitt wanted students to possess a modern, critical
spirit, which could foster the modification, the transcendence, or even the
rejection of prior models.[110] Dismissing the idea that people in the contemporary world can afford to be "mere traditionalists," he argued, "Our
holding of tradition must be in the highest degree critical; that is, it must
involve a constant process of hard and clear thinking, a constant adjust-
ment, in other words, of the experience of the past to the changing needs of
the present."[111]

[108] Livingstone 1916: 58–59.
[109] See Nevin 1984: 39. Nevin also mentions (80) that Babbitt saw ancient Greece as a warning as
much as an example for later societies. After all, it had fostered anti-humanists such as the sophists.
[110] On this topic, see the astute views of Ryn 1995a: 10–13 and 1995b: xxix–xxx.
[111] Babbitt 1940: 44. See also Babbitt 1930: 42 and 1977: 362, 364.

In this respect, Babbitt broke ranks with many traditionalistic defenders of the antebellum classical colleges, who often supported curricular prescription in the hope that it would help demonstrate the truth of a particular interpretation of Christianity. As we discussed in Chapter 2, at many American colleges by the conclusion of the colonial period, obligatory senior capstone courses in moral philosophy had allowed these institutions to provide an intellectual and spiritual summation for undergraduates, which would reconcile their sacred and secular studies along approved doctrinal lines. Babbitt, who wanted students to refuse to take anything on authority—including the authority of tradition—inhabited a very different intellectual universe.

For the Renaissance humanists, the key to the classical humanities was the inculcation of received wisdom from the ancients.[112] Babbitt, borrowing selectively from his modernist opponents, envisioned a more active pedagogical process, in which students would engage their imaginations to accept, modify, or even reject the models of the past. "The task of assimilating what is best in the past and present," he contended, "and adapting it to one's own use and the use of others, so far from lacking in originality, calls for something akin to creation."[113] For this reason, one can find in Babbitt's oeuvre significant criticisms of classical authors whose philosophies of life he deemed deleterious. This disapproval is especially notable in Babbitt's analysis of the Stoic Marcus Aurelius and the Epicurean Lucretius—both of whom Babbitt associated with naturalism and thus deemed opponents of humanism. About the former, for example, he wrote, "We should, again, be struck by the resemblance between [Hippolyte] Taine's attitude toward life and stoicism, even if we did not know that, like many other nineteenth-century stoics, he actually sought a rule of life in the desolate and pathetic Marcus Aurelius."[114] Babbitt, unlike many earlier humanists, encouraged a contemporary,

---

[112] On this topic, see, e.g., Adler 2016: 45 and previous.

[113] Babbitt 1986: 125. Babbitt's pedagogical philosophy was also more active than that of the ancient Greeks and Romans; see Marrou 1956: 305. For another example of Babbitt's vouching for an active approach to pedagogy, see Babbitt 1991: 387–88.

[114] Babbitt 1940: 85. For another criticism of Aurelius, see Babbitt 1977: 241. Leander (1937: 116–17, 177) expounds on Babbitt's dislike of Stoicism as "a classical equivalent of modern humanitarianism" (117). For Babbitt's criticisms of Lucretius, see, e.g., Babbitt 1977: 260. For other examples of Babbitt's criticisms of classical antiquity, see, e.g., Babbitt 1910: 38, 250–52, 1977: 116, 320, 382–83, 1986: 74–76, 83–84, and 1991: 77.

questioning spirit among students reflecting on the masterpieces of the past.[115]

A War over New Humanism

For decades Babbitt elaborated on his philosophy of life, penning many books and essays, and cobbling together a small academic movement, which included numerous former pupils of his at Harvard. By all accounts a charismatic teacher who treated the issues discussed in his classroom as matters of life-or-death importance, toward the conclusion of his career Babbitt was one of Harvard's pedagogical shining lights, and for many students there enrolling in one of his courses was tantamount to a rite of passage. Thanks in part to his inclination to blend Eastern and Western wisdom, Babbitt was especially attractive to Asian students, many of whom attended Harvard chiefly to study with him.[116]

By the 1920s, both Babbitt and More had won impressive reputations for themselves in the history of American letters. Some younger New Humanists, principally Stuart P. Sherman (1881–1926), a spirited and pugnacious literary and social critic,[117] helped bring even more recognition to the movement. Sherman's polemical jousting with the famed libertarian journalist H. L. Mencken (1880–1956), for example, attracted much attention among the American reading public.[118] Once Norman Foerster (1877–1972), one of Babbitt's former undergraduate students who maintained strong interests in higher education, had managed to get his edited collection *Humanism and America* in print in 1930, the scene was set for an intellectual ruckus that often generated more heat than light. For a year or so, it seemed as if every

---

[115] See, e.g., Babbitt 1991: 120, 258–59. Cf. Babbitt 1924: 314.

[116] For discussions of Babbitt in the classroom, see the contributions to Manchester and Shepard 1941. On Babbitt's popularity with Asian students, see, e.g., Aldridge 1993: 332.

[117] On Sherman, a student of Babbitt who ultimately moved away from New Humanism, see, e.g., Foerster 1930b: ix; Elliott 1938: 66–85; Hoeveler 1977: 14–16. For an example of Sherman's educational populism, see Sherman 1963: 147–68. For Humanist criticism of Sherman's criticism, see Munson 1930: 233–39.

[118] On the literary feud between Sherman and Mencken, see, e.g., Hoeveler 1997: 98–100. Babbitt also tangled with Mencken. For Mencken's criticisms of Babbitt, see, e.g., Mencken 1924. For Babbitt's criticisms of Mencken, see, e.g., Babbitt 1924: 274, 1968: 201–34, and 1940: 218–19. Cf. Jones 1928, which criticizes Babbitt's criticisms of Mencken. Much rancor surrounding New Humanism focused on some Humanists' harsh criticisms of contemporary literature. Babbitt mostly stayed away from such feuds; see, e.g., Hoeveler 1977: 100–1.

learned American periodical, and at least a few unlearned ones, had devoted column space to this brouhaha.

Unfortunately, the polemical character of the debate ensured that New Humanism seldom received a fair hearing.[119] The bellicose essays that aimed to criticize Babbitt's ideas, in fact, often displayed misimpressions and distortions. Many critics characterized New Humanism as a strictly backward-looking endeavor, disconnected from the vicissitudes of the present. In the pages of *The New Republic*, for example, Howard Mumford Jones opined, "Mr. Babbitt has built himself a cloud-city, compounded out of Buddha, Aristotle, Plato, and other favorite masters, from which he mournfully surveys the degradation of the humanitarian dogma."[120] Henry Hazlitt, in his contribution to *The Critique of Humanism*, characterized Babbitt's creed as a prime example of "neophobia" that amounted to "special pleading for the genteel tradition."[121]

Detractors also excoriated the perceived ethics of New Humanism, wrongly contending that Babbitt's notion of an inner check suggested a strictly negative approach to morality. For instance, the famed literary critic Edmund Wilson asked, "And how can one take seriously a philosophy which enjoins nothing but negative behavior?—as if humanity were not, now as always, as much in need of being exhorted against coldness and indifference and routine as against irresponsible exuberance—especially Anglo-Saxon humanity."[122] The Southern Agrarian poet Allen Tate demonstrated his sympathy for Wilson's position on this score when he presumed that according to New Humanism, "The good man is he who 'refrains from doing' what the 'lower nature dictates,' and he need do nothing positive."[123] Although Babbitt had also stressed the affirmative possibilities of the higher will, his opponents mischaracterized the morality of New Humanism as support for pure abstention.[124]

[119] On the many misunderstandings of New Humanism, see, e.g., Panichas and Ryn 1986a: 2, 12–13, 15; Ryn 1997b: 10.
[120] Jones 1928: 158. For similar views, see, e.g., Canby 1930: 1122; Blackmur 1955: esp. 147; Dewey 1984: 264. Some progressive scholarship on American higher education has presented similar views of Babbitt's ideas: see, e.g., Harris 1970: 49–79; Butts 1971: 261–62, 270–72.
[121] Hazlitt 1930: 96. The (misleading) idea that New Humanism was an exemplar of "the genteel tradition" came from the work of Santayana (1998: 154–96). Babbitt himself criticized the genteel tradition and distanced himself from such notions; see, e.g., Babbitt 1986: 123–24 and 1968: 3.
[122] Wilson 1930: 46.
[123] Tate 1930: 141. For similar misimpressions, see, e.g., Cowley 1930: 67–68; Mumford 1930: 345–46, 348, 351; McMahon 1931: 81. Cf. Lovejoy 1920: 308.
[124] See, e.g., Mather 1930: 159; Ryn 1977: 254, 1991: xxxvi, and 1997: 31–32; Jamieson 1986: 158. According to Panichas and Ryn (1986a: 15), Babbitt's unclear writing was the responsible for the confusion surrounding his views on the inner check. On this topic, see the section "Babbittian Blemishes," this chapter.

Literary Fascism?

A good deal of the controversy that first reared its head in the late 1920s surrounded the presumed political bona fides of New Humanism. For all his talk of moderation, the law of measure, and the middle path, Babbitt's political philosophy, most fully articulated in his book *Democracy and Leadership* (1924), appeared to possess little in common with the American political center. Indeed, in this book Babbitt demonstrated that his approach to humanism dovetailed with his anti-statist, anti-imperialist political commitments. To be sure, in many places Babbitt proved critical of reactionaries and he nowhere embraced the label *conservative*.[125] Further, in his books he discussed political matters on a theoretical plane, almost entirely steering clear of the quotidian concerns of the day's political parties. Yet, from a pragmatic standpoint, Babbitt's desire to link Humanism to his political outlook both opened up his educational views to criticism and of necessity limited their appeal.

Critics of Babbitt's approach to politics could zero in on a few passages in his work that seemed troubling when removed from their contexts to cast aspersions on the movement as a whole.[126] In one spot in *Literature and the American College*, for example, Babbitt wrote, "The eager efforts of our philanthropists to do something for the negro and the newsboy are well enough in their way; but a society that hopes to be saved by what it does for its negroes and newsboys is a society that is trying to lift itself by its own bootstraps. Our real hope of safety lies in our being able to induce our future Harrimans and Rockefellers to liberalize their own souls, in other words to get themselves rightly educated."[127] A careful reader of *Literature and the American College* would have recognized that Babbitt did not take exception to aiding these groups but rather to the spirit in which modern humanitarians discussed such philanthropy. Babbitt himself had worked as a newsboy as a

---

[125] For Babbitt's criticisms of reactionary politics, see, e.g., Babbitt 1910: xiii, 1940: 90, and 1977: 40, 381. Hoeveler (1977: 125–51) discusses the politics of New Humanism and notes (134 n. 15) that Babbitt was at least partially sympathetic to the plight of laborers and (144) that New Humanism did not naturally lead to political conservatism. Cf. Nevin 1984: 39–40, 91, 100–24; Hovey 1986: 207; Brennan and Yarbrough 1987: 112; Ryn 1995b: xxix. Others have claimed that Babbitt was a conservative: e.g., Grattan 1930b: 12; Harrison 1941: 279; Kariel 1951: 431; Hindus 1994: 3.

[126] They often did so without providing the broader context surrounding them, though in some cases this broader context at least partly exonerated him.

[127] Babbitt 1986: 108. For another potentially racist view in his work, see Babbitt 1924: 209–10. But this remark seems anathema to Babbitt's consistent skepticism of racial thinking. Contra Brennan and Yarbrough 1987: 126, whose views on Babbitt and race lack nuance.

youth in New York City[128] and his skepticism of eugenics demonstrated his animus toward racists in his day. In his book *The Masters of Modern French Criticism*, for example, Babbitt wrote,

> The endless theorizing that has gone on about race during the past century may indeed be seen in retrospect to have been the happy hunting-ground of the pseudo-scientist. And this pseudo-science is often used to produce a sort of emotional intoxication that may take the form either of exultation at one's own superiority or else of contempt for the (supposedly) inferior breeds. It gives a man a fine expansive feeling to think that he is endowed with certain virtues simply because he has taken the trouble to be born a Celt or a Teuton or an Anglo-Saxon.[129]

Babbitt's impulse to detect a unity of human knowledge ("a central core of normal human experience")[130] among disparate cultures, furthermore, was clearly a reaction against the Darwinian-Spencerian impulse of his day to split up and rank human beings along racial lines. Despite such critiques of racism, however, Babbitt failed to express sufficient appreciation for the plight of black Americans.[131] His high regard for syncretism demonstrates implicit hostility to segregation, but it would have been helpful if Babbitt had made a critique of anti-black racism a more prominent component of his thought. Although this omission was, unfortunately enough, a common failing in Babbitt's era (it was also rife among Babbitt's pedagogical opponents), it opened him up to some reasonable criticisms.

Less fairly, some critiques of Babbitt during the kerfuffle over New Humanism focused heavily on guilt-by-association. The writings of Babbitt's friend More, for example, contain some views on women and feminism that have, at the very least, aged poorly.[132] Additionally, the temporary association of a man called Seward Collins (1899–1952) with New Humanism harmed the movement.[133] This wealthy socialite and journal editor drifted

---

[128] D. Babbitt in Manchester and Shepard 1941: ix.
[129] Babbitt 1977: 30–31. For further examples of Babbitt's criticisms of racism and/or eugenics, see, e.g., Babbitt 1924: 210, 1968: 235–37, and 1977: 161. Similarly, Babbitt (1940: 36) claimed that he opposed "ethnic essentialism."
[130] Babbitt 1924: 163.
[131] As Withun 2017: 36–37 correctly notes.
[132] See, e.g., More 1915: 143, 241–42. According to Dakin (1960: 126), More opposed women's suffrage.
[133] On Collins and his fleeting interest in New Humanism, see, e.g., Frohock 1940: 327–29; Hoeveler 1977: 24, 181; Brennan and Yarbrough 1987: 71–72. For an example of linking New Humanism to Collins, see Brody 1930.

in his affiliations from Southern Agrarianism, to New Humanism, to a self-described American Fascism. Although Babbitt and More appear to have found him an oddball,[134] various followers of New Humanism, to their discredit, continued to contribute to Collins's periodical *The American Review* after Collins had departed Humanism in favor of a flirtation with Fascism.

This left New Humanism open to charges of dubious extremism, despite the fact that Babbitt, given his stalwart anti-imperialism,[135] antinationalism,[136] and anti-militarism, despised fascist politics.[137] The radical writer V. F. Calverton, in the pages of the Marxist magazine *New Masses*, for instance, maintained that "the new humanists are intellectual fascists of the present (and the forthcoming) generation," adding that "Babbitt is, in every way, the fit leader for the intellectual fascism that humanism represents."[138] Admittedly, Calverton embodied an extreme position, but more moderate critics provided critiques of New Humanism that were based primarily on the perceived political underpinnings of the movement.[139]

Other criticisms of Babbitt's politics demonstrate that the polemical character of the debate over New Humanism led to unfounded charges. According to C. Hartley Grattan, the editor of *The Critique of Humanism* and a dogged opponent of Babbitt, "Mr. Babbitt lives in a most unholy awe of State Street."[140] Given Babbitt's skepticism of big business[141] and suspicions of the discipline of economics,[142] Grattan's contention is simply unsound.

Such debates over the politics of New Humanism, while more conducive to the culture warriors who took part in the spirited rows over the movement, appear to have been something of a sideshow. As Lewis Mumford justly recognized in his contribution to Grattan's collection, there was nothing inherently conservative about New Humanism. Mumford stressed, "While the New Humanism has been allied, more or less overtly, with a defense of the privileged classes—I would cite, for example, Professor Babbitt's

---

[134] Hoeveler (1977: 24 n. 35) notes that More, in a letter to Babbitt, wondered how "stable" Collins was. For Babbitt's correspondence with Collins, see IBP, Box 11, "Collins, Seward, 1929–1932."

[135] For examples of Babbitt's criticisms of imperialism, see, e.g., Babbitt 1924: 18–20, 273, 1940: 208–9, 1968: 239–40, and 1977: 129.

[136] For Babbitt's criticisms of nationalism, see, e.g., Babbitt 1940: 192–93, 1986: 170–72. On this topic, see Hoeveler 1977: 146–48.

[137] On Babbitt's disdain for Fascism, see Chalmers 1941: 390; Hoeveler 1977: 181.

[138] Calverton 1930: 10. Cf. anonymous 1930.

[139] E.g., Burke 1930: 171–73; Cowley 1930: 68–69, 73–74; Grattan 1930b: 12; Blackmur 1955: 157.

[140] Grattan 1930b: 12.

[141] For his criticisms of business leaders, see, e.g., Babbitt 1940: 214–15 and 1986: 92, 107. Cf. Babbitt 1910: 233.

[142] For his criticism of economics, see Babbitt 1940: 214.

shrill vituperations against those who would endanger the sanctity of private property by a social interpretation of the Constitution—the connection is a social accident, rather than a logical necessity, and it is conceivable that a New Humanist might hold most of Mr. Babbitt's doctrines without being any more impressed by the sacredness of private property than Plato was."[143] Indeed, this belief was not just conceivable but undeniably the case. In a review of *The Critique of Humanism* in *The New Republic*, Frank Jewett Mather, Jr., (1868–1953), an art historian at Princeton who had been among Babbitt's friends and followers since they were both faculty members at Williams College in the 1890s, deemed himself "a Humanist of the extreme left."[144] Especially in regard to Babbitt's approach to higher education, moreover, there were many reasons for people of varying ideological orientations to find elements of New Humanism attractive. Had he focused less attention on political theory, Babbitt might have won a larger audience for his powerful criticisms of American higher education.

Is Humanism a Religion?

The perceived political character of New Humanism was not the lone issue that distracted critics from a discussion of Babbitt's pedagogical philosophy. Whereas some on the Left found fault with Babbitt chiefly for his anti-statism, a variety of conservatives took issue with Babbitt's failure to declare his devotion to Christianity.[145] Some right-wing critics of Humanism saw it as a meager replacement for religion. In an essay from 1929 titled "Is Humanism a Religion?," the famous British Catholic convert G. K. Chesterton, for instance, concluded, "I do not believe that Humanism can be a complete substitute for Superhumanism."[146] Similarly, Allen Tate announced, "Humanism is not enough," adding that "if the values for which the Humanist pleads are to be made rational, even intelligible, the parallel condition of an objective religion is necessary."[147] Even T. S. Eliot, for whom Babbitt served as a mentor

---

[143] Mumford 1930: 341.

[144] Mather 1930: 156.

[145] This charge did not exhaust right-wing criticisms of New Humanism. Mencken, for example, found many other faults with the movement. On this topic, see the section "A War over New Humanism," this chapter.

[146] Chesterton 1929: 236. This opinion hints at the international interest in New Humanism. Although the debate over Babbitt's movement was chiefly confined to the US, New Humanism also had for a time a sizable influence abroad, including in Britain, France, and China.

[147] Tate 1930: 160.

and inspiration since the former's undergraduate days, although sympathetic to many Humanist views, fretted that "humanism is the *alternative* to religion."[148] "You cannot," he stressed, "make humanism itself into a religion."[149] Indeed, Eliot even found fault with Babbitt's cosmopolitan learnedness. Babbitt, he argued, "knows too many religions and philosophies, has assimilated their spirit too thoroughly (there is probably no one in England or America who understands Buddhism better than he) to be able to give himself to any. The result is humanism."[150]

Such criticisms stemmed in large measure from Babbitt's complex and, at times, cagily expressed relationship with revealed religion. According to Paul More, Babbitt was more critical of the Christian Church than his writings expressed and was closest to Buddhism in his religious outlook.[151] Although he was supportive of ideas associated with Christianity in his work, Babbitt's inclination to keep doctrinal and institutional religion at arm's length, combined with his obvious affection for Buddhism and, to a much lesser extent, Hinduism, made many religious conservatives uncomfortable.[152]

The discomfort of religious conservatives was largely based on misunderstandings. In his contribution to Foerster's *Humanism and America*, Babbitt underscored that he did *not* view Humanism as a religion. "For my own part," he wrote, "I range myself unhesitatingly on the side of the supernaturalists. Though I see no evidence that humanism is necessarily ineffective apart from dogmatic and revealed religion, there is, as it seems to me, evidence that it gains immensely in effectiveness when it has a background in religious insight."[153] As if this were not sufficiently clear, he added, "It is an error to hold that humanism can take the place of a religion."[154] Among

[148] Eliot 1964: 420.

[149] Ibid. 423. The New Humanist Shafer (1935: 283–85), supportive of Paul More's later embrace of Christianity, similarly concluded that Babbitt aimed to make Humanism a substitute for religion.

[150] Eliot 1964: 428. For Babbitt's responses to T. S. Eliot's criticisms, see, e.g., Babbitt 1928, 1930: 37, 49, and 1940: 204.

[151] More in Manchester and Shepard 1941: 332. Cf. Shafer 1935: 224 n. 7; Leander 1937: 156–57; Hamm in Manchester and Shepard 1941: 314; Dakin 1960: 282–83; Hoeveler 1977: 42; Hindus 1994: 29; Ryn 1995b: xii; Smilie 2010: 173 n. 80. Babbitt was greatly influenced by Buddhism (especially in its Lesser Vehicle formation) but denied that he was a Buddhist; see Brennan and Yarbrough 1987: 17. Still, Warren (1956: 159), a former student, claims that despite denials Babbitt was a Buddhist.

[152] For various views on Babbitt's approach to religion, see, e.g., Mercier 1928: v–vi and 1936: 171–200; Grattan 1930b: 22; Rascoe 1930: 119; Grabo 1933: 31–32; More 1936: 16; Leander 1937: 147–61; Elliott 1938: 22, 86–125; Dakin 1960: 282–83, 338, 341; Veysey 1965: 204–5; Harris 1970: 50; Ryn 1977: 252, 1986: 58–61, 1991: xi, xiv, xxxviii–xli, 1995b: xii, xxx–xxxii, and 1997: 38; Nevin 1984: 125–43; Panichas 1986: 27–49 and 1999: 37–38, 77; Brennan and Yarbrough 1987: 129–41. According to Maynard (1935: 575), many New Humanists were Unitarians.

[153] Babbitt 1930: 39.

[154] Ibid. 43. See also Babbitt 1940: 203.

the proponents of Humanism from the early twentieth century one notes a range of religious views, from the Catholic Louis J. A. Mercier, the Protestant G. R. Elliott, to the seeming atheist Norman Foerster. All the same, some social conservatives proved ill at ease with Babbitt's ecumenism; such devoted followers as T. S. Eliot and even Paul More partly retreated from the movement because of their more robust commitment to Anglicanism.[155]

Critics of Babbitt's approach to religion appear not to have recognized the pragmatic value of his tactics. Babbitt aimed to fight scientism on its own terms, providing a defense of Humanism that did not rely on recourse to religious dogma. Had he advertised a devotion to, say, Catholicism, it is likely that many potential Humanist sympathizers from other religious traditions would have shunned the movement. Babbitt wanted to provide a modern, critical case for Humanism first of all, but also for religion, and this necessitated the avoidance of arguments based on revealed religion. At the same time, he attempted to make his philosophy reasonably compatible with a variety of faiths—and even no faith at all. In contrast to his discussion of politics, on the religious front Babbitt aimed to attract as wide an audience as possible.

"The Saving Remnant"

Much disapproval of New Humanism surrounded the caustic literary criticism of some of its devotees. This was an aspect of the controversy in which Babbitt, less interested in contemporary literature, played little part. But faultfinders spied in the anti-romantic literary criticism of younger Humanists such as Stuart Sherman and Robert Shafer (1889–1956)[156] a studied disconnect from modern life coupled with an elitism they found appalling. Malcolm Cowley, for example, linked such criticism to its authors' troubling academic haughtiness. "The American humanists," he wrote, "less paradoxical than Socrates and more faithful to the usage of the city, have adopted the older conventions of the universities where most of them teach. One of these conventions is a snobbery both intellectual and social—a snobbery

---

[155] On More's move toward Anglicanism at the end of his life, see, e.g., Dakin 1960: 88. Ryn has written helpfully on misunderstandings on the relationship between Humanism and religion: see, e.g., Ryn 1991: xxvii–xli and 1995b: xxxiii–xxxvi.

[156] For an example of such criticism from Shafer, see his contribution to Foerster's collection (Shafer 1930), which is an attack on Theodore Dreiser.

which does not seem out of place in a professor's drawing-room, but which becomes grotesque when applied to literature and art."[157]

Babbitt's Humanism was indeed semi-aristocratic in spirit, based on a concern for the proper education of a group he, fastening on Matthew Arnold's phrase, labeled "the saving remnant."[158] Yet Babbitt's personal background undercuts common reproofs of Humanism's social and economic elitism. As we have already discussed, Babbitt himself had graduated from a public high school in the Midwest, and he barely scraped the money together to attend Harvard. By no means did Babbitt believe that a college education should be the sole prerogative of an economic and social elite. Rather, like Arnold, he favored what one might term an aristocracy of intellect and character. As Babbitt put it in *Literature and the American College*, American higher education must stay true to humane standards and liberal culture, so it can "do its share toward creating that aristocracy of character and intelligence that is needed in a community like ours to take the place of an aristocracy of birth, and to counteract the tendency toward an aristocracy of money."[159]

Foerster, who grew increasingly favorable to pedagogical populism after Babbitt's death,[160] attempted to refute the notion that New Humanism was needlessly elitist. About the sorts of students who should be encouraged to study the liberal arts, he wrote, "The intellectually robust are, I think, a much larger body than is usually supposed. The mind that is capable of enough liberal education to justify the effort is not rare; it is common."[161] New Humanists such as Babbitt and Foerster hoped to attract undergraduates who were sufficiently intellectually engaged to benefit from the rigorous, inner-focused humanism that they advocated. As the historian David Withun perceptively noted, Babbitt's regard for an intellectual aristocracy had much in common with W. E. B. Du Bois's concerns about the humanistic education of his so-called Talented Tenth.[162]

It must also be noted that many of Babbitt's intellectual opponents, such as Charles Eliot, Babbitt's pedagogical bête noire, were open to charges of elitism, sexism, and ethnocentrism. As we detected in the previous chapter,

---

[157] Cowley 1930: 72. Later generations of progressive scholars of American higher education echoed such conclusions, pillorying New Humanism for its educational elitism: see, e.g., Harris 1970: 57–61; Butts 1971: 347–48. Cf. Hoeveler 1977: 117–18; Spanos 1985: 29–50. For some examples of Babbittian elitism, see, e.g., Babbitt 1920: 64, 1924: 263–64, 1940: 63. Cf. Babbitt 1986: 111–12, 164.

[158] See, e.g., Babbitt 1921: 89.

[159] Babbitt 1986: 127. See Leander 1937: 94.

[160] See, e.g., Foerster 1946: esp. v–vii.

[161] Foerster 1937: 185.

[162] Within 2017.

Eliot's approach to education had been greatly shaped by the social Darwinist Herbert Spencer.[163] Eliot supported segregated schools for blacks and whites,[164] opposed co-education,[165] and touted Zionism's potential to "contribute to the eradication of the undesirable qualities in Jews."[166] According to the historian Samuel Eliot Morison, in response to concerns that the free-elective system would turn some students into dabblers, Eliot countered that such students were unserious and thus of minimal concern to a university.[167] Indeed, Eliot believed in an aristocracy of intellect, thinking that only those among its ranks should attend high school and college.[168] The educational disputes of the early twentieth century, which took place prior to the dramatic increases in the college-going population that resulted from the passage of the G.I. Bill in 1944, were mired in more elitism than one often finds in contemporary debates.

Babbittian Blemishes

The problematic nature of many criticisms expressed in the battle over New Humanism does not imply that Babbitt's educational views lack downsides. Babbitt, for example, was guilty of treating Rousseau and the romantic movement in a one-sided manner. Although he deliberately did not supply "a rounded estimate" of some figures he discussed and was knowingly selective in dealing with them in order to clarify distinctions,[169] Babbitt failed to

---

[163] Eliot (1911: viii) labeled Spencer "a true educational pioneer," but thought that Spencer was incorrect to see science as "the universal staple" of education (ix). On Spencer's intellectual and political influence on Eliot, see, e.g., Boyd 1934: esp. 34; Hawkins 1972: 143; Hoeveler 1977: 115 n. 15; Egan 2002: 122, 141–45.

[164] Few 1909: 185; Hawkins 1972: 190–93. Hawkins also notes that Eliot occasionally linked ethnicity and mental ability (182), supported anti-miscegenation laws (183), harbored paternalistic views on Catholic education (189), spoke disparagingly of white ethnics while he was touring the South (189), and may have believed that blacks were genetically inferior to whites (191). Eliot did, however, want Harvard to be open to all creeds and colors (181) and disliked racial pseudoscience (191). But see also Eliot 1911: xiv, in which he laments the neglect of eugenics.

[165] Eliot 1969: 17–18; Hawkins 1972: 193–97. Eliot believed that women's education should prepare them for motherhood alone: see, e.g., Eliot 1926: 164–65.

[166] Eliot 1924: 253. When writing for a Jewish audience, he avoided such objectionable language: see Eliot 1915.

[167] Morison 1942: 344.

[168] See Hawkins 1972: 103, 111, 167, 196, 233–34. Cf. 147–48. Hawkins also notes that Eliot opposed more money for the Morrill Act (152) and originally opposed tuition-free high schools (226). On Eliot's educational elitism, see, e.g., Hindus 1994: 55.

[169] Babbitt 1986: 69–70 (quotation on 70). Babbitt also realized that Rousseau was a writer of great power and value, even though Babbitt focused on what he perceived as the negative aspects of Rousseau's philosophy: see, e.g., Babbitt 1910: 122 and 1940: 226. Cf. Ryn 1991: xx and 1995b: xxxvii.

appreciate the richness and even the countervailing tendencies in romanticism.[170] In fact, he did not appear to realize that he himself was partly a
product of the romantic movement: as the political philosopher Claes Ryn
has ably demonstrated, both Babbitt's approach to aesthetics and his theory
of knowledge demonstrate important romantic influences.[171] Intriguingly
for a writer so critical of this movement, Babbitt, like the romantics, vastly
preferred classical Greece to Rome,[172] though one might have thought that
he would have shown greater appreciation for Roman authors' creative imi-
tation of their forebears. More generally, Babbitt was capable of simplifying
the views of his intellectual opponents; in his analyses of the philosophers
Benedetto Croce and John Dewey, for instance, he underplayed significant
points of agreement that could have helped him cobble together additional
support for his ideas and suggest paths forward for educational reformers.[173]

Irked by insinuations that modern humanistic study was an inherently
feminine undertaking, Babbitt, attuned to the tendency of his time to equate
a sound college education with manliness,[174] also occasionally displayed
his sexism. He, for example, criticized literary dilettantism as effeminate
and attempted to strengthen the notion that culture was a masculine pursuit.[175] Most importantly for our purposes, Babbitt did not go far enough
in his intellectual ecumenism for the twenty-first century. He neglected

---

[170] See Hoeveler 1977: 43–44, 54; Hovey 1986: 203–4; Ryn 1991: xx–xxi.

[171] See Ryn 1991: xxi, 1995b: xliv, and 1997: 45–46, 52. Lovejoy (1920) contended that Babbitt was
a romantic, a view that appears to have influenced Jones (1928: 159) and Dewey (1984: 265). Ryn
(1997: 50) notes, however, that Lovejoy's later work betrays Babbitt's influence.

[172] E.g., Babbitt 1977: x, 24, 1986: 113–14, 143, 159. Cf. Babbitt 1940: 81–82, 1968: xvi, 12, and
1991: 16, 204, 386. According to Warren in Manchester and Shepard 1941: 217, Babbitt would have
wanted to live in Athens during the age of Pericles; cf. Warren 1956: 155. See also Clark in Manchester
and Shepard 1941: 265. Knapp (1911: 73) criticized Babbitt's romantic preference for the Greeks.
But Babbitt did demonstrate his esteem for some Roman authors: e.g., Babbitt 1918: 139 (Vergil),
1991: 77 (Horace).

[173] For Babbitt's criticisms of Croce, see, e.g., Babbitt 1910: 223–27, 238, 1940: 66–72. Cf. More
1930. Leander (1986: esp. 90) notes that Babbitt never studied Croce closely enough to recognize the
later correspondence of their views; likewise, Ryn (1995b: xli–xliv and 1997: 45–46, 50) demonstrates
that Babbitt's criticisms of Croce's aesthetics were unfair. For Babbitt's criticisms of Dewey, see, e.g.,
Babbitt 1924: 312–13, 1940: 211–12, and 1991: 388. Dewey had also criticized New Humanism: see
Dewey 1984: 263–66. On the correspondences of some of Babbitt's and Dewey's educational views,
see Ryn 1997b: 49; Smilie 2010: 11, 64, 122–23, 137, 170–99 and 2016. Winterer (2002: 109) mentions
that Dewey was not an anti-classicist. Indeed, Dewey (1969: 76) saw intellectual value in studying
Latin literature. He also (1938: 21–22) criticized the unlimited free election of coursework. Dewey
did (1940: 16), however, stress that education's goal was service, subordinate the humanities to the
scientific method (22), oppose dualism (48; cf. 1969: 98), criticize the concept of culture as prescien-
tific (1969: 97), and support vocationalism (1969: 103–4).

[174] See, e.g., Geiger 2015: 376–80.

[175] For examples of Babbitt's sexism, see, e.g., Babbitt 1986: 112, 125, 134–35, 139. See Nevin
1984: 28–29.

whole continents and sundry intellectual and spiritual traditions. His interest in the problem of the One and the Many demonstrates that he believed in a common humanity and universality in lived experience; thus his work can suggest ways forward for today's humanists. But his decision to focus chiefly on the West and the Far East at the expense of other human traditions renders his work insufficiently inclusive for an educational program in the contemporary US.

Babbitt also overemphasized the impact of the professionalization of philology in the nineteenth century on the marginalization of the classical humanities. Although he was correct to contend that this professionalization contributed mightily to Americans' perceptions of the classics as recondite and unappealing,[176] Babbitt did not sufficiently stress that the study of the ancient languages had degenerated from humanist standards far earlier.[177] As we have suggested in previous chapters, the turn to defend Latin and ancient Greek on the basis of their fostering mental discipline appears related to the pedagogical realities of the antebellum colleges, in which an obsession with grammatical minutiae trumped the study of literature as a source of humane insight.

We should also recognize that critics' misimpressions of Babbitt's views are to some degree understandable. Although his punchy and humorous prose style makes him appear at first glance to be a straightforward writer, his work can prove quite difficult to grasp.[178] Babbitt did not organize his thoughts in a typical essayistic style,[179] with the result that one must read large swaths of his work in order to determine his broader contentions; further, decontextualized quotations from Babbitt's writing are especially susceptible to misinterpretation.[180] Babbitt typically failed to define his terms carefully, and thus readers must wade through much of his work to get an accurate sense of what he means by such key concepts as "higher will," "inner check," "positivism,"

---

[176]   On this topic, see Babbitt 1986: esp. 151–67.

[177]   Babbitt recognized, however, that the neoclassical formalism of the old American colleges trivialized the study of the classics. See, e.g., Babbitt 1986: 109, 121; Smilie 2010: 161–62.

[178]   On this subject, see, e.g., Leander 1986: 76–77; Hindus 1994: 39. Dakin (1960: 170 n. 65) quotes from a 1917 letter from More to Babbitt, in which More suggests that Babbitt's writing style was responsible for rendering his work less effective. Cf. Dakin 1960: 105 n. 60. Elliott (1938: 55–56, 88 and Elliott in Manchester and Shepard 1941: 149), suggests that Babbitt was a better conversationalist than a writer.

[179]   See Ryn (1995b: xiv). Cf. Warren 1956: 160.

[180]   See Nevin 1984: 25, 29. Babbitt, given his penchant for wit and sententiousness, remains an eminently quotable writer, and thus only magnifies the possibility that his broader contentions will be misunderstood.

"naturalism," "normal," and "discipline"—concepts that do not necessarily reflect definitions customary among other authors.[181]

As a thinker more given to philosophical contemplation upon predominantly literary subjects than the specificities of pedagogical reform, moreover, Babbitt never provided his own curriculum.[182] Although the disinclination to offer a curricular blueprint had a strong pragmatic rationale (his readers, after all, could fixate on the details of a proposed curriculum and ignore his broader arguments),[183] it seems to have led critics to presume that he aimed to reintroduce the old prescribed curriculum of the antebellum colleges.[184] Careful attention to his ideas demonstrates that this conclusion is incorrect: clearly, as we have seen, Babbitt's avant-garde impulse to blend Eastern and Western thought puts him in an intellectual milieu different from that inhabited by American educators in the nineteenth century.

Even fellow thinkers associated with New Humanism appear not to have recognized fully the implications of Babbitt's educational philosophy. Thus, for example, Paul More partly defended the classical humanities through recourse to arguments about faculty psychology that Babbitt had rightly discarded. In an essay titled "Academic Leadership," More argued, "The sheer difficulty of Latin and Greek, the highly organized structures of these languages, the need of scrupulous search to find the nearest equivalents for words that differ widely in their scope and meaning from their derivatives in any modern vocabulary, the effort of lifting one's self out of the familiar rut of ideas into so foreign a world, all these things act as a tonic exercise to the brain."[185] Similarly, in his book *The American State University*, Foerster demonstrated great sympathy for faculty psychology;[186] the proper justification

---

[181] On this score, see Ryn (1986: 53–54 and 1995a), who discusses Babbitt's confusing references to himself as a "positivist." Cf. Hazlitt 1930: 91–92; Barney 1974: 134 n. 50; Ryn 1997b: 91. See also Nevin 1984: 40. For confusion stemming from Babbitt's use of the word *normal*, see Chamberlain 1930: 262.

[182] See Davis 2006: 54; Smilie 2010: 6–7, 43.

[183] Additionally, it should be noted that Babbitt's attempt to introduce a specific reform to Harvard's curriculum, in the form of an A.M. degree with honors based on assimilative learning, was soundly defeated by the modern language faculty in 1930. See Babbitt 1908 and 1986: 145–47; Hoeveler 1977: 117 n. 18; Brennan and Yarbrough 1987: 111; February 10, 1930, document noting the 15-to-2 vote against the proposal (IBP, Box 6, "Harvard Correspondence, 1886–1936"). Babbitt also supported major reforms to the humanities Ph.D.: see Babbitt 1986: 130, 141–42, 150.

[184] See, e.g., Harris 1970: 49–79, who groups Babbitt among the "educational counterrevolutionists" of his era. Cf. Rudolph 1977: 239, who sees Babbitt and fellow proponents of liberal culture as educational reactionaries.

[185] More 1915: 48. See also More 1972: 262 for a similar sentiment. On this topic, see Duggan 1966: 82–83. Cf. 84, where More more closely approximates Babbitt's rationale for the required study of classical literature; the same is true of More 1972: 182.

[186] Foerster 1937: 202–4.

for a liberal education, he maintained, was the "culture of the mind, comparable with the culture of the body for its health and vigor."[187]

Pedagogical Potential

Unfortunately, the raucous debates over New Humanism that took place in the late 1920s and early 1930s focused so much on the movement's perceived political, aesthetic, and religious character that Babbitt's philosophy of education was seldom featured in it.[188] Few at the time expressed convincing criticisms of the New Humanist vision of an appropriate college education. Soon after *Literature and the American College* appeared in print, the classicist Paul Shorey (1857–1934) provided an anonymous assessment of the book in the pages of *The Nation*.[189] "With Babbitt's main idea we are in cordial sympathy," Shorey wrote.[190] But, in a review that failed to note the book's main thesis,[191] Shorey also thought that *Literature and the American College* went too far; "our general impression," he claimed, "is that Professor Babbitt is not quite fair or generous in his treatment of American classical scholarship."[192]

Shorey seemed not to recognize the crucial differences between Babbitt's case for the classical humanities and those of traditionalists during the Battle of the Classics. An examination of Shorey's own defenses of ancient Greek and Latin helps explain this important failure on his part. In "The Case for the Classics," one of his many examples of classical apologetics from the

---

[187] Ibid. 203. Such sentiments led Hoeveler (1977: 110, 110 n. 4) to surmise incorrectly that New Humanism advanced outdated views on mental discipline as the lynchpin of its curricular arguments.

[188] Significantly, no contribution to the edited collection *The Critique of Humanism* focused on Babbitt's educational philosophy. Had he lived, Babbitt might have fulfilled his aim to write another book on education; see Babbitt 1940: vi; Brennan and Yarbrough 1987: 111–12.

[189] Shorey 1908. More, then the literary editor of the magazine, chose Shorey for the review, a choice that irked Babbitt. In a May 17, 1908, letter to More, Babbitt complained about the substance of the review (IBP, Box 9, "Babbitt-More Correspondence, December 1895–April 1914, pages 1–167").

[190] Shorey 1908: 403.

[191] To be fair, as More noted in a May 27, 1908, letter to Babbitt, Shorey's review was originally twice its published length, but Hammond Lamont, the editor of *The Nation*, cut it drastically, apparently including the portion in which Shorey dealt with Babbitt's main thesis (IBP, Box 1, "Family Correspondence, 1865, 1884–1937").

[192] Shorey 1908: 403. For other reviews of *Literature and the American College*, see, e.g., anonymous 1908b; Mims 1908; Knapp 1911. Cf. anonymous 1908a. According to Hoeveler (1977: 118), this monograph became increasingly popular in the 1920s. Rudolph (1977: 239) suggests that in the book Babbitt articulated criticisms that the student counterculture would also take up. See also Graff 1987: 240.

era, Shorey showed that he centered his defense of the ancient languages around the conventional approach to faculty psychology. Shorey maintained that "the critical interpretation of [ancient Greek] supplies the simplest and most effective all-round discipline of the greatest number of faculties."[193] He believed, as he put it, "that there is such a thing as intellectual discipline, and that some studies are better mental gymnastics than others."[194]

His article ably demonstrates some of the downsides of this shopworn rationale for the classics. Although he recognized that social scientists could test empirically which subjects most effectively promoted mental discipline, Shorey feebly attempted to undercut such studies. "There are in general," he claimed, "no laboratory experiments that teach us anything about the higher mental processes which we cannot observe and infer by better and more natural methods."[195] This generalization was merely an attempt on Shorey's part to hide the fact that he had no proof of the superior mental discipline inculcated by the study of ancient Greek.

Overall, Babbitt's educational philosophy was the most consistently praised aspect of New Humanism. Even many of Babbitt's ardent critics proved enthusiastic about his pedagogical views. In his contribution to *The Critique of Humanism*, the poet and literary critic Yvor Winters (1900–68), otherwise condemning of New Humanism, announced, "I am particularly grateful for Mr. Babbitt's brilliant exposition of our educational chaos."[196] Similarly, in his essay expressing "Second Thoughts about Humanism," T. S. Eliot contended that "Humanism has done no greater service than its criticism of modern education."[197] In a postmortem estimation of the movement, the professor of English Theodore Maynard appears to have been correct when he concluded that "Irving Babbitt's educational theories seem not only sound but are shared by many who would not call themselves Humanists."[198]

Despite this common opinion about the strengths of its educational philosophy, after the early 1930s New Humanism, though it has never disappeared, quickly faded from the forefront of American intellectual life. Given the value of his pedagogical ideas, it is unfortunate that Babbitt has

---

[193] Shorey 1910: 598.
[194] Ibid. 607.
[195] Ibid. 607.
[196] Winters 1930: 329.
[197] Eliot 1964: 434 n. 2.
[198] Maynard 1935: 578. Canby (1930: 1122) and Colum (1930: 1064), critics of Humanism, see value in Babbitt's critique of academia. Hindus (1994: 45), an admirer of Babbitt, believes that Babbitt's best work was on the subject of education.

had so little influence on the American academy. To some extent, this lack must be related to the fact that by the time he began contributing books and essays, Babbitt was embarking on a lost cause. The prescribed undergraduate curriculum of the antebellum colleges was already a goner, the victim of previous losses in the Battle of the Classics.[199] More's and Foerster's inclination to ground their case for the classics in mental discipline and therefore muddying Babbitt's views did not help matters. Ultimately, the Great Depression rendered Babbitt's anti-statist political ideas unpopular in America. Babbitt's early death in 1933 surely did not help matters.[200] And America's entrance in World War II likely hammered the last nail in New Humanism's coffin. Although Babbitt has remained influential among a small circle of traditionalistic conservatives such as Russell Kirk and his name graces an endowed professorship in comparative literature at Harvard, he is nowhere near as well-known as he should be. One of Babbitt's primary achievements is that in the early twentieth century he presented the most cogent attack on the scientific democrats who midwifed the American research university and sidelined the humanities.

Babbitt aimed for a transformation of higher learning in the US—a transformation steeped in an appreciation of the best of the past, but also linked to relating a much-expanded humanistic tradition to the needs of the present and future. Unlike those who vouch for the humanities on the basis of "mental discipline" or "critical thinking," Babbitt gave humanists an exclusive duty in the pedagogical process. The others on a college's or a university's faculty—its natural and social scientists, its vocationalists—may concern themselves with improving the material conditions of life; the humanist's job is the crucial balancing work of humanism.[201] This philosophy does not imply (as some of his critics have asserted)[202] that Babbitt saw no role for

---

[199] One should also note that Babbitt believed that ancient and modern language instructors should work together for a common purpose: see, e.g., Babbitt 1920: 69–70, 1940: 195–96, and 1986: 131, 179–80.

[200] On Babbitt's death from ulcerative colitis on July 15, 1933, see D. Babbitt in Manchester and Shepard 1941: xiii; Slayton 1986: 235; Ryn 1991: xvii and 1995b: xix; Panichas 1999: 205.

[201] The partial exception appears to be the discipline of psychology, which in many instances focuses on a human being's interior life. But see Proctor 1998: 113–16. The goal of psychoanalysis, Proctor contends, is to be *healthy*, not necessarily to be *good*. Moreover, Proctor argues that Freud's discovery of the unconscious ultimately undermined the humanist belief that one can know one's true self in an effort to improve it (114). Cf. Baumeister and Tierney 2011: 8. Nussbaum (2008) examines some of the downsides associated with so-called positive psychology, given the failure of its practitioners to examine the concept of happiness with philosophical rigor.

[202] E.g., Harris 1970: 79.

natural science or utilitarian intellectual pursuits in higher education.[203] But Babbitt granted to humanists a unique and foundational job: helping students to cultivate their higher selves through the examination of literary, religious, philosophical, and artistic masterworks, thereby aiding them in living sounder and happier lives. In short, he demonstrated that the humanities, broadly conceived, far from merely promoting occupationally desirable skills, provide the young with the opportunity—central to personal and civilizational flourishing—to elevate and enrich their souls.

As we have already noted, Babbitt's pedagogical philosophy is not above criticism and in important respects seems insufficiently capacious to meet the intellectual and moral needs of the present. Although exhibiting considerable broadmindedness for his time, Babbitt did not underscore the potential contributions to the humanities of sundry cultural traditions. But Babbitt's writings, with their emphasis on the unity of human experience and knowledge, can help supporters of an inclusive humanism find a way forward. Humanists can craft an undergraduate curriculum that foregrounds life's great questions without the Western triumphalism often associated with the Great Books tradition.

Thankfully, one need not agree with all Babbitt's ideas in order to find value in his detailed re-centering of the humanistic tradition around great works of world culture. Unlike so many traditionalists in the Battle of the Classics and proponents of the modern humanities today, his vision of education relies on specific content—masterworks that can inspire a drive for personal perfection.[204] Although by no means a panacea for the contemporary university, Babbitt's educational program, which need not be tied to his political philosophy, can help us envision the most effective ways to rescue the modern humanities from oblivion on today's college campuses.

How can it do so? How can we use Babbitt's pedagogical philosophy as a springboard for a novel, yet genuinely humanistic, plan for the modern humanities? Our final chapter aims to show the way.

---

[203] See Babbitt 1986: 127 and 1991: 368. For his approval of humanitarianism, see, e.g., Babbitt 1986: 105, 113, 127, 209. Cf. Hovey 1986: 207. In his writings Babbitt also made clear that he saw value in the natural sciences: see, e.g., Babbitt 1912: 452, 1924: 258, 1930: 32, and 1986: 105. *Pace* Grattan 1930b: 24.

[204] Babbitt thus often vouched for the value of particular humanistic works over others: see, e.g., Babbitt 1986: 75, 122, 164; Connely in Manchester and Shepard 1941: 185 (quoting Babbitt).

6

Toward a Truly Ecumenical Wisdom

The fact, recognized from ancient times onward, that individuals differ has been dwelt upon latterly till we have almost forgotten a much more important fact, that they resemble each other.
—Norman Foerster, *The Future of the Liberal College* (1938)

Everyone recognizes that the Occident has been amazingly successful in its pursuit of power, but the question may be asked whether it has not got its power at the expense of wisdom.
—Irving Babbitt, "Humanistic Education in China and the West" (1921)

The Substance of an Education

Throughout this book we have detected that contemporary defenses of the humanities radically undersell their value and role in higher education. By relying solely on instrumental rationales for the modern humanistic disciplines, today's defenders have repeated the missteps traditionalists made during the Battle of the Classics. In both cases, apologists, discarding humanistic justifications for the study of ancient Greek and Latin advanced as far back as the early Renaissance, failed to underscore what is unique about the humanities. Instead, they highlighted their ability to inculcate skills that other disciplines outside the humanities' orbit could also claim to instill. This change of course of necessity renders the humanities superfluous: since they supposedly provide students only with nebulously defined aptitudes that various sciences and vocational subjects can also reasonably profess to offer, there is no need for the modern humanities in an undergraduate curriculum.

Worse still, in both the Battle of the Classics and today's debates over the value of the humanities, humanists unwittingly turned social scientists into the rightful judges of educational value. If the humanistic disciplines are merely conduits for skills, social scientists, with their ability to test empirically which subjects most effectively inculcate such skills, become our educational umpires. This situation places the fate of the humanities in the hands of scholars who may have little regard for them and have pragmatic incentives to undercut their curricular opponents.[1] Ever since the academic revolution of the late nineteenth century, when election took the place of prescription as the dominating force in undergraduate education, higher learning in America has become a popularity contest, according to which disciplines, like salespeople, must rope in as many customers as possible in order to survive. In such an academic environment, the tendency for humanists to outsource the task of proving the value of what they teach to other actors who have their own agendas seems especially fraught. Turning social scientists into the arbiters of higher education also suggests to observers that humanists lack any intrinsic ability to assess quality. Why should students study subjects so feeble that their devotees cannot credibly vouch for the courses' value on their own terms? Although proponents of the humanities, duty-bound to counter vocationalist fears, may occasionally need to muster skills-based defenses,[2] these sorts of defenses cannot serve as the humanities' foundation.

As humanists such as Petrarch, Bruni, and Babbitt recognized, *the humanities need substance*. Their special contribution to the educational process is their ability to offer to young people the invitation to improve themselves through the use of models from the past. Profound works of art, literature, philosophy, and religion provide the best means of shaping students' souls—contributing visions of the good, the true, and the beautiful that can allow human beings to lead sounder, happier, and more responsible lives.

This goal does not suggest that non-humanistic disciplines cannot help with this endeavor. Indeed, the social sciences, for instance, can furnish us with key insights about human nature that reflect our age. And growing interest in social-science coursework that moves beyond the teaching of methods and gestures toward the concept of the Good Life hints at a deep hunger among undergraduates for humanistic wisdom. At Yale University,

---

[1] Academic administrators may also lack appreciation for the broader purpose of humanistic training. Since such administrators often have the power to make the ultimate decisions regarding the fate of academic departments, failing to provide them with rationales for the humanities that humanists can best judge is dangerous.

[2] It is imperative to note that the nebulousness that has dogged the modern humanities since their birth in the second half of the nineteenth century has rendered it essentially impossible to provide a defense that will ring true in all circumstances. This challenge is particularly salient in regard to disciplines such as history, which are typically seen as only partially linked to the modern humanities. On this subject, see Chapter 2, this volume.

for example, "Psychology and the Good Life" has become the most popular undergraduate class in the institution's entire history.[3] But this contemporary wisdom derived from the social sciences is itself insufficient to the task at hand and can serve as only one component of *the wisdom of all the ages*: a core of common human experience gleaned from cultural masterworks that can inform students about the human condition in all its diversity and encourage them to ponder sound ethical standards.[4] As Cicero taught us, to disregard this wisdom is knowingly to cut oneself off from the past, to remain forever a child. Further, as Babbitt justly noted, "The notion that in spite of the enormous mass of experience that has been accumulated in both East and West we are still without light as to the habits that make for moderation and good sense and decency, and that education is therefore still purely a matter of exploration and experiment is one that may be left to those who are suffering from an advanced stage of naturalistic intoxication."[5] Unfortunately, contemporary American higher education offers much evidence of such intoxication, evidence that suggests even more urgently the need for the humanities to serve as a counterweight to the naturalistic tendencies of our age.

All this means that the *content* encountered in the humanistic classroom is of crucial import and cannot be determined by either a faculty member's research agenda or a student's whims. As has been recognized since antiquity, some works of culture provide more profound models for reflection than do others. Some encapsulate visions of life that are more powerful than do others. Some speak to what is both particular and, more importantly, universal in human experience more successfully than do others.

---

[3] See Shimer 2018.

[4] On this topic, see the valuable insights of Kupperman (1991: 159–72), a philosopher who discusses the comparative strengths and weaknesses of humanistic and social scientific approaches to moral psychology. Kupperman points to Confucius, Aristotle, La Rochefoucauld, Hume, and Dostoevsky as examples of thinkers whose insights into moral psychology are especially valuable. On the value of fictional works to an understanding of moral psychology, Kupperman writes, "A central point is that depictions in novels and plays can be taken as modeling aspects of reality. A model brings out detail and relevant connections, enabling us better to focus on the reality it models. This accounts for the way in which novels and plays often allow us to perceive events and connections in the real world that we otherwise might not have taken in, so that people sometimes murmur that life imitates art. A novelist or playwright can look like a great moral psychologist, if she or he gets us to see fundamental connections—either in the psychology of people or in everyday life—that we otherwise would not have grasped" (170). Nussbaum (2008) proposes another key reason that social scientists investigating the Good Life need to rely on the work of humanists. She keenly demonstrates that scholars associated with the so-called positive psychology movement often advance simplistic and problematic conceptions of happiness. This conclusion suggests the urgent need for psychologists to bolster their ideas through the study of philosophy.

[5] Babbitt 1991: 388.

It is important here to pose crucial and increasingly sensitive questions: How ought this process of selection occur? Who decides which works of culture are "more profound" than others, or which most satisfyingly engage both the particular and the universal in human experience? Naturally, different sorts of colleges and universities will require different answers to these questions.[6] No individual can—or should—dictate a curriculum for all American higher education. This book aims not to prescribe an ironclad course of studies but rather to highlight the prevailing—and problematic—tendency for humanist scholars to relinquish their responsibility to *debate* such matters in an open and transparent way, secure in the knowledge that what they teach matters.

Undoubtedly faculty members can disagree endlessly about which works are the best vehicles for the wisdom of the ages. Notions of the good, the true, and the beautiful can and do evolve, and thus institutions need not put forward a single vision.[7] What is required is curricular debates of this nature to take place and for humanists to rise to the occasion and say what they think is most profound—and *why*. Such debates are integral to the humanities' survival and thus well worth having. In fact, the abdication of faculty members' role in crafting an undergraduate curriculum of substance that provides a clear vision of what it means to be a well-educated person amounts to one of our age's most devastating attacks on the humanistic tradition.

As we have seen in earlier chapters, so-called scientific democrats in the late nineteenth century pioneered curricular models that dismissed the value of education's content precisely in order to supplant the humanities. Continued support for such curricular models today is a recipe for destruction. If humanists leave the substance of an education to a student's fancy, they thereby reinforce the contemporary university's chimerical notion that we need not guide the young to focus their attention on self-improvement. The goal of self-perfection—though surely never fully attainable—is too important to human happiness and civilizational flourishing to be cast aside as a

---

[6] There are so many pragmatic concerns associated with the realities of disparate colleges and universities that it seems foolhardy to dictate a core humanities curriculum for all of them. Factors that influence the eventual shape of such a curriculum include institutional support for these courses; the makeup of the humanities faculty; and the financial resources of the institutions. This chapter thus includes broad suggestions for crafting an intellectually and morally sound humanities core. The specifics will depend on the humanities faculty at different institutions and the vicissitudes of their institutions.

[7] As Babbitt (1991: lxxiii) emphasized, "Life does not give here an element of oneness and there an element of change. It gives a *oneness that is always changing*. The oneness and the change are inseparable" (emphasis in the original).

relic of the past. But this is precisely what the American academy, with its romantic vision of innate human altruism, its distrust for anything other than scientific fact, and its concomitant embrace of vocationalism, has achieved. The instrumental defenses of the modern humanities so often championed today feed our culture's naturalistic inclination to dismiss the past and, in accordance with Charles Eliot's dangerously one-sided advice, to look forward and not backward, to look outward and not in.[8] If we aspire to produce future generations that are not only efficient but also happy and morally grounded, we must counsel them to look forward *and* backward, outward *and* in. To meet this goal, of course, we need a humanistic revival.

Professionalized Pragmatism

If instrumental defenses of the humanities prove so underwhelming and are antithetical to the flourishing of the humanistic disciplines, why, one might reasonably ask, have they proven so popular? In the context of the Battle of the Classics, at least, we can hazard a guess. Proponents of the classical humanities in the nineteenth century focused their arguments on skills because the dreary, gerund-grinding pedagogy associated with ancient Greek and Latin in America left them unable to advance humanist defenses of the classics. The appeal to mental discipline was, if you will, the easy way out: as challenging as Greek grammar can be, using classical literature to explore the moral principles by which to live is far tougher. The shift from genuinely humanist to instrumental defenses of the classical humanities appears to have been primarily pragmatic in inspiration.[9]

Many may suggest that more ideological reasons lie behind the contemporary flight from substance. Ever since the late political philosopher Allan Bloom, in his bestseller *The Closing of the American Mind*,[10] excoriated the relativism he spied in modern American higher education, culture warriors have harped on the crippling effects of postmodern theory on the humanities. Undoubtedly, as even less fault-finding critics such as Mark Edmundson

---

[8] On this advice, see Chapters 4 and 5, this volume.

[9] Bolgar (1973: esp. 10–12) notes, however, that to a lesser extent even Renaissance humanists often failed to live up to their pedagogical theories in the classroom. This failure appears to be a pervasive problem: teachers can maintain that instruction in their subject matter has a moral effect on pupils but not make good on this claim. On the need for pedagogical approaches that foreground the moral component of the humanities, see the following text.

[10] Bloom 1987.

and Michael Roth have observed, contemporary humanists often seem wary about offering qualitative assessments of writers and artists.[11] Paradoxically, this reluctance may also stem from a scientistic compulsion to view neutral analysis as the only goal of literary study—a compulsion that discourages scholars from any efforts to assess which works best engage the most fundamental questions of life. In fact, many scholars now appear skeptical of any claims to literary "greatness,"[12] regardless of whether such skepticism stems from a postmodern theoretical orientation or a literary scientism. The result is a crippling failure to judge—a curious phenomenon for a profession in which peer review remains the gold standard and ensures that colleagues are constantly assessing one another's work.

But one gathers, as was the case during the Battle of the Classics, that much of the impetus for instrumental apologetics stems from pragmatic motives. Skills-based justifications do not disturb the contemporary curricular smorgasbord. Although educators often suggest that opposition to a core curriculum for undergraduates is based on ideological distaste for the Great Books model, Babbitt has ably demonstrated that there remain no reasons to restrict a core curriculum to a canon of dead white males. In fact, as we have detected in the previous chapter, his insistence on solving the problem of the One and the Many provides compelling reasons *against* doing so.

Still, rather than propose a truly multicultural core, many humanists appear content with the choose-your-own-adventure curriculum that has dominated general education in the US since the late nineteenth century and has helped assure the increasing irrelevance of the humanities. Why might humanists esteem a curricular model that sidelines their own disciplines? As was the case during the Battle of the Classics, we are taking the easy way out. Core courses, after all, require broad, assimilative learning that is not a hallmark of contemporary graduate education, with its fixation on specialized knowledge. Unlike courses nominally devoted to inculcating vaguely defined skills with their bureaucratically determined learning outcomes, moreover, classes that aim to serve a humanist purpose work best when they focus on specific content—masterworks that explore life's great questions with humane insight. Such courses thus fight against professors' training and necessitate a greater amount of pedagogical preparation. Thanks to the priorities of the professionalized university, many professors would prefer to teach

---

[11] Edmundson 2013: 22–23; Roth 2015: 141.
[12] On this topic, see Edmundson 2013: 22–23 and Chapter 1, this volume.

narrow courses that maximize their publication goals at the expense of fostering a genuinely humanistic classroom.[13]

From a strictly pragmatic standpoint, then, it seems unwise for humanities professors to rebel against the distribution requirements system. But, as we have seen, the humanities cannot revive in the midst of a curricular free-for-all. Such a course of studies fights against humanistic values: it stresses the ahistorical will of the individual over the wisdom of the past and mandates a skills-based approach to education that values method over substance. If, in the context of general education, all content will suffice, then content does not matter. And if content does not matter, skills become education's raison d'être and, as we have seen, the humanities will continue to wither.

The pragmatic distaste for core curricula can also be illustrated by pondering the intellectual inspiration for the free-elective system. As we have noted in this book, the original American university reformers—the first generation of scientific democrats—popularized curricular models inspired by free-market capitalism and social Darwinism. The free-elective system—much like the distribution requirements system, which amounts to a paltry modification of it—treats students as customers and provides the stimulus for what critics call the neoliberal university, according to the dictates of which everything—and everyone—is valued on the grounds of economic efficiency alone.

It is singularly peculiar that the insightful literature criticizing the neoliberal turn in American higher education so often overlooks *curricular neoliberalism*. Thus, for example, *How the University Works*, Marc Bousquet's valuable book-length assault on free-market fundamentalism in our nation's colleges and universities, fails to link the consumerization of higher education to our romantic, consumerized course of studies.[14] Why are books that are so deeply—and justly—critical of our laissez-faire universities so reluctant to touch upon their laissez-faire curriculum? A proper answer to this

---

[13] The faculty breakdown of the two main courses that make up the Core at Columbia University, "Literature Humanities" and "Contemporary Civilization," both year-long classes required of all first- and second-year students respectively, bear witness to the effects of this incentive structure. Roosevelt Montas, the former Director of the Center for the Core Curriculum at Columbia, informed me that for at least a decade, only one-third of these courses have been taught by tenure-track or tenured faculty members: the other two thirds have been led by either Columbia Ph.D. candidates working on their dissertations or postdoctoral fellows chosen from among former students at Columbia. Especially at an institution such as Columbia, which makes significant research demands of its faculty, tenure-stream professors have pragmatic incentives to eschew such broad coursework.

[14] Bousquet 2008. The same can be said about similarly valuable books decrying the neoliberal university, such as Kirp 2003 and Donoghue 2008. For a fuller examination of such works and their disinclination to discuss curricula, see Adler 2018.

question hints at the pragmatic rationales lurking behind humanists' acquiescence to free election and distribution requirements.

We need not scapegoat humanities professors, however, who are simply responding rationally to the incentives the architects of the American research universities established for our nation's higher learning. Contemporary professors of the humanities, after all, did not pioneer the system that fetishizes research productivity at the expense of good teaching. They did not create the environment in which most of our nation's colleges offer perilously little guidance to undergraduates, counterintuitively leaving it up to the uneducated to determine what it means to be educated. Humanities professors merely inhabit this world; they did not manufacture it. This world, moreover, awash in a romantic presentism, by design tilts the scales in favor of vocationalism and the sciences, to the humanities' detriment. In addition, the ever-increasing price tag for a bachelor's degree further pushes many students in the direction of vocationalism, even if narrow, strictly occupation-based training makes decreasing sense in an economic and technological environment in which specific categories of jobs are constantly in jeopardy of being outsourced or automated.

Training for Wisdom and Character

It is a mark of how successful the original shapers of the American university movement have been that humanities professors in America have now become so professionalized that their careers have scarcely little to do with the humanistic tradition. Thus, for example, the English professor Stanley Fish, discussing his vision of the proper approach to the collegiate classroom, cautioned that "teachers cannot, except for a serendipity that by definition cannot be counted on, fashion moral character, or inculcate respect for others, or produce citizens of a certain temper."[15] Here an influential American humanities professor—likely without recognizing it—dismissed the spirit of Renaissance humanism that played the chief role in shaping the American college curriculum from the colonial period to the middle of the nineteenth century. Even more astonishingly, he openly denied the moral component of education that has proved crucial to the liberal arts tradition for millennia. Do literary, philosophical, artistic, and religious masterpieces

[15] Fish 2008: 14.

really have *no power to influence human beings' moral lives*, except in seren-dipitous circumstances?

Naturally, Fish's minimalist view of education's effects on the young radi-cally undercuts the humanistic tradition.[16] And we should not deny the al-lure of his skepticism. Many pessimists, for example, could point to highly cultured but ethically challenged humanities professors to conclude that ex-posure to the humanities does not assure the transformation of young people into decent human beings. Great works, however, can be studied in a variety of ways. Just as Babbitt complained about the arid formalist approach to the ancients, which treats classical masterworks as "literary playthings rather than the basis of a philosophy of life,"[17] so the study of masterpieces can de-volve into sterile esteem for cultural capital. If, as Fish has counseled, we teach merely in order to offer students "the analytical skills—of argument, statistical modeling, laboratory procedure—that will enable them . . . to en-gage in independent research after a course is over,"[18] humanists are guilty of undermining the capability of cultural masterworks to shape lives.

"Truly great art," the philosopher Claes Ryn has stressed, "is never di-dactic, but it helps us understand who we are. It attunes us to the real world and prepares us for acting within it."[19] As the ancients recognized long ago, the young must have values and models of conduct. "In the absence of good models," Babbitt wrote, "the child will imitate bad ones, and so, long before the age of intelligent choice and self-determination, become the prisoner of bad habits."[20] We should therefore select models from works that offer the most profound visions of human experience. Such models need not offer—in fact, they ought *not* offer—a uniform guide for self-improvement. Instead, they should reflect both the reassuring sense of unity (the One) and the rich diversity (the Many) of human experience over time.

Fish's minimalist recommendations for the college classroom also fail to appreciate how a curriculum shapes students' souls. A course of studies, after all, is not merely a list of classes or a convenient agreement brokered by var-ious academic departments. On the contrary: an institution's curriculum

---

[16] Fish's view is also undercut by social science research (e.g., Heckman and Kautz 2013) suggesting that educational programs *do* have long-term effects on character development, though such re-search tends to view "character" in terms of skills (e.g., grit, emotional resilience) rather than the humanistic, substance-based approach advocated here.

[17] Babbitt 1991: 118.

[18] Fish 2008: 13.

[19] Ryn 1997a.

[20] Babbitt 1991: 387.

provides the philosophical blueprint for the sorts of adults it aims to produce. As we have traced in this book, during the late nineteenth century this philosophical blueprint fundamentally altered, from a semi-aristocratic conception rooted in the classical humanities to a vision of Americans as democratic customers. Our laissez-faire course of studies has helped create laissez-faire Americans: rootless, isolated, utilitarian, and possessed of an impoverished view of the Good Life. To revitalize American society, we need to train students not just for service and power, but also for wisdom and character.

Toward a Modern, Critical Spirit

To do this training, we as teachers must have sufficient respect for our students to allow them to come to their own conclusions about the essential questions of life. One of the modernists' most successful lines of attack against the old prescribed curriculum during the Battle of the Classics focused on its cultivation of passivity: undergraduates were to drink in the wisdom of the ancients, unquestioningly accepting the college's doctrinal vision of the good. Reformers justly criticized this model, which implicitly viewed students as receptacles for information, rather than active participants in the search for standards. Heavy-handed approaches in the classroom—in which the syllabus or the lectern is transformed into an instrument of proselytization—revive this old spirit of student passivity, effectively robbing undergraduates of their role in the most crucial educational opportunity of their lives. How can we argue that the humanities serve as a bulwark against, as the political scientist Ruth O'Brien maintained, "the power of blind tradition and authority"[21] if we ask students blindly to follow our authority in the classroom?[22]

It remains difficult to determine how serious a problem this is in contemporary American academia. Naturally, we cannot monitor every classroom to see how much professors strive to cultivate a modern, critical spirit among undergraduates. One should note, moreover, that the picture of radicalized humanities instructors bent on brainwashing the young has become a feature of political demagoguery, which often relies more on anecdote

---

[21] O'Brien 2010: ix.
[22] Cf. Kupperman 1991: 174: "Education of character should stimulate reflection and suggest possible directions; once beyond the core of social morality that is taught to very small children, it should not dictate answers."

than evidence.[23] But surely *some* humanists fail to encourage in students a modern, critical attitude toward their pet ideologies (whatever they may be). Just as we must inspire students to reflect creatively on the masterworks of the past, thus we must motivate them to question received wisdom in the classroom. If, for all their genius, great creators do not deserve to be placed on metaphorical pedestals as purveyors of peerless insight, surely we humble professors do not deserve such treatment either.

All these points suggest that a shift in apologetics for the humanities requires more than a mere change in argumentative tactics. The re-centering of the humanities on their substance must also encourage a salubrious revolution in the classroom. As we have discussed in earlier chapters, essential to the humanistic tradition from the Renaissance forward is the use of prior models to perfect the individual. This striving for perfection can most easily be accomplished if we study cultural masterworks. But it also depends on how a class is taught. We humanists must ask ourselves, are we encouraging students to grapple with life's animating questions? Or are we merely compelling them to think like contemporary humanities professors?[24]

Unfortunately, the buffet-style approach to general education that dominates America's colleges and universities can be counted on to reinforce the latter over the former. My own institution, for instance, has pioneered a general education requirement it calls "Scholarship in Practice." Contrary to the spirit of well-roundedness integral to the liberal arts tradition, the requirement aims to turn undergraduates into proto-professors. A glossy brochure highlighting the "innovative" character of Scholarship in Practice announces, "Areas such as architecture, business, education, and journalism offer courses in this area that lead to products such as architectural designs, new technologies, innovative publications, new computer software, business plans, advertising campaigns, and educational curricula."[25] Reinforcing our culture's penchant for encouraging premature specialization, the requirement turns unwitting undergraduates into Baconian researchers-in-training.

[23] E.g., Kimball 2019, who cavalierly maintains that the humanities "at most colleges and universities have devolved into cesspools of identity politics and grievance studies" and thus "should be starved of funding and ultimately shut down."
[24] Particularly in my role as a language teacher, this is an issue that constantly concerns me. Am I focusing too much attention on grammar and translation, rather than using the language as a vehicle for more important matters? In my advanced undergraduate Latin courses, I have abandoned research papers in favor of essays in which students must examine the worldviews of the authors we read and compare them with their own. This is but one strategy for attempting to inculcate humanist values in the classroom. Other professors can surely pioneer their own.
[25] Anonymous 2010: 18.

Humanists must fight against such preprofessional presentism in general education, with curricula and teaching strategies that foreground sound standards for living.

We cannot vouch for the essential role of the humanities in higher education if we fail to live up to our pedagogical promises. Re-centering our concerns on substance offers humanists the exciting possibility to use the classroom to focus on issues of paramount concern to all people who aim to lead a serious life. This is one essential means of battling against charges of the humanities' elitism. Demonstrating that the humanities provide training for life turns the tables on their pseudo-populist critics. As Norman Foerster maintained, "The utilitarian specialists who control most of our state universities are not content that the common man should be a worker: he should be nothing else, he should be kept a mere worker. They will not recognize and develop his humanity."[26] By denying to all but privileged undergraduates the opportunity to shape their souls, vocationalists implicitly broadcast their elitism. Babbitt's impulse to home in on the ways in which great works of culture from various traditions speak to our common humanity helps showcase the humanities' populist potential. Rightly taught, after all, the modern humanities highlight universality in human experience. Without granting students access to this human drama writ large, utilitarians encourage the young to see themselves as little more than cogs in a machine.

Humanists should also advertise the fact that eschewing character development in favor of strict vocationalism is a danger to society. We cannot presume—as pedagogical romantics such as Charles Eliot and John Dewey have presumed—that young people will naturally use their pragmatic training for altruistic purposes. As Babbitt cautioned, by avoiding the ethical component of education, America's colleges and universities run the risk of creating "efficient megalomaniacs," whose resistance to introspection can cause great misery.[27] Our current generation of Silicon Valley tech giants, certain that their new inventions will "make the world a better place,"[28] even though those inventions often appear to increase depression and anxiety,[29] provides ample warning about the threats posed by an amoral, Darwinian approach to higher learning.

---

[26] Foerster 1946: vi.
[27] Babbitt 1991: 366.
[28] See Marantz 2016.
[29] On the negative impact of social media, see, e.g., Hunt, Marx, Lipson, and Young 2018.

An Educational Law of Measure

As we have suggested, the crucial goal of re-grounding the humanities in substance requires a humanist revolt against what Foerster humorously termed "required electives."[30] The impetus, he rightly maintained, "to 'pass the buck' to the student" when it comes to the undergraduate course of studies demonstrates "the intellectual bankruptcy" inherent in pushing such a vacuous curricular model.[31] As Babbitt reminds us, "The very word curriculum implies a running together. Under the new educational dispensation, students, instead of running together, tend to lounge separately."[32]

This conclusion does not imply that we should return to the spirit of the old classical colleges, with their intellectual myopia, their sectarianism, and their curricular rigidity. But humanists should fight for *an educational law of measure*. American higher education requires *both* humanitarianism *and* humanism—the drive to improve the material conditions of the world *and* to improve oneself. Without the former, we potentially encourage in the young an anchoritic disconnect from society; without the latter, we leave the world in the hands of those who lack an ethical center. Bereft of the humanities, then, our colleges and universities can accomplish only half of what they should. To create an educational law of measure, our institutions of higher learning require novel approaches to the course of studies—approaches that place humanism and humanitarianism on equal footing.

Undergraduates must thus experience the natural and social sciences as part of their general education. How they are led to do so should be a matter for an institution's natural and social scientists to determine. But, for reasons we have elaborated on throughout this book, the humanities cannot rely on "required electives"—a choice between, say, Plato and pornography. Rather, we must fight for approaches to humanistic general education that undercut pure naturalism by demonstrating to students the unparalleled necessity of determining sound standards for living. For the same reason, humanists must insist on a robust language requirement for all undergraduates to provide to them the experience of reading at least part of one great work in a language other than English. Such an experience helps reinforce both the familiar and unfamiliar aspects of other cultures and, that is to say, emphasizes

---

[30] Foerster 1969: 47, 68.
[31] Ibid. 68.
[32] Babbitt 1924: 303–4.

the cardinal importance of the One and the Many to personal and civilizational flourishing.

Self-improvement should not be the sole concern of humanities majors. One unfortunate byproduct of our Darwinian curriculum and impoverished vision of general education is our tendency to assess pedagogical success strictly according to the number of majors in a given discipline. Indeed, our lackluster required electives well-nigh force students to consider their concentrations the singular focus of their intellectual concerns. By comparison, students typically view the fulfillment of distribution requirements as the mental equivalent of jumping through hoops. To balance their souls, *all students must grapple with life's animating questions.* "We figure our pupils as eventual pedagogues, clerks, salesmen, journalists, landscape-gardeners, library-assistants, and so forth," wrote the philosopher R. M. Wenley (1861–1929). "It seldom occurs to us that, first and foremost, they are, and must continue, human beings, and that our prime responsibility is to inoculate them with an estimate of life commensurate with this, their privileged calling."[33]

For this, we need humanists of a certain spirit. The professionalization of the faculty in the nineteenth and early twentieth centuries greatly improved American academia in important respects, raising the level of scholarly seriousness and accuracy. Obviously, then, reasonable criticisms of this professionalized temper should not lead to a wistful return to the pedagogical olden days, with their mind-numbing fixation on mental discipline. Though we need careful scholars, however, their scrupulousness should not come at the expense of a humanist emphasis on character-building. The urgent revival of the humanist classroom should not only center around the study of great works but also encourage us to pioneer ways to fixate less on scholarly minutiae and focus more on ethics.

Promises and Pitfalls

How can we develop a salubrious approach to humanistic general education in the contemporary academic environment? As we have discussed at length, the almost omnipresent laundry lists of courses that meet various skills-based distributional requirements will prove incapable of revivifying the humanities. But how should humanists interested in rescuing their disciplines best

---

[33] Wenley 1910: 517–18.

proceed? Naturally, as we have stressed, different sorts of institutions will call for different solutions. But one recent high-profile attempt to revamp a humanistic curriculum suggests some important promises and pitfalls for prospective reformers.

Reed College in Portland, Oregon, attracted headlines when its long-standing team-taught core course, Humanities 110, encountered prolonged student protests. This year-long sequence, required of all first-year students, dates back to 1943.[34] Undergraduate activists, some of whom were members of a group called Reedies Against Racism, launched an in-class sit-in of sorts in 2016 and even began disrupting lectures. Although the class, which focused chiefly on the ancient Mediterranean, included some readings from cultures not normally deemed "Western,"[35] protestors charged that the syllabus was, in the words of the reporter Colleen Flaherty, "too white, too male and too Eurocentric."[36]

As one might imagine, culture warriors of various stripes, getting wind of the increasingly disruptive protests, chimed in about the situation. Some conservative critics excoriated the protesters as the typical identity-obsessed "snowflakes" of the politically correct university. *National Review*'s Stanley Kurtz, for example, fretted that "The Hum 110 requirement may soon be fatally weakened. Signs point to faculty capitulation to these disruptions. That will spell the end of Reed's distinctive character, and the loss of a unique choice for American students."[37]

The faculty at Reed, compelled to start its decennial review of Hum 110 a year early, soon announced major reforms to the institution's signature humanities course. It now focuses on "four thematic modules" over the course of an academic year: the ancient Mediterranean and Athens in the fifth and fourth centuries BC during the fall semester; and Mexico City and the Harlem Renaissance in the spring.[38] Campus radicals seem to have been no more impressed with the alterations than were conservative pundits. In a response on Facebook, Reedies Against Racism pilloried the revised sequence, lamenting the continued focus on ancient Greece and Rome. The group announced that "we're calling for the Humanities 110 faculty to pick

---

[34] Flaherty 2017a. Rudolph (1977: 241) specifies that Reed inaugurated mandatory core humanities courses for all freshmen and sophomores as part of its reforms in 1921.

[35] For the syllabus, see https://www.reed.edu/humanities/hum110/syllabus/2016-17/fall.html.

[36] Flaherty 2017a.

[37] Kurtz 2017.

[38] For further details on the new Hum 110, see https://www.reed.edu/humanities/hum110/index.html. See also Patel 2018.

different cities from the old syllabus for the first two semesters. We feel that these cities should be outside of Europe, as reparations for Humanities 110's history of erasing the histories of people of color, especially black people."[39]

The controversy at Reed (essentially a replay of the quarrel surrounding Stanford's changes to its Western Culture program in the late 1980s)[40] demonstrates how fraught the creation or re-envisioning of a humanities core curriculum can be in our ideologically charged climate. But it also helps accentuate some of the benefits of the Babbittian approach to higher learning proposed here. The conservative inclination to bemoan any revisions to what was, at its heart, a "Western civilization" sequence seems shortsighted. As the New Humanists pointed out long ago, a chief goal of the modern humanities is to determine whether there are any standards for living apart from the dictates of scientific fact. For this assessment, we need to study a variety of human civilizations, rather than privilege one concatenation of societies first lumped together as "Western" in the mid-nineteenth century.[41]

All the same, Reed's revised core, despite the obvious good intentions of its authors, is a work in progress and at present may not live up to the full promise of greater inclusiveness.[42] By adding modules devoted to Mexico City and the Harlem Renaissance, Reed's faculty likely fed fears that the revisions to Hum 110 amounted to a capitulation to contemporary American identity politics. With its focus on two groups—Hispanic and black Americans—whose exclusion has been among the most deep-seated concerns for the diversity movement in the US, the new sequence reinforces the sense that the reforms, nominally aimed at a genuine cosmopolitanism, instead underscore American provincialism. This reinforcement is deeply unfair to the civilizations the faculty saw fit to include in the new course, which have obviously produced works well worth serious contemplation.

A New Humanist might have stressed, moreover, that at its root, education, as the word's Latin derivation implies, should be a drawing out of oneself toward that which is universal in human experience. This definition suggests that the most effective approach to the modern humanities will

---

[39] See https://www.facebook.com/reediesagainstr4cism/photos/a.1216652598413611/ 1690731074339092/?type=3&theater.

[40] On the feverish debate over Stanford's Western Culture program during the academic culture wars, see Adler 2016: 19, 23, 26, 38.

[41] On this topic, see Chapter 2, this volume.

[42] Elizabeth Drumm, the program chair of Hum 110 during the decennial review, suggested to me that the faculty aims to add and subtract different modules in the future. So, the current grouping of four is not set in stone.

focus on masterworks from sundry cultures—rather than merely the West or the West and a handful of groups that happen to be woefully underrepresented in the contemporary American academy.

What do philosophers, novelists, poets, artists, musicians, and religious figures from manifold societies tell us about how we ought to live our lives? This question can serve as the backbone for an intellectually and morally sound approach to pluralism. Many contemporary American students, romantics at heart, merely hunger for the curriculum to represent *them*. By contrast, a salutary humanities curriculum should feature a diversity of human traditions precisely because it must *force all students to look beyond the particular toward what we as human beings have in common*.[43]

A promising approach to the humanities, then, could focus on required coursework dedicated to questions of broad interest surrounding the human condition, with results that could help students elevate and enrich their souls. There need not be rigid requirements to represent all groups from all time periods—a quixotic goal at best. Rather, works should be selected on the basis of their capacity to shed light on life's animating concerns, from a variety of different cultures and perspectives. To model this Babbittian approach and provide some specific examples of what it could imply, we might anchor a curriculum in some of these foundational issues: the problem of mortality (e.g., selections from the Egyptian *Book of the Dead*, Shakespeare's *Hamlet*, Dostoyevsky's *Crime and Punishment*, Virginia Wolf's *To the Lighthouse*, and García Márquez's *One Hundred Years of Solitude*); ethical codes (e.g., selections from the Bible, the *Analects* of Confucius, the *Bhagavad Gita*, Aristotle's *Nicomachean Ethics*, the *Dhammapada*, and the Quran); the opportunities and challenges of love, family, and friendship (e.g., Sappho, Rumi, Jane Austen's *Pride and Prejudice*, and Ralph Ellison's *Invisible Man*); the realm of human imagination (e.g., Homer's *Odyssey*, *One Thousand and One Nights*, Boccaccio's *Decameron*, Cervantes' *Don*

---

[43] In an introduction to his great novel *Invisible Man*, Ralph Ellison (1995: xx) offered a congruent impression of the value of imaginative literature for such unifying purposes: "By way of imposing meaning upon our disparate American experience the novelist seeks to create forms in which acts, scenes and characters speak for more than their immediate selves, and in this enterprise the very nature of language is on his side. For by a trick of fate (and our racial problems notwithstanding) the human imagination is integrative—and the same is true of the centrifugal force that inspirits the democratic process. And while fiction is but a form of symbolic action, a mere game of 'as if,' therein lies its true function and its potential for effecting change. For at its most serious, just as is true of politics at its best, it is a thrust toward a human ideal." Although Ellison focused these remarks on a democratic and American context, they seem applicable to a broader conception of the humanities as a whole.

Quixote, and Mary Shelley's *Frankenstein*); the problem of living together (e.g., Plato's *Republic*, Ibn Khaldun's *Muqaddimah*, and the *Narrative of the Life of Frederick Douglass*); and the pitfalls of power (e.g., Tacitus' *Agricola*, Murasaki Shikibu's *The Tale of Genji*, Machiavelli's *The Prince*, and Chinua Achebe's *Things Fall Apart*).

In such a curriculum, diversity and inclusiveness remain important organizing principles. Yet they are not attained by a relentless, tokenizing pursuit of representativeness for its own sake. On the contrary: they emerge from a more intellectually serious investigation of how we as a species have sought to answer the most fundamental questions of life.

The Wisdom of All *the Ages*

We inhabit a society obsessed with difference. The romantic impulse to foreground our uniqueness, combined, one worries, with a Darwinian desire to classify and rank disparate groups, has left us enraptured with diversity. To a great extent, the current fetishization of human difference stems from a condign recognition of previous and contemporary injustices. But our infatuation with distinctiveness amounts to a dangerous half-truth. Civilizations, Babbitt teaches, have fallen due to their inability to harmonize the One and the Many.[44] We urgently require a humanist curriculum that does not simply reinforce the half-truth of difference, but also juxtaposes it with the consummate truth of similarity. For the contemporary world to turn back from the abyss of tribalism and warmongering, we are in desperate need of syncretism.

Is there a central core of human wisdom—across the ages, from manifold traditions—that can guide us as we grapple with the best ways to live? We can find out only by experiencing masterworks of art, literature, religion, and philosophy from a broad range of cultures. This is *not* an exercise in intellectual tokenism; nor does it presume a single way of living that is best. Rather, it provides the soundest means by which to investigate life's meaning. The future health of human civilization relies upon the rejuvenation of the humanistic tradition. We cannot improve the world if we cannot improve ourselves.

---

[44] Babbitt 1986: 84.

Bibliography

"A Recent Graduate." 1883. "Greek at Harvard [Letter to the Editor]." *The Nation* 37.949 (Sept. 6): 207.

Adams, Charles Francis, Jr. 1861. "The Reign of King Cotton." *The Atlantic Monthly* 7 (April): 451–65.

Adams, Charles Francis, Jr. 1868. "Boston." *The North American Review* 106.219 (April): 557–91.

Adams, Charles Francis, Jr. 1883. "A College Fetich." *The Independent* 35 (Aug. 9): 997–1000.

Adams, Charles Francis, Jr. 1884. *A College Fetich: An Address Delivered before the Harvard Chapter of the Fraternity of the Phi Beta Kappa in Sanders Theatre, Cambridge, June 28, 1883* (3rd edition). Boston: Lee and Shepard.

Adams, Charles Francis, Jr. 1893. "Preparatory School Education: The Classics and Written English." *Harvard Graduates' Magazine* 1 (Jan.): 177–89.

Adams, Charles Francis, Jr. 1900. *Charles Francis Adams*. Boston and New York: Houghton Mifflin.

Adams, Charles Francis, Jr. 1904. "The Proposed Increase of the Tuition Fee." *Harvard Graduates' Magazine* 13 (Sept.): 6–22.

Adams, Charles Francis, Jr. 1906. "Reflex Light from Africa." *The Century* 72: 101–11.

Adams, Charles Francis, Jr. 1907. *Three Phi Beta Kappa Addresses*. Boston and New York: Houghton, Mifflin and Company.

Adams, Charles Francis, Jr. 1916. *Charles Francis Adams 1835–1915: An Autobiography*. Boston and New York: Houghton Mifflin.

Adams, Henry. 1973. *The Education of Henry Adams*, edited and introduced by Ernest Samuels. Boston: Houghton Mifflin. Originally published in 1918.

Adler, Eric. 2016. *Classics, the Culture Wars, and Beyond*. Ann Arbor: The University of Michigan Press.

Adler, Eric. 2018. "The Neoliberal University and the Neoliberal Curriculum." *Humanitas* 31.1–2: 113–25.

Agard, Walter R. 1953. "Classical Scholarship." In *American Scholarship in the Twentieth Century*, edited by Merle Curti. 146–67. Cambridge: Harvard University Press.

Aldridge, A. Owen. 1993. "Irving Babbitt in and about China." *Modern Age* 35.4 (summer): 332–39.

Allardyce, Gilbert. 1982. "The Rise and Fall of the Western Civilization Course." *The American Historical Review* 87: 695–725.

Allen, Walter. 1969. *Governor Chamberlain's Administration in South Carolina: A Chapter of Reconstruction in the Southern States*. Freeport, NY: Books for Libraries Press.

Anonymous. 1870. *Catalogue of the Officers and Students of the College of New Jersey for the Academical Year, 1869–'70*. Princeton: The Standard Office.

Anonymous. 1878. *Catalogue of the College of New Jersey for the Academical Year 1878–'79*. Princeton: The Press Printing Establishment.

Anonymous. 1882. *The Harvard University Catalogue, 1882–83*. Cambridge: Charles W. Sever.

Anonymous. 1883a. "Averse to Attic Salt." *The* (Baltimore) *Sun* (July 5): 2.

Anonymous 1883b. "Charles Francis Adams Jr. Denounces Greek as a 'College Fetich.'" *Chicago Daily Tribune* (June 29): 3.

Anonymous. 1883c. "The College Idol." *Detroit Free Press* (Oct. 20): 4.

Anonymous. 1883d. "A College Reform." *The* (Meadville) *Chautauquan* 4.2 (Nov.): 116–17.

Anonymous. 1883e. "The Colored People Clamor for Greek." *Detroit Free Press* (July 19): 4.

Anonymous. 1883f. "Current Topics." *The Albany Law Journal* 28.18 (Nov. 3): 341.

Anonymous. 1883g. "The Dead Languages: An Address at Harvard on the Futility of a Classical Education." *The Washington Post* (July 1): 6.

Anonymous. 1883h. "Education—Classical and Practical." *The Atlanta Constitution* (July 4): 4.

Anonymous. 1883i. "A Fetich of the College: The Proper Mental Equipment of To-day." *The New York Times* (June 29): 3.

Anonymous. 1883j. "Greek and Anti-Greek." *Boston Daily Globe* (Oct. 14): 4.

Anonymous. 1883k. "The Greek Language Humbug." *Chicago Daily Tribune* (June 30): 4.

Anonymous. 1883l. "Languages in Colleges: A Meeting of College Presidents to Discuss 'A College Fetich.'" *Chicago Daily Tribune* (Nov. 18): 14.

Anonymous. 1883m. "Latin and Greek Must Go." *Christian Union* 28.1 (July 5): 19.

Anonymous. 1883n. "A Little Latin and Less Greek." *Detroit Free Press* (July 4): 4.

Anonymous. 1883o. "Lord Coleridge on the Classics." *The New York Times* (Oct. 28): 8.

Anonymous 1883p. "Modern Education: The Dead-Language Superstition." *Saturday Press* (Honolulu) (Sept. 22): 1.

Anonymous 1883q. "Notes." *The Nation* 37.942 (July 19): 54.

Anonymous. 1883r. "The Old and the New." *New York Tribune* (July 1): 6.

Anonymous. 1883s. "A Plea for Greek." *Detroit Free Press* (July 10): 4.

Anonymous. 1883t. "Practical Education." *Maine Farmer* 51.34 (July 12): 2.

Anonymous. 1883u. "R. W. Emerson's Word about Dead Languages." *Detroit Free Press* (Aug. 29): 2.

Anonymous. 1883v. "School and College." *The Independent* 35 (July 19): 9.

Anonymous. 1883w. "The Study of the Classics." *Massachusetts Ploughman and New England Journal of Agriculture* 42.43 (July 28): 2.

Anonymous. 1883x. "The Study of the Classics: An Opinion on the Subject from President Carter of Williams College." *The Washington Post* (July 22): 6.

Anonymous. 1883y. "Study of Greek and Latin: Charles Francis Adams, Jr., on 'A College Fetich.'" *Boston Daily Globe* (June 29): 5.

Anonymous. 1883z. "That College Fetich: A Professional View of the Phi Beta Kappa Oration." *Boston Daily Globe* (July 8): 2.

Anonymous. 1883ab. "Town Talk." *The Manhattan* 2.3 (Sept.): 286–88.

Anonymous. 1883ac. "The University Convocation: Needs of American Colleges." *New York Tribune* (July 13): 2.

Anonymous. 1883ad. "[Unititled.]" *The Michigan Argonaut* 2.1 (Oct. 6): 4.

Anonymous. 1883ae. "Voices." *The Nassau Literary Magazine* 39.3 (Sept.): 135.

Anonymous. 1884a. "Greek Not a College Fetich: Mr. Chamberlain's Address to Yale Students in Answer to Mr. Adams." *The New York Times* (March 12): 4.

Anonymous 1884b. "The Popular Science Monthly and the Classics." *The Independent* (New York) (March 13): 336–37.

Anonymous. 1884c. "That Alleged College Fetich." *Hartford Daily Courant* (April 5): 2.

Anonymous. 1884d. "The Value of Greek: Eightieth Commencement of the University of Vermont." *Boston Daily Globe* (June 25): 3.

Anonymous. 1885a. "Admission to Harvard: Another Blow at the Greek Incubus." *Chicago Daily Tribune* (Feb. 24): 7.

Anonymous. 1885b. "The American University." *The Critic* 3.61 (Feb. 28): 103.

Anonymous. 1885c. "Brief Mention." *Zion's Herald* 62.11 (March 18): 84.

Anonymous. 1885d. "College Presidents Disagree." *The* [New York] *Sun* (Feb. 25): No pagination.

Anonymous. 1885e. "Dr. McCosh's Reply." *The Independent* 37.18 (March 26): 17.

Anonymous 1885f. "[Editorial.]" *The Princetonian* 9.27 (March 6): 279–80.

Anonymous 1885g. "Elective Studies." *The New York Times* (Feb. 26): 4.

Anonymous. 1885h. "Electives in Colleges." *The Evening Critic* [Washington, DC] (March 3): 2.

Anonymous. 1885i. "Freedom in Higher Education." *New York Evangelist* 56.31 (July 30): 4.

Anonymous. 1885j. "The Graduates of Brown: Few Advocates of Harvard's New Departure." *The New York Times* (Feb. 28): 2.

Anonymous. 1885k. "The Harvard Plan." *Hartford Daily Courant* (Feb. 28): 2.

Anonymous. 1885l. "The Ideal University: For and Against Harvard's New Methods." *The New York Times* (Feb. 25): 5.

Anonymous. 1885m. "Liberty of Choice in Colleges." *New York Daily Tribune* (Feb. 26): 4.

Anonymous. 1885n. "Modern Ideas at Harvard: The System of Examinations for Admission Revised." *The New York Times* (Feb. 19): 3.

Anonymous. 1885o. "Presidential Debate: Harvard's Changes and Dr. McCosh's Comments." *Cornell Daily Sun* 5.89 (Feb. 26): 1.

Anonymous. 1885p. "Progress versus Reaction: Contrasting Principles of University Management Upheld by President Eliot and Dr. McCosh." *The Boston Globe* (Feb. 25): 2.

Anonymous. 1886a. *Catalogue of the College of New Jersey, Princeton: One Hundred and Fortieth Year, 1886–87*. Princeton: The Princeton Press.

Anonymous. 1886b. "Dr. Holmes's Harsh Words." *The New York Times* (Nov. 16): 1.

Anonymous. 1886c. "Electives in College Study." *New Princeton Review* 2: 284–85.

Anonymous. 1886d. *The Harvard University Catalogue, 1886–87*. Cambridge: Harvard University Press.

Anonymous. 1886e. "McCosh and Eliot: The Presidents of Princeton and Harvard." *Crawford Almanac* 33 (Dec. 9): 1.

Anonymous. 1886f. "Religion in Colleges: Discussion by Drs. McCosh and Eliot." *New York Daily Tribune* (Feb. 4): 7.

Anonymous. 1887. "Mr. Lowell on Education." *New Princeton Review* 3: 131–33.

Anonymous. 1891. *Officers, Members and Constitution of the Nineteenth Century Club and a List of Lectures and Discussions before the Club Since Its Formation*. New York: Albert B. King.

Anonymous. 1906a. "College Systems Wrong: Charles Francis Adams Calls for Radical Reforms." *The Washington Post* (June 13): 6.

Anonymous. 1906b. "Mr. Adams on Colleges." *New York Daily Tribune* (June 17): 6.

Anonymous. 1906c. "The Revised Views of Charles Francis Adams." *Hartford Courant* (June 4): 10.

Anonymous. 1908a. "Humanism in Education." *The Dial* 45.536 (Oct. 16): 237–39.

Anonymous. 1908b. "[Review of Babbitt 1986.]" *The Journal of Education* 67.13 (March 26): 357.

Anonymous. 1917. "The Battle of the Classics." *The Nation* 104 (June 7): 676.

Anonymous. 1930. "Humanists Start Wordy War." *The Boston Globe* (June 15): C7.

Anonymous. 2010. *Transforming General Education at the University of Maryland: The University of Maryland Plan for General Education*. (Dec.): http://gened.umd.edu/documents/TranformingGeneralEducation.pdf.

Anonymous. 2013. *Humanities Report Card: 2013*. American Academy of Arts and Sciences: https://www.amacad.org/sites/default/files/publication/downloads/hum_report_card.pdf.

Anonymous. 2016. "STEM Education Is Vital—But Not at the Expense of the Humanities." *Scientific American* (Oct. 1): https://www.scientificamerican.com/article/stem-education-is-vital-but-not-at-the-expense-of-the-humanities/

Armitage, David, Homi Bhabha, Emma Dench, Jeffrey Hamburger, John Hamilton, Sean Kelly, Carrie Lambert-Beatty, Christie McDonald, Anne Shreffler, and James Simpson. 2013. *The Teaching of the Arts and Humanities at Harvard College: Mapping the Future* (May 31): http://artsandhumanities.fas.harvard.edu/files/humanities/files/mapping_the_future_31_may_2013.pdf.

Arnold, Matthew. 1869. *Culture and Anarchy: An Essay in Political and Social Criticism*. London: Smith, Elder and Co.

Arum, Richard and Josipa Roksa. 2011. *Academically Adrift: Limited Learning on College Campuses*. Chicago and London: The University of Chicago Press.

Astin, Alexander W. 2011. "In 'Academically Adrift,' Data Don't Back Up Sweeping Claim." *The Chronicle of Higher Education* (Feb. 14): http://www.chronicle.com/article/Academically-Adrift-a/126371.

Atkinson, Dwight. 1997. "A Critical Approach to Critical Thinking in TESOL." *TESOL Quarterly* 31.1: 71–94.

Atwater, Lyman H. 1882. "Proposed Reforms in Collegiate Education." *The Princeton Review* 4 (July): 100–20.

Axtell, James. 2016. *Wisdom's Workshop: The Rise of the Modern University*. Princeton and Oxford: Princeton University Press.

Babbitt, Irving. 1897. "The Rational Study of the Classics." *The Atlantic Monthly* (March): 355–66.

Babbitt, Irving. 1908. "Culture and Scholarship [Letter to the Editor]." *The Nation* 87 (July 2): 7–8.

Babbitt, Irving. 1910. *The New Laokoon: An Essay on the Confusion of the Arts*. Boston and New York: Houghton Mifflin.

Babbitt, Irving. 1912. "Bergson and Rousseau." *The Nation* 95 (Nov. 14): 452–55.

Babbitt, Irving. 1918. "Genius and Taste." *The Nation* 100 (Feb. 7): 138–41.

Babbitt, Irving. 1920. "English and the Discipline of Ideas." *The English Journal* 9.2 (Feb.): 61–70.

Babbitt, Irving. 1921. "Humanistic Education in China and the West." *The Chinese Students' Monthly* 17 (Dec.): 85–91.

Babbitt, Irving. 1924. *Democracy and Leadership*. Boston and New York: Houghton Mifflin.

Babbitt, Irving. 1928. "The Humanistic View [Letter to the Editor]." *The Forum* 80 (Oct.): 638.

Babbitt, Irving. 1930. "Humanism: An Essay at Definition." In Foerster 1930a: 25–51.

Babbitt, Irving. 1936. *The Dhammapada: Translated from the Pāli with an Essay on Buddha and the Occident.* New York: New Directions Publishing Company.

Babbitt, Irving. 1940. *Spanish Character and Other Essays.* Boston and New York: Houghton Mifflin.

Babbitt, Irving. 1968. *On Being Creative and Other Essays.* New York: Biblo and Tannen. Originally published in 1932.

Babbitt, Irving. 1977. *The Masters of Modern French Criticism.* Westport, CT: Greenwood Press. Originally published in 1912.

Babbitt, Irving. 1986. *Literature and the American College: Essays in Defense of the Humanities.* Washington, DC: National Humanities Institute. Originally published in 1908.

Babbitt, Irving. 1991. *Rousseau and Romanticism.* New Brunswick, NJ: Transaction Publishers. Originally published in 1919.

Babbitt, Irving. 1995. *Character and Culture: Essays on East and West.* New Brunswick, NJ and London: Transaction Publishers.

Bailin, Sharon, Roland Case, Jerrold R. Coombs, and Leroi B. Daniels. 1999. "Common Misconceptions of Critical Thinking." *Journal of Curriculum Studies* 31.3: 269–83.

Barney, Joseph Aldo. 1974. *The Educational Ideas of Irving Babbitt: Critical Humanism and American Higher Education.* Diss. Loyola University of Chicago.

Bascom, John. 1885. "The Part Which the Study of Language Plays in a Liberal Education." *Journal of Proceedings and Addresses of the National Educational Association, Session of the Year 1884, at Madison, Wisconsin.* 273–84. Boston: National Education Association.

Bauerlein, Mark. 2013. "What Dido Did, Satan Saw and O'Keefe Painted." *The New Criterion* 32.3 (Nov.): 4–9.

Bauerlein, Mark. 2014. "Humanities: Doomed to Lose?" *The New Criterion* 33.3 (Nov.): 10–14.

Bauerlein, Mark. 2015. "A Lesson in Western Civ." *The New Criterion* 34.3 (Nov.): 32–36.

Baumeister, Roy F. and John Tierney. 2011. *Willpower: Rediscovering the Greatest Human Strength.* New York: Penguin Books.

Beard, Mary. 2013. *Confronting the Classics: Traditions, Adventures and Innovations.* London: Profile Books.

Belkin, Douglas. 2016. "Liberal Arts Lose Luster." *The Wall Street Journal* (April 25): A3.

Ben-David, Joseph. 1972. *American Higher Education: Directions Old and New.* New York: McGraw-Hill.

Bennett, William J. 1984. *To Reclaim a Legacy: A Report on the Humanities in Higher Education.* Washington, DC: National Endowment for the Humanities.

Berman, Russell A. 2006–2007. "The Humanities, Globalization, and the Transformation of the University." *ADFL Bulletin* (fall): 8–12.

Berrett, Dan. 2016. "If Skills Are the New Canon, Are Colleges Teaching Them?" *The Chronicle of Higher Education* (April 3): http://www.chronicle.com/article/If-Skills-Are-the-New-Canon/235948.

Bérubé, Michael. 2015. "Value and Values." In Bérubé and Ruth 2015: 27–56.

Bérubé, Michael and Jennifer Ruth. 2015. *The Humanities, Higher Education, and Academic Freedom: Three Necessary Arguments.* London: Palgrave Macmillan.

Bishop, Morris. 1962. *A History of Cornell.* Ithaca: Cornell University Press.

Blackmur, R. P. 1955. *The Lion and the Honeycomb: Essays in Solicitude and Critique*. New York: Harcourt, Brace and Company.

Bloom, Allan. 1987. *The Closing of the American Mind: How Higher Education Has Failed Democracy and Impoverished the Souls of Today's Students*. New York: Simon and Schuster.

Bloomer, W. Martin. 2011. *The School of Rome: Latin Studies and the Origins of Liberal Education*. Berkeley, Los Angeles, and London: University of California Press.

Bolgar, R. R. 1973. "From Humanism to the Humanities." *20th Century Studies* 9 (Sept.): 8–21.

Bolles, Albert S. 1883. "What Instruction Should Be Given in Our Colleges?" *The Atlantic Monthly* 53 (Nov.): 686–94.

Bonner, Stanley Frederick. 1977. *Education in Ancient Rome: From Cato the Elder to the Younger Pliny*. Berkeley: University of California Press.

Bousquet, Marc. 2008. *How the University Works: Higher Education and the Low-Wage Nation*. New York and London: New York University Press.

Bow, Charles Bradford. 2013. "Reforming Witherspoon's Legacy at Princeton: John Witherspoon, Samuel Stanhope Smith and James McCosh on Didactic Enlightenment, 1768–1888." *History of European Ideas* 39.5: 650–69.

Bowen, James. 1972. *A History of Western Education*. Vol. 1, *The Ancient World: Orient and Mediterranean, 2000 B.C.–A.D. 1054*. London: Methuen and Company.

Bowker, R. R. 1884. "The College of To-Day." *The Princeton Review* (Jan.): 89–110.

Boyd, William. 1934. "President Eliot and Herbert Spencer." *Harvard Teachers Review* 4 (Feb.): 33–36.

Brennan, Stephen C. and Stephen R. Yarbrough. 1987. *Irving Babbitt*. Boston: Twayne Publishers.

Brodhead, Richard H., John W. Rowe, et al. (Commission on the Humanities and Social Sciences). 2013. *The Heart of the Matter: The Humanities and Social Sciences for a Vibrant, Competitive, and Secure Nation*. Cambridge: American Academy of Arts and Sciences.

Brody, Alter. 1930. "Humanism and Intolerance [Letter to the Editor]." *The New Republic* 61 (Jan. 29): 278.

Broome, Edwin Cornelius. 1903. *A Historical and Critical Discussion of College Admission Requirements*. New York: Macmillan.

Brown, Richard. 1991. *Church and State in Modern Britain, 1700–1850*. London and New York: Routledge.

Brubacher, John S. and Willis Rudy. 1997. "Professional Education." In Goodchild and Wechsler 1997: 379–93.

Bruce, Philip Alexander. 1920. *History of the University of Virginia, 1819–1919: The Lengthened Shadow of One Man*, vol. 2. New York: The Macmillan Company.

Büchner, Karl. 1967. "Humanitas." In *Der Kleine Pauly: Lexicon der Antike*, vol. 2, edited by Konrad Ziegler and Walter Sontheimer. 1241–44. Stuttgart: Alfred Druckenmüller.

Burke, Colin B. 1982. *American Collegiate Populations: A Test of the Traditional View*. New York: New York University Press.

Burke, Kenneth. 1930. "The Allies of Humanism Abroad." In Grattan 1930a: 169–92.

Burstein, Stanley M. 1996. "The Classics and the American Republic." *The History Teacher* 30.1: 29–44.

Burton, R. W. 1880. "Should the High School Be Organized as Supplementary to the Common School, or as Preparatory to the University or College?" *Wisconsin Journal of Education* 10: 183–90.

Butts, R. Freeman. 1971. *The College Charts Its Course: Historical Conceptions and Current Proposals.* New York: Arno Press and *The New York Times.* Originally published in 1939.

Calder, William M., III. 1966. "Die Geschichte der klassischen Philologie in den Vereinigten Staaten." *Jarbuch für Amerikastudien* 11: 213–40.

Calverton, V. F. 1930. "Humanism: Literary Fascism." *New Masses* 5 (April): 9–10.

Canby, Henry Seidel. 1930. "Post Mortem." *The Saturday Review of Literature* 6.47 (June 14): 1121–23.

Carnochan, W. B. 1993. *The Battleground of the Curriculum: Liberal Education and the American Experience.* Stanford: Stanford University Press.

Cary, John D. 1885. "The Value of Classical Training." *The Hamilton Literary Magazine* 19 (Jan.): 165–68.

Chalmers, Gordon Keith. 1941. "Rediscovery of a Radical [review of Babbitt 1940]." *The Kenyon Review* 3.3 (summer): 388–92.

Chamberlain, D. H. 1876. "The Value of Classical Studies." *The New Englander* 35 (April): 222–50.

Chamberlain, D. H. 1884. *Not "A College Fetish." An Address in Reply to the Address of Charles Francis Adams, Jr., Delivered before the Harvard Chapter of the Fraternity of the Phi Beta Kappa, at Cambridge, June 28, 1883.* Boston: Willard Small.

Chamberlain, D. H. 1885. "The German University and Gymnasium and the American College [Letter to the Editor]." *The New York Times* (Feb. 27): 2.

Chamberlain, D. H. 1886. "The Elective Policy." *The New Englander* 45 (May): 459–63.

Chamberlain, D. H. 1904. *Present Phases of Our So-Called Negro Problem: Open Letter to the Right Honorable James Bryce, M. P., of England.* [Place and name of publisher not identified.]

Chamberlain, D. H. 1907. "Some Conclusions of a Free-Thinker." *The North American Review* 186.623 (Oct.): 174–94.

Chamberlain, John. 1930. "Drift and Mastery of Our Novelists." In Grattan 1930a: 257–77.

Cheney, Lynne V. 1988. *Humanities in America: A Report to the President, the Congress, and the American People.* Washington, DC: National Endowment for the Humanities.

Chesterton, G. K. 1929. "Is Humanism a Religion?" *The Bookman* 69 (May): 236–41.

Christes, Johannes. 2004. "Enkyklios paideia." *Brill's New Pauly: Encyclopaedia of the Ancient World*, vol. 4, edited by Christine F. Salazar. 982–84.

Clark, Albert Curtis, ed. 1911. *M. Tulli Ciceronis Orationes*, vol. 5. Oxford: Clarendon Press.

Cohan, Peter. 2012. "To Boost Post-College Prospects, Cut Humanities Departments." *Forbes* (May 29): https://www.forbes.com/sites/petercohan/2012/05/29/to-boost-post-college-prospects-cut-humanities-departments/#885110d55bf0.

Colum, Mary M. 1930. "Debating Humanism." *Scribner's Magazine* 87 (May 24): 1063–64.

Connor, W. Robert. 2013a. "Misled by the Majors." WRobertConnor.com (July 25): http://www.wrobertconnor.com/blog/misled-by-the-majors.

Connor, W. Robert. 2013b. "The New Story about the Humanities." WRobertConnor.com (July 20): http://www.wrobertconnor.com/blog/the-new-story-about-the-humanities.

Connor, W. Robert. 2013c. "The Only Statistics about the Humanities That Really Matter." WRobertConnor.com (Oct. 31): http://www.wrobertconnor.com/blog/the-only-statistics-about-the-humanities-that-really-matter.

Cooke, Josiah Parsons. 1883. "The Greek Question." *Popular Science Monthly* 24 (Nov.): 1–6.

Cooke, Josiah Parsons. 1884. "Further Remarks on the Greek Question." *Popular Science Monthly* 25 (Oct.): 772–77.

Cowley, Malcolm. 1930. "Humanizing Society." In Grattan 1930a: 63–84.

Cowley, W. H. and Don Williams. 1991. *International and Historical Roots of American Higher Education.* New York and London: Garland Publishing.

Cremin, Lawrence A. 1997. "College." In Goodchild and Wechsler 1997: 35–52.

Curry, Daniel. 1883. "The 'College Fetich.'" *Western Christian Advocate* (Aug. 8): 249.

Cuyler, Theodore L. 1885. "Dr. McCosh and the New Departure." *New York Evangelist* 56.13 (March 26): 1.

Dakin, Arthur Hazard. 1960. *Paul Elmer More.* Princeton: Princeton University Press.

Damon, William. 1989. "Learning How to Deal with the New American Dilemma: We Must Teach Our Students about Morality and Racism." *The Chronicle of Higher Education* (May 3): B1–B3.

Davis, Glenn A. 2006. "Irving Babbitt, the Moral Imagination, and Progressive Education." *Humanitas* 19.1–2: 50–64.

Delbanco, Andrew. 2012. *College: What It Was, Is, and Should Be.* Princeton and Oxford: Princeton University Press.

DeNicola, Daniel R. 2012. *Learning To Flourish: A Philosophical Exploration of Liberal Education.* New York and London: Continuum Books.

Dewey, John. 1938. *Experience and Education.* New York: Simon and Schuster.

Dewey, John. 1940. *Education Today.* New York: Greenwood Press.

Dewey, John. 1969. *The Educational Situation.* New York: Arno Press and *The New York Times.* Originally published in 1904.

Dewey, John. 1984. *The Later Works, 1925–1953, Vol. 5: 1929–1930*, edited by Jo Ann Boydston. Carbondale and Edwardsville: Southern Illinois University Press.

Di Leo, Jeffrey R. 2013. *Corporate Humanities in Higher Education: Moving beyond the Neoliberal Academy.* New York: Palgrave Macmillan.

Dillon, James J. 2006. "Irving Babbitt's 'New Humanism' and Its Potential Value to Humanistic Psychology." *The Humanist Psychologist* 34.1: 59–73.

Dix, Willard. 2018. "It's Time to Worry When Colleges Erase Humanities Departments." *Forbes* (March 13): https://www.forbes.com/sites/willarddix/2018/03/13/its-time-to-worry-when-colleges-erase-humanities-departments/#1a359081461a.

Donoghue, Frank. 2008. *The Last Professors: The Corporate University and the Fate of the Humanities.* New York: Fordham University Press.

Duggan, Francis X. 1966. *Paul Elmer More.* New York: Twayne Publishers.

Dyer, Louis. 1884. *The Greek Question and Answer: A Paper Read before the Harvard Club of Rhode Island in Providence, February 25th, 1884.* Boston: James R. Osgood.

Earnest, Ernest. 1953. *Academic Procession: An Informal History of the American College, 1636 to 1953.* Indianapolis and New York: The Bobbs-Merrill Company.

Edmundson, Mark. 1993. "Introduction: The Academy Writes Back." In *Wild Orchids and Trotsky: Messages from American Universities,* edited by Mark Edmundson. 3–28. New York: Penguin.

Edmundson, Mark. 2013. *Why Teach? In Defense of a Real Education*. New York: Bloomsbury.

Edwards, Mary Morgan. 2016. "Humanities Professors Blame OSU for Declining Enrollments." *Dayton Daily News* (Feb. 12): B2.

Egan, Kieran. 2002. *Getting It Wrong from the Beginning: Our Progressive Inheritance from Herbert Spencer, John Dewey, and Jean Piaget*. New Haven and London: Yale University Press.

Eggert, C. A. 1884a. "A Plea for Modern Languages." *The North American Review* 138.329 (April): 374–82.

Eggert, C. A. 1884b. "Science *Versus* the Classics." *Popular Science Monthly* 24 (March): 674–75.

Eliot, Charles W. 1869a. "The New Education: Its Organization," part 1. *The Atlantic Monthly* 23 (Feb.): 203–20.

Eliot, Charles W. 1869b. "The New Education: Its Organization. II." *The Atlantic Monthly* 23 (March): 358–67.

Eliot, Charles W. 1891. "Educational Changes and Tendencies," reported by I. M. Metcalf. *Journal of Education* 34 (Dec. 24): 403.

Eliot, Charles W. 1899. "Recent Changes in Secondary Education." *The Atlantic Monthly* 94 (Oct.): 433–44.

Eliot, Charles W. 1893. "Undesirable and Desirable Uniformity in Schools." In *National Educational Association Journal of Proceedings and Addresses, Session of the Year 1892*. 82–95. New York: National Education Association.

Eliot, Charles W. 1897. *American Contributions to Civilization and Other Essays and Addresses*. New York: The Century Co.

Eliot, Charles W. 1898. *Educational Reform: Essays and Addresses*. New York: The Century Co.

Eliot, Charles W. 1908. *University Administration*. Boston and New York: Houghton Mifflin.

Eliot, Charles W. 1911. "Introduction." In *Essays on Education and Kindred Subjects*, by Herbert Spencer. Vii–xvi. New York: E. P. Dutton.

Eliot, Charles W. 1914–15. "Tribute." *Massachusetts Historical Society Proceedings* 48: 387–92.

Eliot, Charles W. 1915. "The Potency of the Jewish Race." *Menorah Journal* 1.3 (June): 141–44.

Eliot, Charles W. 1916. "Mr. Eliot's Comments [on Herbert Spencer's 'Specialized Administration']." In *The Man versus the State*, by Herbert Spencer, edited by Truxton Beale. 287–95. New York: Mitchell Kinnerley.

Eliot, Charles W. 1917. "The Case against Compulsory Latin." *The Atlantic Monthly* 119 (March): 352–61.

Eliot, Charles W. 1923. *Harvard Memories*. Cambridge: Harvard University Press.

Eliot, Charles W. 1924. *A Late Harvest: Miscellaneous Papers Written between Eighty and Ninety*. Freeport, NY: Books for Libraries Press.

Eliot, Charles W. 1926. *Charles W. Eliot: The Man and His Beliefs*, vol. 1, edited by William Allan Nelson. New York and London: Harper and Brothers Publishers.

Eliot, Charles W. 1969. *A Turning Point in Higher Education: The Inaugural Address of Charles William Eliot as President of Harvard College, October 19, 1869*. Cambridge: Harvard University Press.

Eliot, T. S. 1964. *Selected Essays*. San Diego, New York, and London: Harcourt Brace Jovanovich.

Elliott, G. R. 1938. *Humanism and Imagination*. Port Washington, NY: Kennikat Press.

Ellis, John M. 1997. *Literature Lost: Social Agendas and the Corruption of the Humanities*. New Haven and London: Yale University Press.

Ellison, Ralph. 1995. *Invisible Man*. New York: Vintage Books. Originally published in 1952.

F. F. 1883. "The Critics of Mr. C. F. Adams, Jr. [Letter to the Editor]." *The Nation* 37.952 (Sept. 27): 271–72.

Ferrall, Victor E., Jr. 2011. *Liberal Arts at the Brink*. Cambridge and London: Harvard University Press.

Fernald, Frederik A. 1884. "German Testimony on the Classics Question." *Popular Science Monthly* 26 (Nov.): 20–30.

Few, William P. 1909. "President Eliot and the South." *The South Atlantic Quarterly* 8: 184–91.

Finkelstein, Martin. 1997. "From Tutor to Specialized Scholar: Academic Professionalization in Eighteenth and Nineteenth Century America." In Goodchild and Weschler 1997: 80–93.

Fish, Stanley. 2008. *Save the World on Your Own Time*. Oxford and New York: Oxford University Press.

Fisher, George P. 1884. "The Study of Greek." *The Princeton Review* 4.13 (March): 111–26.

Flaherty, Colleen. 2017a. "Occupation of Hum 110." *Inside Higher Ed* (Sept. 11): https://www.insidehighered.com/news/2017/09/11/reed-college-course-lectures-canceled-after-student-protesters-interrupt-class.

Flaherty, Colleen. 2017b. "Proposed Cuts to Humanities at SUNY Stony Brook." *Inside Higher Ed* (May 9): https://www.insidehighered.com/quicktakes/2017/05/09/proposed-cuts-humanities-suny-stony-brook.

Flaherty, Colleen. 2018. "U Wisconsin-Stevens Point to Eliminate 13 Majors." *Inside Higher Ed* (March 6): https://www.insidehighered.com/quicktakes/2018/03/06/u-wisconsin-stevens-point-eliminate-13-majors.

Flexner, Abraham. 1930. *Universities: American, English, German*. New York, London, and Toronto: Oxford University Press.

Foerster, Norman, ed. 1930a. *Humanism and America: Essays on the Outlook of Modern Civilisation*. New York: Farrar and Rinehart.

Foerster, Norman. 1930b. "Preface." In Foerster 1930a: v–xvii.

Foerster, Norman. 1937. *The American State University: Its Relation to Democracy*. Chapel Hill: The University of North Carolina Press.

Foerster, Norman. 1946. *The Humanities and the Common Man: The Democratic Role of the State Universities*. Chapel Hill: The University of North Carolina Press.

Foerster, Norman. 1969. *The Future of the Liberal College*. New York: Arno Press and *The New York Times*. Originally published in 1938.

Frantzman, Seth J. 2013. "Decline of the Humanities: Don't Believe It." *The Jerusalem Post* (July 17): 15.

Freedman, James O. 2003. *Liberal Education and the Public Interest*. Iowa City: University of Iowa Press.

Frohock, W. M. 1940. "What about Humanism." *Southwest Review* 25.3 (April): 322–34.

Frost, William G. 1885. "Greek among Required Studies." *The Bibliotheca Sacra* 165 (April): 327–50.

Fuess, Claude M. 1950. *The College Board: Its First Fifty Years*. New York: Columbia University Press.

Gaggi, Silvio. 2011. "Assault on Humanities Weakens Us as a People." *Tampa Bay Tribune* (Feb. 12): 15.

Geiger, Roger L., ed. 2000a. *The American College in the Nineteenth Century*. Nashville: Vanderbilt University Press.

Geiger, Roger L. 2000b. "The Crisis of the Old Order: The Colleges in the 1890s." In Geiger 2000a: 264–76.

Geiger, Roger L. 2000c. "The Era of Multipurpose Colleges in American Higher Education, 1850–1890." In Geiger 2000a: 127–52.

Geiger, Roger L. 2000d. "Introduction: New Themes in the History of Nineteenth-Century Colleges." In Geiger 2000a. 1–36.

Geiger, Roger L. 2000e. "The Rise and Fall of Useful Knowledge: Higher Education for Science, Agriculture, and the Mechanical Arts, 1850–1875." In Geiger 2000a: 153–68.

Geiger, Roger L. 2000f. "The 'Superior Instruction of Women,' 1836–1890." In Geiger 2000a: 183–95.

Geiger, Roger L. 2015. *The History of American Higher Education: Learning and Culture from the Founding to World War II*. Princeton and Oxford: Princeton University Press.

Geiger, Roger L. 2016. "From Land-Grant Tradition to the Current Crisis in the Humanities." In Hutner and Mohamed 2016b: 18–30.

Goodchild, Lester F. and Harold S. Wechsler, eds. 1997. *The History of Higher Education*, 2nd edition. Boston: Pearson Custom Publishing.

Gordon, Ted and Wahneema Lubiano. 1992. "The Statement of the Black Faculty Caucus." In *Debating PC: The Controversy over Political Correctness on College Campuses*, edited by Paul Berman. 249–57. New York: Laurel.

Grabo, Carl H. 1933. "The Case of Mr. Babbitt." *The New Humanist* 6: 29–34.

Graff, Gerald. 1987. *Professing Literature: An Institutional History*. Chicago and London: The University of Chicago Press.

Graff, Gerald. 1990. "Teach the Conflicts." *The South Atlantic Quarterly* 89: 51–67.

Grafton, Anthony. 1981. "Prolegomena to Friedrich August Wolf." *Journal of the Warburg and Courtland Institutes* 44: 101–29.

Grafton, Anthony. 1983. "Polyhistory into *Philolog*: Notes on the Transformation of German Classical Scholarship, 1780–1850." *History of Universities* 3: 159–92.

Grattan, C. Hartley, ed. 1930a. *The Critique of Humanism: A Symposium*. New York: Brewer and Warren.

Grattan, C. Hartley. 1930b. "The New Humanism and the Scientific Attitude." In Grattan 1930a: 3–36.

Green, James. 1908. *Personal Recollections of Daniel Henry Chamberlain, Once Governor of South Carolina*. Worcester, MA [publisher not identified].

Grendler, Paul F. 2002. *The Universities of the Italian Renaissance*. Baltimore and London: The Johns Hopkins University Press.

Gummere, Francis B. 1883. "President Porter on the Study of Anglo-Saxon [Letter to the Editor]." *The Nation* 37.950 (Sept. 13): 226–27.

Gutting, Gary. 2013. "The Real Humanities Crisis." *The New York Times* (Dec. 1): http://opinionator.blogs.nytimes.com/2013/11/30/the-real-humanities-crisis/.

Gwynn, Aubrey. 1926. *Roman Education: From Cicero to Quintilian*. Oxford: Clarendon Press.

H. G. P. 1883. "The Place of Greek in a College Course [Letter to the Editor]." *The Nation* 37 (Aug. 30): 183–84.

Haar, Charles M. 1948. "E. L. Youmans: A Chapter in the Diffusion of Science in America." *Journal of the History of Ideas* 9.2: 193–213.

Hall, Peter Dobkin. 2000. "Noah Porter Writ Large? Reflections on the Modernization of American Education and Its Critics, 1866–1916." In Geiger 2000a: 196–220.

Harloe, Katherine. 2013. *Winckelmann and the Invention of Antiquity: History and Aesthetics in the Age of Altertumswissenschaft.* Oxford: Oxford University Press.

Harpham, Geoffrey Galt. 2011. *The Humanities and the Dream of America.* Chicago and London: The University of Chicago Press.

Harr, Charles M. 1948. "E. L. Youmans: A Chapter in the Diffusion of Science in America." *Journal of the History of Ideas* 9.2: 193–213.

Harris, Michael R. 1970. *Five Counterrevolutionists in Higher Education: Irving Babbitt, Albert Jay Nock, Abraham Flexner, Robert Maynard Hutchins, Alexander Meiklejohn.* Corvallis: Oregon State University Press.

Harris, W. T. 1880. "Equivalents in a Liberal Course of Study." In *The Addresses and Journals of Proceedings of the National Educational Association.* 167–75. Salem, OH: National Educational Association.

Harrison, William. 1941. "Babbitt's Early Essays [Review of Babbitt 1940]." *The Sewanee Review* 49.2 (April–June): 279–81.

Hawkins, Hugh. 1960. *Pioneer: A History of the Johns Hopkins University, 1874–1889.* Ithaca: Cornell University Press.

Hawkins, Hugh. 1964. "Charles W. Eliot, University Reform, and Religious Faith in America, 1869–1909." *The Journal of American History* 51.2: 191–213.

Hawkins, Hugh. 1972. *Between Harvard and America: The Educational Leadership of Charles W. Eliot.* New York: Oxford University Press.

Hazlitt, Henry. 1930. "Humanizing and Value." In Grattan 1930a: 87–105.

Hecht, Marie B. 1972. *John Quincy Adams: A Personal History of an Independent Man.* New York: Macmillan.

Heckman, James J. and Tim Kautz. 2013. "Fostering and Measuring Skills: Interventions That Improve Character and Cognition." *National Bureau of Economic Research Working Paper no. 19656*: https://nber.org/papers/w19656.

Herbermann, C. G. 1885. "The Classics in Modern Higher Education." *The American Catholic Quarterly Review* 10.37 (Jan.): 140–62.

Herbst, Jurgen. 1996. *The Once and Future School: Three Hundred and Fifty Years of American Secondary Education.* New York and London: Routledge.

Herzog, Reinhart. 1983. "On the Relation of Disciplinary Development and Historical Self-Preservation—The Case of Classical Philology since the End of the Eighteenth Century." In *Functions and Uses of Disciplinary History*, vol. 7, edited by Loren Graham, Wolf Lepenies, and Peter Weingart. 281–90. Boston: Reidel.

Heyl, John D. and Barbara S. Heyl. 1976. "The Sumner-Porter Controversy at Yale: Paradigmatic Sociology and Institutional Crisis." *Sociological Inquiry* 46.1: 41–49.

Hindus, Milton. 1994. *Irving Babbitt, Literature, and the Democratic Culture.* New Brunswick, NJ and London: Transaction Publishers.

Hirsch, E. D, Jr. 1987. *Cultural Literacy: What Every American Needs to Know.* Boston: Houghton Mifflin.

Hitchcock, Henry-Russell. 1930. "Humanism and the Fine Arts." In Grattan 1930a: 195–233.

Hoeveler, J. David, Jr. 1977. *The New Humanism: A Critique of Modern America, 1900–1940*. Charlottesville: University Press of Virginia.

Hoeveler, J. David, Jr. 1981. *James McCosh and the Scottish Intellectual Tradition: From Glasgow to Princeton*. Princeton: Princeton University Press.

Hoeveler, J. David, Jr. 2002. *Creating the American Mind: Intellect and Politics in the Colonial Colleges*. Lanham, Boulder, New York, and Oxford: Rowman and Littlefield.

Hoeveler, J. David, Jr. 2007. *The Evolutionists: American Thinkers Confront Charles Darwin, 1860–1920*. Lanham, MD: Rowman and Littlefield.

Hofstadter, Richard. 1959. *Social Darwinism in American Thought*. New York: G. Braziller.

Hovey, Richard B. 1986. "*Literature and the American College*: Irving Babbitt Yesterday and Today." In Panichas and Ryn 1986: 201–25.

Hofmann, August Whilhelm. 1883. *The Question of a Division of the Philosophical Faculty: Inaugural Address on Assuming the Rectorship of the University of Berlin*. Boston: Ginn, Heath, and Company.

Hofstadter, Richard. 1959. *Social Darwinism in American Thought* (revised edition). New York: George Braziller.

Howard, Thomas Albert. 2006. *Protestant Theology and the Making of the Modern German University*. Oxford and New York: Oxford University Press.

Howe, Daniel Walker. 1970. *The Unitarian Conscience: Harvard Moral Philosophy, 1805–1861*. Cambridge: Harvard University Press.

Howe, Irving. 1991. "The Value of the Canon." *The New Republic* (Feb. 18): 40–47.

Humphreys, E. R. 1883. "Greek, a Prime and Necessary Factor of Scientific Education." *Journal of Education* (Boston) 18 (Aug. 9): 87.

Hunt, Melissa G., Rachel Marx, Courtney Lipson, and Jordyn Young. 2018. "No More FOMO: Limiting Social Media Decreases Loneliness and Depression." *Journal of Social and Clinical Psychology* 37.10: 751–68.

Hutchins, Robert Maynard. 1995. *The Higher Learning in America*. New Brunswick, NJ and London: Transaction Publishers. Originally published in 1936.

Hutner, Gordon and Feisal Mohamed. 2013. "The Real Humanities Crisis Is Happening at Public Universities." *The New Republic* (Sept. 6): http://www.newrepublic.com/article/114616/public-universities-hurt-humanities-crisis.

Hutner, Gordon and Feisal Mohamed. 2016a. "Introduction." In Hutner and Mohamed 2016b: 1–17.

Hutner, Gordon and Feisal Mohamed, eds. 2016b. *A New Deal for the Humanities: Liberal Arts and the Future of Public Higher Education*. New Brunswick, NJ and London: Rutgers University Press.

Isaac, Benjamin. 2004. *The Invention of Racism in Classical Antiquity*. Princeton: Princeton University Press.

Jacobs, Alexander I. 2015. "The Humanities at the End of the World." *The Chronicle of Higher Education* (Sept. 28): http://www.chronicle.com/article/The-Humanities-at-the-End-of/233355.

Jaeger, Werner. 1943. *Humanism and Theology*. Milwaukee: Marquette University Press.

James, Edmund J. 1884. "The Classical Question in Germany." *Popular Science Monthly* 24 (Jan.): 290–306.

James, Henry. 1930. *Charles W. Eliot: President of Harvard, 1869–1909*, 2 vols. Boston and New York: Houghton Mifflin.

Jamieson, T. John. 1986. "Babbitt and Mauras as Competing Influences on T. S. Eliot." In Panichas and Ryn 1986b: 155–77.

Jarrett, James L. 1973. *The Humanities and Humanistic Education*. Reading, MA: Addison-Wesley.

Jaschik, Scott. 2017. "Humanities Majors Drop." *Inside Higher Ed* (June 5): https://www.insidehighered.com/news/2017/06/05/analysis-finds-significant-drop-humanities-majors-gains-liberal-arts-degrees.

Jaschik, Scott. 2019a. "Carroll College Cuts 5 Majors and 10 Minors." *Inside Higher Ed* (Feb. 25): https://www.insidehighered.com/quicktakes/2019/02/25/carroll-college-cuts-5-majors-and-10-minors.

Jaschik, Scott. 2019b. "Disappearing Language Offerings." *Inside Higher Ed* (Jan. 24): https://www.insidehighered.com/news/2019/01/24/research-documents-decline-languages-offered-over-three-year-period.

Jaschik, Scott. 2019c. "McDaniel College Eliminates 5 Majors and 3 Minors." *Inside Higher Ed* (Feb. 25): https://www.insidehighered.com/quicktakes/2019/02/25/mcdaniel-college-eliminates-5-majors-and-3-minors.

Jay, Paul. 2014. *The Humanities "Crisis" and the Future of Literary Studies*. New York: Palgrave Macmillan.

Jay, Paul and Gerald Graff. 2012. "Fear of Being Useful." *Inside Higher Ed* (Jan. 5): https://www.insidehighered.com/views/2012/01/05/essay-new-approach-defend-value-humanities.

Jeff. 1883. "Boston." *Detroit Free Press* (July 16): 11.

Jencks, Christopher and David Riesman. 1968. *The Academic Revolution*. Garden City, NY: Doubleday.

Jewett, Andrew. 2012. *Science, Democracy, and the American University: From the Civil War to the Cold War*. Cambridge and New York: Cambridge University Press.

Johnson, Eldon L. 1997. "Misconceptions about the Early Land-Grant Colleges." In Goodchild and Weschler 1997: 222–33.

Johnson, Ralph H. and Benjamin Hamby. 2015. "A Meta-Level Approach to the Problem of Defining 'Critical Thinking.'" *Argumentation* 29: 417–30.

Jones, Howard Mumford. 1928. "Professor Babbitt Cross-Examined." *The New Republic* (March 21): 158–60.

Kallendorf, Craig W., ed. and trans. 2002. *Humanist Educational Treatises*. Cambridge and London: Harvard University Press.

Karabel, Jerome. 2005. *The Chosen: The Hidden History of Admission and Exclusion at Harvard, Yale, and Princeton*. Boston and New York: Houghton Mifflin.

Kariel, Henry S. 1951. "Democracy Limited: Irving Babbitt's Classicism." *The Review of Politics* 13.4 (Oct.): 430–40.

Kelley, Donald R. 1991. *Renaissance Humanism*. Boston: Twayne Publishers.

Kemeny, P. C. 1998. *Princeton in the Nation's Service: Religious Ideals and Educational Practice, 1868–1928*. New York and Oxford: Oxford University Press.

Kimball, Bruce A. 1995. *Orators and Philosophers: A History of the Idea of Liberal Education*. New York: College Entrance Examination Board.

Kimball, Roger. 1990. *Tenured Radicals: How Politics Has Corrupted Our Higher Education*. New York: Harper and Row.

Kimball, Roger. 2019. "PC Insanity May Mean the End of American Universities." *New York Post* (May 31): https://nypost.com/2019/05/31/pc-insanity-may-mean-the-end-of-american-universities/.

King, Clarence. 1888. "Artium magister." *The North American Review* 147.383 (Oct.): 369–84.

Kirkland, Edward Chase. 1965. *Charles Francis Adams, Jr., 1835–1915: The Patrician at Bay*. Cambridge: Harvard University Press.

Kirp, David L. 2003. *Shakespeare, Einstein, and the Bottom Line: The Marketing of Higher Education*. Cambridge and London: Harvard University Press.

Kleinman, Daniel Lee. 2016. "Sticking up for Liberal Arts and Humanities Education: Governance, Leadership, and Fiscal Crisis." In Hutner and Mohamed 2016b: 86–100.

Klinkenborg, Verlyn. 2013. "The Decline and Fall of the English Major." *The New York Times Sunday Observer* (June 23): 10.

Knapp, Charles. 1911. "[Editorial: Professor Babbitt's *Literature and the American College*.]" *The Classical Weekly* 5.10 (Dec. 23): 73–74.

Kraus, Joe W. 1961. "The Development of a Curriculum in the Early American Colleges." *History of Education Quarterly* 1.2: 64–76.

Kristeller, Paul Oskar. 1961. *Renaissance Thought: The Classic, Scholastic, and Humanist Strains*. New York: Harper and Row.

Kronman, Anthony T. 2007. *Education's End: Why Our Colleges and Universities Have Given Up on the Meaning of Life*. New Haven and London: Yale University Press.

Krug, Edward A. 1969. *The Shaping of the American High School, 1880–1920*. Madison, Milwaukee, and London: The University of Wisconsin Press.

Kuklick, Bruce. 1990. "The Emergence of the Humanities." *The South Atlantic Quarterly* 89.1 (winter): 195–206.

Kupperman, Joel J. 1991. *Character*. New York and Oxford: Oxford University Press.

Kurtz, Stanley. 2017. "The Campus Free-Speech Crisis Deepens." *National Review* (Sept. 27): https://www.nationalreview.com/corner/campus-free-speech-crisis-deepens/.

LaFleur, Richard A. 2000. "Latin and Greek Enrollments in America's Schools and Colleges." *ADFL Bulletin* 3.13 (spring): 53–58.

Leander, Folke. 1937. *Humanism and Naturalism: A Comparative Study of Ernest Seillière, Irving Babbitt and Paul Elmer More*. Gothenburg: Göteborgs Högskola.

Leander, Folke. 1974. *The Inner Check: A Concept of Paul Elmer More with Reference to Benedetto Croce*. London: Edward Wright.

Leander, Folke. 1986. "Irving Babbitt and Benedetto Croce." In Panichas and Ryn. 75–102.

Lemann, Nicholas. 2016. "What Should Graduates Know?" *The Chronicle of Higher Education* (Jan. 8): http://www.chronicle.com/article/What-Should-Graduates-Know-/234824.

Leventhal, Robert S. 1986. "The Emergence of Philological Discourse in the German States, 1770–1810." *Isis* 77: 243–60.

Leverette, William E., Jr. 1963. *Science and Values: A Study of Edward L. Youmans' Popular Science Monthly, 1872–1887*. Diss. Vanderbilt University.

Leverette, William E., Jr. 1965. "E. L. Youman's Crusade for Scientific Autonomy and Respectability." *American Quarterly* 17.1: 12–32.

Levermore, Charles H. 1886. "The 'New Education' Run Mad." *Education* 6: 290–98.

Levin, Harry. 1966. *Refractions: Essays in Comparative Literature*. New York: Oxford University Press.

Levin, Harry. 1991. "From Bohemia to Academia: Writers in Universities." *Bulletin of the Academy of Arts and Sciences* 44.4 (Jan.): 28–50.

Levin, Phyllis Lee. 2015. *The Remarkable Education of John Quincy Adams*. New York: Palgrave Macmillan.

Levine, George, Peter Brooks, Jonathan Culler, Marjorie Garber, E. Ann Kaplan, and Catharine R. Stimpson. 1989. *Speaking for the Humanities*. New York: American Council of Learned Societies.

Levine, Lawrence W. 1996. *The Opening of the American Mind: Canons, Culture, and History*. Boston: Beacon Press.

Livingstone, R. W. 1916. *A Defence of Classical Education*. London: Macmillan and Co.

Long, [John Davis]. 1914–15. "Tribute." *Massachusetts Historical Society Proceedings* 48: 384–86.

Lovejoy, Arthur O. 1920. "[Review of Babbitt 1991.]" *Modern Language Notes* 35.5 (May): 302–8.

Lucas, Christopher J. 1994. *American High Education: A History*. New York: St. Martin's Press.

MacDonald, Heather. 2014. "The Humanities Have Lost Their Humanity." *The Wall Street Journal* (Jan. 4): A11.

Malamud, Margaret. 2016. *African Americans and the Classics: Antiquity, Abolition and Activism*. London and New York: I. B. Tauris.

Manchester, Frederick and Odell Shepard, eds. 1941. *Irving Babbitt: Man and Teacher*. New York: G. P. Putnam's Sons.

Marantz, Andrew. 2016. "How 'Silicon Valley' Nails Silicon Valley." *The New Yorker* (June 9): https://www.newyorker.com/culture/culture-desk/how-silicon-valley-nails-silicon-valley.

Marchand, Susan L. 1996. *Down from Olympus: Archaeology and Philhellenism in Germany*. Princeton: Princeton University Press.

Marcus, Steven. 2006. "Humanities from Classics to Cultural Studies: Notes toward the History of an Idea." *Daedalus* 135.2: 15–21.

Marrou, H. I. 1956. *A History of Education in Antiquity*, translated by George Lamb. New York: Sheed and Ward.

Marsden, George M. 1994. *The Soul of the American University: From Protestant Establishment to Established Nonbelief*. New York and Oxford: Oxford University Press.

Mason, Mark. 2007. "Critical Thinking and Learning." *Educational Philosophy and Theory* 39.4: 339–49.

Mather, Frank Jewett, Jr. 1930. "The Babbittiad [Review of Grattan 1930a]." *The New Republic* 63 (June 25): 156–59.

Mattingly, Paul H. 2017. *American Academic Cultures: A History of Higher Education*. Chicago and London: The University of Chicago Press.

Maynard, Theodore. 1935. "The Rise and Decline of American Humanism." *Studies: An Irish Quarterly Review* 24.96 (Dec.): 573–88.

McCaughey, Robert A. 1974. "The Transformation of American Academic Life: Harvard University, 1821–1892." *Perspectives in American History* 8: 239–332.

McCosh, James. 1868. *Inauguration of James McCosh, D.D., LL.D., as President of the College of New Jersey, Princeton, October 27, 1868*. New York: Robert Carter and Brothers.

McCosh, James. 1874. *The Scottish Philosophy: Biographical, Expository, Critical, from Hutcheson to Hamilton*. New York: Robert Carter and Brothers.

McCosh, James. 1878. "Discipline in American Colleges." *The North American Review* 126.262 (May–June): 428–41.

McCosh, James. 1884. *The Course of Study in Princeton College: Being a Report to the Trustees of the College, November 13th, 1884, by the President*. [No information about publisher.]

McCosh, James. 1885a. *Herbert Spencer's Philosophy as Culminated in His Ethics*. New York: Charles Scribner's Sons.

McCosh, James. 1885b. *The New Departure in College Education: Being a Reply to President Eliot's Defence of It in New York, Feb. 24, 1885*. New York: Charles Scribner's Sons.

McCosh, James. 1885c. *What an American University Should Be*. New York: J. K. Lees.

McCosh, James. 1886a. *Religion in a College: What Place It Should Have, Being an Examination of President Eliot's Paper, Read before the Nineteenth Century Club, in New York, Feb. 3, 1886*. New York: A. C. Armstrong and Son.

McCosh, James. 1886b. "A Statement by Dr. M'Cosh [Letter to the Editor]." *The New York Times* (Nov. 17): 4.

McCosh, James. 1888. *Twenty Years of Princeton College: Being Farewell Address Delivered June 20th, 1888*. New York: Charles Scribner's Sons.

McCosh, James. 1890. *The Religious Aspect of Evolution*, 2nd edition. New York: Charles Scribner's Sons.

McCosh, James. 1896. *The Life of James McCosh: A Record Chiefly Autobiographical*, edited by William Milligan Sloane. New York: Charles Scribner's Sons.

McCumber, John. 2016. "How Humanities Can Help Fix the World." *The Chronicle of Higher Education* (Oct. 2): http://www.chronicle.com/article/How-Humanities-Can-Help-Fix/237955.

McMahon, Francis E. 1931. *The Humanism of Irving Babbitt*. Diss. Catholic University of America.

Melin, Charlotte. 2016. "Speaking the Languages of the Humanities." In Hutner and Mohamed 2016b: 101–14.

Menand, Louis. 2010. *The Marketplace of Ideas: Reform and Resistance in the American University*. New York and London: W. W. Norton.

Mencken, H. L. 1924. "The State of the Country [Review of Babbitt 1924]." *The American Mercury* 3 (Sept.): 123–25.

Mercier, Louis J.-A. 1928. *Le Mouvement humaniste aux États-Unis: W. C. Brownell, Irving Babbitt, Paul Elmer More*. Paris: Librarie Hachette.

Mercier, Louis J.-A. 1936. *The Challenge of Humanism: An Essay in Comparative Criticism*. New York: Oxford University Press.

Meriwether, Coyler. 1907. *Our Colonial Curriculum: 1607–1776*. Washington, DC: Capital.

Merrill, George B. 1883. "Small Latin and Less Greek." *The Overland Monthly* 2.10 (Oct.): 417–30.

Meyer, Donald H. 1972. *The Instructed Conscience: The Shaping of the American National Ethic*. Philadelphia: University of Pennsylvania Press.

M[ims], E[dward]. 1908. "[Review of Babbitt 1986.]" *The South Atlantic Quarterly* 7: 294–96.

More, Paul Elmer. 1915. *Aristocracy and Justice: Shelburne Essays, Ninth Series*. Boston and New York: Houghton Mifflin.

More, Paul Elmer. 1930. "The Humility of Common Sense." In Foerster 1930a: 52–74.

More, Paul Elmer. 1936. *On Being Human: New Shelburne Essays*, vol. 3. Princeton: Princeton University Press.

More, Paul Elmer. 1972. *The Essential Paul Elmer More: A Selection of His Writings*, edited by Byron C. Lambert. New Rochelle, NY: Arlington House.

Morgan, Teresa. 1998. *Literate Education in the Hellenistic and Roman Worlds*. Cambridge: Cambridge University Press.

Morison, Samuel Eliot. 1935. *The Founding of Harvard College*. Cambridge: Harvard University Press.

Morison, Samuel Eliot. 1936. *Harvard College in the Seventeenth Century*, vol. 1. Cambridge: Harvard University Press.

Morison, Samuel Eliot. 1942. *Three Centuries of Harvard, 1636–1936*. Cambridge: Harvard University Press.

Morris, Matthew. 2014. "We Know in Part: James McCosh on Evolution and Christian Faith." *Journal of the History of Biology* 47: 363–410.

Morse, J. H. 1883a. "Greek in American Colleges." *The Critic* (Aug. 25): 341–42.

Morse, J. H. 1883b. "Mr. Adams on the Classics." *The American* 6.153 (July 14): 214–15.

Mumford, Lewis. 1930. "Towards an Organic Humanism." In Grattan 1930a: 337–59.

Munson, Gorham B. 1930. "Our Critical Spokesmen." In Foerster 1930a: 231–57.

Nemo. 1885. "New York Letter." *Zion's Herald* 62.14 (April 8): 1.

Nevin, Thomas R. 1984. *Irving Babbitt: An Intellectual Study*. Chapel Hill and London: The University of North Carolina Press.

Newfield, Christopher. 2008. *Unmaking the Public University: The Forty-Year Assault on the Middle Class*. Cambridge and London: Harvard University Press.

Newfield, Christopher. 2016. "What Are the Humanities For? Rebuilding the Public University." In Hutner and Mohamed 2016b: 160–78.

Newton, James King. 1885. "A Plea for a *Liberal* Education." *Bibliotheca Sacra* 165 (Jan.): 139–64.

Nikopoulos, James. 2017. "Stop Defending the Humanities." *Times Higher Education* (Feb. 25): https://www.timeshighereducation.com/blog/stop-defending-humanities.

Nussbaum, Martha C. 1997. *Cultivating Humanity: A Classical Defense of Reform in Liberal Education*. Cambridge and London: Harvard University Press.

Nussbaum, Martha C. 2008. "Who Is the Happy Warrior? Philosophy Poses Questions to Psychology." *The Journal of Legal Studies* 37.S2 (June): S81–S113.

Nussbaum, Martha C. 2010. *Not for Profit: Why Democracy Needs the Humanities*. Princeton and Oxford: Princeton University Press.

O'Boyle, Lenore. 1983. "Learning for Its Own Sake: The German University as Nineteenth-Century Model." *Comparative Studies in Society and History* 25: 3–25.

O'Brien, Michael. 2004. *Conjectures of Order: Intellectual Life and the American South, 1810–1860*, 2 vols. Chapel Hill: The University of North Carolina Press.

O'Brien, Ruth. 2010. "Foreword." In Nussbaum 2010: ix–xi.

Pak, Michael S. 2008. "The Yale Report of 1828: A New Reading and New Implications." *History of Education Quarterly* 48.1: 30–57.

Palmer, Courtlandt. 1886. "The Irrepressible Conflict [Letter to the Editor]." *The Independent* 38.194 (Feb. 25): 3.

Panichas, George A. 1986. "Babbitt and Religion." In Panichas and Ryn 1986b: 27–49.

Panichas, George A. 1999. *The Critical Legacy of Irving Babbitt: An Appreciation*. Wilmington, DE: ISI Books.

Panichas, George A. and Claes G. Ryn. 1986a. "Introduction." In Panichas and Ryn 1986b: 1–16.

Panichas, George A. and Claes G. Ryn, eds. 1986b. *Irving Babbitt in Our Time*. Washington, DC: The Catholic University of America Press.

Patel, Vimal. 2018. "Students Said a Keystone Course Was Racist. Here's What Professors Did about It." *The Chronicle of Higher Education* (April 11): https://www.chronicle.com/article/Students-Said-a-Keystone/243095.

Patton, F. L. 1885. "Dr. McCosh on the New Departure in College Education." *Presbyterian Review* 6: 341–47.

Payton, Phillip W. 1961. "Origins of the Terms 'Major' and 'Minor' in American Higher Education." *History of Education Quarterly* 1.2: 57–63.

Peabody, A. P. 1884. "The Study of Greek." *The Atlantic Monthly* 53 (Jan.): 71–79.

Pearcy, Lee T. 2005. *The Grammar of Our Civility: Classical Education in America*. Waco, TX: Baylor University Press.

Peckham, Irvin. 2010. *Going North Thinking West: The Intersections of Social Class, Critical Thinking, and Politicized Writing Instruction*. Logan: Utah State University Press.

Pfeiffer, Rudolph. 1976. *History of Classical Scholarship: From 1300 to 1850*. Oxford: Clarendon.

Phillips, D. E. 1901. "The Elective System in America." *Pedagogical Seminary* 8.2 (June): 206–30.

Philo. 1886. "'A College Fetich' Vindicated." *Boston College Stylus* 5.2 (Dec.): 19–20.

Phinney, Edward. 1989. "The Classics in American Education." In *Classics: A Discipline and Profession in Crisis?*, edited by Phyllis Culham and Lowell Edmunds. 77–87. Lanham, MD: University Press of America.

Pierson, George Wilson. 1952. *Yale College: An Educational History, 1871–1921*. New Haven: Yale University Press.

Porter, Noah. 1883. "A College Fetich." *The Princeton Review* 4.12 (Sept.): 105–28.

Porter, Noah. 1884. "Greek and a Liberal Education." *The Princeton Review* 4.14 (Sept.): 195–218.

[Porter, Noah?]. 1885. "Criticism from Yale of the Last Harvard Educational Move— Greek and the Bachelor's Degree." *New Englander and Yale Review* 44 (May): 424–35.

Portolano, Marlana. 2013. "John Quincy Adams's Higher Learnings: Rhetoric, Science, and Intellectual History." In *A Companion to John Adams and John Quincy Adams*, edited by David Waldstreicher. 422–44. Malden, MA: John Wiley and Sons.

Potts, David B. 2000. "Curriculum and Enrollment: Assessing the Popularity of Antebellum Colleges." In Geiger 2000a: 37–45.

Potts, David B. 2010. *Liberal Education for a Land of Colleges: Yale's Reports of 1828*. New York: Palgrave Macmillan.

Proctor, Robert E. 1998. *Defining the Humanities: How Rediscovering a Tradition Can Improve Our Schools*. Bloomington: Indiana University Press.

Proctor, Robert E. 2014. "The Debate over Liberal Arts Education in English-Speaking Countries: Martha Nussbaum's *Not for Profit* and Its Nineteenth-Century Predecessors." *ClassicoContemporaneo* 0: 9–41.

Proctor, Robert E. Forthcoming. *From Violence to Beauty: The Roman Origins of the Liberal Arts Tradition*.

Prose, Francine. 2017. "Humanities Teach Students to Think. Where Would We Be without Them?" *The Guardian* (May 12): https://www.theguardian.com/commentisfree/2017/may/12/humanities-students-budget-cuts-university-suny.

R. 1883. "Greek and English [Letter to the Editor]." *The Nation* 37.950 (Sept. 13): 226.

Rand, E. K. 1932. "The Humanism of Cicero." *Proceedings of the American Philosophical Society* 71.4: 207–16.

Rascoe, Burton. 1930. "Pupils of Polonius." In Grattan 1930a: 109–27.

Rawlings, Hunter, III and Lillian Aoki. 2013. "A College Education Is about More Than a First Job." The Huffington Post (Jan. 31): http://www.huffingtonpost.com/hunter-r-rawlings-iii/college-education-value_b_2593826.html.

Reese, William J. 1995. *The Origins of the American High School*. New Haven and London: Yale University Press.

Reinhold, Meyer. 1984. *Classica Americana: The Greek and Roman Heritage in the United States*. Detroit: Wayne State University Press.

Richard, Carl J. 1994. *The Founders and the Classics: Greece, Rome, and the American Enlightenment*. Cambridge and London: Harvard University Press.

Richard, Carl J. 2009. *The Golden Age of the Classics in America: Greece, Rome, and the Antebellum United States*. Cambridge and London: Harvard University Press.

Roberts, Jon H., and James Turner. 2000. *The Sacred and the Secular University*. Princeton: Princeton University Press.

Rogers, Walter P. 1942. *Andrew D. White and the Modern University*. Ithaca and New York: Cornell University Press.

Roth, Michael S. 2015. *Beyond the University: Why Liberal Education Matters*. New Haven and London: Yale University Press.

Rothblatt, Sheldon. 2016. "Old Wine in New Bottles, or New Wine in Old Bottles? The Humanities and Liberal Education in Today's Universities." In Hutner and Mohamed 2016b: 31–50.

Rousseau, Jean-Jacques. 1979. *Emile: or On Education*, translated by Allan Bloom. New York: Basic Books. Originally published in 1762.

Rudolph, Frederick. 1962. *The American College and University: A History*. New York: Alfred A. Knopf.

Rudolph, Frederick. 1977. *Curriculum: A History of the American Undergraduate Course of Study since 1636*. San Francisco: Jossey-Bass Publishers.

Rudy, Willis. 1960. *The Evolving Liberal Arts Curriculum: A Historical Review of Basic Themes*. [New York]: Bureau of Publications, Teachers College, Columbia University.

Ryn, Claes G. 1977. "The Humanism of Irving Babbitt Revisited." *Modern Age* 21 (summer): 251–62.

Ryn, Claes G. 1986. "Babbitt and the Problem of Reality." In Panichas and Ryn 1986b: 51–74.

Ryn, Claes G. 1991. "Introduction to the Transaction Edition." In Babbitt 1991: ix–lxvii.

Ryn, Claes G. 1995a. "How We Know What We Know: Babbitt, Positivism and Beyond." *Humanitas* 8.1: 6–25.

Ryn, Claes G. 1995b. "Introduction to the Transaction Edition." In *Character and Culture: Essays on East and West*, by Irving Babbitt. Ix–l. New Brunswick, NJ and London: Transaction Publishers.

Ryn, Claes G. 1997a. "Imaginative Origins of Modernity: Life as Daydream and Nightmare." *Humanitas* 10.2: https://css.cua.edu/humanitas_journal/imaginative-origins-modernity-life-daydream-nightmare/.

Ryn, Claes G. 1997b. *Will, Imagination and Reason: Babbitt, Croce and the Problem of Reality*, 2nd edition. New Brunswick, NJ: Transaction Publishers.

Samuels, Ernest. 1965. *The Young Henry Adams*. Cambridge: Harvard University Press.

Santayana, George. 1998. *The Genteel Tradition: Nine Essays by George Santayana*, edited by Douglas L. Wilson. Lincoln and London: University of Nebraska Press.

Saul, Scott. 2013. "Resilience of the Humanities." *The International Herald Tribune* (July 5): 6.

Saveth, Edward N. 1988. "Education of an Elite." *History of Education Quarterly* 28.3: 367–86.

Schadewaldt, W. 1973. "Humanitas Romana." *Aufstieg und Niedergang der römischen Welt* 1.4: 43–62.

Schmidt, Ben. 2013a. "A Crisis in the Humanities?" *The Chronicle of Higher Education* (June 10): http://chronicle.com/blognetwork/edgeofthewest/2013/06/10/the-humanities-crisis/.

Schmidt, Ben. 2013b. "The Data Shows There's No Real Crisis." *The New York Times* (Nov. 4): http://www.nytimes.com/roomfordebate/2013/11/04/the-fate-of-the-humanities/the-data-shows-theres-no-real-crisis-in-the-humanities.

Schmidt, Ben. 2018. "Mea Culpa: There *Is* a Crisis in the Humanities." *Sapping Attention* (July 27): https://sappingattention.blogspot.com/2018/07/mea-culpa-there-is-crisis-in-humanities.html.

Schmidt, George P. 1936. "Intellectual Crosscurrents in American Colleges, 1825–1855." *The American Historical Review* 42.1: 46–67.

Schneider, Hans Josef. 2006. "Artes Liberales." *Brill's New Pauly: Encyclopaedia of the Ancient World*. Vol. 16 *Classical Tradition*, vol. 1, edited by Manfred Landfester. 298–302.

Schrecker, Ellen. 2010. *The Lost Soul of Higher Education: Corporatization, the Assault on Academic Freedom, and the End of the American University*. London and New York: The New Press.

Seaver, [Edwin Pliny]. 1914–15. "Tribute." *Massachusetts Historical Society Proceedings* 48: 416–19.

Segrest, Scott Philip. 2010. *America and the Political Philosophy of Common Sense*. Columbia and London: University of Missouri Press.

Selden, Daniel L. 1990. "Classics and Contemporary Criticism." *Arion* n.s. 1.1: 155–78.

Seltzer, Rick. 2017. "Philosophy Department on Chopping Block at Mills." *Inside Higher Ed* (June 12): https://www.insidehighered.com/quicktakes/2017/06/12/philosophy-department-chopping-block-mills.

Sewall, Gilbert T. 2019. "Twilight of the Humanities." *The American Conservative* (Feb. 13): https://www.theamericanconservative.com/articles/twilight-of-the-humanities/.

Shafer, Robert. 1930. "An American Tragedy." In Foerster 1930a: 149–69.

Shafer, Robert. 1935. *Paul Elmer More and American Criticism*. New Haven: Yale University Press.

Sherman, Stuart P. 1963. *The Genius of America*. Port Washington, NY: Kennikat Press. Originally published in 1923.

Shimer, David. 2018. "Yale's Most Popular Class Ever: Happiness." *The New York Times* (Jan. 26): https://nytimes.com/2018/01/26/nyregion/at-yale-class-on-happiness-draws-huge-crowd-laurie-santos.html.

Shipman, Paul R. 1880. "The Classics That Educated Us." *Popular Science Monthly* 17 (June): 145–55.

[Shorey, Paul.] 1908. "[Review of Babbitt 1986.]" *The Nation* (April 30): 403–4.

Shorey, Paul. 1910. "The Case for the Classics." *The School Review* 18.9 (Nov.): 585–617.

Shorey, Paul. 1919. "Fifty Years of Classical Studies in America." *TAPA* 50: 33–61.

Sill, E. R. 1883. "Herbert Spencer's Theory of Education." *The Atlantic Monthly* 51 (Feb.): 171–79.

Sill, E. R. 1885. "Should a College Educate?" *The Atlantic Monthly* 56 (Aug.): 207–15.

Slayton, Mary E. 1986. "Irving Babbitt: A Chronology of His Life and Major Works, 1865–1933." In Panichas and Ryn 1986: 227–37.

Small, Helen. 2013. *The Value of the Humanities*. Oxford: Oxford University Press.

Smilie, Kipton Dale. 2010. *Irving Babbitt's New Humanism: An Outsider's Perspective on Curricular Debates at the Turn of the 20th Century*. Diss. University of Kansas.

Smilie, Kipton Dale. 2012. "Humanitarian and Humanistic Ideals: Charles W. Eliot, Irving Babbitt, and the American Curriculum at the Turn of the 20th Century." *Journal of Thought* 47.2 (summer): 63–84.

Smilie, Kipton Dale. 2013. "Bookends of the Twentieth Century: Irving Babbitt, E. D. Hirsch, and the Humanistic Curriculum." *American Educational History Journal* 40.1: 153–70.

Smilie, Kipton Dale. 2016. "Unthinkable Allies?: John Dewey, Irving Babbitt, and 'the Menace of Specialized Narrowness.'" *Journal of Curriculum Studies* 48.1: 113–35.

Smith, Wilson. 1956. *Professors and Public Ethics: Studies of Northern Moral Philosophers before the Civil War*. Ithaca: Cornell University Press.

Smyth, Herbert Weir. 1930. "The Classics, 1867–1929." In *The Development of Harvard University since the Inauguration of President Eliot, 1869–1929*, edited by Samuel Eliot Morison. 33–64. Cambridge: Harvard University Press.

Spanos, William V. 1985. "The Apollonian Investment of Modern Humanist Education: The Examples of Matthew Arnold, Irving Babbitt, and I. A. Richards." *Cultural Critique* 1 (autumn): 7–72.

Spencer, Herbert. 1865. *Education: Intellectual, Moral, and Physical*. New York: D. Appleton and Company. Originally published in 1861.

Stanic, George A. 1986. "Mental Discipline Theory and Mathematics Education." *For the Learning of Mathematics* 6.1: 39–47.

Stein-Hölkeskamp, Elke. 2003. "Artes Liberales." *Brill's New Pauly: Encyclopaedia of the Ancient World*, vol. 2. 71–74.

Stone, Donald D. 1998. "Matthew Arnold and the Pragmatics of Hebraism and Hellenism." *Poetics Today* 19.2 (summer): 179–98.

Storch, Helmut. 2005. "Humanitas." *Brill's New Pauly: Encyclopaedia of the Ancient World*, vol. 6: 560–63.

Summit, Jennifer. 2012. "Renaissance Humanism and the Future of the Humanities." *Literature Compass* 9.10: 665–78.

Sumner, William G. 1884. "Our Colleges before the Country." *Princeton Review* 13 (March): 127–40.

Tate, Allen. 1930. "The Fallacy of Humanism." In Grattan 1930a: 131–66.

Thayer, [William Roscoe]. 1914–15. "Tribute." *Massachusetts Historical Society Proceedings* 48: 405–6.

Thompson, Daniel Greenleaf. 1888. "Obituary: Courtlandt Palmer." *The Independent* 40.2070 (Aug. 2): 23.

Thorndike, E. L. 1924. "Mental Discipline in High School Studies." *The Journal of Educational Psychology* 15.1: 1–22, 83–98.

Turk, Milton Haight. 1933. "Without Classical Studies." *The Journal of Higher Education* 4: 339–46.

Turner, James. 1992. "Secularization and Sacralization: Speculations on Some Religious Origins of the Secular Humanities Curriculum, 1850–1900." In *The Secularization of the Academy*, edited by George M. Marsden and Bradley J. Longfield. 74–106. New York and Oxford: Oxford University Press.

Turner, James. 1999. *The Liberal Education of Charles Eliot Norton*. Baltimore and London: Johns Hopkins University Press.

Turner, James. 2014. *Philology: The Forgotten Origins of the Modern Humanities*. Princeton and Oxford: Princeton University Press.

Turner, James and Paul Bernard. 2000. "The German Model and the Graduate School: The University of Michigan and the Origin Myth of the American University." In Geiger 2000a: 221–241.

Turner, R. Steven. 1974. "University Reformers and Professional Scholarship in Germany, 1760–1806." In *The University and Society*, vol. 2, edited by Lawrence Stone. 495–531. Princeton: Princeton University Press.

Turner, R. Steven. 1980. "Prussian Universities and the Concept of Research." *Archiv für Sozialgeschichte der deutschen Literatur* 5: 68–93.

Turner, R. Steven. 1981. "The Prussian Professoriate and the Research Imperative, 1790–1840." In *Epistemological and Social Problems of the Sciences in the Early Nineteenth Century*, edited by Hans Niels Jahnke and Michael Otto. 109–21. Dordrecht: Reidel.

Tworek, Heidi. 2013. "The Real Reason the Humanities Are in 'Crisis.'" *The Atlantic* (Dec. 18): https://www.theatlantic.com/education/archive/2013/12/the-real-reason-the-humanities-are-in-crisis/282441/.

Vanderbilt, Kermit. 1959. *Charles Eliot Norton: Apostle of Culture in a Democracy*. Cambridge, MA: Belknap Press.

Verene, Donald Phillip. 2002. *The Art of Humane Education*. Ithaca and London: Cornell University Press.

Veysey, Laurence R. 1965. *The Emergence of the American University*. Chicago and London: The University of Chicago Press.

Veysey, Laurence R. 1979. "The Plural Organized Worlds of the Humanities." In *The Organization of Knowledge in Modern America, 1860–1920*, edited by Alexandra Oleson and John Voss. 51–106. Baltimore and London: The Johns Hopkins University Press.

W. M. G. 1883. "Exclusive Preference for the Classics [Letter to the Editor]." *The Nation* 37.958 (Nov. 8): 391.

[Walker, James]. 1855. *Twenty-Ninth Annual Report of the President of Harvard College to the Overseers, Exhibiting the State of the Institution for the Academical Year 1853–54*. Cambridge: Metcalf and Company.

[Walker, James]. 1856. *Thirtieth Annual Report of the President of Harvard College to the Overseers, Exhibiting the State of the Institution for the Academical Year 1854–55*. Cambridge: Metcalf and Company.

[Walker, James]. 1857. *Thirty-First Annual Report of the President of Harvard College to the Overseers, Exhibiting the State of the Institution for the Academical Year 1855–56*. Cambridge: Metcalf and Company.

Warren, Austin. 1956. *New England Saints*. Ann Arbor: The University of Michigan Press.

Wechsler, Harold S. 1977. *The Qualified Student: A History of Selective College Admission in America*. New York, Sydney, and Toronto: John Wiley.

Wenley, R. M. 1910. "The Classics and the Elective System." *The School Review* 18.8 (Oct.): 513–29.

Wertenbaker, Thomas Jefferson. 1946. *Princeton, 1746–1896*. Princeton: Princeton University Press.

West, Andrew F. 1884. "Must the Classics Go?" *The North American Review* 138.327 (Feb.): 151–62.

West, Andrew F. 1885. "What Is Academic Freedom?" *The North American Review* 140 (May): 432–44.

West, Andrew F. 1886. *A Review of President Eliot's Report on Elective Studies*. New York: J. K. Lees.

Wicks, John. 1883. "A Question or Two for Charles Francis Adams, Jr." *Detroit Free Press* (July 20): 7.

Wiesen, David. 1981–82. "Cornelius Felton and the Flowering of Classics in New England." *Classical Outlook* 59.2: 44–48.

Wilkins, A. S., ed. 1902. *M. Tulli Ciceronis Rhetorica*, vol. 1. Oxford: Clarendon Press.

Wilson, Edmund. 1930. "Notes on Babbitt and More." In Grattan 1930a: 39–60.

Wilson, Marilyn. 1988. "Critical Thinking: Repackaging or Revolution?" *Language Arts* 65.6: 543–51.

Winterer, Caroline. 2002. *The Culture of Classicism: Ancient Greece and Rome in American Intellectual Life, 1780–1910*. Baltimore: Johns Hopkins University Press.

Winters, Yvor. 1930. "Poetry, Morality, and Criticism." In Grattan 1930a: 301–33.

Winthrop, John. 1883. "Our Boston Letter." *The Independent* 35 (July 19): 5.

Withun, David. 2017. "W. E. B. Du Bois and Irving Babbitt: A Comparative Evaluation of Their Views on Education, Leadership, and Society." *Phylon* 54.1 (summer): 25–42.

Witt, Ronald G. 2000. *"In the Footsteps of the Ancients": The Origins of Humanism from Lovato to Bruni*. Leiden, Boston, and Cologne: Brill.

Witt, Ronald G. 2015. *The Two Latin Cultures and the Foundation of Renaissance Humanism in Medieval Italy*. New York: Cambridge University Press.

Wright, John Henry. 1886. *The College in the University and Classical Philology in the College: An Address at the Opening of the Eleventh Academic Year of the Johns Hopkins University, October 7, 1886*. Baltimore: The Publication Agency of the Johns Hopkins University.

Wright, Louis B. 1940. *The First Gentlemen of Virginia: Intellectual Qualities of the Early Colonial Ruling Class*. San Marino, CA: Huntington Library.

Wriston, Henry M. 1939. "A Critical Appraisal of Experiments in General Education." In *The Thirty-Eighth Yearbook of the National Society for the Study of Education, Part II: General Education in the American College*, edited by Guy Mongrose Whipple. 297–321. Bloomington, IL: Public School Publishing.

[Youmans, E. L.]. 1880a. "Sewage in College Education." *Popular Science Monthly* 17.37 (Sept.): 693–707.

[Youmans, E. L.]. 1880b. "Sir Josiah Mason's Science College." *Popular Science Monthly* 18.2 (Dec.): 265–67.

[Youmans, E. L.]. 1881. "The Study of Sewerage in London." *Popular Science Monthly* 18.3 (Jan.): 414–15.

[Youmans, E. L.]. 1883a. "The Current Study of Classics a Failure." *Popular Science Monthly* 24 (Nov.): 117–22.

[Youmans, E. L.]. 1883b. "Dead-Language Studies Necessarily a Failure." *Popular Science Monthly* 24 (Dec.): 265–69.

[Youmans, E. L.]. 1883c. "The Dead-Language Superstition." *Popular Science Monthly* 23 (Sept.): 701–8.

[Youmans, E. L.]. 1883d. "Greek and Latin against Nature and Science." *Popular Science Monthly* 23 (May): 116–20.

[Youmans, E. L.]. 1883e. "Queer Defenses of the Classics." *Popular Science Monthly* 24 (Dec.): 269–71.

[Youmans, E. L.]. 1884a. "Collegiate Influence upon the Lower Education." *Popular Science Monthly* 24 (March): 702–6.

[Youmans, E. L.]. 1884b. "The College Fetich Once More." *Popular Science Monthly* 25 (Sept.): 701–4.

[Youmans, E. L.]. 1884c. "Education without Dead Languages." *Popular Science Monthly* 24 (Feb.): 558–60.

[Youmans, E. L.]. 1884d. "President Eliot on Liberal Education." *Popular Science Monthly* 25 (July): 412–14.

[Youmans, E. L.]. 1884e. "Yale Professors on College Studies." *Popular Science Monthly* 25 (May): 124–29.

Youmans, E. L. 1900. "Mental Discipline in Education." In *The Culture Demanded by Modern Life: A Series of Addresses and Arguments on the Claims of Scientific Education*, edited by E. L. Youmans. 1–56. New York: D. Appleton. Originally published in 1867.

Zakaria, Fareed. 2015. *In Defense of a Liberal Education*. London: W. W. Norton.

Index

For the benefit of digital users, indexed terms that span two pages (e.g., 52–53) may, on occasion, appear on only one of those pages.